NEGOTIATING RELIGION

NEGOTIATING RELIGION

Perspectives from Indian History

Edited by

RAMESHWAR PRASAD BAHUGUNA
RANJEETA DUTTA
FARHAT NASREEN

MANOHAR
2012

First published 2012

ISBN 978-81-7304-924-8

Published by
Ajay Kumar Jain *for*
Manohar Publishers & Distributors
4753/23 Ansari Road, Daryaganj,
New Delhi 110 002

Printed at
Salasar Imaging Systems
Delhi 110 035

Contents

Acknowledgements 7

Note on Transliteration 9

Introduction 11

PART I: TEXTS, TRADITIONS AND DISCOURSE

1. Of Binaries and Beyond: The Dialectics of Buddhist-Brahmanical Relations in India
   Uma Chakravarti 41

2. Tradition and Memory: Filiation and Identity in Early Sanskrit Literature and Philosophy
   Heeraman Tiwari 61

3. Representations of a Past: The Life of Rāmānuja and the Śrīvaiṣṇava Community
   Ranjeeta Dutta 85

4. Culture Under Interpretative Stress: Bankim Chandra and the Re-Formulation of '*Dharma*' in Colonial Bengal
   Amiya P. Sen 119

PART II: DIVINITY AND THE FEMININE: REPRESENTATIONS OF GENDER AND GENDER RELATIONS

5. A Home for the Goddess: Structural Shrines for Independent Female Deities in Early Medieval Tamiḻakam, *c.* CE 600-1300
   R. Mahalakshmi 141

6. Rādhā and Radhaism: Neutralizing Gender in *Brajmaya* Krsnaism of Medieval Braj
Farhat Nasreen 169

PART III: RELIGIOUS IDENTITIES: NEGOTIATING CONFLICT AND ACCOMMODATION

7. Understanding Sufi-Sant Interaction in Medieval India
Rameshwar Prasad Bahuguna 211

8. Saiyid Ahmad Barelvi, Altaf Husain Hali and the Formation of Muslim Identity in the Nineteenth Century
N.R. Farooqi 233

9. Exclusive Resources and Inclusive Objectives: Islam in the Making of Indian Nationalism: 1857-1922
Rizwan Qaiser 261

10. Christianity and the Mizo Identity: A Review of Sociological and Historical Circumstances
Joy L.K. Pachuau 291

11. Religion and Social 'Subversion': Re-examining Colonial Orissa
Biswamoy Pati 325

12. Religious Rhetoric, Mercantile Strategies and a Community in Revolt: A Study on the Conflicts between the St. Thomas Christians and the Portuguese *Padroado*
Pius Malekandathil 353

13. Sufis and Communal Harmony: A Case Study of Indian Sufis
S.M. Azizuddin Husain 383

List of Contributors 395

Acknowledgements

The articles in this work are some of the presentations made in a seminar, 'Religion in Indian History: Ideas, Practice and Change', held under the aegis of UGC's DRS-SAP programme in the Department of History and Culture, Jamia Millia Islamia. We are thankful to Professor R. Gopinath, Coordinator, DRS-SAP Programme, for his approval and support in organizing the seminar and bringing out this volume. A very special word of thanks goes to Professor Irfan Habib who was kind enough to take time off his busy schedule to deliver the key-note address of this seminar. We are grateful to Professor T.N. Madan for giving the valedictory lecture. We are also thankful to Professor Amiya Sen and Professor Lakshmi Subramanian for the academic advice and guidance. The organization of this seminar was possible due to the assistance of the committee comprising Professor Sunita Zaidi, Dr. Nishat Manzar and Rajneesh Kumar. We are thankful to Mohammad Bilal, Shabana and Mohammad Ashfaq for all the help that they extended. The administrative staff of Jamia Millia Islamia was extremely helpful and cooperative in providing logistical support to this endeavour. We are grateful to Manohar Publishers & Distributors for providing all possible help and cooperating at every stage of the publication of this volume.

EDITORS

Note on Transliteration

In this volume, an attempt has been made to maintain consistency in spelling and transliteration. Uniform diacritical marks have been used for those texts that have been cited in the various contributions here. Specific texts exclusive to a single contribution follow the relevant linguistic spellings and diacritics. Modern names, places and common terms follow the widely accepted anglicized spellings.

Introduction

The diversity of religious practices in India within a changing historical context and their intersection with complex social processes and institutions, especially in the context of the politics of religious identities, has generated considerable scholarship in recent years. A variety of perspectives from anthropologists, sociologists and political scientists has resulted in important insights about understanding religion in Indian history, generating an interdisciplinary approach.[1] The essays in this volume comprise revised versions of selected papers presented in a two-day conference titled, 'Religion in Indian History: Ideas, Practice and Change', organized by the Department of History and Culture, Jamia Millia Islamia and funded by the UGC-DRS SAP programme. In view of the complexities and vast subjectivity in understanding religion, religious experience and religious phenomena, the essays here have focused on the mutual interactions and negotiations of the religious with extra-religious themes like caste, gender, state, commerce and politics. Further, the subsequent ramifications of such an interface have been analysed in texts, traditions and religious dialogues, as reflected in conversion, representations and contestations—all contextualized in the religious dynamics of various phases in Indian history, ranging from the early period to the colonial period.

Earlier researches on the history of Indian religions comprised the philological and ethnological study of texts, especially the Vedas, a sociological and anthropological analysis of religion, and studies written from the Marxist perspective in which religion was seen as part of the material milieu and social formation.[2] However, the essays presented here, while keeping in view the importance of these studies, stress the issue of religion and the sacred and their negotiations with the profane and secular, or the non-religious sphere.[3] The essays also attempt to point out that 'any religion or religious system has to be seen as it was understood by its followers (and different groups of them), as well as by outsiders, at each different point of time'.[4] The exploration of the relations between different religious communities in pre-colonial and colonial times has been central to most recent researches in religion in Indian history. The heightening of religious tensions since the mid-1980s and the consolidation of homogenized versions of religious communities coupled with epoch-making events such as the destruction of the Babri Masjid in 1992 (and the communal riots that followed it), the tragedy of 9/11 in the USA and the Gujarat carnage of 2002 have led scholars, albeit in divergent ways, to revisit the themes of religious conflict and accommodation in Indian history.[5] The essays in the present collection emanate from contemporary scholarly engagement with issues of religious identity and conflict. Yet they try to eschew, as far as possible, the prevailing communal, secular and nationalist ways of interpreting the religious history of India that have been reductionist in their respective approaches.

Recent studies of Indian religious history, including those using Marx's insightful ideas about religious phenomena, have moved away from the conventional way of treating religion as part of a superstructure that is determined by an economic base. In his inaugural address at the conference which gave rise to the present collection of essays, Irfan Habib made the following observations about the role of religion as an active historical agent in shaping the social order and the course of social change:

> Religion may be outside the realm of reason, but the historian's study of religion is not outside the realm of reason. Religion does affect human action. It is history's duty to study these effects. . . . It is important to examine the question whether religion forms or creates the social order that it sanctifies. To what extent is it true that religion creates a social order? For instance, class society, gender differences and so on . . . how much of it is created by religion? Such an approach becomes important for meanings differ today in the twenty-first century from what they were perceived to be in the twelfth and thirteenth centuries. Religious ideas change and therefore can be studied historically. . . . Even the religious ethics and beliefs are factors

of social change. Hence, some aspects of religion remain immutable, but these aspects get re-casted in the new ethos while other aspects transform themselves. Thus, it becomes crucial to understand that religion has never been a static, monolithic structure.[6]

Elsewhere, in his essay on Kabir, Habib again emphasizes the relative autonomy of the religious sphere and its impact on the social structure:

> The time is past—if ever there was one, except in the case of a very simplistic variant of Marxism—when one could dismiss religion as either too insignificant a factor in history or, alternatively, see its various forms as mere reflexes of social environments, which could be narrowed to a few standard 'modes'. Contemporary events have retold us with renewed force that ideas, prejudices, superstitions, that is, the entire complex that constitutes the mental part of religion, does not arise automatically out of certain economic phenomena, or disappear with them, but has a life, a momentum of its own, which acts upon as well as responds to the whole social structure.[7]

I

Is it from the standpoint of a secular age that we find the inseparability of religions and social change unacceptable? Isn't it important to analyse the various ways in which religious traditions, communities and so on are invented? In what ways and how far can the mutual involvement of the 'religious' and 'extra-religious' in pre-modern India and the range of phenomena called 'religion' be understood? Are our modern Indian preoccupations with religious strife and aspirations to communal harmony leading us to misread our past? These are some of the questions that arise inevitably in the course of interrogation of what happens to the domain of religion in the modern period. Such questions have a bearing on discussions on religion in this volume. The essays here are a part of ongoing political and academic debates on three of the following issues: the relevance of secularism as a political doctrine and the relation between the sacred and the secular; trends in history writing where the modern-day cultural and political concerns of community consciousness have encouraged a particular reading of the past, the construction of stereotypes that essentialize religious communities, particularly religious minorities; and finally, the complex issue of religious identities itself.

As an ideological concept and political doctrine, secularism evolved in the context of the intellectual developments that accompanied the Protestant Reformation and Enlightenment in Europe.[8] Advocating the strict separation of the church from the state, secularism emerged as the essence of modernity and the nation state that attempted 'to define a political ethic independent of religious conviction altogether'.[9] Thus, religion was considered to be irrational and backward and consigned to an exclusive, personalized, private sphere, divorced from the public domain that was to be dominated by a rational and scientific outlook. This political doctrine became the core of governance that attempted to prevent and manage religious conflicts and fanaticism.

In India, secularism was adopted in the Constitution as a part of the ideals of a democratic state that would not interfere with its pluralistic religious life nor favour any religion at the expense of another, thus ensuring 'equal respect for all'.[10] However, despite state measures to create institutions and implement programmes that articulated the Indian brand of secularism, communal conflicts and the persecution of religious minorities as the 'others' continued unabated, often with the open or tacit acquiescence of the Indian nation state. The crisis of Indian secularism was further underscored by the Hindutva attack on secularism that focused on accusing the 'pseudo-secularists' of pandering to the non-Hindu minorities. It is not only in India that secularism is in crisis. Even in the liberal democratic nations of the West, the birthplace of secularism, this crisis is reflected in the difficulties faced by their state systems in grappling with the issues of multiculturalism.[11]

The assault by the Hindutva ideology on secularism and the failure of the Indian state to safeguard minority rights have generated academic debates among sociologists, anthropologists, political scientists and political philosophers on secularism and the relevance of religion in countering fundamentalism and violence.[12] According to some of these scholars, the solution lies in using the indigenous resources of 'religious toleration' and interreligious communications to resolve communal conflicts and prevent their occurrence in future. This would entail, according to them, a dialogue that would acknowledge religion in the public domain, thus doing away with the Western idea of separation between the state and religion, where the former is 'secular' and the latter 'private'.

However, it is emphasized here that despite all its problems and inherent contradictions, 'the desirability and inescapability of secularism' cannot be denied and attempts have to be made to work out 'an alternative conception of secularism rather than simply an alternative to it'.[13] Thus, in a pluralistic society like India, separation between the state and religion is imperative in order to prevent the hegemonization by the majoritarian communalism and discrimination against minorities. However, such a separation does not imply the negation of religion in the public arena. In fact, religion never disappeared from the public domain and has always been an integral part of social identities. Any attempted separation is artificial and flawed. It is suggested here that perhaps one of the ways to counter fundamentalism is to understand the historical processes of the evolution of religions, religious communities and identities.

The essays in this volume, while being sensitive to the debates on secularism, emphasize the need to study religious experiences and processes in conjunction with the social and political processes of the historical past. It becomes important to understand the dynamics of religion and assert the idea that there is a historical past that has to be analysed in its own terms and that preoccupations with contemporary issues of religious conflicts and identities should not influence our readings of it. Just as communal historians and fundamentalists make use of the past to legitimize their contemporary political agenda, secular historiography in post-independent India has sought to ideologically prop up contemporary Indian secularism by tracing its historical origins to the existence of religious syncretism, composite culture and harmony in pre-colonial India. Laudable as the secular historigraphical project was in terms of its objectives, it tended to overlook the evidence for the existence of various kinds of religious conflict in the pre-colonial period, for the sake of establishing a secular harmonious society in the post-Independence period. Thus, in a way, both the 'avenging the grievous injustice' approach and the 'religious toleration' approach sacrificed evidence for wanting to establish an Indian state and society of their respective visions. The secular historians' preoccupation with syncretism and religious toleration meant that areas of religious conflict would become 'the special preserve of sectarian and "communal" '.[14] Through the analysis of historical processes, the essays show that there were moments of religious conflicts and negotiations, but these were complex and their ramifications different from those of present-day tensions, and were not negotiated through rigid community polarizations with the tacit or obvious compliance of the state.

Since the past plays an important role in creating a shared history and a common memory to forge nationalist identities, the discipline of history always becomes a site of political contestation. This is the next underlying theme of this volume. The articles of N.R. Farooqi, Rizwan Qaiser and Uma Chakravarti point out the communalization and homogenization of the historical past that have influenced our historical consciousness today. The contestations generated by such history writing have been influenced by the context in which respective ideological formulations took place. The Orientalist perspective of history glorified Sanskrit and the ancient period of Indian history. Utilitarians like James Mill divided Indian history into Hindu, Muslim and British periods.[15] The nationalists and the communalists were influenced by these perceptions and constructed the stereotype of the 'Golden Age' characterized by just kings, a 'non-violent' Brahmanical religion (often synonymous with Hinduism), and philosophical spiritualism was contrasted with an equally stereotyped construct of the 'Dark Age' marked by invasions, temple destruction and conversions by the 'Muslim' rulers. Thus, the concepts of the 'the Sword of Islam' and Muslims as 'foreigners' and 'iconoclasts' became an integral part of history writing, especially in the regional languages in the nineteenth century.[16] Since the nationalist agenda required a specific notion of history that was homogeneous, with continuities between old and new cultural forms, these ideas became significant in propitiating national pride and honour.[17] Thus was constructed a glorious ancient past comparable to the classical antiquity of European civilization. Further projection of national identity was sought through the concept of 'national heroes'. Prithviraj Chauhan, Rana Pratap, Shivaji and others were valourized in stories and plays. Such writings influence till this day the popular public domain of textbooks, films and television serials.[18]

However, there has also been a large corpus of historical research that has questioned such polemical sectarian stereotypes. One of the earliest historians in this regard was Mohammad Habib. Writing from the perspective of a secular nationalist historian who believed in India's composite culture, Habib asserted that the plundering of India's wealth and not a religious war against the Hindus was the prime motive of Mahmud of Ghazni's invasions of northern India in the late tenth and early eleventh centuries.[19] However, it was difficult to counter the widely prevalent image of Mahmud of Ghazni as a villain, an image that was further highlighted in the descriptions of his raids into Indian territory and looting of the Somanātha temple.

The temple's synonymity with national pride has often been asserted and this was done again in 1990 when L.K. Advani started his *rathayātrā* from Somanātha. While analysing five kinds of narratives, viz., the Turko-Persian chronicles, Jaina texts from the eleventh to the thirteenth century, Sanskrit inscriptions from Somanath, debates in the British House of Commons and the nationalist perception of the event, Romila Thapar points out that the Jaina and Sanskrit inscriptions make marginal allusions to the event. It is the Turko-Persian chronicles that describe the raid at great length.[20] According to Thapar, seen in the framework of literary style, the narratives projected Mahmud of Ghazni as a model for the rulers of the Delhi Sultanate and the Mughal Empire.[21] While analysing the narratives, Thapar not only throws light on the contradictions and exaggerations in these texts, but also brings to notice the fact that the hostility of Mahmud was also against the Shias whose mosques he destroyed—a fact that is hardly ever highlighted.[22]

Advocating a contextual analysis of temple looting and desecration in history, researches emphasize a more nuanced understanding of different genres of historical sources that goes beyond simplistic notions of Islamic iconoclasm and religious zeal. According to Richard Davis, plundering of temples cannot be merely attributed to the advent of Islam and the Turks. He cites evidence to show that it was also an important political phenomenon in the early medieval period (that is, prior to the fourteenth century). Since temples and divine images were patronized by rulers, they symbolized royal legitimation and sovereignty and were, therefore, political in character.[23] Hence, as a part of political aggrandizement and the assertion of hegemony, attacking the temples of enemies, looting their images and displaying them as trophies of war were important strategies in the consolidation of the early medieval state. Davis provides several illustrations of looting of temple idols that, for a change, are not associated with Islamic iconoclasm. For instance, the looting of the golden image of the Buddha (a symbol of Sinhalese royalty) from the Abhayagiri monastery in Anurādhapura in Sri Lanka by the Pāṇḍyan ruler of Madurai in the ninth century, the looting of the image of Viṭṭhala after ransacking the temple at Pandharpur in the Adil Shahi kingdom by the Vijayanagara ruler, Kṛṣṇadevarāya, and many other examples show that attacking temples was a political practice that the Turks and Mughals continued to follow in order to delegitimize erstwhile royal authorities. Similarly, Richard Eaton argues that the Turks and Mughals destroyed only those temples that were on the 'frontiers of the invading army'. Temples that were not perceived as threats were left untouched, like the temples at Khajuraho. Eaton points out that there were several instances of the Turks and Mughals patronizing and protecting temples, especially those that were within their territorial control, and that this was an attempt to highlight their status as righteous rulers, an important component of medieval kingship. Even Aurangzeb's reign, notorious in history textbooks and popular perception for temple desecration, saw widespread temple-building activities.[24]

The essays here do not deal directly with the issues of temple desecration and the Babri Masjid demolition. However, they focus on the problematic representations of religious communities and their identities that not only homogenize but also hegemonize the idea of 'Hindu' by using it synonymously with 'Indian' . These issues came to be discussed extensively in historical scholorship, especially after the destruction of the Babri Masjid in 1992. Uma Chakravarti's essay emphasizes on treating Buddhism as an independent religious tradition and not as an appendage to Hinduism, as done by several nationalists and historians. The articles of Farooqui and Qaiser speak of the creation of the binary categories of Hindus and Muslims resulting in the image of disadvantaged Muslims. S.M. Azizuddin Husain's essay on the 'Sufis and Communal Harmony: A Case Study of Indian Sufis' has been written in a polarized context, in which Islam has been essentialized, especially after 9/11.[25] While tracing the evolution of Sufism within Islam and its growth in the medieval Indian context, Husain feels that many current socio-cultural conflicts can be resolved if we draw lessons from the lives and teachings of the Sufis, who, in his opinion, believed in peaceful co-existence.

The issue of identities is the dominant theme in this volume. Certain ideas have emerged while trying to understand religious identities as a consequence of negotiations, accommodations and conflicts in a given set of historical circumstances. The dissemination of religious exegesis and traditions in religion has evoked reactions from many of the followers. Such responses often influenced religious ideas and shaped religious attitudes. The range of interpretations and readings of the same cultural practice indicated the diversity of a religious tradition that often contradicted its claim of being homogeneous. The dominant idea of universality while attempting to create a notion of a uniform community marginalized various aspects of heterogeneity, and represented a consistent and uncontested depiction of religious identities. However, internal contradictions always remained and the many voices of heterogeneous representations kept asserting themselves and reshaped those identities. In this sense, religious identities were always in the making, assumed complex forms and never remained static.

Neither Hinduism nor Islam was monolithic nor were they always mutually antagonistic. Several researches show that Hindus as a uniform religious community were absent in early India.[26] The idea that diverse social groups with multi-layered identities based on different regions, castes, occupations and sects referred to themselves as Hindus, and their religion as Hinduism in the early period is questionable.[27] It is only from the eleventh century onwards that Arab texts like Al-Beruni's *Al-Hind* used the word 'Hindu' not only in a geographical sense but also in a religious sense to distinguish a religion different from Christianity and Islam.[28] Similarly, Islam's monolithic identity in South Asia is also questioned, as it comprises a variety of social, ethnic and linguistic groups with a range of ideas and practices.[29] In fact, to encapsulate the range of cultural practices and socio-religious identities within the category of 'Hindus' and 'Muslims' seems to convey a sense of 'reductive religious orientations'.[30] Therefore, new terms like 'Islamicate' and 'Indic' have gained academic currency as both go beyond the normative religious doctrines of Hinduism and Islam, and take into account the diverse cultural and civilizational interactions and influences in each micro-context where different groups and traditions relate differentially to either Hinduism or Islam and often both.[31]

The interaction of these diverse religious traditions today grouped as 'Hindus' and 'Muslims' have been complex and cannot be discussed here. However, some trends need to be pointed out with special reference to the medieval period in Indian history. First, in the period between the seventh and fourteenth centuries, with the advent of the Arabs in Sindh and the establishment of the Delhi Sultanate by the Turks, the term 'Muslim' does not seem to be in use in Sanskrit sources for denoting a religious community. Sanskrit inscriptions during this period contain terms like *turuṣkas*, *yavanas*, *mlechchhas*, *tulukkas*, *pārasikas* and so on for groups who were followers of Islam. These terms did not refer to a unified religion of Islam; rather these were ethnic, geographical and cultural terms, reflecting diverse perceptions devoid of any religious connotation.[32] Second, the writings of court historians during the Sultanate and Mughal periods in Indian history, while using the term 'Hindu' referred to the non-Muslim elites.[33] The term 'Hindu' in these writings was thus also used in a political sense. The evidences also shows that neither the rulers of Delhi Sultanate nor the Mughal Empire based their administrative policies on the *sharia*. Political expediency was the basis of governance. Neither is there any evidence that the medieval Muslim rulers were engaged in the large-scale conversion of Hindus to Islam.[34] Third, this interaction shows mutual influence both at the level of politics as well as in the socio-religious sphere. For instance, Mahmud of Ghazni stamped the image of Goddess Lakshmi on some of his gold coins. In the fifteenth century, Rana Kumbha got 'Allah' carved in Arabic on the Hindu deities sculpted in his famous Victory Tower at Chittor. The titles *Hindu Suratrāṇa*, that is 'Hindu Sultan' and *Hindurāya-Suratrāṇa*, that is 'Sultan amongst the Hindu kings' were adopted by the Rajput and Vijayanagara rulers, respectively. There has been a considerable discussion on the influence of Islam on Hinduism, especially in relation to the Sufi-*bhakti* relationship. Historiography, particularly of the nationalist variety, emphasizes a two-way interaction between the medieval Indian Sufis and the bhakti saints, both 'syncretically' influencing each other. This interaction is seen as an important building block of the medieval composite culture. This historiographical trend, which began about eight decades ago with Tara Chand's pioneering study of the medieval Indian religious movements, continues to inform most of the scholarly work on the theme even today.[35] However, an analysis of these interactions shows that they were not only intricate but also transgressed simplistic binaries. The traditions grouped as bhakti were not the representatives of the 'Hindu' religion. Nor were they interested in any mutual interaction between Islam and Hinduism. Their encounters can, in fact, be related to the larger world of medieval Indian religious life where different religious formations were competing for patronage, resources and followers.[37]

That the all-embracing, universal religious categories of modern times cannot be projected back into a past in which the dynamics of religious identity formation were different is brought out here in varied themes on interactions of the religious with the non-religious sphere. The concerns discussed in these essays question the notion of a homogeneous religion. For example, the essay of Pius Malekandathil focuses on conflicts within the same religious tradition reflecting multiple contradictory interests that went beyond mere religious affiliations. The essays of Amiya Sen, Heeraman Tiwari, Ranjeeta Dutta, N.R. Farooqi and Joy Pachuau focus on self-reflexive modes of articulating the self within the community through a dialogue, showing that there were varied ways in which an individual or a group related to the same religious tradition. The perspective of gender becomes important for it brings out the complexities in the identity question, further challenging the notion of homogeneity. R. Mahalakshmi and Farhat Nasreen's articles bring out the gendered nature of devotion and religious practice.

II

The first theme that articulates the importance of indigenous categories that question the stereotyped binaries of identities is *Text, Traditions and Discourse*. The texts analysed in the essays here are written ones that primarily articulate the community tradition, ideology and opinions within the changing context. In Uma Chakravarti's essay, larger contextual and inter-textual borrowings have been emphasized. While reflecting upon ideas of the communities in changing times, the essay emphasizes on inter-borrowings and dialogues between religious traditions, thus questioning the idea of absolute binaries between Hinduism and Buddhism. Uma Chakravarti points out that there are other ways of examining the relationship between Buddhism and Hinduism as it was played out in early India. It was a dialectical relationship, including a somewhat unacknowledged influence of the Buddhist tradition upon Brahmanism, in thinking about renunciation, on the one hand, and birth-based claims to superiority, on the other. The paper not only analyses the Buddhist-Brahmana dialogues in early Pali texts but also highlights that an extension of these dialogues can be found in the Buddhist hybrid Sanskrit text, the *Vajrasūcī*, attributed to the great Buddhist writer, Asvaghosha.

The author also maps the circulation of the text in western India and its impact on the early formation of a critique of caste in nineteenth-century Maharashtra. Such a study becomes important as the relationship between Buddhism and Brahmanism, or Brahmanic Hinduism, has been somewhat clouded by what may be called the politics of appropriation. Since Buddhism has been India's greatest cultural export of early times, those investing in the innate greatness of the Indian tradition have sought to treat Buddhism as one stream in the Indian/Hindu way of thinking. Others, such as the Ambedkarite Dalits, have regarded the Hindu and Buddhist traditions as essentially opposed to each other, and have sought to establish this difference by exiting from Hinduism and 'converting' to Buddhism.

Heeraman Tiwari's essay on early Sanskrit literature and philosophy brings out the idea of tradition as delineated in Sanskrit texts, and the method of transmission through the use of mnemonic strategies that transformed the nature of these texts. The focus has been on the epic, *Rāmāyaṇa,* whose oral tradition and transmission through memory to subsequent generations created an individual and collective tradition. According to Tiwari, when information or knowledge is planned to be transmitted through a disciplined process of memorizing, it becomes a deliberate and disciplined memory which 'thus appears to be a specialization of the more natural process of acquiring knowledge and techniques, religious or otherwise, that unconsciously determine a person's membership in a particular tradition'.[37] Such a membership then becomes essential in the interest of continuity of tradition. Further, accuracy in memorizing becomes essential, particularly for religious texts or the exegeses which represent the tradition and identity of a society. Such multiplicities in the transmission of the *Rāmāyaṇa* go against the unilinear epic tradition and the fixity of the text and identities around it.

The texts not only represented the past but also re-ordered it, thus significantly influencing religious identities. This has been highlighted in Ranjeeta Dutta's essay on hagiographies that delineated a particular past while narrating the life history of Rāmānuja, a medieval bhakti *ācārya* and the founder leader of the Śrīvaiṣṇava community of south India. The essay discusses that while the hagiographies or *guruparamparās* provided a cogent narrative woven with myths and metaphors, they also simultaneously constructed an ancient past, perpetuated it and provided a sense of continuity, putting forth the notion of a *sampradāya*. In this context, the texts developed a charismatic image of Rāmānuja, concentrating on his qualities of a philosopher (*ācārya*) who propounded the idea of Viśiṣṭādvaita and organized the community, primarily by instituting temple reforms that incorporated non-brāhmaṇa participation. Therefore, hagiographical narratives, while delineating the life of Rāmānuja, evolved the idea of a uniform identity that implied belonging to a single Śrīvaiṣṇava community with Rāmānuja as its head. This idea became the dominant theme in all the Śrīvaiṣṇava sectarian hagiographies. In this manner, each sectarian group with its lineage claimed to represent the uniform Śrīvaiṣṇava community and drew legitimacy from this claim during contests over power and control of resources in temples. The hagiographical texts in this manner reflected the 'social location and ideology' of different groups and sub-sects. While they established these multiple identities, they nonetheless had some common perception of the Śrīvaiṣṇava community and its past, and drew from a common pool of ideas and events in their respective narratives.

Amiya Sen's essay is an attempt to examine the way in which the Bengali intelligentsia reformulated certain indigenous categories of thought and modes of self-expression in the mid-nineteenth century. Contextualized within the circumstances of the growing dissemination of English education, the Bengali lexicon reinvented itself by introducing new words. However, this 'hermeneutical enterprise', as Sen puts it, 'put greater faith on investing traditional idioms or categories of thought with somewhat untypical meanings rather than creating or popularizing altogether new modes of cultural self-expression'. Such an exercise was evident in a nineteenth-century text, *Dharmatattva*, written by Bankim Chandra Chattopadhyaya (1838-94), where a theological dialogue is explicated between a traditional guru and a Western educated pupil, and a detailed exposition takes place on the word *Dharma*. The text attempted to harmonize the individual and his interests with that of the community in several ways. Disagreeing with the pessimism of certain Hindu and Buddhist thoughts, Bankim emphasized that the quest for *Dharma* was not simply about *sukha* which was ephemeral; rather it was for *sadhana*, an intense personal quest for realizing the truth, which comes only after a lifetime of sustained self-questioning, and was, therefore, an enduring reality.

These essays reflect a continuous process of redefining the self within a particular paradigm that, instead of discarding traditional categories, gave them different meanings. The Buddhists never discarded the category of the brāhmaṇa but redefined it, even when they were engaged in a confrontationist dialogue with the Brahmanical tradition. The revoking of tradition through memory was important while breaking grounds with older ones, and this was an attempt to express continuity with the older tradition even when such a continuity did not exist. For instance, a particular past was constructed to legitimize the Śrīvaiṣṇava existence by using the structure of a tradition. Finally, the Bengali intelligentsia in the nineteenth century reformulated some indigenous categories like *Dharma*, rather than investing in new categories of self-expression.

The second theme in this volume, 'Divinity and the Feminine: Representations of Gender and Gender Relations', comprising two essays refers to the complexities of gender and gender discourse in various religious traditions.[38] There are several notable issues relating to gender and religion. These include both religious comments on secular society and views regarding traditional forms of religious communities. Gender relations, often expressed in patriarchal terms in various forms of religious practice and representations of divinities, were based on complex relations of power and subordination and represented the kinship structure of a particular religious community. Therefore, studying gender relations in religion goes beyond the mere delineation of the status of women in society. Both the essays in this volume analyse the religious representation of gender relations, which when framed within the idea of devotion and spirituality internalizes the patriarchal norms. Appropriation and representations of female divinities did not imply an exalted status of a woman. Rather, it emphasized the process of incorporation of the cultural group devoted to the worship of the feminine divinity.

In her paper, R. Mahalakshmi focuses on the construction of structural shrines for independent goddesses in the Tamil region. According to her, even a cursory survey of the inscriptions related to goddesses in early medieval *Tamiḻakam* or the Tamil region (*c*. CE 600-1300) reveals instances where the goddess was being accommodated spatially within the Śaiva pantheon, through the building of a shrine for her in the precincts of the Śiva temple. However, the names of goddesses and the fact that they were not identified as the spouses of Śiva in the inscriptions revealed their status as independent deities, organically linked to localities and communities, which could perhaps be traced to earlier tribal cults and belief systems. Documenting the interaction between the Śaiva temples and the cultic belief systems, Mahalakshmi presents a comprehensive analysis of inscriptions to map out the presence of goddesses in terms of shrines built in their honour. In her essay on Krsnaite Vaisnavism in medieval Braj, Farhat Nasreen focuses on the significance of the cult of Rādhā in the specific context of regional culture. Her influence grew over time and an inadvertent fallout of Radhaism was the idea of neutralizing genders. A *bhakta*, male or female, was ideally meant to emote and feel like a *gopī*, *sakhī* or *mañjarī*, who are female associates of Rādhā in the Brajmaya Kṛṣṇa devotion. Love and sensuality, as in a female psyche, were to be emulated in the formation of a relationship with Kṛṣṇa, the 'only' male of Braj. Radhaism did not conform to orthodox Vaiṣṇava norms. However, the theologians of Brajmaya Krsnaism resolved the paradox by drawing line between the theory of psychological emulation of the female psyche in an adulterous situation and actual life in which loyalty and obedience of women towards their husbands was emphasized.

The third theme, 'Religious Identities: Negotiating Conflict and Accommodations' comprises six essays. Rameshwar Prasad Bahuguna takes up the theme of the complex processes of competition and interaction between the followers of medieval *sants* and Sufis. Interrogating the dominant assumptions of the secular nationalist historiography, prevalent since the publication of Tara

Chand's pioneering study, Bahuguna disagrees with the view that medieval *sants* like Kabir championed the cause of Hindu-Muslim unity and religious synthesis.[40] He points to the virtual non-existence of any direct interaction or common meeting ground between medieval *sants* and Sufis, and underlines the different social backgrounds and ideological agenda of the two groups of devotees. While most Sufis of established orders were firmly rooted in the Islamic system of belief and piety, the *sants* rejected both Brahmanical Hinduism and Islam. Bahuguna, however, makes the interesting observation that the followers of the Sufis and *sants* brought them together in hagiographic narratives due to their increasing popularity during the course of the sixteenth and seventeenth centuries, thereby engaging in the process of mutual interaction and appropriation. The outcome of this two-way interaction was that the followers began to look upon the Sufis and *sants* as part of the same religious universe.

N.R. Farooqi's paper looks at how issues of identities get reshaped and reformulated with the construction of a particular past that becomes the basis of a contemporary identity. The paper further emphasizes the historical circumstances in which the past is recovered, constructed and represented. However, the past is always contested or may be used in a variety of ways to articulate contemporary concerns of the community. While examining the response of Indian Muslims of the nineteenth century to British rule in India, the paper examines the attitudes of Saiyid Ahmad Barelvi (1786-1831) and Altaf Husain Hali (1837-1914). Their ideas were crucial to a proper understanding of the process of the identity formation among Indian Muslims in the nineteenth century. While the colonial historiography denigrated India's past, the response of these two to British rule and the consequent plight of the Muslilms was to utilize the past for the construction of an identity aimed at the regeneration of the Muslim community and the restoration of its lost prestige in society. The former adopted violent means to accomplish his objectives, used the symbolism of *jihad*, and promoted *hajj* and widow remarriage. The latter, on the other hand, endeavoured to construct an identity for Muslims in a non-violent and peaceful manner by extolling the former glory of Islam and lamenting its subsequent degeneration in his famous poem, *Musaddas*. While Saiyid Ahmad failed in his objectives and died for his cause, Hali succeeded in his mission, given the unprecedented response his poem received from all classes and categories of Muslims.

Perhaps one of the crucial ways to understand religious identities is to analyse the context in which they were located, and their reaction to the context and negotiations with it. In many ways, identities were constructed around certain metaphors, themes and symbols that often changed the character of the religious community concerned. Questioning existing academic theories of primordial and constructionist identities, Rizwan Qaiser tries to bring out the experience of South Asian Muslims against anti-colonial struggles, with special reference to the revolt of 1857 and the Khilafat movement. He emphasizes that in either of the two contexts in which the Muslims participated, the aim was not to seek an autonomous political space. Rather, the struggles were directed towards a historical condition where it would be possible to integrate themselves into a nation along with other religious communities. The process was complex as it is seen in the analyses of *jihad* by Qaiser. Qaiser points out that during the revolt of 1857, Muslim leaders like Begum Hazrat Mahal and many others never gave this call. Nor did they invoke any religious metaphor to mobilize the masses. Their strategies and methods attempted to include both Hindus and Muslims through the passionate call against the oppression and tyranny of British colonial rule. Similarly, the support to the Khilafat movement, on the one hand, was apart of a pan-Islamic movement but, on the other, it was an anti-colonial struggle within the country which never had any exclusivist boundaries. The resources were certainly exclusive but not the larger objective that attempted to constitute an inclusive political society or nation. Qaiser argues that the Muslims did not always rely on religion; they also drew from other sources of political energy like the immediate historical experience of subjugation and exploitation. While discussing a set of intellectual, political, social and religious responses of Muslims to the British presence, the essay establishes that there were, in fact, multiple leaders and multiple identities within the Muslim fold. Thus, both

Farooqui and Qaiser establish that a 'one size fits all' approach towards the study of religious experience and the religiosity of Indian Muslims is problematic. Rather, a pluralistic, multifaceted approach is needed that can recognize broad similarities and unique differences in religious experience. This uniqueness is also reflected in Joy Pachuau's essay on Christianity in Mizoram. Pachuau points out that the adoption of Christianity in Mizoram was as recent as the last decade of the nineteenth century, with the earliest conversions from traditional forms of belief, often referred to as animism. The paper addresses the issue as to why and how this almost-total identification with Christianity, albeit in a local idiom, took place. The context could be traced to the historical circumstances of the arrival of Christianity and the impact of colonialism in the region, when ideas of modernity and English education coalesced with the Mizo social structure and belief, thus facilitating the shift to a new form of religious identity. In this way, historical and sociological factors become crucial in trying to understand why an adopted religion, which is just a little more than 100 years old, becomes an intrinsic part of the Mizo identity today.

Among the two essays on religious conflicts, the first focuses on the idea that these need not be always be disruptive leading to fissures. Built within the process of conflict are elements of negotiations and accommodations which have to be recognized. Often, such conflicts become close to the established structures and even legitimize them. This point is emphasized in Biswamoy Pati's paper that probes the 'making' of the plebeian Mahima cult and the Munda rebellion by weaving in diverse dimensions of social history, ranging from the fallout of the colonization of the region, the famine of 1866 (*Nanka Durbikhya*) and the activities of missionaries. Critical of what he considers the elitist approach of certain scholars associated with Subaltern Studies, who depict tribal/peasant revolts as 'autonomous' and marked by 'territoriality', Pati shows how both these movements transgressed the boundaries ascribed to them. As delineated, both strategically employed a discourse of equality to fight their immediate oppressors. Thus, the Mahima movement represented an anti-caste, monotheistic order that sought to delegitimize the *rājās* and brāhmaṇas. Similarly, the Munda protest (led by the Mundas who had converted to Christianity) in 1939 opposed the princely state of Gangpur and also confronted colonialism. In discussing these movements, this paper aims to delineate fascinating aspects of popular imagination and interrogate some of the assumptions of the subaltern historiography. Pati further states that by interrogating the Brahmanical order and delegitimizing it, both these struggles, particularly the Mahima movement, posed a serious threat to the caste system. At the same time, by 'otherizing' some castes, the Mahima movement drew upon some oppressive features that it had set out to contest. Its patrons included some of the elite sections of society and, in fact, its major centre was at Dhenkanal, a princely state.

Another important aspect of religious conflicts is the use of the religious rhetoric of persecution and hatred that is often linked to larger socio-economic and political interests. Pius Malekandathil's paper discusses the religious idioms and languages used by the Portuguese against the St. Thomas Christians of Kerala. The central purpose of this paper is to see how the cultural and mercantile strategies of the commercially-oriented Portuguese to bring the spice-producing community of the St. Thomas Christians under the control of *Padroado Real* were resisted and challenged by the latter, despite both belonging to the same faith, Christianity. Malekandathil feels that the use of the religious rhetoric of persecution and hatred by the Portuguese should be viewed within the frame of their larger mercantile interests of creating an atmosphere that would help to maximize their trade with Lisbon. A chain of accusations of 'Nestorian heresy' was levelled against the spice-producing indigenous Christians, whose age-old customs, practices and rituals were labelled 'heretical' by the Portuguese. Such a religious rhetoric was intensively used to erase the indigenous culture, ritual practices and traditions prevalent amongst the St. Thomas Christians. The core areas of conflict and resistance often moved from diverse religious platforms to the domain of economics, with the spice-producing indigenous Christians blocking the flow of pepper and other spices from inland production centres to Portuguese factories on the coast, and diverting the trade to the Coromandel ports through Ghat-routes. The final outcome of this conflict was the open revolt against the Portuguese in 1653.

On the whole, this volume has attempted to bring together different perspectives on religion, and its negotiations and interactions with changing historical contexts. Caste, gender, class, politics and commerce came to influence religion and religious discourse and were, in turn, influenced by them. The essays argue that the structured, well-defined, universal religious identities of modern times cannot be superimposed on to the historical past. The essays, while focusing on a multi-dimensional framework of analysing religious processes and identity formation, point to the complex interactions and negotiations between the 'sacred' and 'secular' and go beyond the simplistic binarism that informs large number of modern historical works on Indian religions.

NOTES

1. Some of the works with an interdisciplinary approach on religion in Indian history are: Richard Eaton, *Sufis of Bijapur, 1300-1700: Social Role of the Sufis in Medieval India*, Princeton: Princeton University Press, 1978; Romila Thapar, 'Imagined Religious Communities? Ancient History and Modern Search for a Hindu Identity', in *Interpreting Early India*, Delhi: Oxford University Press, 1992, pp. 60-88; Richard Eaton, *The Rise of Islam and the Bengal Frontier, 1204-1760*, Berkeley: University of California Press, 1993; Harjot Oberoi, *The Construction of Religious Boundaries: Culture, Identity and Diversity in the Sikh Tradition*, Delhi: Oxford University Press, 1994; David N. Lorenzen, ed., *Bhakti Religion in North India: Community, Identity and Political Action*, Delhi: Mahohar, 1996; Kunal Chakrabarti, *Religious Process: The Puranas and the Making of a Regional Tradition*, Delhi: Oxford University Press, 2001; David Ludden, ed., *Making India Hindu: Religion, Community, and the Politics of Democracy in India*, 2nd edn., Delhi: Oxford University Press, 2005; Satish Saberwal and Supriya Varma, eds., *Traditions in Motion: Religion and Society in History*, Delhi: Oxford University Press, 2005; Irfan Habib, ed., *Religion in Indian History*, Delhi: Tulika Books, 2007; and Christian Lee Novetzke,

History, Bhakti, and Public Memory: Namdev in Religious and Secular Traditions, Ranikhet: Permanent Black, 2008.

2. It may be added here that D.D. Kosambi's collection of essays entitled *Myth and Reality*, Bombay: Popular Prakashan, 1962, is the first major attempt to understand India's religious history from the Marxist standpoint, although his *An Introduction to the Study of Indian History*, Bombay: Popular Prakashan, 1956 had already offered a few glimpses of his use of the Marxist ideology to study ancient Indian religious beliefs, practices and institutions. For an overview of various approaches to religion and studies in religion in Indian history, see Krishna Mohan Shrimali, *Religion, Ideology and Society*, Presidential Address, Indian History Congress, 49th Session, Dharwad: Karnataka University, 1988; and Kunal Chakrabarti, 'Recent Approaches to the History of Religion in Ancient India', in Romila Thapar, ed., *Recent Perspectives of Early Indian History*, Mumbai: Popular Prakashan, 1995, pp. 185-245.
3. For details, see Mircea Eliade, *Sacred and the Profane: The Nature of Religion*, tr. from French by William R. Trask, London: Harvest Book, 1957, rpt.; Talal Asad, *Formations of the Secular: Christianity, Islam and Modernity*, Stanford: Stanford University Press, 2003; and Giorgio Agamben, *Profanations*, New York: Zone Books, 2007. The notions of 'sacred', 'profane' and 'secular' in these works are conceptually analysed. However, in this collection, the theoretical aspects are not highlighted. In keeping with the central idea of these works, it is emphasized here that both the sacred and profane and the sacred and secular are not dichotomous categories as Emile Durkheim has suggested. They interact with each other, influencing and transforming each other in the process. Also see Emile Durkheim, *The Elementary Forms of Religious Life*, tr. from French by Joseph Ward Swain, George Allen, 1964; and T.N. Madan, ed., *Religion in India*, Delhi: Oxford University Press, 1993, pp. 1-22.
4. Irfan Habib, 'Kabir: The Historical Setting', in Irfan Habib, ed., op. cit., 2007, p. 143.
5. A large number of historical researches was published after 1992. The central theme of these works was the Hindu-Muslim relation and the historical basis of the communal antagonism. For details, see, Gyanendra Pandey, *Hindus and Others: The Question of Identity in India Today*, Delhi: Oxford University Press, 1993; Cynthia Talbot, 'Inscribing the Other, Inscribing the Self: Hindu-Muslim Identities in Pre-Colonial India', in *Comparative Studies in Society and History*, vol. 37, 1995, pp. 692-722; Phillip B. Wagoner, 'Sultan Among Hindu Kings: Dress, Titles and Islamicization of Hindu Culture at Vijayanagar', in

Journal of Asian Studies, vol. 55, no. 4, 1996, pp. 851-80; Brajadulal Chattopadhyaya, *Representing the Other? Sanskrit Sources and the Muslims (Eighth to Fourteenth Century)*, Delhi: Manohar, 1998; David Gilmartin and Bruce B. Lawrence, eds., *Beyond Turk and Hindu: Rethinking Religious Identities in Islamicate South Asia*, Gainesville: University Press of Florida, 2000; Richard Eaton, *Essays on Islam and Indian History*, Delhi: Oxford University Press, 2000; Muzaffar Alam, *The Poltical Language of Islam*, Delhi: Permanent Black, 2002; Shahid Amin, 'On Retelling the Muslim Conquest of North India', in Partha Chatterjee and Anjan Ghosh, eds., *History and Present*, Delhi: Permanent Black, 2002; Richard Eaton, ed., *India's Islamic Traditions*, Delhi: Oxford University Press, 2003; Romila Thapar, *Somanath: The Many Voices of a History*, Delhi: Viking/Penguin, 2004; David N. Lorenzen, *Who Invented Hinduism? Essays on Religion in History*, Delhi: Yoda Press, 2005; Mushirul Hasan and Asim Roy, eds., *Living Together Separately: Cultural India in History and Politics*, Delhi: Oxford University Press, 2005; Satish Saberwal and Mushirul Hasan, eds., *Assertive Religious Identities: India and Europe*, Delhi: Manohar, 2006; Finbarr Barry Flood, ed., *Piety and Politics in the Early Indian Mosques*, Delhi: Oxford University Press, 2008; and Sunil Kumar, ed., *Demolishing Myths or Mosques and Temples?: Readings on History and Temple Desecration in Medieval India*, Delhi: Three Essays, 2008.

6. The editors are grateful to the rapporteurs, Samuel Philip and Shyba Babu, students of the postgraduate programme in the Department of History and Culture, Jamia Millia Islamia for recording the inaugural address delivered by Professor Irfan Habib.
7. Irfan Habib, in Irfan Habib, ed., op. cit., p. 142.
8. For details, see, Talal Asad, op. cit., 2003; Rajeev Bhargava, ed., *Secularism and Its Critics*, Delhi: Oxford University Press, 1998; Hent de Vries and Lawrence E. Suvillan, *Political Theologies: Public Religions in a Post-Secular World*, Delhi: Social Science Press and Orient Longman, 2007, abridged edition; and Asim Roy, 'Introduction', in Mushirul Hasan and Asim Roy, eds., op. cit., pp. 1-25.
9. Talal Asad, op. cit., 2003, p. 2.
10. Asim Roy, op. cit., p. 12.
11. Scholars argue that Western nations never subscribed to secularism as a political doctrine to begin with. For details, see, Asim Roy, op. cit., p. 11; Talat Asad, op. cit., pp. 6-8.
12. Ashis Nandy, 'Counter-statement on Humanistic Temper', *Mainstream*, 10 October 1981, pp. 16-18; *The Intimate Enemy: Loss and Recovery of Self under Colonial Rule*, Delhi: Oxford University Press, 1983;

'The Politics of Secularism and the Recovery of Religious Toleration', in Rajeev Bhargava, ed., op. cit., pp. 321-44; T.N. Madan, 'Whither Secularism in India?', in *Modern Asian Studies*, 27: 3, 1993; *Modern Myths, Locked Minds, Secularism and Fundamentalism in India*, Delhi: Oxford University Press, 1997; 'Secularism in Its Place', in Rajeev Bhargava, ed., op. cit., pp. 297-320; and Partha Chatterjee, 'Secularism and Tolerance', in Rajeev Bhargava, ed., op. cit., pp. 345-79. There are some scholars who, while being skeptical about the relevance of secularism in the Indian context, have a different point of view. For details, see, Akeel Bilgrami, 'Secularism, Nationalism, and Modernity', in Rajeev Bhargava, op. cit., pp. 380-417; and Stanley J. Tambiah, 'The Crisis of Secularism in India', in Rajeev Bhargava, op. cit., pp. 418-53.

13. Rajeev Bhargava, op. cit., p. 28; Rajeev Bhargava, 'What is Secularism For?', pp. 486-542; Asim Roy, in Mushirul Hasan and Asim Roy, eds., op. cit., p. 17.
14. Shahid Amin, in Partha Chatterjee and Anjan Ghosh, eds., op. cit., p. 32.
15. Romila Thapar, Harbans Mukhia and Bipan Chandra, *Communalism and the Writing of Indian History*, Delhi: People's Publishing House, 1969.
16. Partha Chatterjee, *The Nation and Its Fragments: Colonial and Postcolonial Histories*, Delhi: Oxford University Press, 1994, pp. 73-4, 76-94; and Shahid Amin in Partha Chatterjee and Anjan Ghosh, eds., op. cit., pp. 23-9.
17. Also see Shireen Ratnagar, 'A Past to Mirror Ourselves', XXVII M.A. Ansari Memorial Lecture, Delhi: Department of History and Culture, Jamia Millia Islamia, 25 February, 2009.
18. Spearheaded by right-wing political forces that subsequently came to power, rhetoric developed advocating the avenging of a past in which the Muslims had destroyed temples, causing immense trauma to the Hindu psyche. Such rhetoric dominated history writing, particularly in the revised version of the NCERT history textbooks. For details, see Mushirul Hasan, 'The BJP's Intellectual Agenda: Textbooks and Imagined History', in *South Asia*, December 2003. Also reprinted in Mushirul Hasan, ed., *Will Secular India Survive?*, Gurgaon: Imprint One, 2004, pp. 157-76; Sunil Kumar, 'Introduction', in Sunil Kumar, ed., pp. 1-21. For television serials that echo such views, see Uma Chakravarti, 'Inventing Saffron History: A Celibate Hero Rescues an Emasculated Nation', in *Everyday Lives, Everyday Histories: Beyond the Kings and Brahmanas of 'Ancient' India*, Delhi: Tulika, 2006.
19. Mohammad Habib, "Sultan Mahmud of Ghazni', in K.A. Nizami, ed., *Politics and Society during the Early Medieval Period: Collected Works*

of Professor Mohammad Habib, vol. I, Delhi: People's Publishing House, 1981, pp. 36-104.

20. Romila Thapar, 2004, op. cit.
21. Romila Thapar, 'Narratives of a History', in Sunil Kumar, ed., op. cit., pp. 70-1.
22. Ibid., pp. 68-74.
23. Richard Davis, *Lives of Indian Images*, Delhi: Motilal Banarsidass, 1999, rpt.; first published in Princeton: Princeton University Press, 1997; and Richard Davis, 'Indian Art Objects as Loots', in *The Journal of Asian Studies*, vol. 52, 1993, pp. 22-48; also in Sunil Kumar, ed., op. cit., pp. 23-64.
24. Richard Eaton, 'Temple Desecration and Indo-Muslim States', in David Gilmartin and Bruce B. Lawrence, eds., 2000, op. cit., pp. 246-81; also see in Richard Eaton, 2000, op. cit., pp. 94-132; in Sunil Kumar, ed., op. cit., pp. 93-139. For further details on the critical analysis of Aurangzeb as a 'temple destroyer' and a 'religious bigot' who re-imposed *jaziya*, see Carl W. Ernst, 'Admiring the Works of the Ancients: The Ellora Temples as Viewed by Indo-Muslim Authors', in David Gilmartin and Bruce Lawrence, eds., op. cit., pp. 98-120; Satish Chandra, '*Jiziya* and the State in India during the Seventeenth Century', in Richard Eaton, ed., 2003, pp. 133-49; S.M. Azizuddin Husain, '*Jaziya*: Its Re-imposition during the Reign of Aurangzeb: An Examination', in *Structure of Politics under Aurangzeb, 1658-1707*, Delhi: Kanishka, 2002, pp. 92-130.
25. See Ayesha Jalal, *Partisans of Allah: Jihad in South Asia*, Ranikhet: Permanent Black, 2009 for an analysis of the concept of *jihad.*
26. Romila Thapar, 1992, op. cit., pp. 13-18.; Irfan Habib, in Irfan Habib, ed., 2008, op. cit., p. 143.
27. Ibid.
28. For a different view, see, David N. Lorenzen, 'Who Invented Hinduism?', in *Comparative Studies in Society and History*, vol. 41, no. 4, October, 1999, pp. 630-59; also reprinted in David N. Lorenzen, 2000, op. cit., pp. 1-32.
29. Richard Eaton, 'Introduction', in Richard Eaton, ed., 2003, p. 2.
30. David Gilmartin and Bruce Lawrence, 'Introduction', in David Gilmartin and Bruce Lawrence, eds., 2000, op. cit., p. 2.
31. The term 'Islamicate' was coined by the American historian Marshall G.S. Hodgson to refer to Africa and Eurasia that were not inhabited by large numbers of Muslims but registered the influence of Muslim rulers, leading to a cosmopolitan broad-based interface of civilizations. For details, see Marshall G.S. Hodgson, *The Venture of Islam: Conscience and History in a World Civilization*, Chicago: University of Chicago

Press, 1974, pp. 57-60. For works that use these terms for various case studies, see David Gilmartin and Bruce Lawrence, eds., 2000, op. cit.; Richard Eaton, 2000; Richard Eaton, ed., 2003 and Meenakshi Khanna, ed., *Cultural History of Medieval India*, Delhi: Social Science Press, 2007, p. xxv.

32. Romila Thapar, 1992, op. cit., pp. 77-81; Brajadulal Chattopadhyaya, 1998, op. cit.
33. See, for instance, Zia-uddin Barani, *Fatawa-i-Jahandari*, English tr. Prof. M. Habib and Mrs Afsar Khan under the title *Political Theory of the Delhi Sultanate*, Allahabad: Kitab Mahal, n.d.; see also Harbans Mukhia, 'Medieval Indian History and the Communal Approach', in Romila Thapar, Harbans Mukhia and Bipan Chandra, 1967, op. cit., pp. 22-35; Harbans Mukhia, *Historians and Historiography During the Reign of Akbar*, Delhi: Vikas, 1976; and Harbans Mukhia, *Perspectives on Medieval History*, Delhi: Vikas, 1993, pp. 33-45.
34. Some of the works on religion and state, with special reference to the religious policy of Akbar, are: Osamu Kondo, 'Akbar and the Theologians' Declaration (Mahzar) of 1579', in Irfan Habib, ed., op. cit., pp. 158-66; Shireen Moosvi, 'The Road to *Sulh-i-Kul*: Akbar's Alienation from Theological Islam', in Irfan Habib, ed., op. cit., pp. 167-76; Irfan Habib, ed., *Akbar and His India*, Delhi: Oxford University Press, 1997; Irfan Habib, 'A Political Theory of the Mughal Empire: A Study of the Ideas of Abu'l Fazl', *Proceedings of the Indian History Congress, 59th Session*, Patiala, 1998, pp. 329-40; Iqtidar Alam Khan, 'The Nobility Under Akbar and the Development of His Religious Policy', in *Journal of the Royal Asiatic Society of Great Britain and Ireland*, 1968, pp. 29-36. Also reprinted in Richard Eaton, ed., 2003, op. cit., pp. 120-32.
35. Tarachand, *Influence of Islam on Indian Culture*, Allahabad: Indian Press Publication, 1963 (2nd edn.); Yusuf Hussain, *Glimpses of Medieval Indian Culture*, Bombay: Asia Publishing House, 1959.
36. There is considerable scholarship on conflicts between the different bhakti traditions and intolerance towards each other, as well as towards Jainism and Buddhism. These conflicts have strong sectarian and violent overtones that question the popular understanding of Hinduism as a 'tolerant' and 'non-violent' religion. Some of the essays are Romila Thapar, 1992, op. cit., pp. 60-71; David N. Lorenzen, ed., 1996, op. cit.; R. Chamapakalakshmi, 'From Devotion and Dissent to Dominance: The *Bhakti* of the Tamil Alvars and Nayanars', in R. Champakalakshmi and S. Gopal, ed., *Tradition, Dissent and Ideology: Essays in Honour of Romila Thapar*, Delhi: Oxford University Press, 1996, pp. 135-63; D.N. Jha, 'Constructing the Hindu Identity', in Irfan Habib, ed.,

2008, op. cit., pp. 210-37; Rameshwar Prasad Bahuguna, 'Conflict and Assimilation in Medieval North Indian Culture', Jamia Millia Islamia, Delhi.

37. Phillippe Borgeaud, *Encyclopedia of Religion*, Mircea Eliade, ed., New York: Collier Macmillan, 1987, vol. 9: 366, entry *Memorization.*
38. For reasons beyond the control of the editors, it was only possible to solicit two essays out of the five presented in the conference.

PART I

Texts, Traditions and Discourse

ONE

Of Binaries and Beyond

The Dialectics of Buddhist-Brahmanical Relations in India

Uma Chakravarti

Examining the relationship between Buddhism and Brahmanism has a long history, going back to the nineteenth century when the historical analysis of texts and textual traditions was first seriously undertaken in India.[1] The subject continues to have relevance even today with numerous scholars focusing attention on the relationship. What then could one be saying that is meaningful to our understanding of religious or ethical systems in the past or in the present? I would argue that we need to rethink the two systems as discrete binaries that are also persistently opposed to each other, an idea that many of us have conventionally worked with. We need to do this even as we may continue to position ourselves in one or other binary, broadly in a mutually antagonistic relationship with the other. Thus, I would locate myself in a position that acknowledges the antagonism between the two while insisting that we need to open up lines of enquiry on the extent and nature of the interaction, as well as the opposition between the two and the ensuing textual dialogue that was generated thereby.

Certain simplistic positions have obstructed our possible understanding because they have come from highly esteemed intellectuals with a wide influence in the public sphere. For example, we carry the baggage of the nationalist regeneration of 'Hinduism' visible from the late nineteenth century wherein Buddhism could not be granted an autonomous existence. As India's best known 'export item' in the past, contributing immensely to the culture of East and

South-East Asia, it needed to be claimed within Hinduism, or at least treated in harmony with it, or regarded as a reform movement within it that invigorated the main religious tradition, and finally being incorporated within it. A classic example of this position is represented by S. Radhakrishnan, the erstwhile President of India. In his words 'The Buddha did not feel that he was announcing a new religion. He was born, grew up and died a Hindu. He was restating with a new emphasis the ancient ideals of the Indo-Aryan civilization. . . .'[2]

And again:

> Buddhism did not start as a new and independent religion. It was an offshoot of the more ancient faith of the Hindus, perhaps a schism or a heresy. . . .[3]

> The Buddha's main object was to bring about a reformation in religious practices and return to the basic principles. All those who adhere to the essential framework of the Hindu religion and attempt to bring it back to the essential framework . . . are treated as *avatāras*. The Buddha was regarded as an *avatāra* who reclaimed Hindus from erroneous practices and purified their religion. . . .[4]

> The Buddha utilized the Hindu inheritance to correct some of its expressions. He came to fulfill, not to destroy. *For us in this country, the Buddha is an outstanding representative of our religious tradition* [emphasis added].[5]

In a similar vein, the well-known Indologist and art historian, Ananda Coomaraswamy, firmly believed that in all essentials, Buddhism and Brahmanism formed a single system.[6]

At the other end, part of the problem in exploring the relationship between Buddhism and Brahmanism is also the baggage of the more recent past wherein many secular and rationalist figures from the late nineteenth century onwards found Buddhism to be an attractive and humane alternative to Brahmanism/Hinduism, even seeing it on occasion as a powerful way to exit an oppressive religious tradition that denied humanity to large sections within its fold. It is this position that informed Ambedkar's 'conversion' to Buddhism in 1956 and its political fallout has had repercussions in writings about the relationship between Buddhism and Brahmanism.[7] Drawing broadly from the latter position and distancing myself from those who collapse the difference between the two,

I suggest that we see the two systems in a dialectical relationship with each other and explore the negotiations and tensions on both sides. Thus, we should examine the critical dialogue between the two over the centuries even though such a dialogue is often oblique rather than direct or confrontational at most times.

BUDDHIST-BRAHMANA DIALECTICS

Buddhist-Brahmanical dialogues pepper the Buddhist texts and what is notable is that sometimes the same brāhmaṇa characters appear in a number of *suttas*,[8] even asking the same question on different occasions. The brāhmaṇas confine their questions to their claims to birth-based superiority. This entitles them to the highest reverence and the right to draw services from all others, particularly the śūdras. One finds reference to these themes in the *Ambaṭṭha Sutta* of the *Dīgha Nikāya* and the *Madhura Sutta* of the *Majjhima Nikāya*, respectively.[9] In the former, the main protagonist is Ambaṭṭha, a young brāhmaṇa who was being trained in all the subtleties of Vedic-brahmanic lore under the wealthy brāhmaṇa, Pokkharasādi. Ambaṭṭha was also the recipient of richly endowed lands granted by the king in the prosperous village Ikkhānankala. Curious to test the prowess of the Buddha, Ambaṭṭha was sent to literally 'suss' him out by his teacher, Pokkharasādi. Ambaṭṭha went off in a richly caparisoned horse accompanied by a retinue of young brāhmaṇas. Clearly there were huge stakes involved in this intellectual testing of wits. The churlish and proud Ambaṭṭha tried to provoke the Buddha by calling the Sākyans *bandhupadapakka* literally meaning a menial. From the initial interaction between Ambaṭṭha and the Buddha, it appears that there was an ongoing war of words between the Sākyans and brāhmaṇas with the latter clearly rattled by the Buddhist refusal to accept their superiority.[10]

Indeed throughout this long and rich *sutta* with many twists in the argument, an important issue came up which would finally figure in later texts, particularly the *Vajrasūcī*. This issue was the impossibility of maintaining purity of birth by restricting the marriage circle without which the brāhmaṇa claim to birth-based superiority could not stand. Before the proud Ambaṭṭha was humbled, there was the impending threat of his head splitting into pieces for his failure to sustain his intellectual challenge against the Sākyans, used here in the sense of the followers of the Buddha.[11] Then, as the brāhmaṇa gang began to revile Ambaṭṭha for his own low birth, the Buddha turned the discussion to another plane, first establishing more rigid marriage practices amongst the kṣatriyas and then, more pertinently, showing why such questions were in any case irrelevant in the context of *dhamma*. The Buddha pointed out that questions such as the purity of lineage, or who is superior and who inferior, were brought up only while negotiating a marriage! For those seeking wisdom, these were mundane matters and must be shunned. Material possessions, taking grants of land from kings for personal use, and indulging in sensual pleasures took one away from the pursuit of salvation and hence, must be renounced by those seeking the righteous life. Both Ambaṭṭha and Pokkharasādi were then convinced of the Buddha's teachings. The pride of pure birth was finally humbled by the use of arguments that highlighted the higher ethics of the Buddhists who privileged conduct and high values over birth-based claims to special reverence and privileges.[12]

Amongst the most interesting of the Buddhist-brāhmaṇa dialogues is the *Agganna Sutta.*[13] This *sutta* comprises two parts. In the first, set in the Buddhist present, the usual claim of superiority was made by a number of brāhmaṇas who reviled and abused two *bhikkhus*, Vāseṭṭha and Bhāradvāja. These *bhikkhus* were erstwhile brāhmaṇas before they joined the *sangha* and appear in various *suttas* as the askers of stock questions on the brāhmaṇa claim of supremacy. They began with the statement that the brāhmaṇas claimed they were born from Brahma, the creator's mouth, and therefore were the purest of men and the heirs of Brahma. Thus, the dominant version in the Puruṣa Sūkta hymn of the *Ṛgveda* describing the origin of the varṇa system was circulated in this text. According to the hymn, when the primeval man was sacrificed he produced a brāhmaṇa from the mouth, a kṣatriya from his arms, a vaiśya from his thighs and a śūdra from his feet.[14] This was an important statement of legitimation both for the hierarchy of the four social divisions and for its divine origin, and difficult to challenge. In response, the Buddha used the Durkheimian social fact[15] approach by drawing attention to the sameness of birth processes of the brāhmaṇas as well as all other women and men. According to the Buddha, brāhmaṇa women, too, menstruated, got pregnant, brought forth babies and then nursed them. In claiming to be born from Brahma's mouth rather than from a woman's womb, they slandered Brahma and forgot their own great heritage.[16] The Buddha then proceeded to redefine what was primary, or to be placed first, i.e. the *bhikkhu*, for his virtues and his wisdom. Here we see the familiar Buddhist argument that it were the ancient brāhmaṇa values such as the practice of *dhamma*, now possessed by the *bhikkhus*, constituted brāhmaṇahood, and entitled someone to be called a brāhmaṇa.

In a long and interesting telling of the origin of the world, the account takes us from a state of being when there were no forms to the evolution of materiality, to gross forms, the earth with a skin-like substance on it, and plants which could be eaten to satisfy hunger. In this telling, the human beings evolved finally with stable gender divisions, making for male and female who experienced heterosexual desire which they consummated. They proceeded to build huts and, in the fall from an earlier state of ethereal beings, individual greed developed. This led to the emergence of households, 'private' property and the state in the form of a king who maintained a social order in which theft was punished. The state and the king gave rise to the category of kṣatriyas. Later, different groups of beings took to different modes of existence. Those who led moral lives, refrained from lies, lived on alms and devoted themselves to meditation were called brāhmaṇas. But they soon descended to being mere reciters of *mantras*. Others took up skills of various kinds and were called *vessas*, and still others pursued cruel occupations such as hunting and came to be called *suddas*.[17] Then finally some members left from all classes and became *bhikkhus*. The *bhikkhus* were primary, the highest type of beings, because they practised righteousness both in this life and the next.[18] This kind of argument was widely interspersed in Buddhist texts, many of which have been put together in a collection called the *Brāhmaṇa Vagga* in the *Dhammapada*.[19]

Here is a sample from the *Brāhmaṇa Vagga* where the Buddha defines brāhmaṇa very pointedly not as a caste but as a set of values, acquired by individuals through strenuous effort:

> A man does not become a *brāhmaṇa* by his plaited hair, or by birth;
> In whom there is truth and righteousness, he is blessed; he is a *brāhmaṇa*[20]
> I do not call a man a *brāhmaṇa* because of his origin or of his mother
> He is indeed arrogant and he is wealthy;
> But he who is without possessions, who is free from all attachments, him I call indeed a *brāhmaṇa*[21]
> Him I call indeed a *brāhmaṇa* who does not cling to sensual pleasures, like water on a lotus leaf, like mustard on the point of a needle[22]
> Him I call indeed a *brāhmaṇa* whose knowledge is deep who possesses wisdom, who knows the right way and the wrong, and has attained the highest end.[23]
> He who is thoughtful, blameless, settled, without passions and who has attained the highest end, him indeed I call a *brāhmaṇa*.[24]
> Him I call indeed a *brāhmaṇa* who without hurting creatures, whether feeble or strong, does not kill, does not cause slaughter.[25]
> Him I call indeed a *brāhmaṇa* who in this world, having abandoned all desires travels about without a home, [and] in whom all covetousness is extinct.[26]
> Because a man is rid of evil he is called he is called a *brāhmaṇa*
> Because he walks quietly he is called a *samaṇa*
> Because he has sent away his own impurities he is called a *pabbajita*.[27]

We can see from the above verses that for the Buddha the term brāhmaṇa represented a set of values in which non-attachment, a basic requirement of the *bhikkhu*, had a central place and he firmly and unambiguously rejected any birth-based claims which was based on reverence from others. The true brāhmaṇa was above pride and must earn his right to being respected. Most notably, he must renounce possessions and be like the *samaṇa*, a wanderer who lived righteously.

Renouncing home and possessions implied a *bhikkhu*-like existence, a withdrawal from production and reproduction without which one could not enter the journey towards *nibbāna*. It was asserted that the world of production set-up attachment to wealth and material possessions and the world of reproduction set-up attachments to sensual pleasures and kin. Both obstructed the goal of *nibbāna*. The brāhmaṇas who claimed privileges were enmeshed in both spheres of activity and were, therefore, least entitled to any special privileges as they had fallen from the true path. This was the context for a lively dialogue between the Buddha and a brāhmaṇa aptly named 'Kāśībhāradvāja', that is an agriculturist brāhmaṇa named Bhāradvāja.[28]

The narrative tells us that on a routine round of alms-seeking, the Buddha came across an energetic sowing activity in a village called Ekanala. A team of about 500 ploughmen who had undertaken the activity of ploughing and sowing were taking a break for their midday meal when the Buddha approached the area where the food distribution was taking place and stood silently apart. The brāhmaṇa, Kāśībhāradvāja, noticed him and said to him pointedly: 'I, oh *samaṇa*, both plough and sow, and having sown I eat; you also should plough and sow and having done so you should eat.' The implication clearly is that only those who work to produce food were entitled to eat. When the Buddha responded by saying that he, too, ploughed and sowed and then he ate, the brāhmaṇa flashed back ironically that he saw no instruments of production being handled by the Buddha—he had no ploughshare, no yoke, no plough! This provided the Buddha the opportunity to metaphorically allude to the work that he actually did in cultivating the mind by using a series of agricultural operations that paralleled them in the road to *nibbāna*. Kāśībhāradvāja was convinced of the merit of this argument and offered him milk *payasa* which the Buddha turned down saying that he did not want anything acquired by the recitation of the *mantras*—something all brāhmaṇas did to gain wealth, thereby introducing a sharp twist in the dialogue that put the prosperous and proud brāhmaṇa in the dock instead of the Buddha.[29]

More irony and humour was deployed in making a critique of animal sacrifices spearheaded by brāhmaṇas for their own gain, but which also implicated the kings since they were rewarded with grants of land, gold, cattle and corn for the performance of these sacrifices. The brāhmaṇa in the narrative was called Kūṭadanta,[30] literally sharp-toothed, who was making preparations for a huge sacrifice. The preparations coincided with a visit by the Buddha to the village where Kūṭadanta intended to perform the sacrifice. The huge response to the Buddha's visit, however, awakened Kūṭadanta's curiosity, so he, too, visited the Buddha. This was the occasion for a veiled critique of the Brahmanical practice of large-scale animal sacrifice with another tale about the past when the good brāhmaṇa counsellor of the king—who was the Buddha in a previous life—advised the king first to distribute resources to those who needed them (a familiar theme in Buddhist texts), and then to substitute the slaughter of animals in the sacrifice with other items. The Buddha also introduced the value of giving *dāna* to the *bhikkhus* for the acquisition of merit, and finally he exhorted the adoption of righteous conduct as a way of life instead of the performance of rituals that required a bloody slaughter of animals. At the end of the account of this past, Kūṭadanta was convinced of the Buddha's arguments against animal sacrifice and the merit of almsgiving. We see here a subtle humour and irony at work in drawing attention to a new ethical and humane set of values using, as in the *Agganna Sutta*, two moments of time—an ethical past and a degenerate present—to debunk Brahmanical rituals and animal sacrifices. These practices were particularly heinous because they used coercion against the *dāsa-karmakāras* in the execution of the rituals.[31] Violence against two sets of helpless beings was, thus, terminated through the ethical intervention of the Buddha who spoke for those who were voiceless in the Brahmanical regime.

Two accounts in the *Jātakas* carried the Buddhist critique of Brahmanical practices into the humbler public domain in which they circulated. The first was a critique of the Brahmanical obsession with purity and pollution taboos, the observance of which was the basis of their claims to superior status. A brāhmaṇa, Setaketu, who considered himself very pure had to cross paths with a *cāṇḍāla.* Fearing that he would be polluted if the wind struck the latter first and then went towards him, he called out in panic, 'Curse you! You ill-omened *cāṇḍāla*, get to leeward!' and quickly went to the windward side himself. But the *cāṇḍāla* was too quick for him and stood to his windward side, clearly defying and teasing the brāhmaṇa for his silly beliefs. The *cāṇḍāla* then offered that he would follow the brāhmaṇa's command if the latter could prove his mettle with him in a debate. Clearly believing himself to be superior, the brāhmaṇa agreed but was unable to stand his ground intellectually and was defeated. The *cāṇḍāla* forcibly made the brāhmaṇa bow before him to rub his pride in. In the usual style of the *Jātakas*, the *cāṇḍāla* was identified as Sariputta (born in a brāhmaṇa household but now representing the higher vaves of a *bhikkhu*) in a previous birth and Setaketu as a false priest.[32]

In the *Therīgāthā*, we have the story of a young *dāsī* called Puṇṇā, which literally means 'little'. Puṇṇā was a *kumbhadāsī*, a slave girl in a rich merchant's house. She used to bring water from the river for the merchant's house throughout the year. During the winter she noticed a brāhmaṇa man shivering while taking his dips in the water and said to him:

> Drawer of water, I [go] down to the water
> Even in winter in fear of blows,
> Harassed by fear of blame from mistresses,
> What *brāhmaṇa* fearest thou that ever thus
> Thou goest down to the water
> Why with shivering limbs dost thou suffer bitter cold?

The brāhmaṇa explained that he suffered bitter cold in order to wash off his sins and release him of his ill-deeds. Puṇṇā responded with gentle irony, asking a very commonsensical question: 'Why then, the fishes and the tortoises, frogs and water snakes must straight to heaven go?'

The irony gets even better because she suggests that the water would wash away the merit too, not just the sin, unless it was very discerning and knew exactly what to wash off and what to leave. Surely that was not the case, so Puṇṇā advised that it was better to give up the shivering and muttering and the pursuit of meaningless rituals.[33]

Significantly, this is a classic argument that surfaces in many counter-Brahmanical traditions in later times too, one of which was recounted to me when I talked about Puṇṇā in Pakistan, as forming a stock theme in Sufi poetry. Together, the 'popular' tradition rebutted the core of Brahmanical beliefs, caste purity rules and rituals that maintained their superior claims in society, which were rejected by the Buddhists as false. It is not surprising then that Dharmakīrti, the Buddhist scholar of the fourth century CE, should sum up Brahmanism as: the vanity of caste, belief in the Vedas and a creator, the ritual of sacrifice, taking the holy dip to get merit, and torturing the body to redeem sins. According to him, these were the five characteristics of the stupidity of Brahmanism.[34] Such themes also surfaced in the bhakti literature of medieval times, particularly in the poetry of Kabir. Clearly Buddhism left a powerful legacy for all counter-traditions in the subcontinent.

READING THE *VAJRASŪCĪ*

Roughly half a millennium after the Buddha lived and taught his ethico-religious philosophy of suffering and its cessation, of righteous conduct and the cultivation of the self, of rejecting rituals and birth-based claims by the brāhmaṇas to monopolizing knowledge and drawing services from other social groups, an important text in hybrid Sanskrit titled the *Vajrasūcī* was composed. The text is attributed to Aśvaghoṣa although scholars are not in agreement over its authorship. This is a text that critiques caste but does so drawing almost entirely—at least on the face of it—from Brahmanical texts and Brahmanical myths. According to literary tradition, Aśvaghoṣa (*c.* first century BC) was born in a brāhmaṇa family[35] but was drawn to Buddhism. This gave him an understanding of both traditions which he seemed to have used to good effect in the *Vajrasūcī*, which literally means diamond needle, referring here perhaps to the cutting of the Brahmanical position on caste.

In his famous compendium of Indian literature compiled in the early twentieth century, Maurice Winternitz regards Aśvaghoṣa's method as most effective since he uses texts produced by the brāhmaṇas themselves to refute their claims to pure birth, by drawing suitable and selected quotations from the Vedas, the

Mahābhārata and the *Manusaṁhitā*. All these texts are till today the canonical texts of the brāhmaṇa tradition. The internet version of *Vajrasūcī* shows how fragile such claims are.[36] For its style of refutation, its familiarity with Brahmanical texts and its persuasive logic, Sukumari Bhattacharji regards it as a work of Aśvaghoṣa.[37] I am inclined to accept this position even though there is conflicting evidence within the Buddhist tradition itself.[38] Although we may never settle the issue of authorship, we may be fairly certain of its Buddhist origins, as its arguments are derived from the Buddhist style of rebuttal. The special feature in this case is that it does not always use the common sense positions that underwrite early Buddhist arguments attributed to the Buddha, examples of which I have already included here, but are a combination of common sense reasoning and more intellectual modes of arguing.

Although the *Vajrasūcī* has circulated among certain circles that I will examine below, it has not received much scholarly attention in contemporary works, even though there is an interesting history of its circulation in the last two centuries. The reasons for this are not clear. There is an even longer history of its circulation as a text. In Maharashtra today, there is a popular tradition that Bahinabai, the brāhmaṇa woman bhakti poet of the thirteenth century, translated the text into Marathi and this would have made the text accessible to other bhakti poets from humbler backgrounds. Bahinabai was a disciple of Sant Tukaram, one of the best known bhakti poets of Maharashtra. According to the 'religious historian' R.C. Dhere, this 'fiercely anti-Brahmanic text' is believed to have influenced an eighteenth-century bhakti poet Śrīśyāmrāja. In the nineteenth century, it appeared in the writings of Gurav, a śūdra, who wrote the *Nāthalīlāmara* and 'who paraphrased parts of the *Vajrasūcī* in it'.[39] Clearly it had been kept alive in the anti-Brahmanic tradition in Maharashtra by the bhakti poets, many of whom were drawn from the poorer and lower castes of Maharashtra.

Rosalind O'Hanlon has also traced the history of the *Vajrasūcī* as it was picked up and circulated amongst colonial scholars/ administrators and other literary compilers. The British resident at Kathmandu, B.M. Hodgson, received a copy from a Buddhist friend. The work was first translated into English under his aegis and Hodgson read it to the Royal Asiatic Society of Great Britain and Ireland in 1831. The translated work was published as *The Wajrasuchi or The Refutation of the Argument upon Which the Brahmanical Institution of Caste is Founded* in 1839. It contained an introduction to the work by Lancelot Wilkinson, the political agent in Bhopal, with a letter from Hodgson detailing the contents of the pamphlet.[40] With all this in circulation, it is not surprising that Rammohun Roy found support for his reformist position in the *Vajrasūcī* and enhanced its circulation by translating it into Bengali. The 'recovery' of the text in the nineteenth century and the notice that it received from the colonial authorities, as well as its circulation in European Indological circles, must have produced great anxiety amongst Sanskrit pandits who received patronage from the colonial state by virtue of their caste as learned brāhmaṇas particularly in western India.[41] It is notable that the brāhmaṇa pandit who probably helped to edit and translate the text with Wilkinson, refused to be part of the project unless his 'refutation' of the *Vajrasūcī* was published alongside its English translated version.

Wilkinson's version was accompanied by an indignant response from Soobajee Bapoo, titled *Tanku: Being a Response to the Vajrasūcī.* Winternitz, Sylvain Levi and Huber in the *History of Sanskrit Buddhism* point out that Aśvaghoṣa would have been delighted by Soobajee's response. In any case, the 'argument was not dulled by the offended *brāhmaṇa's* reply....' Thus, the violent polemist who had so frequently and so cruelly humiliated the pride of the brāhmaṇas, once more enters the scene, after centuries of silence in the shock of religious controversy.[42]

Much like the growing patronage by kings in the days of the Buddha for the Buddhists, which may have been the reason why the brāhmaṇas constantly brought up the issue of their purity in discussions with him, here, too, the stakes were high. The interest taken by the colonial powers and the Christian missionaries in the text could have had serious implications, unlike the circulation of the *Vajrasūcī* amongst dissenting bhakti poets which could be more easily ignored. In contrast, the *Vajrasūcī* was received in Europe with admiration by scholars who were astonished at the 'democratic spirit of Europe' displayed by the text. There started a journey from being a historical memory to becoming a text that began to re-circulate for its anti-brāhmaṇa critique of caste-based superiority. The text made its impact within a relatively short of period of twenty years.[43] Ironically though, during the same period, a position from the other end of the spectrum was advanced by Albrecht Weber who located the *Vajrasūcī* within a Brahmanic tradition. He argued that since the text was placed in the respectable category of an Upaniṣad, which is how it is often described, it was of Brahmanical origin. Even more startling was its attribution to the great anti-Buddhist, Śaṅkarācārya, by Weber.[44] We see here the usual tendency to deny the Buddhist tradition an autonomy of voice within a dialogic field, denude it of its rational basis and fold it back somehow into the Brahmanic/ Hindu tradition via Śaṅkarācārya, believed to be the greatest opponent of Buddhism.

What does the text actually say that impelled it to be quietly erased or rebutted when 'rediscovered', or sought to be appropriated for its empirical and rational critique of the caste system, particularly of the brāhmaṇa claims to birth-based superiority?[45] At a fundamental level, the text rehearses the Buddhist position that the values and qualities of human beings alone distinguish one from the other. Those who are righteous in their conduct, morally upright, living the kind of life adopted by *bhikkhus* having renounced the world of family, kin, production and reproduction and living off alms, can be called brāhmaṇas. This term will apply then to righteous śūdras, too, as indeed to anyone else, whatever their so-called origins might be. But at another level, the strategies adopted to debunk the claims of the brāhmaṇas to superiority are noteworthy. Using the model of the analysis of language adopted by the Sanskrit commentator, Patanjali, on the word *gau*, not in terms of its individual parts—such as the horns, legs, colour and so on—but in terms of its essential meaning, the *Vajrasūcī* begins to disaggregate the word brāhmaṇa. So is it *śarīra*? No, it is not because if it is, then Agni would be responsible for *brahmahatyā* (killing of brāhmaṇas when the dead brāhmaṇa is burnt). Then is brāhmaṇa knowledge? No, it is not, because śūdras who have wisdom would then become brāhmaṇas. Is it good conduct? Then all the śūdras living righteously would become brāhmaṇas. Is it *karma* that is brāhmaṇa? No, because those kṣatriyas, vaiśyas and śūdras who perform good actions are not actually regarded as brāhmaṇas. Is it knowledge of the Vedas then? No, it is not because then Rāvaṇa who knew the Vedas thoroughly would be regarded as brāhmaṇa and that he is certainly not! The *Vajrasūcī* poses the question: how is brāhmaṇahood acquired? Not through the Dharmaśāstras, birth or family; nor through the Vedas, or *karmas*, but through purity of conduct and self-control. The text reiterates that only one who has renounced lies, pride and worldly possessions can be called a brāhmaṇa.[46]

Another line of debunking brāhmaṇa claims in the *Vajrasūcī* is similar to early Buddhist texts, showing lines of continuity albeit with a few distinctive flourishes. Since purity of birthing practices is said to be the basis of brāhmaṇa claims to superior status, the impossibility of strictly upholding endogamous re-production, reflected in the mythical lineages of various *ṛṣis*, is taken up. Some are said to be born from a fisherwoman's womb, or are *apsarā*-born, or deer-born, or born of a *cāṇḍālī*. So no one is of pure birth and yet they are regarded as brāhmaṇas. The claim of pure birth is, thus, false. The myth of the sacrifice of the primeval man giving rise to a hierarchical ordering of the four varnas is demolished as absurd. If all were born from the same progenitor, then how can they be unequal? We see here a development of mythology and a refinement of the rational argument, common sense and Durkheimian social fact to a different level of argument. Even normative practices such as incest rules are brought up to demonstrate the ridiculousness of the claims of the brāhmaṇas.[47]

The double-pronged move to reject the Brahmanical emphasis on caste divisions and caste purity draw from early Buddhist tropes. While the brāhmaṇas treat varṇa as originating with birth, wherein the brāhmaṇa is the repository by virtue of birth in a brāhmaṇa family, the Buddhists insist on the status of brāhmaṇa as acquired. In the early canonical literature, the term brāhmaṇa, therefore, was a shifting category that moved along a dual axis according to the context, with the brāhmaṇas using it to describe a birth-based identity and the Buddhists regarding it as an acquired value. The *Vajrasūcī* retains this duality but since it is a text written from the Buddhist standpoint, it takes up the Brahmanical position and debunks it in a conceptual debate with a 'hidden' adversary. The brāhmaṇa does not speak directly but through the author of the text, splitting himself into two parts. The first takes up the position of the unseen brāhmaṇa. The second rebuts his position by using older Buddhist arguments defining who is a real brāhmaṇa but now uses subtle irony and common sense to draw attention to the ridiculousness of Brahmanic mythology, and, therefore, of its claims to order the world into fixed and immutable hierarchies with the brāhmaṇa at the top.

The impact of the publication of the *Vajrasūcī* in the first half of the nineteenth century has already been discussed. In Maharashtra, it has had special significance and played an important role in the anti-caste movement spearheaded by Jotiba Phule who helped the publication of Tukaram Tatya Padval's critique of caste titled *Jatibhed Viveksar* or a *Critique of Caste Divisions.* This text was published in 1861 and drew heavily upon the *Vajrasūcī*.[48] What is significant is that the text continues to be appropriated even today, most recently in a Hindutva takeover on the internet.[49] Already in the early twentieth century, Veer Savarkar had found the text useful in presenting Hinduism as a rationalist religion.[50] It is still playing out the Buddhist-brāhmaṇa dialectic as a single, broad, cultural stream where Buddhism is not granted an autonomous ethical position, both in philosophical and social terms. This may partly be a consequence of the indirect ways in which Brahmanism has confronted the Buddhist challenge in its drive towards hegemony in early centuries, a phenomenon that continues even today, especially in terms of achieving a non-hierarchical society. We may bear in mind that the position on caste was an unresolved tension between Buddhism and Brahmanism/Hindusim, a tension that we do not see in the Jaina-Brahmanical relationship to the same extent. The Buddhist position on caste failed to critically impact the Indian social order based on caste. On other fronts, Buddhism was more successful in impacting religious and philosophical ideas such as on the centrality of the *yajña* in Brahmanical rituals.

This is a field that has been written about and can be explored further.

For the moment, I want to conclude this essay by drawing from recent studies of the *Mahābhārata* which outline the dialogic field of the Buddhist-brāhmaṇa relationship.[51] A well-known dimension of the *Mahābhārata* is its expansion from a core narrative about a fratricidal war between cousins with a decidedly kṣatriya flavour on to a huge text with a large corpus of 'ancillary' stories. These stories transform the *Mahābhārata* into a Brahmanical text that privileges the brāhmaṇas and places their values in a dominant position.[52] This is done in three major ways: by the issues and values that the ancillary tales foreground, by raising questions about the validity of war, killing and large-scale devastation, and finally the propriety of animal sacrifice as a part of rituals.[53] The latter two positions are a response to Buddhist ethics on how the ideal king should conduct himself, expanding territory only by the persuasive power of *dhamma*, and the critique of animal sacrifice in the *Kūṭadanta Sutta* that has been discussed earlier in the essay. The figures that embody the debate on these two issues are Yudhiṣṭhira, Arjuna, Kṛṣṇa and Bhīṣma. What is interesting is that, at different points in the text, Arjuna and Yudhiṣṭhira articulate the Buddhist position on violence—or rather non-violence, silently addressed through the unseen presence of Aśoka who, as a king with a distinctive vision, left an uncomfortable legacy for the diehard upholders of an older Vedic-Brahmanism. The rebuttal of his legacy is expounded by Kṛṣṇa to Arjuna on the battlefield, and by Bhīṣma to Yudhiṣṭhira in the Śānti Parvan of the *Mahābhārata* after the war is over. The grand old patriarch teaches a thoroughly Brahmanized politics to Yudhiṣṭhira who has been unable to reconcile himself to the killing entailed by the war. Bhīṣma's teachings are the core of the Brahmanical version of *rājadharma*, the duties of a king in an ideal kingdom.

We can see that the dialogues between the Buddhists and brāhmaṇas are frontally handled by the former but are often obliquely dealt with by the Brahmanical tradition. This ensures that the Buddhist positions may be countered without acknowledging that they are influential, have a wide circulation, and pose a challenge to the hegemony of the brāhmaṇas. By placing some of these primarily Buddhist positions within the body of an influential text produced by the brāhmaṇas themselves, they can both apparently deny the force of the argument of the Buddhists as well as retain ideological control, simultaneously assimilating and countering the force of the Buddhist critique of Brahmanism.

NOTES

1. See, for example, H. Oldenberg, *The Buddha: His Life, His Doctrine, His Order*, London: Williams and Norgate, 1882; Max Weber, *The Religion of India*, Glencoe: Free Press, 1960; A.K. Warder, 'On the Relationship Between Buddhism and Other Contemporary Systems', *Bulletin of the School of Oriental and African Studies*, vol. XVIII, 1956, p. 51; Uma Chakravarti, *The Social Dimensions of Early Buddhism*, Delhi: Oxford University Press, 1987, pp. 36-7.
2. Dr. S. Radhakrishnan, 'Introduction', in P.V. Bapat, *2500 Years of Buddhism in India*, Delhi: Publications Division, 1956, p. ix. This was a Government of India publication and given that Radhakrishnan was the president at the time the volume was published, we may treat this view as the official position of the Government of India to the rest of the Buddhist world.
3. Ibid., p. xiii.
4. Ibid., p. xiv.
5. Ibid., p. xv.
6. Ananda Coomaraswamy, *Buddha and the Gospel of Buddhism*, Bombay: Asia Publishing House, 1956, p. 219.
7. See, for example, B.R. Ambedkar, *The Buddha and His Dhamma*, Bombay: Siddhartha College, 1957; Kancha Ilaiah, *God as Political Philosopher*, Calcutta: Samya, 2001; and Gail Omvedt, *Buddhism in India: Challenging Brahmanism and Caste*, Delhi: Sage, 2003. Earlier scholars and activists who found Buddhism attractive include Iyothiadass, the Tamil dalit scholar, the Marxist, Rahul Sankrityayan, and the socialist, Acharya Narendra Deva.
8. Steve Collins, *Agganna Sutta: The Discourse on What is Primary*, Delhi: Sahitya Akademi, 2001, p. 17.
9. The *Dīgha Nikāya*, tr. T.W. Rhys Davids as *The Dialogues of the Buddha*, vol. I, London: Pali Text Society, 1978, pp. 108 ff.; the *Majjhima Nikāya*, tr. I.B. Horner as *The Middle Length Sayings*, vol. II, London: Pali Text Society, 1976, pp. 273 ff.

10. The stakes in maintaining superiority over all others is nicely brought out in another *sutta* called the *Sonadanda Sutta*. Sonadanda, a brāhmaṇa well-versed in the three Vedas who enjoyed lands granted to him by the king of Magadha was convinced of the Buddha's teachings but could not make a public declaration of it because he would then lose his own reputation, and perhaps his entitlement to special privileges. For details, see *Dialogues of the Buddha*, vol. I, op. cit., p. 158.
11. Ibid., p. 117.
12. Ibid., pp. 108-36.
13. Ibid., vol. III, pp. 77-94.
14. *Rigveda*, tr. R.T.H. Griffiths, Varanasi: Chaukhamba Sanskrit Series, 1971, vol. II, 10.90.12. The relevant passage states: the brāhmaṇa was his mouth, of both his arms was the kṣatriya made, his thigh became the vaiśya, from his feet the śūdra was produced.
15. Collins, op. cit., p. 16.
16. *Dialogues*, vol. III, pp. 78-9.
17. The allegorical account of the origin of the world, and especially its social divisions, is an important way in which the Buddhist texts counter the sacred legitimation for caste in Brahmanical texts. As Gombrich says, the *Agganna Sutta* is full of parody, but it also seriously debunks the Brahmanical view of caste by showing that it is nothing but a human invention (cited in Steve Collins, op. cit., p. 13).
18. *Dialogues*, vol. III, pp. 78-9.
19. *The Dhammapada*, tr. Max Müller, Sacred Books of the East, Delhi: Motilal Banarsidass, 1977, pp. 90-6.
20. Ibid., p. 91.
21. Ibid., p. 92.
22. Ibid., p. 93.
23. Ibid.
24. Ibid., p. 91.
25. Ibid., p. 93.
26. Ibid., p. 95.
27. Ibid., p. 91.
28. *The Sutta Nipata*, tr. Max Müller, Sacred Books of the East, op. cit., pp. 11-15.
29. Ibid.
30. *Dialogues*, vol. I, pp. 172-85.
31. Ibid., p. 180.
32. *The Jatakas*, tr. E.B. Cowell, vol. III, Delhi: Motilal Banarsidass, 2005, pp. 153-63.
33. *The Therīgāthā*, tr. C.A.F. Rhys Davids as *Psalms of the Sisters*, London: Pali Text Society, 1948, pp. 116-19.

34. Rahul Sankrityayan et al., *Buddhism: The Marxist Approach*, Delhi: People's Publishing House, 1970, p. 8.
35. Maurice Winternitz, *A History of Indian Literature*, vol. II, Calcutta: University of Calcutta, 1933, p. 257.
36. Ibid., p. 265.
37. Sukumari Bhattacharji, *Buddhist Sanskrit Literature*, Calcutta: The Asiatic Society, 1992, p. 48.
38. According to Winternitz, Chinese accounts attribute the *Vajrasūcī* to Dharmakīrti. For details, see Winternitz, op. cit., p. 266. One view suggests that Dharmakīrti completed an earlier version of the text. This might account for the familiarity with the *Manusmriti* and the *Mahābhārata*, both of which would have been known to scholars by the time of Dharmakīrti.
39. Rosalind O'Hanlon, *Caste, Conflict and Ideology*, Delhi: Orient Longman, 1985, p. 225.
40. Ibid., pp. 225-6.
41. Uma Chakravarti, *Rewriting History: The Life and Times of Pandita Ramabai*, Delhi: Kali For Women, 1998, Chapter 2.
42. M. Winternitz et al., *Literary History of Sanskrit Buddhism*, http://www.archive.org/stream/lit, pp. 178-9. I owe this reference to S. Anand.
43. Ibid., p. 179.
44. Ibid., p. 178.
45. The analysis of the text provided below is drawn from its reading by Mrs. Sushila Ambike (who conducts a Sanskrit class at Manana, a trust and library set-up in the name of my Ph.D. supervisor, Dr. D. Devahuti) during the year 2007-8. I am grateful for the mutually enriching class participation which was reading a Buddhist text for the first time in an eight-year long interaction in this once a week Sanskrit class held since 2001.
46. The text we used in the class was the only version available in book stores. It was translated into Hindi. For details, see *The Vajrasūcī of Aśvaghoṣa*, ed. and tr. Ramayan Prasad Dwivedi, Varanasi: Chaukhamba Amarbharati Prakashan, 1985.
47. Ibid., p. 32. The text says that if all brāhmaṇas were born from the mouth of the primeval man and married within themselves, then it would imply that they married their own sisters!
48. Rosalind O'Hanlon, op. cit., p. 226.
49. A Google search on the internet yields a version that claims it to be within the Hindu fold, thus emptying the text of its Buddhist origins.
50. Rosalind O'Hanlon, op. cit., p. 226.
51. Nicholas Sutton, 'Ashoka and Yudhishthira: A Historical Setting for the Ideological Tensions of the *Mahābhārata*?', *Religion*, vol. 29,

1997, pp. 331-41; and Israel Selvanayagam, 'Aśoka and Arjuna as Counterparts Standing on the Field of Dharma: A Historico-Hermeneutical Perspective', *History of Religions*, vol. 32, 1, 1992, pp. 59-79.

52. Barbara Gombach, *Ancillary Stories in the Sanskrit Mahābhārata*, Ph.D. thesis, New York: Columbia University, 2000.
53. Mary Caroll Smith, *The Warrior Code of India's Sacred Song*, New York: Garland Press, 1992.

TWO

Tradition and Memory

Filiation and Identity in Early Sanskrit Literature and Philosophy

Heeraman Tiwari

> The memory which our culture reserves of the past is depressingly fragmentary, distorted, and incoherent in the fortuitous survival of evidence; there is so very much we should like to know and will never known, so very little we can be sure about. No wonder that dreams and myths often take over where facts are elusive, no wonder, in other words, that to the critical eye much of the humanities looks like the indulgence of subjectivity and that the search has arisen for more objective criteria.[1]

Count Leo Tolstoy famously said: 'History is like a deaf man replying to questions which nobody puts to him.'[2] Although Tolstoy seems to suggest here that history as a subject is not worth wasting one's time for, if one reads through his novels, journals and letters to his famous friends in Russia, who curiously came from both sides of the intellectual divide, one would notice that he was tormented by the kind of history that was being taught and written in Europe those days. As I understand it, Tolstoy was not interested in the answers to questions like 'what?' and 'where?'. He was anxious to get the answers to the question 'why?' in history. In other words, Tolstoy as an imaginative giant was not interested in what the ninth-century Indian literary critic, Abhinavagupta, had called a 'mere chronicle of events' or 'a systematic attempt to answer non-existent questions with all the real issues carefully left out'.[3] For Tolstoy, the real issues were the spiritual—'inner' events, which were the most real, the most immediate experience of human beings; they, and only they, are what life, in the last analysis, is made of; and the purpose of history, Tolstoy suggests, should be 'the discovery of truth'.[4]And I believe language and literature do help in the discovery of truth.

TRADITION AND AFFILIATION

In ancient Indian literature and philosophy, the concept of underlining affiliation to the tradition is very strong indeed. Scholars may have produced absolutely new ideas but still wish to maintain that what they are doing is not more than collating, scrutinizing and repeating what has already been said by the elders. For instance, Jayantabhaṭṭa, the ninth-century Indian philosopher, says about his otherwise fairly revolutionary ideas in Indian logic:

> *kuto vā nūtanaṃ vastu vayam utprekṣituṃ kṣamāḥ* |
> *vaco vinyāsavaicitryamātram atra vicāryatām* ||

> Whence can I discover new things?
> What I am going to say here, therefore,
> Will be no more than a *novel representation*
> Of what has already been said.[5]

It is interesting to note how the father of the Telugu language, Appakavi, received inspiration from the god of language to compose Nannaya grammar in Telugu, a grammar that is different from that of Sanskrit.

> I am delighted at your awakening.
> Let me introduce my two wives, Wealth and Earth,
> And myself—the god with lotus eyes.
> I have come to you, good Brahmin, in affection,
> To bring you certain fortune.
> Make Nannaya's book into Telugu, with my help,
> To the poets' astonishment and praise.
> Don't ask me how you are to turn into Telugu
> A book you've never heard or seen. I'll tell you
> All about that book and how it will come to you.[6]

A few verses later, the god with the lotus eyes explains why Appakavi had to compose the grammar of Nannaya in Telugu:

In the language of the gods, one can pack dense meaning
Into *sūtras* of minimal syllables. If you do not elaborate
In Telugu, will anyone understand?
Nannaya composed the rules of word-making
In the impenetrable coconut mode.
Mere Telugu speakers won't find their way through them.
You must write them in a style soft as grapes.
Also, since the lawmaker of language was composing in Sanskrit,
Where no Telugu can be used, he gave the rules alone
Without even one example. That's why some rules
Were unintelligible.
Can anyone—even the Creator, even his lovely wife,
The goddess of Words—count the words generated
Out of a single *sūtra*? Still, you can show a few.
Because your book will be helpful to poets,
You will store up merit and true fame which will lead you
To heaven. What could be more wonderful?
Than making it into Telugu?

Let me recount a twelfth-century Jaina story from the *Prabhāvakacarita* of Prabhācandra, which tells us of the two versions of the same episode from the *Mahābhārata*:

[Once during the rainy season, Hemacandra gave an exposition about the life of Lord Nemi, in the course of which he told how the Pāṇḍava brothers of the *Mahābhārata* had renounced the world and became Jaina monks. The Brahmins of the city, jealous of Hemacandra's popularity, protested: 'The *Mahābhārata* says that devoted to Lord Śiva the Pāṇḍavas went wandering into the Himalayas at the end of their lives.' The king summoned Hemacandra to arbitrate the matter and asked:] 'Is it true, according to the scriptures, the Pāṇḍavas renounced the world according to the Jaina rules?' The venerable *ācārya* said, 'This has been said by our ancient *ācāryas* in our scriptures, and it is equally true that their sojourn in the Himalayas is described in the *Mahābhārata*. But we do not know that those [Pāṇḍavas] who are described in our scriptures are the same as those who are described in the work [*Mahābhārata*] of sage Vyāsa, or yet still by other authors in different works.'

To this the king said, 'But then, O sage, were there more than one of these persons, and were they born in ancient times?' Then the teacher said, 'O king, . . . In the narrative of Vyāsa himself there is the following episode about Bhīṣma the grandfather, who is also known as the descendant of the Ganges. At the time of entering the battlefield he told his attendants, 'At my death cremate my body only on a piece of earth which has always been pure, a place where no-one has ever been cremated.' [After Bhīṣma's death, his] attendants remembered his words and, lifting his body, took it to a hill [which they thought has never been visited by any man]. When they readied the body [for cremation] a divine voice spoke:

'A hundred Bhīṣmas have been cremated here,
And three hundred Pāṇḍavas,
And a thousand Droṇācāryas.
As for Karṇas [cremated here],
Their number is beyond counting!'

[Having quoted this verse from the *Mahābhārata*] Hemacandra said, 'Hearing this [verse] in our minds we believe that among the hundreds of Pāṇḍavas mentioned here it is possible that some may have been Jainas.[7]

THE PHILOSOPHICAL BASIS OF MEMORY

The debate in Indian texts, both classical and later, is intense over whether memory should be accorded the status of a 'valid or accredited means' of knowledge that is *pramāṇa*. Even perceptual knowledge cannot succeed without enlisting help from the memory. In fact, perception itself is half-memory. Yet, for all its utility in acquiring knowledge, the memory has failed to attain such a status. In discussing poetics, Aristotle says that memory or 'recognition' is 'a change from ignorance to knowledge, tending either to affection or enmity', and 'when one's awareness is roused by seeing something', for example, when seeing a picture or listening to some song or music, the person bursts into tears because that picture or music brings about a recognition of his or her past experience.[8]

The Indian philosophical tradition, too, has a long history of debate on the status of 'memory', where memory brings about the knowledge by which we can either accept or reject (*heya* and *upādeya*) the thing recognized. Philosophers argued amongst themselves whether memory should be treated as a valid means of knowledge. The Nyāya school, for example, defines memory as 'the cognition born from, attained through, the traces of the past', that is, *saṃskāramātrajanyaṃ jñānaṃ smṛtiḥ*, where *saṃskāra* means 'impressions' or 'traces' of the past.[9] *Saṃskāra* in general, too, means 'an unbroken chain of impressions from the past times/ lives'; in other words, *saṃskāra* means tradition. It also refers to *vāsanā* which means 'the smells of the past'.[10]

Let us briefly see what the various schools of Indian philosophy have to say about memory. The Naiyāyikas rejected memory as a valid means of knowledge because as realists they thought that it cannot be an instrument of veridical knowing. Also, although memory has the same content as perception and inference, it may fail to present its contents/objects correctly. It leaves out some of the properties noted previously or adds others not initially present. Praśastapāda, the fourth-century Vaiśeṣika and commentator of the *Vaśeṣikasūtras*, on the other hand, says that memory is *vidyā*, a form of true knowledge. However, it is not a *pramāṇa*. For example, when we remember *x*, it is the trace produced by the *x* and not the *x* itself. In perception, one recollects the resemblance in the thing perceived with one's own experience of that thing in the past: 'One remembers because one sees a partial similarity between the object present and an object one has seen before.'[11] And Jayantabhaṭṭa who straddled both the Nyāya and Vaiśeṣika schools of Indian philosophy, says that memory is a form of perception. Thus, we can say that memory has a symbiotic relationship with the three important means of accredited knowledge: perception, inference and verbal testimony. In other words, the relationship between memory and the other three means of knowledge depends on mutualism. The Mīmāṃsaka believes that all true judgements have their content objects not previously known but memory has contents that are previously known. One can appreciate why the Mīmāṃsaka would like to hold such a view for, otherwise, it would be difficult for him to claim that Vedic knowledge was previously not known. The Vaiṣṇavas accepted memory as 'a true knowledge'. For example, Vedāntadeśika, one of the major figures of this tradition in thirteenth-century south India, equates the position of a devotee, a *bhakta*, with that of a poet and says that both require memory to attain their goal:

> *smṛtyā hi kavayaḥ kāvyāni kavayanti, smṛtyā hi śabdānumānayoḥ pravṛttiḥ parabhaktyādiniṣpattiś ca*

> With the power of memory alone can poets compose their poetry, with the power of memory alone is the cognition through inference and verbal testimony possible; and it is with the process of memory that devotees can regain their lost relationship with the supreme Lord.[12]

However, when the Vaiṣṇavas were pressed to declare whether memory was a *pramāṇa*, a valid means of knowledge, they referred to the tradition, which in itself is based on memory, and said that memory was not accepted by the elders as a *pramāṇa*.

The Vedānta philosophy, as we know, espouses the soul's relationship with the world, *saṃsāra* or *jagat*, as engulfed in illusion. Illusion or *māyā* causes a sort of amnesia to the soul, *jīvātmā*. As a result, the soul fails to recognize its link with *Brahman*, the ultimate reality. The therapy to cure this amnesia of illusion for the soul is, as taught in the Vedānta philosophy, rumination, *nididhyāsana*, on the nature of both the world and the *Brahman*, the scriptures and other texts of great learning. Guide or a teacher helps in this process. If I may be allowed to borrow here a medical terminology for my metaphor, then I would say that the teacher (*guru*) is the physician, the scriptural knowledge the remedy and the tradition (*paramparā*) the nurse who administers that remedy.[13] Once the amnesia of illusion is removed through this process of Vedantic cure, the soul immediately recognizes its true relationship with the *Brahman*, ultimate reality.[14] What the recognition of the past experiences (memory) requires, therefore, is a sign or *hetu*. *Hetus* may be in the form of *saṃskāras* or *vāsanās*, that is, the 'tradition' or 'smells' of the past. The Śaivite accepts *pratyabhijñā*, 'recognition', the main focus of the bhakti, as true knowledge because he was previously acquainted with it. In Buddhism, too, the *Sangha* or the Order founded by the Buddha is an institution (tradition, *paramparā*), which 'not only consists of those who have decided to devote their lives to striving for Enlightenment but also preserves the memory of the Buddha's teaching'.[15] Tradition is our ancient warehouse from which it is easy to recall what we need and when we need it. The Buddhist scholar, Richard Gombrich says:

If we were too rigorous, we can doubt most of our knowledge about the past, certainly about ancient India, where the evidence is sparse and rarely dated. I am not urging that we should claim certainty when we do not have it, but that we should provisionally accept tradition till we have something to put in place—all the while preserving a modest awareness of our uncertainty.[16]

THE PROCESSES OF PRESERVING TRADITION

It is a well-known fact that the passing on of knowledge in ancient India depended for centuries, even millennia, entirely on oral tradition or memory, which included both individual and collective tradition. The structure of the *Rāmāyaṇa*, for example, suggests levels and narrators at various times in history. The legend has it that Vālmīki, the original composer of the story, gets it from Nārada and then makes Lava and Kuśa, the children of Rāma and Sītā, memorize it, who, in turn, recite it at the court of Rāma. In an oral tradition, the same narrator or teller may continue to repeat one story on every occasion, or, alternatively, choose to change the character and repeat the same plot, as brilliantly shown by A.K. Ramanujan in his study of the *Mahābhārata*.[17] However, when information or knowledge is planned to be transmitted through a disciplined process of memorizing, it becomes a deliberate memory, which 'thus appears to be a specialization of the more natural process of acquiring knowledge and techniques that, religious or otherwise, unconsciously determine a person's membership in a particular tradition'.[18]

Such a membership then becomes essential in the interest of continuity of tradition. When writing is a luxury, the knowledge is preserved (if it is to be preserved), through oral tradition (deliberate and disciplined memorization). Accuracy in memorizing becomes essential, particularly for the religious texts or the exegeses which represent the tradition and identity of a society. In ancient Greece, Homer was learnt by heart; the reciter of the *Odyssey* and the *Iliad* who recited from memory to the public audience was rewarded by the ruler and admired by the society.

In ancient India, too, the story was not dissimilar. Vedic scholars were specialists in memorizing the Vedas. Even today, oral recitation (chanting from memory) is valued, particularly of the religious texts. Memorizing of religious texts is extolled as a good deed, *puṇya.*[19] In this way, the past is resurrected by means of recitation, which merges the past into the present. Both the reciter and listener fuse into one to become a tradition.[20] Time and change are immaterial to memory; remembering is the backbone of a tradition. 'To learn,' Ramanujan wrote, 'is to remember (whether it is the self or the Vedas), and to remember is to know the self, to forget is to be unaware of the self.'[21] When memory is committed to scriptural texts, it takes the form of an authoritative tradition. So who makes a tradition? Perhaps the answer will come from the tradition itself.

Basavanna, the twelfth-century Vīraśaiva saint of Karnataka, announces to the world that there could be a tradition within a tradition which will show a new path to the society. This *vacana* verse in Kannada refers to a non-Sanskritic tradition. But the local and vernacular traditions flourished and prospered alongside the so-called grand Sanskrit tradition, which, wherever it went or was taken, never supplanted the local tradition.[22] On the contrary, it kept on learning from its experiences, and encouraged the local traditions to create and develop their own literary and social cultures. The Telugu literary tradition and the *Maṇipravālam* of the Malayalam tradition are a couple of examples.[23]

THE *RĀMCARITMĀNAS* OF TULSĪDĀS

Like many *Rāmāyaṇa* writers before him, the medieval Indian saint, Tulsīdās, too, invokes memory in telling the story of Rāma, which he calls the *Rāmacaritmānas* or 'The Charming Lake of the Holy Acts of Rāma'. Tulsī explains in the beginning of his *Rāmāyaṇa* how he received the story of Rāma, and lists the long tradition through which it has reached him:[24]

> First Śiva composed it and then told it to Pārvatī, also to the celestial sage, Muni Nārada. Śiva also tells it to Sage Agastya and Kākabhuśuṇḍi, the wise crow and the emancipated devotee of Rāma. Then Kākabhuśuṇḍi tells it to Muni Yājñavalkya, also to Śiva along with other saints, the lord of the birds, Garuḍa, and other birds and animals who regularly congregate in the *āśrama*

of Kākabhuśuṇḍi. Then Sage Yājñavalkya narrates it to Sage Bhāradvāja. From Sage Bhāradvāja it is passed on to many saints who memorize it for the 'Tradition' (*paramparā*) of the *Rāmāyaṇa.*[25] The Tradition itself consists of sages, twice born, poets, bards and so on. Narharyānanda, the *guru*, the teacher of Tulsī, receives it from the Tradition. And, finally, Narharyānanda tells the story of Rāma to Tulsī:

> *main puni nij guru san sunī kathā so sūkarkhet* |
> *samujhī nahi tasi bālpan tab ati raheun acet* || (1.30a)
>
> And I heard (received) this story from my teacher (Narharyānand) in the land of *Sūkarkhet*. However, I could not properly understand (the importance and richness of) it then, for I was not mature enough and was in fact very young.

THE LITERARY BASIS

Let us search for examples from the two ancient epics. How do they begin? Like the *Rāmāyaṇa*, the *Mahābhārata*, too, begins with recalling the vicissitudes of the Kuru family, particularly Pāṇḍava family. When he learns what had happened to his ancestors King Janamejaya, the son of Parīkṣita, takes a vow to avenge his father's killing by snake bite, by performing a sacrifice in which all the reptile species of the world would be incinerated. Parīkṣita, the son of Uttarā and Abhimanyu, was the sole male survivor of the Great War.

The *Mahābhārata* is also considered by the tradition as a book of history, *itihāsa,* 'that's the way it was', *iti iha āsa*, to quote Ramanujan's very attractive rendering of the term.[26] The stories of the *Mahābhārata* have been recalled by generations through the process of both written as well as social memory. Ramanujan suggests that a certain structure in the epic allows it to be recalled 'in bits and pieces that fit together and make a whole in the learner's mind', and only by denying it a structure could a poem be seen or accepted as a 'history' or 'chronicle of events'.[27] One is not entirely sure why a structured poem cannot be called a history; the poetic and literary works of Kālidāsa and others, which are based on various episodes from the epics and Purāṇas, would surely be considered as literary histories or meta-histories for they do recall the events of their source stories, albeit with certain variations and expansions. The same can be seen in the *Rājataraṅgiṇī* of Kalhaṇa, a poem that has been accepted as an authentic source of the early medieval history of Kashmir. Velcheru Narayan Rao, David Shulman and Sanjay Subrahmanyam have suggested that 'authority, and the right to produce history, are dispersed within the body of the social group, which seems less suspicious than certain other traditions. . . . In other words, the authority that guarantees the accuracy of transmission is vested in the image of a person who is by definition a repository of complete cultural knowledge.'[28] There are scholars who have argued successfully that 'anything can be literature', as the famous literary critic of recent times Terry Eagleton has done. Sheldon Pollock says, while commenting on critics like Eagleton, that 'literature is not some permanent and essential feature of a text but a way the reader relates to it. Texts come into and go out of literary being (as when Plato is read as drama and Homer as history) depending on what we want to do with them. In this "literature" is like a "weed": one person's pest is another's flower and yet another's dinner.'[29] We can, thus, turn this argument round and say that a book on history could also be a poem or a literary work; many of the travel writings by famous literary figures, which are written with the purpose of political and social history as well as of literature, and many ancient and medieval Indian court poems, will fall within this category. The *Rājataraṅgiṇī* of Kalhaṇa has already been mentioned. On the other hand, some critics believe that a poem or a literary work cannot sacrifice its main objective, i.e. poetry, for the sake of history; it has a different priority and genre. As Ānandavardhana, the ninth-century literary critic from Kashmir, has pointed out: 'A poet has no need to carry out a mere chronicle of events. That is a task accomplished by the historians.'[30] However, Pollock has suggested:

> What is crucial for historical literary scholarship is not the fact that the literary is the functional rather than an ontological category, comprising something people do with a text rather than something a text truly and everlastingly is, but the fact that people are constantly induced to do whatever that something is, and to do it variously because every specific situation is historical.[31]

Tradition is also what some have called a 'constitutive imagination'.[32] So, Vālmīki, Vyāsa, Kālidāsa and other writers of Itihāsa and Purāṇa all rely on tradition and memory to create their work. The story of the *Rāmāyaṇa*, too, was apparently reproduced by Vālmīki on the basis of Sītā's narration of the story of her life. Vālmīki, in other words, acts as Sītā's (albeit the Ikṣvāku clan's) biographer. When the story is chanted in bardic fashion by the two young ascetics, Lava and Kuśa, in the palace of Rāma during the festival of the *Aśvamedha* sacrifice, Rāma feels strangely uneasy for the tale was cryptically so similar to his own life-story. Rāma's suspicions are eventually confirmed when he comes to fight Lava and Kuśa in the battlefield and finds Sītā dissuading them from fighting the mighty Rāma. As I mentioned earlier in the context of the tradition of the *Tulsī Rāmāyaṇa*, the first poet, Vālmīki, was persuaded by the two celestial figures, Nārada and his father Brahmā, to compose the story into a poem.[33] These details are part of the main body of the *Rāmāyaṇa* of Vālmīki. Brahmā says to the sage:

mac chandād eva te brahman pravṛtteyaṃ sarasvatī |
rāmasya caritaṃ kṛtṣnaṃ kuru tvaṃ ṛṣisattama ||

(*Vālmīki Rāmāyaṇa*, 1.2.30)

Brahman, it was by my will alone that you produced this elegant speech. Greatest of seers, you must now compose the entire history of Rāma.[34]

Here, I deliberately take *caritam* to mean 'history'. Thus, the first poet commits himself to composing the story of Rāma in lyrical verse. Even he needed a teacher or two to guide him so that he could recall the entire story of the *Rāmāyaṇa*—he needed an assurance from his superior, in this case the representatives of the world of the gods, that what he was going to compose in that grammar was, in fact, inspired by the higher being who may have been the origin of the tradition. There is a parallel to this kind of assurance, even invocation, from the higher being in the cultural tradition of medieval south India. David Shulman talks of grammar as 'something given, not discovered' without which 'one cannot speak; and without speech, there is no world'.[35] What I am trying to suggest here is that there is a 'splendid working' of the process of transmission of traditional texts, through what Ramanujan calls 'intertextuality', the way in which Indian texts engage in conversation with one another.[36]

KĀLIDĀSA'S REWORKING OF THE EPISODES FROM THE *MAHĀBHĀRATA*

Although the story of Śakuntalā and Duṣyanta is first told in the *Mahābhārata* (1: 62-9, in the Śakuntalopākhyāna of the Sambhavaparvan of the Ādiparvan, in eight chapters and 305 verses), in Kālidāsa's drama, the *Abhijñānaśākuntalam*, the same story has acquired a most dramatic and abiding flavour. The *Mahābhārata* episode of Śakuntalā and Duṣyanta, too, revolves around forgetting and remembering but in the *Śakuntalā* of Kālidāsa, the story has been turned entirely into a mesmerizing play on memory.[37] In the *Mahābhārata*, though, 'after being forced by a voice from heaven to recognise his son, the king [Duṣyanta] says to Śakuntalā,'[38] 'O Śakuntalā! I had married you secretly (*lokaparokṣa*, i.e. "without the knowledge of my people"), it was to purify you [i.e. to convince my people of your purity], therefore, that I did this.'[39]

kṛto lokaparokṣo 'yaṃ sambandho vai tvayā saha |
tasmād etan mayā devi tvac chuddhy arthaṃ vicāritaṃ ||
(*The Mahābhārata*, 1:69:40)

To point out one reason why Kālidāsa may have changed the plot a little to suit his version of the tale, let me quote Daniel H.H. Ingalls who analyses Ānandavardhana's *Dhvanyāloka*, a major work of literary criticism of ninth-century Kashmir, where the latter suggests how a literary transformation of a story [memory!] should take place in a different genre. Ānandavardhana has Kālidāsa in mind when he makes this suggestion and Ingalls points to a specific example from Kālidāsa's Śakuntalā:

> In exhibiting the heroism of a human king, for example, one should not engage him in adventures that could be accomplished only by a god. If a plot given in the epics and Purāṇas contains a trait that is inappropriate to the character of the hero or to the intended *rasa* [literary flavour or taste], one must either omit it or add some element to the plot to achieve the needed

appropriateness. . . . So Kālidāsa invented the story of the ring of recognition, by losing which Śakuntalā unhappily brings upon the king his involuntary forgetfulness.[40]

All this is happening, one would assume, at the level of memory/tradition, both of the epic tale as well as of the literary guidelines of a play that is to be composed for the connoisseurs (*sahṛdayas*). V.S. Naipaul speaks of the 'folk memory' of the nineteenth-century Indian immigrants in Trinidad:

. . . from the objects the immigrants brought with them, and the religious rites and festivals they carried in their memory—taken together, like a folk memory—it would have been possible for the civilisation to be reconstructed, more than is possible for the Mayan or the Etruscan. So in one way it cannot be said that the immigrants brought little from India: they brought their civilisation. They could not describe it perhaps, except in those details that were available to them—the epics to which they could refer nearly all human behaviour; the complicated rituals and festivals that dramatized the year and kept their calendar separate from the other calendars of the island; and, above all, they deeply held ideas of propriety.[41]

Also, an example from the *Adhyātma Rāmāyaṇa*, a fourteenth-century *Rāmāyaṇa* written in Sanskrit, will show how in the process of transmitting information—in this case the story of Rāma—through tradition and memory, the narrator plays on the tradition of the *Rāmāyaṇa* telling.[42] In the episode in question, which is available in every version of the *Rāmāyaṇa*, on being exiled, Rāma is dissuading Sītā from accompanying him to the hard life of the forest. When a long argument between them appears to be going in Rāma's favour, an exhausted Sītā thunders one last argument. Here is what the composer of the *Adhyātma Rāmāyaṇa* makes Sītā say to Rāma:

anyat kiñ cit pravakṣyāmi śrutvā māṃ naya kānanam |
rāmāyaṇāni bahuśaḥ śrutāni bahubhir dvijaiḥ ||
sītāṃ vinā vanaṃ rāmo gataḥ kiṃ kutra cid vada |
atas tvayā gamiṣyāmi sarvathā tvatsahāyinī ||

(*Adhyātma Rāmāyaṇa*, 2.4.77-8)

Let me tell you one more reason hearing which you must take me to the forest with you. Many *Rāmāyaṇas* have been heard many a time by many twice borns in the past. Can you tell me one instance where Rāma has gone to the forest without Sītā? Therefore, I shall have to go with you for I have always been by your side (*and for the sake of honouring the tradition*).[43]

This is what may happen when a poet attempts to say something new in representing a well-established story, or, alternatively, the narrator wants to be brutally faithful to a text which is very famous in society, so much so that it may have acquired a religious status. In the contexts, however, Sītā appears to have invoked the tradition in favour of her arguments. Compare this with the process of preserving and transmitting the story in the *Vālmīki Rāmāyaṇa*, as we have just seen above. The process of composition and transmission itself becomes part of the main text, that is, it confers and communicates with tradition; it becomes what Ramanujan calls 'a microcosmic replica for the whole text'.[44] Another example of transmission and transformation through tradition (*paramparā*) or 'a kind of textual chain' of a particular story can be seen through the process of working and reworking of the episodes of the *Mahābhārata*, as has been shown by Wendy Doniger in her illuminating essay, 'Echoes of the *Mahābhārata*'.[45]

A UTOPIAN VĀLMĪKI: THE CHAMPION OF AN ALTERNATIVE TRADITION?

Isaiah Berlin has suggested two kinds of Utopias: the poet's Utopia, and the thinker's Utopia; while the poets believe that 'the golden age is in a past which can never return' and the thinkers believe that 'the golden age is still to come',[46] Berlin goes on to quote the Hebrew prophet, Isaiah, who tells us that,

> . . . in the last days men shall beat their swords into ploughshares, and their spears into pruning hooks: nation shall not lift up sword against nation, neither shall they learn war anymore . . . the wolf also shall dwell with the lamb, and the leopard shall lie down with the kid . . . the desert shall rejoice, and blossom as rose . . . and sorrow and sighing shall flee away.[47]

Such a theme of Utopia is also present in the Sanskritic tradition.[48] Vālmīki, who would struggle in his epic for change in social tradition, apparently established it for generations, and it continued even after the story of Rāma was popular among people. The entire narrative of the story is what Sheldon Pollock calls an 'emotional response to violence and unrighteousness' and, thus, 'the ethics he [i.e.Vālmīki] advocates would have been thought as equally pronounced innovation'.[49] It certainly seems so when one compares the narrative and plots of the *Rāmāyaṇa* with those of the *Mahābhārata*. In the *Mahābhārata*, the narrative appears to suggest the struggle for a continuity of tradition, while, in the *Rāmāyaṇa*, the narrator invents new traditions at the cost of the old one. Let us look at the first major innovation of Vālmīki. As you read along and reach the point where Rāma is exiled to the forest for fourteen years, the traditional reader would expect him not to give up his rightful throne so easily. But that is precisely what Rāma does. Not only does he not feel anguished or cheated but he expresses extreme satisfaction and happiness to see his younger brother, Bharata, become king.[50] When Lakṣmaṇa, enraged by the news of Rāma's exile and in order to restore the kingdom to him, vows to fight not only Bharata but his father, Daśaratha, as well, Rāma counsels him: 'Give up this ignoble notion that is based on the code of the *kṣatriyas* . . . base your actions on righteousness, not on violence' (*tad enāṃ visṛjānāryāṃ kṣatradharmāśritāṃ matim* | *dharmam āśraya mā taikṣṇyam* . . . 2.18.36). And to his desolate mother, Rāma says: 'Only for the sake of mere kingship shall I not turn my back on glory, which facilitates greater returns; nor would I acquire this paltry, insignificant land through unfair means' (*yaśo hy ahaṃ kevalarājyakāraṇān na pṛṣṭhataḥ kartum alaṃ mahodyam* | *adīrghakāle na tu devi jīvite vṛṇe'varām adya mahīm adharmataḥ* || 2.18.39).

Bharata, on the other hand, refuses to become king by invoking the 'tradition' and pleads with Rāma not to allow the tradition to be violated, by obeying the wishes of his father and mother: 'It has always been the tradition of our House that the kingship passes to the eldest son. Rāma, our elder brother, shall be the lord of the earth, and I, in turn, shall go to live in the forest for fourteen years' (*jyeṣṭhasya hi rājatā nityam ucitā hi kulasya naḥ* | . . . *rāmaḥ pūrvo hi no bhrātā bhaviṣyati mahīpatiḥ.* | *ahaṃ tv araṇye vatsyāmi varṣāni nava pañca ca* || 2: 73: 7-8).

A despondent Daśaratha tries desperately to suggest to Rāma that even if the latter imprisoned him—or even killed him—for claiming the throne of Ayodhyā, it would not go against the ways of kings (2: 31: 23): 'O, Rāghava! I was deceived by [the charm of] Kaikeyī into granting a boon. [But you can] depose me [even kill me] to become king of Ayodhyā yourself.' However, Rāma counsels his father by saying: 'You must not on my account act untruthfully' (2: 31: 25), and goes on to suggest that Daśaratha should feel no guilt in 'giving Bharata the throne of this land with all its bounties, stores of treasures and peoples which I have happily abdicated; and I shall follow your command and depart for my long sojourn in the forest' (2: 31: 30-33). Bharata, too, is not ready to violate the tradition: 'How could a son born of Daśaratha usurp the kingship? The kingship, and myself, belong to Rāma. Righteous Kākutstha, the eldest son and the best must obtain the kingship just as Daśaratha did, as well as our great ancestors Dilīpa and Nahuṣa before him' (2: 76: 10-12), for 'the other course is an evil one, followed only by ignoble men, and leading to hell. Were I to take it [the kingship] I should become a blot on the house of Ikṣvākus in the eyes of all the worlds' (2: 76: 13). Bharata later reminds Rāma of an ancient tradition of his house: 'There is an ancient practice of righteousness . . . established among us for all time. It is this: with the eldest brother living . . . a younger may not become king' (2: 95: 2). In inventing new traditions, therefore, Vālmīki inverts the existing one; Rāma's story defies the well-established *varṇāśramadharma.* Rāma has to go through the stage of *vānaprastha* before *gṛhastha*; well before he completes *brahmacarya*, he has to take up arms to protect Viśvāmitra's sacrificial deeds in the forest. He barely enters the well-earned *gṛhastha* stage when he is shunted out to the forest again on an excuse that was unheard of before. One can go on to point out many such inventions, inversions or subversions by Vālmīki.

The role of memory in producing a literature which, in turn, allows a tradition to flourish for posterity might not pass a scientific scrutiny. However, every act of writing within a particular tradition draws upon memory and convention which demonstrate its affiliation to that tradition. In this process, many of the early

Indian texts betray the tension between conformity to tradition and suggesting a new convention, but the dialogue about the affiliation of memory to tradition remains alive. The creation of a literature and its legitimization in a tradition, notwithstanding the inherent dilemma, are both aimed at providing meaningful information in a specific context. A literature so produced may have undergone, as indeed it must undergo, transformation over time, but this process brings to life (at least breathes new life into) a vibrant literary tradition which adds dynamism to a historical dimension.[51]

NOTES

1. E.H. Gombrich, *Tributes: Interpreters of Our Cultural Tradition*, Oxford: Phaidon, 1984, p. 13.
2. Isaiah Berlin, 'Tolstoy and Enlightenment', in *Russian Thinkers*, London: The Hogarth Press, 1978, p. 242.
3. Ibid.
4. Isaiah Berlin, 'The Hedgehog and the Fox', in *Russian Thinkers*, London: The Hogarth Press, 1978, p. 33.
5. *Nyāyamañjarī* of Jayantabhaṭṭa, I.8 (ed. S.N. Sukla, Banaras: Chowkhamba, 1936: 1).
6. David Dean Shulman, 'First Grammarian, First Poet: A South Indian Vision of Cultural Origins', *Indian Economic and Social History Review*, vol. 38, no. 4, 2001, pp. 355-7. Cf. also a south Indian folktale: 'One dark night an old woman was searching intently for something in the street. A passerby asked her, 'Have you lost something?' She said, 'Yes, I've lost my keys. I have been looking for them all evening.' 'Where did you lose them?' 'I don't know. Maybe inside the house.' 'Then why are you looking for them here?' 'Because it's dark in there, I don't have oil in my lamps. I can see much better under the street lights,' she said. For details, see A.K. Ramanujan, 'Who Needs Folklore?', in Vinay Dharwadakar, ed., *The Collected Essays of Ramanujan*, Delhi: Oxford University Press, 1999, pp. 532-52. What this folktale suggests to me is that often people find it easy to affiliate themselves with an alternative, new tradition because their old tradition may be dark and difficult to be in. But if one can manage some necessary adjustments, the old, dark tradition may provide new things in a different time and age.
7. S. Padmanabh Jaini, 'Jain Puranas: A Puranic Counter Tradition', in Wendy Doniger, ed., *Purana Perennis: Reciprocity and Transformation in Hindu and Jain Texts*, Albany: SUNY, 1993.

8. D.A. Russell and Michael Winterbottom, ed., *Aristotle*: *Poetics* in *Classical Literary Criticism*, New York: Oxford University Press, 1989 (1972), pp. 64, 71.
9. *Tarkasaṃgraha* of Annaṃbhaṭṭa (ed. S. Vangiya, Varanasi: Chowkhamba, 1969, p. 57).
10. See, A.K. Ramanujan, 'The Ring of Memory: Remembering and Forgetting in Indian Literatures', in *Uncollected Poems and Prose*, Delhi: Oxford University Press, 2001, pp. 84-8.
11. Ibid., p. 88.
12. *Nyāyapariśuddhi* of Vedāntadeśika, ed. Viraraghavacarya with comm. *Nyāyatattvapraveśikā*, Madras: Ubhaya Vedanta Granthamala, 1978, p. 290.
13. I have borrowed the application of these metaphors from medical science from Richard Gombrich, who used them for the Buddha, the *Dhamma* and the *Sangha* in the Buddhist philosophy of attaining Enlightenment, *nirvāṇa*: 'The Buddha is the great physician, the Dhamma is the remedy he prescribes, the Sangha is the nurse who administers that remedy.' For details, see Richard Gombrich, *Theravada Buddhism: A Social History from Ancient Benares* to *Modern Colombo*, London: Routledge & Kegan Paul, 1988, p. 2.
14. Cf. *Muṇḍaka*, 2.8: *bhidyante hṛdayagranthiś chidyante sarvasaṃśayāḥ | kṣīyante cāsya karmāṇi tasmin dṛṣṭe parāvare ||*
15. Richard Gombrich, op. cit., p. 2.
16. Ibid., p. 21.
17. A.K. Ramanujan, 'Repetitions in the *Mahābhārata*', in Vinay Dharwadkar, ed., *The Collected Essays of A.K. Ramanujan*, Delhi: Oxford University Press, 1999, pp. 163-83.
18. Phillippe Borgeaud, '*Memorization*', in Mirçea Eliade, ed., Translated from French by Marie-Claude Hays-Merland, *Encyclopedia of Religion*, vol. 9, New York: Macmillan Publishing Company, pp. 365-70.
19. Kṛṣṇa says in the *Bhagavadgītā*:
ananyacetāḥ satatam yo mām smarati nityaśaḥ |
tasyāham sulabhaḥ pārtha nityayuktasya yoginaḥ ||
(*The Bhagavadgītā*, 8.14)
One who constantly remembers none but me is an ever disciplined *yogin*; I am always available to him.
20. See Gabrielle M. Spiegel, 'Memory and History: Liturgical Time and Historical Time', in *History and Theory*, 41, May 2002, pp. 149-62.
21. A.K. Ramanujan, 'The Ring of Memory: Remembering and Forgetting in Indian Literatures', in *Uncollected Poems and Prose*, Delhi: Oxford University Press, 2001, p. 94.

22. Basavanna, in A.K. Ramanujan, tr., *Speaking of Śiva*, Delhi: Penguin, 1973, p. 50.
The rich
Will make temples for Śiva.
What shall I,
a poor man,
Do?
My legs are pillars,
the body the shrine,
the head a cupola
Of gold.
Listen, O lord of the meeting rivers,
things standing shall fall,
But the moving ever shall stay.
23. The *Bhagavadgīta*, 3.21, which is a part of the *Mahābhārata*, says:
yad yad ācarati śreṣṭhas tat tad deve 'taro janaḥ |
sa yat pramāṇam kurute lokas tad anuvartate ||
'Whatever a great man practises, the people other than the gods, too, follow the same. And whatever standards he sets, the entire world then takes it up.' I am not qualified to talk about the neurological basis of memory. Perhaps as a layperson I can only say that genes do function as the formidable super transport of information (i.e. knowledge!) from generation to generation. And a genetic biologist will be best placed to tell us how this information gets transferred or remains dormant inside the genes.
24. There is another tradition that one can trace in the *Rāmcaritmānas*, which follows the *Vālmīki:*
First Śiva composed it and then told it to Pārvatī, also to the celestial sage, Muni Nārada. Śiva also tells it to Sage Agastya and Kākabhuśuṇḍi, the wise crow and emancipated devotee of Rāma. Muni Nārada tells it to the first poet Vālmīki and Brahmā, the architect and the maker of the worlds, exhorts Vālmīki to turn the story into lyrical poetry. Sage Agastya told it to Kākabhuśuṇḍi, too, and also to Śiva. Kākabhuśuṇḍi tells it to Muni Yājñavalkya, also to Śiva along with other saints, the lord of the birds, Garuḍa, and other birds and animals who regularly congregate in the *āśrama* of Kākabhuśuṇḍi. Sage Yājñavalkya narrates it to Sage Bhāradvāja. From Sage Bhāradvāja it is passed on to many saints who memorize it for the 'Tradition' (*paramparā*) of the *Rāmāyaṇa.* Narharyānanda, the *guru*, the teacher of Tulsī, receives it from the Tradition. And, then, from Narharyānanda it reaches Tulsī. *Rāmāyaṇa* and also adds many later tellers of the story.

This 'Tradition' included *Rāmāyaṇa* tellers like Kamban's Tamil version, *Iramāvtāram*, Kṛttibāsa's Bengali version and many other versions. This tradition also consists of many sages, twice-borns, poets, bards and so on. Like many details in ancient Indian epics and the Purāṇas the tradition of transmission of the story of Rāma provided by Tulsī and other *Rāmāyaṇa* tellers veers into mythology, but what is important for our purpose here is the pattern of telling the story: almost all of them are telling and retelling each other for keeping the story alive, as well as preserving it in the memory for posterity.

25. *sambhu kīnh yah charit suhāvā | bahuri kṛpā kari umahi sunāvā ||*
soi siva kāgabhuśuṇḍihi dīnhā | rām bhagati adhikārī chīnhā ||
tehi san jāgbalik puni pāva | tinh puni bharadvāj prati gāvā ||
(1.29-30a *Caupāī*)
26. A.K. Ramanujan, 'Repetitions in the *Mahābhārata*', in Dharwadkar, ed., op. cit., p. 163.
27. Ibid.
28. Velcheru Narayan Rao, David Shulman and Sanjay Subrahmanyam, *Textures of Time: Writing History in South India 1600-1800*, Delhi: Oxford University Press, 2001, pp. 95-6.
29. Sheldon Pollock, 'Introduction', in Sheldon Pollock, ed., *Literary Cultures in History: Reconstructions from South Asia*, Berkeley: University of California and Delhi: Oxford University Press, 2004, p. 9. Pollock refers to Terry Eagleton. For details, see Terry Eagleton, *Literary Theory: An Introduction*, Minneapolis: University of Minnesota Press, 1983, 6 ff. To justify literature as history, Pollock quotes M.M. Bakhtin. For details, see, M.M. Bakhtin, *The Dialogic Imagination: Four Essays*, Austin: Texas University Press, 1984, p. 33: 'After all the boundaries between fiction and non-fiction, between literature and non-literature and so forth are not laid up in heaven. Every specific situation is historical. And the growth of literature is not merely development and change within the fixed boundaries of any given definition: the boundaries themselves are constantly changing.'
30. Daniel H.H. Ingalls, J.M. Masson and M.V. Patwardhan, tr., *The Dhvanyāloka of Ānandavardhan with the Locana of Abhinavagupta*, Harvard Oriental Series 49, Cambridge Massachusetts: Harvard University Press, 1990, p. 436.
31. Sheldon Pollock. 'Introduction', in Sheldon Pollock, ed., op. cit., 2004.
32. Paul Veyne, *Did the Greeks Believe in Their Myths? An Essay on Constitutive Imagination*, tr. Paula Wissing, Chicago: University of Chicago Press, 1988.
33. *na te vāg anṛtā kāvye kācid atra bhaviṣyati |*
kuru rāmakathāṃ puṇyāṃ ślokabaddhāṃ manoramāṃ ||

yāvat sthāsyanti girayaḥ saritaś ca mahītale |
tāvad rāmāyaṇakathā lokeṣu pracariṣyati || (*Rāmāyaṇa*, 1.2.34-35)
'No utterance of yours in this poem will be false. Now compose the whole story of Rāma fashioned into *ślokas* to delight the heart. As long as the mountains and rivers shall endure upon the earth, so long will the story of the *Rāmāyaṇa* be told among men.'
Robert P. Goldman, tr., *The Rāmāyaṇa of Vālmīki, Volume I: Bālakāṇḍa*, Princeton: Princeton University Press, 1984, p. 129.

34. Ibid.
35. David Shulman, 2001, op. cit., pp. 353-73.
36. See, A.K. Ramanujan, 'Is There an Indian Way of Thinking?' in *The Collected Essays of A.K. Ramanujan*, in Dharwadker, ed., op. cit., pp. 37-40.
37. For a more exciting interpretation, see Ramanujan, 'The Ring of Memory: Remembering and Forgetting in Indian Literature'. The ideas presented here are borrowed from this reference.
38. Ingalls, Masson and Patwardhan, tr., op. cit., fn. 1.
39. Ibid., p. 20, fn. 1.
40. Ibid., pp. 20-1.
41. V.S. Naipaul, *A Writer's People: Ways of Looking and Feeling*, London: Picador, 2007, p. 81.
42. See also A.K. Ramanujan, 'Three Hundred *Rāmāyaṇas*: Five Examples and Three Thoughts on Translation', in Dharwadkar, ed., *The Collected Essays of A.K. Ramanujan*, p. 143.
43. *Adhyātma Rāmāyaṇa*, 2.4.77-8 with a Hindi Translation by Munilal, Gitapress, Gorakhpur Edition, p. 80.
44. A.K. Ramanujan, 'Is There an Indian Way of Thinking?' in Dharwadkar, ed., op. cit., p. 42.
45. Wendy Doniger, 'Echoes of the *Mahābhārata:* Why is a Parrot a Narrator of the *Bhagavata Purana* and the *Devibhagavata Purana*', in Wendy Doniger, ed., *Purana Perennis:Reciprocity and Transformation in Hindu and Jain Texts*, Albany: SUNY Press, 1993, pp. 31-57. See also Ramanujan in Dharwadkar, ed., op. cit., pp. 37-40.
46. Isaiah Berlin, *The Crooked Timber of Humanity Chapters in the History of Ideas*, London: John Murray, 1990, p. 21.
47. Ibid., pp. 21-2.
48. Cf. also, the Hindu or Brahmanic view of life and the world:
    1. The concept of *svarga* in the Vedic and post-Vedic Literature: the *varṇāśrama* system and *yajña* as the means to Utopia.
    2. Through the path of Knowledge: *Karma Yoga* and *Jñāna Yoga* of the *Bhagavadgītā*, and the Upaniṣadic Vedānta and Sāṃkhya.
    3. The Alternative Route: The Buddha and his path to Nirvāṇa.

4. The Saints of Medieval India: the path of *saguṇa* and *nirguṇa* devotion.
5. The *Rāmarājya* of Tulsīdās: from the Kingdom of the Righteous Rāma to a God's Country, Avadhpurī.

daihik daivik bhautik tāpā | rāmarāj nahi kāhuhi byāpā || sab nar karanhi paraspar prītī | calanhi svadharma nirati sruti nītī. || (Tulsī, *Rāmcharitmānas*, 7.20.1).

Also, in the *Vālmīki Rāmāyaṇa*: (*Yuddha Kāṇḍa* or the *Book of War*, the last chapter, 14):

Under Rāma's rule, no one ever heard the wailing of widows, nor was there any fear of disease or poisonous snakes. There was no cruelty or injustice and the old never had to do the work of the young. There was happiness everywhere and *dharma* flourished. People took their example from Rāma and were never violent towards each other. Everybody lived for a thousand years and had a thousand sons. They knew neither disease nor unhappiness. Trees yielded fruit and flowers all year, the rains always came at the right time and the touch of the wind was always pleasant. Everybody did their own work and happily lived the lives prescribed for them. Everyone abided by *dharma* and there was no unrighteousness. (From Arshia Sattar, *The Rāmāyaṇa of Vālmīki, Translated with an Introduction*, Delhi: Penguin, 1996, p. 576)

And then in the Last Book, the *Uttara Kāṇḍa* (chapter 2):

A long time went by as mighty Rāma actively pursued *dharma* and ruled his kingdom wisely and well. The bears, monkeys and *rākṣasas* lived under his control and everyday the vassal kings did what would please Rāma. The rain god sent rain on time and the people in the cities and in the countryside were happy and prosperous. Under Rāma's rule, no one died an untimely death, no calamities occurred and no one acted unrighteously (ibid., p. 595).

49. *The Rāmāyaṇa of Vālmīki, Volume II: Ayodhyākāṇḍa*, tr. Sheldon Pollock, Princeton: Princeton University Press, 1986, p. 16.
50. Ibid. Sheldon Pollock: 'This was the established pattern of behaviour. "There is no brotherly love among heroes," Rāvaṇa is told when urged to take up arms and drive his elder brother Vaiśravana from the throne of Laṇkā . . . which the historical kings throughout the period—the young Aśoka, for example—tried to forestall by the summary execution of virtually all possible claimants, elder brothers among them,' p. 17.
51. I am grateful to the organizers of the conference at Jamia Millia Islamia, Delhi, where an earlier version of the paper was presented and also to the anonymous reader of the article for his/her valuable comments; I wish to express my thanks to Dr. Ranjeeta Dutta, one of the editors of this anthology, for her very useful comments, suggestions and, above

all, her perseverance with my rather delayed responses to her queries regarding the article. I have usually translated most of the Sanskrit and Hindi matter used in this article; for *Vālmīki Rāmāyaṇa*, though, I have used also R.P. Goldman's translation of *Bālakāṇḍa* (vol. I, New Jersey: Princeton University Press, 1984) and Sheldon Pollock's *Ayodhyā Kāṇḍa* (vol. II, New Jersey: Princeton University Press, 1986); I have made occasional changes in their translations, where necessary, which in no way reflect any suggestion on their most magnificent translations of the *Vālmīki Rāmāyaṇa*.

THREE

Representations of a Past

The Life of Rāmānuja and the Śrīvaiṣṇava Community

Ranjeeta Dutta

One of the significant aspects of the religious identity of a community is the representation of a particular past that legitimizes its status and authority, justifying its claims in the contemporary socio-political context. Further, associated with the notions of an antiquated past is the concept of a tradition that become central to the evolution of a community. Thus, the representation of the past and the tradition it embodies provide a sense of history and cultural continuity to the community. In many ways, this past and the tradition that it transmits become representative of the community ideology enabling the building up of the community identity *vis-à-vis* the 'other'.

This paper attempts to analyse the representation of a past and its implications for the Śrīvaiṣṇava community identities by focusing on the delineation of the life of Rāmānuja in the Śrīvaiṣṇava hagiographies. Like all religious communities, Srivaisnavism drew its initial impetus from the religious experience of its saints.[1] The hagiographies, while documenting the biographies of these saints (in this case, Rāmānuja), also delineated the history of the Śrīvaiṣṇava community. Enmeshed with this portrayal of history were the issues of community consciousness, caste, identities, the notion of a tradition and the consolidation of the community—all of which were largely influenced by the contemporary socio-political context from the twelfth to the seventeenth century. This was also the period in which most of these hagiographies were written. These themes in the hagiographical narratives will be discussed here in association with Rāmānuja (eleventh-twelfth century). Rāmānuja has been a source of religious and spiritual inspiration for the Śrīvaiṣṇavas. An important philosopher who founded the Viśiṣṭādvaita philosophy, Rāmānuja was also canonized as a popular bhakti saint. It should be noted that the issues just stated are important till date and have become subjects of secular biographies, theatre, comics like *Amar Chitra Katha*, newspaper articles, chapbooks and documentary films. The hagiographical narratives on these themes may not have had any direct relation with the actual life of Rāmānuja but were articulating the concerns of the Śrīvaiṣṇava community and community identity.

The essay is divided into four sections. Section one discusses the nature of the Śrīvaiṣṇava hagiographies in general. Section two will focuses on the context in which they were composed. Section three discusses the concept of the Śrīvaiṣṇava tradition, comprising Vedic-Upaniṣadic, Puranic and Tamil traditions, as epitomized in the life of Rāmānuja, and the organization of the community with special reference to the construction of a lineage. Section four discusses the organization of the community and its consolidation with special reference to caste and the role of Rāmānuja as a 'social reformer'.

I

The Śrīvaiṣṇavas are a distinct Vaiṣṇava community in south India confined primarily to Tamil Nadu, and the southern parts of Andhra Pradesh and Karnataka. The community considers Viṣṇu and his consort Lakṣmī as their supreme godhead, and Rāmānuja as their spiritual leader. The Śrīvaiṣṇavas regard the Sanskrit Vedas and the *Nālāyira Divya Prabandham* as their main scriptures.[2] The present-day Śrīvaiṣṇavas are divided into sects—the Vaṭakalai and the Teṉkalai. The Vaṭakalais represent the Sanskritic tradition. Kāñcīpuram in Tamil Nadu is their institutional centre and Vedānta Deśika (AD 1268-1369) their spiritual preceptor. They give preference to the Sanskrit Vedas over the Draviḍa Vedas, that is the Tamil hymns of the Āḷvārs. Therefore, they are considered Brahmanical and conservative in their outlook. The Teṉkalais, on the other hand, represent the Tamil tradition. Śrīraṅgam in Tamil Nadu is their centre and Maṇavāḷa Māmuṉi (AD 1370-1442) their religious leader. Since the Teṉkalais regard the Draviḍa Vedas as their scriptures, they are considered to be more broadbased than the Vaṭakalais and have a large non-Brahmanical following. Today, the entire Śrīvaiṣṇava tradition, its texts and institutional structure, viz., temples and *maṭhas*, are aligned as either the Vaṭakalai or Teṉkalai. However, despite their distinct identities, both sects acknowledge their affiliation to the larger Śrīvaiṣṇava community.

One of the important textual representations of the Śrīvaiṣṇavas was through the medium of various hagiographical narratives. Documenting the history of the Śrīvaiṣṇava community for its devotees, the hagiographies or *guru-paramparās*, written from the twelfth century onwards, began with an account of the lives of the Āḻvārs, the early mystics steeped in devotion (fourth to the eighth century), followed by Yāmuna (ninth century), Nāthamuni (tenth-eleventh century) and Rāmānuja (eleventh-twelfth century). The latter three were recognized as the *ācāryas*, whose primary concern was the organization of the community. The post-Rāmānuja phase of the community history was characterized by the religious activities of his various disciples, who perpetuated a lineage that culminated in the institutionalization of the personalities of Vedānta Deśika and Maṇavāḷa Māmuṇi as the acaryic heads of the Vaṭakalai and Teṉkalai sects, respectively.

The hagiographical tradition attempted to achieve the dual task of developing a soteriology and ecclesiology revolving round the biographies of the saints, thereby creating the collective ethos for the Śrīvaiṣṇava community. Composed in the post-Rāmānuja period, these texts projected a tradition which a follower could identify with. The process of mythicization in the life-stories of these Āḻvārs and *ācāryas* projected them as representations of divinity. Such a eulogization of the Āḻvārs and *ācāryas* was associated with an important theological concept of the guru or preceptor who was the spiritual guide, guiding a lay devotee towards the goal of salvation through the experience of bhakti and *prapatti*. The role of Rāmānuja as a guru was developed in detail in these texts and the divinely-ordained Viśiṣṭādvaita philosophy was to be propagated, interpreted by and disseminated through the *guru-śiṣya paramparā* or the preceptor-disciple relationship. In this context, the succession, which involved the passing down of tradition through medium of spiritual leaders, became the major concern of the hagiographical tradition.

Hagiographies therefore became the legitimizing mechanism of succession of these spiritual leaders. The arrangement among the Āl̲vārs themselves (sometimes among the Āl̲vārs and *ācāryas* and sometimes among the *ācāryas*) presented a sense of a 'communitas'. These Āl̲vārs and *ācāryas* notwithstanding their different time periods, were anachronistically depicted as interacting with each other. For instance, the story of the *Mudal* Āl̲vārs meeting together attributes contemporaneity, which otherwise is difficult to establish. According to the texts, the three Āl̲vārs, in the course of their wandering, arrived at Tirukkovalūr one night one after the other, in the same sequence as they are presented in the *guru-paramparās* (viz., Poygai, Bhūdatt, Pēy). They took shelter in a choultry near the Viṣṇu temple at Tirukkovalūr. As the space was just enough for three people to stand, the entry of Viṣṇu created a problem and each Āl̲vār became conscious of the stranger having squeezed in. They realized, subsequently, that it was the lord himself. The Āl̲vārs lit the 'spiritual lamp' and had a *darśana* of Viṣṇu, and instantly composed 100 verses each in Tamil known as *Mudal Tiruvantādi*, *Irantantiruvantādi* and *Mun̲ran Tiruvantādi*, respectively. Similarly, the narrative of Nāthamuni recovering the four thousand hymns of the Āl̲vārs by seeking Nammāl̲vār's personal help and Yāmuna's three-finger story (discussed in section three of this paper) are seen as attempts at establishing a continuous succession between the Āl̲vārs and *ācāryas*. In this context Nāthamuni's pilgrimage to various temples for the collection of hymns of the Āl̲vārs and finally setting them to music, thereby evolving an oral scripture is a crucial narrative:

Once, some Vaiṣṇavas from Kurugur (Āl̲vār Tirunagarī) arrived at Vīra-nārāyaṇapuram and sang the ten verses of Nammāl̲vār's hymn. Nāthamuni heard them and was moved to tears. He immediately left for Kurugūr, the hometown of Nammāḻvār. After paying respect to the god in the temple there, he came to the famous tamarind tree in whose trunk Nammāḻvār was residing. The intense desire to meet Nammāḻvār and learn the rest of the hymns made Nāthamuni recite twelve thousand times the ten stanzas of Madhurakavi's hymns. Finally, Nammāḻvār with Madhurakavi appeared before Nāthamuni and transmitted his four works, which explained the meaning of the four Vedas. On his arrival at Vīranārāyaṇa, Nāthamuni set these Dravida hymns to music in the temple at the behest of the god.[3]

Therefore, the *guru-paramparās* were attempting to build-up and establish a tradition, which, till the twelfth century were in oral circulation. The composition of these texts was a response to a major concern of the ideologues of the community—the transmission of the tradition to the future generation in an acceptable manner. When an oral tradition gets codified into a written one, in this case through the composition of hagiographical texts, then 'history is transformed into legends and myths and illuminates the twilight zone of transition between the handed down memories and patterned imagination'.[4] At such junctures, contemporary socio-religious contexts inevitably influence the constructions of a past. Therefore, the aim of hagiographies was to 'structure at least some parts of social life . . . as unchanging and invariant within the changing context'.[5] A discussion on the changing contextual background of these texts will be taken up in the next section. Hagiographies became the medium of articulation, transmission and redaction of the Śrīvaiṣṇava tradition, emerging a part of the Śrīvaiṣṇava canon. Till today, followers consider these *guru-paramparās* as one of their scriptures.

The Śrīvaiṣṇava tradition articulated in these *guru-paramparās* was that of *ubhaya-vedānta*, or the dual Veda, in which the Tamil hymns of the Āḻvārs (some of whom were non-brāhmaṇas), especially the *Tiruvāymōḷi* of Nammāḻvār, were given the appellation of Draviḍa Veda and put on par with the Sanskrit Vedas. This represented both the linguistic as well as the social sphere, or the Tamil and Sanskrit domains of the Śrīvaiṣṇava community. These developments influenced the writing of Śrīvaiṣṇava texts, in this case the hagiographies. From the late twelfth century, religious literature in general and hagiographies in particular began to be composed in a language which was called Maṇiprāvalam. Tamil words were interspersed with Sanskrit words just as the ruby and coral (*maṇi*—ruby; *pravāla*—coral) were strung alternatively in a necklace. For the first time, a 'vernacular' (Tamil) was used alongside Sanskrit and both were accorded scriptural status. This represented a somewhat radical departure. Moreover, this linguistic approach conformed to the *ubhaya-vedāntic* tradition and, on a more basic level, appealed to non-brāhmaṇa devotee, which was the aim of the hagiographers.

Therefore, Maṇipravālam represented the ideology of the Śrīvaiṣṇava exegesis which was characterized by a dualism, viz., the Sanskrit and Tamil traditions. Hence, being the medium of expression of this ideology, it became very significant for the community identity in the post-Rāmānuja period. The advantage of having a dual linguistic tradition was realized particularly by the Śrīvaiṣṇava *ācāryas*, especially the composers of the hagiographies, when this language became the direct and effective medium of transmission and dissemination of the community's ideology. Therefore, Maṇipravālam was a 'situational language' for while, on the one hand,

> it was a natural type of parlance, in that many of the Sanskrit terms employed are common speech of the *bhāgavatas*, thus ensuring the general intelligibility of the language, it is a situational language, in that it developed in specific circumstances to expound the *ubhaya-vedānta* to a diverse religious community whose mother tongue was Tamil and was used in specific contexts like religious instructions.[6]

Such a tradition of *ubhaya-vedānta* was epitomized in the biographical delineation of Rāmānuja.

Thus, within the framework of the *ubhaya-vedānta* tradition and the language of Maṇipravālam, the narratives that evolved in these hagiographical texts provided a sense of history and continuity to the community, bequeathing, from an antiquated past, ideas and beliefs, and conventions and practices which gave legitimacy and credibility. In addition the texts reflected the 'social location and ideology' of the different groups and sub-sects.[7] They provided legitimacy to multiple identities during the contest over power and the control of resources. While they established these multiple identities, they nonetheless had a common perception of the Śrīvaiṣṇava community. This is indicated by the fact that they drew from a common pool of ideas and events in their texts.

The duality in the Śrīvaiṣṇava tradition, however, could not reconcile to the Sanskritic ethos of the community. The authors of the complex textual tradition were the *ācāryas* or spiritual heads who were brāhmaṇas themselves. The tension between the Sanskrit and Tamil were always evident in the texts. There has been, in south India, a certain duality in the construction of religious traditions due to the constant interaction between the mainstream Sanskritic tradition and regional/local or vernacular forms, with shifting emphases between the Sanskritic and vernacular at different points of historical time. This is nowhere better exemplified than in the Śrīvaiṣṇava community's contradictions over Sanskrit and Tamil that finally led to the schism between the Vaṭakalai (northern) and Teṉkalai (southern) sects.

The Śrīvaiṣṇava hagiographical tradition is not a uniform, monolithic one. The hagiographical texts can broadly be categorized into three genres which project their respective affiliations. First, there are some texts which appear to have a non-sectarian, non-partisan approach. Its *Divyasūricaritam* is the only example of this kind. Its non-partisan character may be due to the fact that its composition preceded any sectarian difference within Srivaisnavism. Or, alternatively, it aimed at portraying the undivided or unified perspective of the community until Rāmānuja. Second, certain texts with sectarian overtones presented biographical sketches of important Śrīvaiṣṇava sectarian leaders. These, on the basis of their affiliations, represented a Sanskritic or a Tamil tradition. This duality of Sanskrit and Tamil after the seventeenth century developed schismatic tendencies, and led to the emergence of the Vaṭakalai and Teṉkalai sects. Subsequently the hagiographies also got appropriated as Vaṭakalai or Teṉkalai on the basis of their Sanskritic or Tamil approach, respectively. Henceforth, these texts would be referred to by their sectarian affiliations. The *Teṉkalai Ārayirappaṭi Guruparamparāprabhāvam*, *Teṉkalai Muāyirappaṭi Guruparamparāprabhāvam*, *Vaṭakalai Muāyirappaṭi Guruparamparāprabhāvam*, and the *Vaṭakalai Muāyirappaṭi* are the texts of the Teṉkalai and Vaṭakalai groups respectively.[8] The

Rāmānujadivyasūricaritam (Teṉkalai) and *Yatindrapravaṇa-prabhāvam* (Teṉkalai), the life history of Rāmānuja and Maṇavāḷa Māmunigaḷ, respectively, belonged to the Teṉkalai traditionally.[9] Third category of hagiographic texts are the *guru-paramparās* in this case, genealogies associated with the brāhmaṇa and non-brāhmaṇa families. Through these genealogies, they asserted their individual community identity and emerged as sub-communities within the Śrīvaiṣṇava tradition. However, gradually, each of these became identified with either the Vaṭakalai or Teṉkalai in the seventeenth century.

II

The construction of the past by the ideologues of the Śrīvaiṣṇava community was influenced by contemporary concerns. It was during the twelfth and thirteenth centuries period that the community consciousness developed strengthened structure of the tradition by amalgamating the Tamil (oral) and the Sanskritic (written). This was a significant development for it broadened the scope of the community ideology and tradition, making it relevant for a larger section of society. The notion of being a 'Śrīvaiṣṇava' developed, which determined the normative behavioural pattern of the community. The Śrīvaiṣṇava community inherited two sets of religious ideas and practices in the thirteenth century. They were the Tamil hymns of the Āḻvārs, the *Nālāyira Divyaprabandham* (Corpus of Four Thousand), and the philosophy of Viśiṣṭādvaita of Rāmānuja (eleventh-twelfth century). The Tamil hymns of the Āḻvārs were already in oral circulation. One of the sections of the hymnal corpus, the *Tiruvāymoḷi* of Nammāḻvār, had already been collected and set to music in the Raṅganāthasvāmī temples at Śrīraṅgam and Uttaramērūr in the eleventh century.[10]

The hymns in general and those of Nammāḻvār in particular, were characterized by an unconditional surrender to god, i.e. *prapatti*. The hymns reiterated that the *prapatti* could be attained by anyone, irrespective of the caste status of the individual devotee. The hymns were not only a protest against the exclusive socio-religious sphere of the brāhmaṇas, but also suggested an alternative that placed the community of Vaiṣṇava bhaktas above the affiliation of caste. The community bonds in the hymns were highlighted by emphasizing the merit of recitation in the temple in which the entire community participated. This is best exemplified in Nammāḻvār's *Tiruvāymoḷi*. The consciousness of being a Vaiṣṇava community was further highlighted through the notion of pilgrimage. The descriptions of local cult centres in the hymns as sacred Vaiṣṇava sites charted out a sacred geography for the community. This marked the beginning of the concept of pilgrimage in which each site was visited and sung into prominence. Tirumangai, a ninth-century Āḻvār, in his hymns, the *Periya Tirumatal*, mapped over ninety places. Further, the hymns marginalized Sanskrit as the language of religious expression and emphasized on Tamil, the language of the ordinary Vaishnava devotee. The sacredness of Tamil was further sought to be enhanced in the hymns by claiming to have encapsulated the essence of the otherwise inaccessible Vedas. For the first time, a regional language was placed on par with Sanskrit as a language for scriptures.

All these ideas expressed in the hymns can be related to the marginalized background of the Āḻvārs. For instance, Nammāḻvār was a Vēḷāḷa, and Tirumangai was a non-brāhmaṇa *kalva* chief. Even the Brahmanical background of some of the Āḻvārs like Periyāḻvār was not an exalted one. The transformation of local cult centres into Vaiṣṇava sacred sites was accompanied by the acculturation and assimilation of cultic priests. Since they derived their status from the Agamic forms of worship that were considered inferior to Vedic forms, a low ritual rank was assigned to them within the brāhmaṇa varna.[11] Thus, the Caturvedins (Vedic brāhmaṇas), the Smārtas and Vadamas (those who performed Vedic sacrifices) were superior to the temple priests, the social category to which brāhmaṇa hymnists like Periyāḻvār, Toṉṭaratippoṭi and Madhurakavi belonged. Hence, issues of caste, community, salvation and pilgrimage, as discussed in the hymns, were later dealt with in the hagiographies.

The second religious tradition that the Śrīvaiṣṇavas inherited in the thirteenth century was the Viśiṣṭādvaita philosophy of

Rāmānuja that imparted a theological orientation to the community. Rāmānuja's Viśiṣṭādvaita emerged as a coherent philosophy and inculcated theological ideas of experiencing god, which placed Srivaisnavism on an equal footing with other religious traditions. Although articulated in Sanskrit, it was the first school of thought to challenge Śaṅkara's monistic (i.e. non-dualism) philosophy of Advaita and the concept of the *nirguṇa Brahman*, and presented an alternative model for the perception of the divinity based on 'qualified monism (i.e. Viśiṣṭādvaita) where the divine had attributes that were comprehensible to less intellectual devotees.

Briefly, the Viśiṣṭādvaita philosophy can be summarized into four characteristics. First, it propounded a credible doctrine of complete identity between the god and the absolute. The individual soul was made by god, returned to him and merged with him but was always conscious of its separate existence. If this self-consciousness was lost, it would cease to exist. It was one with god, yet separate; hence, for this reason, the system of Rāmānuja was called Viśiṣṭādvaita.[12] Second, it harmonized god's transcendence (*paratva*) with his accessibility (*saulabhya*). This was very significant for establishing a personal relationship with god. The concept of godhead with attributes, i.e. the *saguṇa Brahman* paved the way for a better socio-ethical approach and made the religion more acceptable to the common man. Rāmānuja's supreme self was one who was extremely compassionate and full of love for his devotees. Unlike the impersonal, attributeless god, i.e. the *nirguṇa Brahman* of Śaṅkara, Rāmānuja's god needed a man and vice versa. Third, it indicated the highest type of devotion without belittling the part of intellectualism and social duties in a man's spiritual life. It taught a way to be away from the phenomenal world but, at the same time, to live within it by surrendering the fruits of action at the feet of god. Fourth, the Viśiṣṭādvaita of Rāmānuja selectively incorporated Śaṅkara's Vedantic tradition with its monism but modified it to make it comprehensible to the non-intellectual, emotionally involved devotee. This was crucial to the social base of the community. Śaṅkara's Advaita preached that salvation could be achieved through abstinence, and the denial of vices and worldly aspects, and that the realization of godhead was possible through introspection. Viśiṣṭādvaita accepted the social obligation of a man. Rāmānuja structured these religious ideas within the framework of the Upaniṣadic tradition through the composition of commentaries in Sanskrit alone. Thus, emerged a new literary tradition, where the exposition of religious philosophy took the form of elaborate interpretations and discourses.

Till the thirteenth century, despite creating an awareness of fraternity among Śrīvaiṣṇava devotees, both the Tamil tradition of the Āḻvārs and the Sanskritic theology of Rāmānuja remained exclusive to each other. It is difficult to judge the influence of the Āḻvārs on Rāmānuja for his writings do not refer to them at all. The two religious traditions continued to be parallel and did not complement each other. Therefore, it was left to the Śrīvaiṣṇava theologians from the thirteenth century onwards to evolve a religious ideology that would combine both. Such an exercise was crucial for, unlike the Śaivas, the Vaiṣṇavas were not a well-developed and organized community with a comprehensive textual tradition in the thirteenth century. Saivism had already evolved an integrative paradigm comprising Tamil bhakti, Brahmanical religious forms and autochthonous cults. The evolution of the Śaiva Āgamas which laid down new forms of worship became the theological basis for converting and finally integrating the local cult centres into Śaiva shrines. The sacred geography as delineated by the Nāyanārs (early Śaiva saints) provided a guide for the identification of these sites, with the maximum concentration in the Kāvērī region. The creation of a Śaiva pantheon with the incorporation of Murukaṉ and Durgā representing a divine family, and the folk analogy of *liṅga* worship, appealed to a larger section of the society and broadened the social basis of Saivism. The presence of aniconic *liṅgas* in canonical temples provided 'a constantly widening orbit for bringing in divergent socio-economic and ethnic groups into Śaiva worship'.[13]

Therefore, for these reasons, Saivism was adopted as the royal cult, which further enabled the consolidation of Śaiva community. In addition, the iconographic forms of Śiva as Yogī (popularly called Dakṣiṇamūrti), Naṭarāja, Bhikṣāṭana and Rāvaṇānugraha (humbling of Rāvaṇa)—all symbolizing the notion of a successful

Puranic hero-appealed to the Cōḷa ideology for establishing power over the Tamil region. From the middle of the tenth to the twelfth century AD, Saivism emerged as a 'state' cult under Rājarāja I (AD 985-1045), Rājendra I and Kulōttunga II (AD 1133-50). The large-scale construction of canonical temples, especially in the royal capital of Gaṅgaikoṇḍacōḷapuram and Tañjāvūr, projected the Cōḷa policy of promoting Śaiva bhakti as an effective ideology for the integration of the society and economy through the expansion of the agrarian order and for establishing royal control. The collection of Śaiva hymns and the composition of hagiographies were a part of the royal project that contributed to the evolution of a Śaiva scripture (*marai*). Nambi Andar Nambi, the compiler of the Tirumurai (scripture), and Cekkilar, the composer of the Śaiva hagiography, the *Periya Purānam*, were associated with the court of Rājarāja I and Kulōttuṅga II, respectively. In fact, the narratives from the hagiographies inspired some of the iconographic themes in the Cōḷa temples.[14] The royal patronage to Śaiva temples expanded the liturgy by introducing the hymns of the four Nāyanārs, viz., Appar, Cuntarar, Campantar and Maṇikkavāccakar, as a part of the ritual singing in them. Their apotheosis took place in the temples around the same time (the tenth century) under royal initiative, mainly of Rājarāja I (985-1014) and Kulōttuṅga II (1133-50).[15]

Royal patronage to Saivism marginalized the development of Vaisnavism. Compared to the Śaiva temples, the construction of Vaiṣṇava ones was not on such a large scale. None of the Āḻvārs, with the exception of Tirumangai, were apotheosized in the Cōḷa temples. Besides, as stated above, unlike the Śaivas, the Vaiṣṇavas were not a well-organized community with a comprehensive textual and scriptural tradition that had a Tamil and Sanskrit base. Attempts were made in the late ninth and early tenth centuries to evolve a text, the *Bhāgavata Purāṇa*. For the first time, the exposition of the Āḻvār bhakti formed the context of this text written in Sanskrit. This 'Sanskritization of the Kṛṣṇa tradition' adopted the popular Puranic style and drew heavily from regional Tamil myths.[16] However, the heavy Sanskritic base of the text coupled with its Advaitic position (to reconcile bhakti with Brahmanical orthodoxy) failed to make an impact on the local population. The world-view of the Ā<u>l</u>vārs regarding community and religion did not achieve a popular base despite their dissent against the established orthodoxy. Perhaps the Viśiṣṭādvaita philosophy of Rāmānuja remained confined to narrow intellectual realm. Consequently, the 'Śrīvaiṣṇavas' remained a discrete, scattered lot in south India. Temple inscriptions refer to the 'Śrīvaiṣṇavas' but it was an honorary prefix of the Vaiṣṇava brāhmaṇas and did not imply a community.

A question that arises is that why, from the twelfth and thirteenth century onwards, was there a conscious attempt to evolve a notion of community, tradition, community consciousness, and cohesive, organized, institutional structures. The answer probably lies in the historical context of this period. The decline of the Cōḷas by the end of the twelfth century AD, the Hoysala occupation of the Tamil region and the establishment of the Vijayanagara Empire by AD 1370 led to the integration of the three cultural zones of Karnataka, Tamil Nadu and Andhra Pradesh. As a result, a network of relations developed between the wetland agricultural settlements and the dry upland zones with a narrow resource base. The fertile Kāvērī delta attracted Telugu warriors as well the dominant agricultural community of the Velamas from the arid northern zones of the Deccan plateau. These two groups gradually became economically and politically powerful, and began impinging upon pre-existing local power groups and their areas of control. The new warrior class, subsequently known as the *nāyakas*, emerged as the patrons of temples and *maṭhas* and promoted various religious groups, especially the Śrīvaiṣṇavas.[17] Migration also brought into prominence a new class of itinerant merchants and traders, several of whom gradually settled down and emerged as powerful landowners. The inscriptional reference to the Kaikkōḷa, Vāniya, Śikku Vāniya, Vyāpārī, Māyilaṭṭi, Ka<u>n</u>mala and Komātti traders from Saurashtra point to the development of a brisk trade and increased craft production, which found a thriving market in the Vijayanagara and post-Vijayanagara kingdoms. Of particular importance were the Kaikkōḷas, an artisan-merchant community of weavers. This group maintained personal armies and organized themselves into supra-local groups called the Mahānāḍus.[18] The emergent mercantile communities were followers of different religious tradition—Śaiva, Vaiṣṇava and Islamic.[19] However, it was primarily Vaisnavism that was the faith of migrant merchants and traders. Their lavish sponsorship to Śrīvaiṣṇava temples was crucial for the development of the community. Simultaneously, with the expansion of trading and political networks, unsettled forested areas and hilly tracts situated on the peripheries of agricultural settlements evolved into major political and economic centres. The population of these inhospitable tracts, comprising hunting tribes with economic prosperity, acquired political power and emerged as important patrons of various religious communities.

Thus, in the context of the changing socio-political milieu and the already defined and well-developed structure of Saivism, the Śrīvaiṣṇava ideology and theology began to reorient itself. There was an attempt to evolve a framework that would provide an integrative structure, unifying disparate social groups within a single community. In this connection, the issue of caste acquired importance. The institutional network, including the temples and *maṭhas*, accommodated non-brāhmaṇa groups and gave them ritual space in temple activities. This will be discussed in the next section.

Such community concerns also underscored the importance of a written textual tradition, codifying pre-existing ideas along with the interpretations and comments of the codifier, modified and added to structure of that tradition. The *guru-paramparā* texts were a part of this textual tradition.[20] As long as the oral tradition circulated, community bonds were fluid and subject to shifting frontiers. The codification of the oral tradition provided a fixed point of reference for scriptures to develop. Perhaps the hagiographies were also codifying Śrīvaiṣṇava ideals and fixing community boundaries. However, the relevance of the orality continued as the only means of dissemination to those denied access to scriptures. For instance, the oral exposition of the philosophy through ritual singing in temples continued to be one of the means of communication in Srivaisnavism.

The textual tradition, of which the hagiographies were a part in a literal sense, may be said to have begun around the ninth-tenth century AD, when, it is believed, the four thousand hymns of the Āḻvārs which were scattered were collected and set to music by Nāthamuni to be sung in the temple. This may be considered the first attempt at creating a text, albeit oral, for developing a community consciousness. However, the collection and compilation of hymns were not enough. These had to be placed in a context to make it relevant to the community. In south India, the context of the transmission of the text was the temple. It provided a physical and ritual space for the recitation of hymns, as the ritual performance of hymns involved the reciters as well as the listeners, i.e. the entire community of devotees, irrespective of their caste status.

The textual tradition entered the second phase from the eleventh century AD onwards when texts on Śrīvaiṣṇava philosophy and hagiographies came to be composed by religious leaders. These focused mainly on theological and biographical issues. They formed the basis of the Viśiṣṭādvaita philosophy of Rāmānuja and the past of the community, which came to be identified with the community and its ideology. The crystallization of philosophical ideas led to soteriological and hermeneutical developments, which later generated further works on philosophy and commentaries. However, in these two stages, the textual tradition, while creating an awareness of fraternity among Śrīvaiṣṇava devotees, remained exclusive in the sense that the Sanskritic and Tamil texts continued to be parallel to each other and not incorporative. The Tamil hymns, it should be pointed out, were still being orally transmitted through temples and the rituals performed in them.

The authors of the complex Śrīvaiṣṇava textual tradition were the *ācāryas*, or spiritual heads, who carefully and cogently presented ideas within a stable and legitimate framework. In this process, several historical situations which emerged as aberrations were justified through various myths and legends. The *ācāryas* themselves derived their positions of authority from the very tradition they built up, which emphasized the importance of the *guru/ācārya* that emerged as a major element in the institutional organization of the community.

Thus, the Śrīvaiṣṇava tradition may be understood as a 'process as well as a product', creating a continuing context for modification, innovation and elaboration. Such reconstructions of the tradition frequently took place because of certain circumstances: one, when the Viśiṣṭādvaita philosophy evolved under the aegis of Rāmānuja, the philosopher-reformer, in a highly Sanskritized scriptural tradition; two, when deviation from Sanskritic norms brought the Tamil hymnal literature to the fore as the Draviḍa Veda, providing sanctity to the 'vernacular' as a scriptural language; three, when sectarian affiliations split the community's coherent organization, resulting in a dual textual tradition.

Hence, under these circumstances, the representation of a particular past became crucial in hagiographical narratives. The hagiographical delineation of Rāmānuja also represented and highlighted community concerns and identity. Some of these were the notion of a tradition, caste and related social issues that became major themes of narratives. The greater concern was to project a superhuman profile of Rāmānuja that would fill the devotees with awe and wonder and present an exalted status of him as the most reverential guru and *ācārya*. Therefore, in this process of idealizing and venerating Rāmānuja, narratives replete with episodes on miracles and divine interventions 'immortalized' him 'by projecting' him 'as larger than life . . . transcending mortal boundaries.'[21] Such an image became so influential that till today he is considered a 'social reformer' and the precursor of modern ones like Periyar and B.R. Ambedkar.[22]

III

Perhaps the central concern of the hagiographers was to explicate the Śrīvaiṣṇava tradition of the *ubhaya-vedānta* not only from a theological point of view but also as the ideological basis of the institutional networks of the temples and the *maṭhas*, both of which provided an arena of interaction for the community. Thus, the dissemination of this tradition was expressed in narratives through issues such as the superiority of the Viśiṣṭādvaita philosophy, lineage and community organization, and the consolidation of the temple and *maṭha* network. These issues were portrayed primarily in the profile of Rāmānuja as the *ācārya* and the organizer of the community. It should be noted that successive *ācāryas* were also portrayed in a similar manner but the narratives on Rāmānuja credit him with a seminal role that had no parallel.

According to the Śrīvaiṣṇava tradition, the appointment of Rāmānuja as the *acaryic* head of the community was divinely pre-ordained. The hagiographical texts inform us that Rāmānuja was born in Śrīperumbūdūr in the Vaḍama sub-caste of brāhmaṇas who were followers of the Smārta tradition. Rāmānuja's family was probably Smārta, i.e. followers of Advaita, the philosophy propounded by Śaṅkara. Rāmānuja's early years were spent in Kāñcīpuram, which was then an important religious and trading centre. The texts inform us about Rāmānuja's extraordinary brilliance in grasping difficult metaphysical ideas and mastering equally difficult texts like the Vedas at a young age.[23] Rāmānuja's guru was Yādavaprakāśa—a famous *advaitin*.[24] In the course of his learning, he often questioned his guru's interpretation of the Upaniṣads.[25] According to the *Divayasūricaritam*, even while Rāmānuja was a student, his fame spread far and wide. The text further informs us that he was utilizing those *śrutis* for expounding Viśiṣṭādvaita that were already being made the reference point for Advaita interpretations, especially by his teacher, Yādavaprakāśa. This brought him into direct opposition with the latter. The tension between teacher and disciple represented the contradictions between the Viśiṣṭādvaita and Advaita systems of philosophy. Therefore, Rāmānuja attempted to formulate a coherent philosophy of Viśiṣṭādvaita and was engaged in constant dialogue with the Advaita disciples of Śaṅkara. This is reflected in narratives that discuss the interface between Rāmānuja and Yādavaprakāśa, reflecting the interaction between the adherents of Advaita and Viśiṣṭādvaita. It should be noted that Śaṅkara was located in eighth-century Kerala and could not have met Rāmānuja. Hence, there must have been some circulation of ideas and philosophical discussions of which Rāmānuja was a part.

Further, the tensions between Yādavaprakāśa and Rāmānuja, or Advaita philosophy and the Viśiṣṭādvaita system of thought, is illustrated through a narrative that highlighted the superiority of Rāmānuja over his teacher:

While he was a disciple of Yādavaprakāśa, during that time the king's son was afflicted by a *brahmarākṣasa*. The king was told of Yādavaprakāśa's occult power and therefore he invited Yādavaprakāśa and his disciples to relieve his son. As soon as Yādavaprakāśa saw the son and the possession of *brahmarākṣasa* over him, he immediately started chanting the *mantras*. On hearing Yādavaprakāśa chanting the *mantras*, the *brahmarākṣasa* was besieged with rage and ridiculed Yādavaprakāśa and declared him completely ignorant. The *brahmarākṣasa* asserted that he knew about all the past births of Yādavaprakāśa and himself. In the course of the argument that ensued, Yādavaprakāśa challenged the *rākṣasa* to reveal all about their respective past births. The *rākṣasa* informed that, 'In the past birth you were a chamaleon (lizard) living near the banks of a pond in an *agrahāra*, named Madurāntaka. When some learned Vaiṣṇava men were on their way to participate in the festivals, they stopped here, rested and ate. Their leftover rice was consumed by you. As a result of the consumption of these sacred leftovers, you were redeemed and hence were born in a human form in this birth. I was a *brāhmaṇa* who along with other *brāhmaṇas* performed the *yajñas*. In one of the *yajñas*, I erred and with the result I was reborn as a *brahmarākṣasa*.'

Pointing towards Rāmānuja, the *rākṣasa* then said, 'This incarnation of *śeṣa* (the snake on which Viṣṇu is resting), who has been sent on this earth to protect mankind, has power over me. If he asks me to leave this body, I will immediately obey. In fact, his sweet words will release me from this body and will give me *mokṣa* or salvation.' After saying this, the *brahmarākṣasa* fell at the feet of Rāmānuja. Thereafter, Yādavaprakāśa ordered Rāmānuja to command the *rākṣasa* to leave the body of the prince. Rāmānuja obeyed his *guru* and commanded politely the aggrieved *brahmarākṣasa* to leave the body, the sign being the breaking of a branch of the *pīpal* tree. The *rakṣasa* left the body of the prince and while going broke the branch of the *pīpal* tree. The king was happy and rewarded Rāmānuja lavishly. Thereafter, Rāmānuja gave all the endowments to his *guru*.[26]

This story states the superiority of the Viśiṣṭādvaita philosophy, as well as the extraordinariness of Rāmānuja. There are several incidents in the hagiographical texts on the intellectual incompatibility between Rāmānuja and Yādavaprakāśa. In fact, the rivalry was so intense that Yādavaprakāśa conspired to take Rāmānuja's life. Consequently, Rāmānuja was saved by none other than Viṣṇu. The *guru-paramparās* are replete with legends on this theme, which is also associated with the organization of the community, conversion and the consequent spread of Srivaisnavism. Sectarianism is not only directed against the Advaitins, but also against the Jainas. Examples of the Hoysala king, Viṣṇuvardhana (twelfth century AD), converting from Jainism and the Muslim princess from Delhi converting from Islam to Srivaisnavism are well-documented.[27] Both these episodes were linked to the establishment of the Narayanaswami temple at Mēlkōṭe and the spread of the community network in the Karnataka region.

The texts, while dealing with the issue of continuity, attempted to portray an uninterrupted acaryic lineage. Historically speaking, Śrīvaiṣṇava leadership had considerable time lags pointing to a disjointed succession of the religious leaders. The role of the hagiographers was to fill these gaps and create a sense of continuity. This was particularly the case when the succession from the last Āḻvār to the first *ācārya*, Nāthamuni, and from the next *ācārya*, Yāmuna or Ālavandar, to Rāmānuja, and from Rāmānuja to his successors was characterized by yawning gaps, which were bridged by fabricated events in a linear, continuous fashion. Hagiography, in this case, thus became the legitimizing mechanism of succession of these spiritual leaders.

In this connection, the texts further inform us that Rāmānuja's independent thinking and the fact that his acharyic position was already pre-ordained attracted Yāmuna's attention. Yāmuna made repeated attempts to meet Rāmānuja but failed. Finally, it was at Yāmuna's funeral that Rāmānuja got the opportunity to know the three last wishes of the *ācārya* (i.e. Yāmuna) as symbolized by his three pointing fingers. Rāmānuja promised to fulfil them. The three wishes were the veneration of Vyāsa, the propagation of the *Tiruvāymoḷi* (the Tamil tradition) and the composition of a commentary on the *Brahmasūtra* of Vyāsa (the Sanskritic tradition). Therefore, the promise made by Rāmānuja implied the synthesis of all the three aspects, which became the basis of the consolidation of Srivaisnavism into one community. Particularly significant in this context were the last two wishes. They became the basis of the subsequent *ubhaya-vedāntic* tradition. Rāmānuja's promise to fulfil Yāmuna's wishes established an element of continuity between the two *ācāryas* (which is otherwise historically missing) and his position as the successive *ācārya* of the community.

Since a direct *guru-śiṣya* relationship was missing between Yāmuna and Rāmānuja, tradition assigned five spiritual preceptors to Rāmānuja who were the direct disciples of Yāmuna and could be said to represent him. This idea emerged clearly in hagiographies when Periya Nambi, one of the gurus, while initiating Rāmānuja stated:

> Of old, Śrī Rāmacandra, being prevented by his promise to his father from reigning in person in Ayodhyā, left with Bharata his sandals as his representatives and proceeded to the forest. Similarly, my master, being prevented from initiating you himself has placed his sacred feet on my head and deputed me the responsibility. So it is he from you [*sic*] have received your initiation and not from me.[28]

The five preceptors individually imparted five different tenets of Srivaisnavism to Rāmānuja. Tirukoṭṭiyūr Nambī (Ghoṣṭipūrṇa) imparted the *dvaya mantra* as well as the secret interpretations of *Tirumantaram.* Tirumalai Āṉḍān (Mālādhār) imparted the text of *Tiruvāymoḷi* and the traditional commentaries on it. Tiruvaranga Perumāḷ (Ranga) disseminated the *stotras* and other customary rituals, while Tirumalai Nambī (Śrī Śaila Pūrṇa) taught the *Rāmāyaṇa* to Rāmānuja at Tirupati. Finally, Periya Nambī (Mahāpūrṇa) performed Rāmānuja's *pañca-saṃskāra* and initiated him formally into Srivaisnavism.[29] Interestingly, Tirukacci Nambī (Kāñcīpūrṇa) is not included in this list though he exercised tremendous influence on Rāmānuja.

This account of Rāmānuja's five preceptors had connotations for the community. First, it established the concept of uniformity in Rāmānuja's profile where all the five elements merged as one. Thereby, it followed that Rāmānuja was the first to organize the community by bringing scattered ideas together into one organization and philosophy. Second, the concept of more than one guru (Rāmānuja officially had five) was a significant deviation from the long established *Orān* tradition, i.e. the single preceptor-disciple *paramparā*.[30] This continued in the post-Rāmānuja period, when the Śrīvaiṣṇava leaders as well as the devotees had more than one guru. This multiplicity of gurus became the basis of multiple identities within the community. Third, the guru was always a brāhmaṇa.

The structuring of the line of descent into a cohesive organization further established the credibility of Rāmānuja as the *ācārya* of the community.[31] A list of special disciples called the Śrīvaiṣṇava Mudalis is given in these texts. However, this list is different from the *guru-śiṣya* lineage, which was the major organizational innovation of Rāmānuja. He is said to have appointed a group of 'seventy-four' to spread the teachings of Srivaisnavism. The hagiographical texts give a list of these seventy-four names, some of which are also repeated in the list of Śrīvaiṣṇava Mudalis. According to the *Yatirāja Vaibhavam* of Āndhra Pūrṇa (Vaḍuga Nambī), the disciple and contemporary of Rāmānuja:

> The great Rāmānujācārya, the chief among the ascetics and *ācāryas* made some persons as the heads of the religious seats known as seventy-four persons.[32] Even among them he made four chief persons for the chair of *Śrībhāṣya* and his spiritual son (Pillān̲) amongst them, as the foremost chief for both the *Vedānta*.[33]

Interestingly, the early preceptors of the Vaṭakalai and Ten̲kalai lineage belonged to this group of seventy-four.[34] Further, the powerful sectarian families in the Vijayanagara period (for instance, the Kanḍāḍai family and the Tātācārya group) also traced their descent from one of the seventy-four and referred to themselves as the *ācāryapuruṣas*.[35] Since this group of seventy-four was personally chosen by Rāmānuja, a claim to their lineage would bestow legitimacy on these sectarian leaders. The issue of succession assumed significant dimensions in the post-Rāmānuja period when various hagiographical texts attempted to establish their credibility through the apostolic line of succession. These texts, thus, emerged as the ideological basis for the subsequent sectarian identity/conflict. The Vaṭakalai and Ten̲kalai *guru-paramparās* became the textual basis for the schism, which, after the sixteenth century AD, ossified into separate sects.

According to the Śrīvaiṣṇavas, these seventy-four were householders, who performed the *pañca-saṃskāra* for their respective disciples. Hence, the claim to being their successors empowered the sectarian leaders, i.e. the *ācāryapuruṣas*, to conduct an initiation that was a privilege. The *maṭha* head, being a *saṃnyāsin* (an ascetic renouncer), could not conduct an initation that required the presence of a fire and touching, according to Dharmashastric laws.[36] Interestingly, at Tirukkovalūr, after the forty-fifth *jīyar*, the subsequent heads became householders and performed *pañca-saṃskāras.*[37] The importance of the seventy-four, therefore, appears to be tremendous for the Śrīvaiṣṇava community. They are referred to as the *siṃhāsanapatīs*, an honorific title which, however, does not find any mention in the hagiographical and *guru-paramparā* texts.[38]

Another factor which led to the dissemination of the faith was the peregrinations of Rāmānuja. His tours to various centres within and outside south India established the supremacy of the Viśiṣṭādvaita faith, and enlarged the limits of the community beyond the geographical boundaries delineated by the Āḻvārs. This endowed the community with a pan-Indian status. During the course of his travels, he is supposed to have impressed upon the people of other faiths the need to voluntarily convert to Srivaisnavism. Rāmānuja achieved further homogenization and uniformity through the introduction of the deification of the Āḻvārs and the *adhyāyanotsava* festival, both of which emerged as important elements in the Śrīvaiṣṇava community identity.[39] The hagiographies assert that Rāmānuja, being well ahead of his times, undertook certain measures for the consolidation and spread of the Viśiṣṭādvaita faith. Noteworthy amongst them were his temple reforms and the establishment of a strong organization to carry on the tradition after him. Rāmānuja is credited with the institutional organization of the community through a series of temple reforms collectively known as the *Code of Uḍaiyavar.*[40] Introduced at Śrīraṅgam, this code was gradually made mandatory in other temple centres. This had three important implications. First, the Raṅganāthasvāmī temple at Śrīraṅgam, being the base of Rāmānuja, emerged as the institutional focus of the community. According to the Śrīvaiṣṇava tradition, Rāmānuja at Śrīraṅgam gave discourses and performed priestly functions as the *ācārya* of the community. However, he was not an ordinary priest (*arcaka*).

The tradition clearly states that Lord Raṅganātha assigned him the control and management of the temple, and gave him the title *Uḍaiyavar*, which meant the possessor or owner:

> Rāmānuja, led by Periya Nambī, entered the sanctum and offered worship. Periya Perumāḷ looked at him pleasingly, honoured him with 'parivattam' and other presents and also offered him the sceptre (of temple management). Then he issued the following *aruḷappāḍu*: 'We have given you all Our wealth and power, to be employed as you wish and desire; and as the "POSSESSOR" and the bestower of eternal bliss (mokṣa) you look after our affairs.'[41]

Second, the pattern of worship and temple organization at Śrīraṅgam was replicated in other Vaiṣṇava centres, thereby integrating the otherwise dispersed groups into one community organization with Rāmānuja as its spiritual head and the Raṅganāthasvāmī temple as its institutional head.

Such a representation of the past through the biographical delineation of Rāmānuja appears to have influenced community practice too. In the post-Rāmānuja period, i.e. from the thirteenth century onwards, every temple had an Uḍaiyavar Emperumānār Koil. The deification of Rāmānuja indicates that he had emerged as the focus of the community. Hagiographical sources inform us that Rāmānuja's deification began during his lifetime. The story goes that the people at Śrīperumbūdūr requested him to consecrate his own *vigraha*. Rāmānuja obliged and installed his own image. According to the *Rāmānujadivyasūricaritam*, the god of Śrīraṅgam ordered the Śrīvaiṣṇavas to perform the *Śatakalaśa Abhiṣekham* of Rāmānuja and take his image in a palanquin around the temple. Thereafter, the god blessed him as the *ubhayavibhūtinātha*, i.e. the lord of both Vaikuntha and Śrīraṅgam. This practice is followed till today and is a part of festival celebrations. The constructions of Rāmānujakutam, Rāmānuja Tiruvīdī and Uḍaiyavar Kalvay Pattadai were all visible marks of Rāmānuja's influence.

IV

Finally, the most important social concern of the hagiographies was related to the question of caste. Caste attributes were presented as secondary to that of faith. The irrelevance of caste was highlighted in the narratives of Rāmānuja, flouting orthodox norms by proclaiming the *Dvaya mantra* (exclusively meant for brāhmaṇas) aloud from the temple tower at Tirukkōṭṭiyūr for everybody to hear. This episode is one of the most popular ones that consolidated the image of Rāmānuja as a social reformer. Further, there are a large number of narratives that portray his attitude towards the caste hierarchy in a radical manner. Hagiographies relate accounts of how his socially conservative wife behaved in a discriminatory manner towards Rāmānuja's non-brāhmaṇa teachers, Tirukacci Nambī (Kāñcīpūrṇa) and Mahāpūrṇa. Rāmānuja is said to have been so upset with her that he consequently became a renunciate. The narratives further highlight his broadmindedness in seeking and persuading Tirukacci Nambī and Tirumalai Nambī, who were non-brāhmaṇas, to become his teachers. His fame as a saint who disregarded caste barriers and made access to god and attainment of salvation possible for everybody appears to have been drawn from an image that was already prominently portrayed in Śrīvaiṣṇava hagiographies.

According to the narratives, he went beyond mere metaphysics and introduced institutional reforms in the temple to incorporate non-brāhmaṇa participation in the ritual as well as organizational aspects of temple worship. The *Code of Uḍaiyavar* as described in the *Koiḷ Oḷugu* broadened the social base of the community by encouraging non-Brahmanical participation in temple affairs. Hagiographical narratives associate this with the catholicity of Rāmānuja.[42] The *guru-paramparās* state that Rāmānuja took the bold step in Mēḷkōṭe of declaring the outcastes as 'Tirukkulattār', or people belonging to the family of Lakṣmī, the divine mother, and accommodating them in the temple organization. These people who belonged to the hunting community had helped Rāmānuja to ward off dacoits in the forest while he was returning from Delhi, bringing back the festival image of the Nārāyaṇasvāmī temple at Mēḷkōṭe looted earlier by the Sultan of Delhi. Rāmānuja is said to have had a large following from all sections of society. The followers comprised 700 *saṃnyāsins*, 12003 *ekāṅgīs* and 300 *koṟṟamai* (women followers).[43] The catholicity of Rāmānuja is further highlighted by showing that *prapatti* was an integral part of his philosophy.

However, in reality, it appears that non-brāhmaṇa groups who were made a part of the temple organization were not accorded any priestly functions. Their activities were mainly confined to:

> Decorating with followers the tirumaṇḍapas during festivals and the Alagiyamanavālan tirumaṇḍapa daily; making garlands and offering them for the starting of procession; raining (see) flowers (on special occasions); proceeding in two rows holding ceasors, two folded cloths, eight gold torches and twenty silver torches and waving two pieces of cloth; forming a rear batch, with hands folded behind the row by the waists reciting the last two lines of each stanza; bearing the Rāmānuja sword and acting as the bodyguard of the *Jīyars* and the Śrīvaiṣṇavas.[44]

That Rāmānuja and other Śrīvaiṣṇava *ācāryas* as well as the *maṭhādhipatis* were brāhmaṇas was no coincidence. In fact, till today, the *ācāryas* and heads of *maṭhas* are always brāhmaṇas. Thus, the brāhmaṇa affiliation was an integral part of the Śrīvaiṣṇava community. This elitist Brahmanical base was responsible for the initial limitations of the community in the pre-twelfth century AD. However, John Braisted Carman concludes that Rāmānuja's temple management policy was more liberal than what existed before and it is this '*relative* liberalism' with reference to caste differences within the Śrīvaiṣṇava community that is emphasized in stories.[45]

As stated before, the philosophy of Viśiṣṭādvaita, by its association with Vedic texts, was structured within a highly Sanskritized framework not comprehensible to the common man. Thus, it was left to the later-day Śrīvaiṣṇava hagiographers and theologians to evolve a Tamil tradition through the structuring of canonical literature, and finally attempt to merge the Tamil and Sanskritic traditions in the personality of Rāmānuja.[46] However, a careful observation would reveal that Rāmānuja's bhakti was more intellectual than popular. The heavy Sanskritic bias cannot be ignored. Perhaps Rāmānuja never intended to address the lay devotee; rather his concern was to evolve a coherent theological base for Srivaisnavism, thereby making it ideationally significant for the community, through a intellectually well-articulated and emotionally more appealing philosophy and theology *vis-à-vis* others, particularly the Advaitins. The principles of *varṇāśrama-dharma* were never questioned in any of his works, nor did he intend to do so. Caste identity was the primordial identity and a complete rejection of it implied disruption of the social order. A social revolution was not what Srivaisnavism needed. It required a strong base with a legitimizing force of brāhmaṇas. In fact, the attribution of *prapatti* to Rāmānuja was a reaction to the viewpoint that it was marginalized in his scheme of religious doctrine. The Śrīvaiṣṇava theologians resolved this controversy in their own way by showing that *prapatti* as a concept was central to Rāmānuja's *Gadyatrayam*.[47]

The hagiographical narratives themselves reflect a discomfort in dealing with the issue of rejecting the caste hierarchy. The tone of the narratives was, in many ways, conservative. According to them, after escaping from the persecution of the Cōḷa ruler, Rāmānuja came to the Hoysala kingdom in Karnataka and took refuge in a forest. The hunting community there was kind to him and provided him with hospitality. The narratives assert that 'the hunters did not ask for undue favours. Rather they were anxious to find a brāhmaṇa who could feed the *ācārya*. The *Gururparamparai Prabhāvam* says that they brought honey and millet which were not ritualistically pollutants. No cooked food served by the hunters was eaten by the *ācārya* and his men. In fact, he received hospitality from one Kongupirāṭṭi, a brāhmaṇa woman who had once received *mantradīkṣā* or initiation from Rāmānuja at Śrīraṅgam.[48]

One of the texts states Rāmānuja's own inhibitions in rejecting the caste hierarchy:

Ālavandar spotted Māranēr Nambī as a spiritually advanced soul and, hence, included him in the pantheon of his disciples. When Māranēr Nambī took on the disease of his master out of sheer devotion, he suffered greatly and was ministered to by Mahā Pūrṇa who brought him the *prasādam* food from the Śrīraṅgam temple. When he died, Mahā Pūrṇa had no hesitation in cremating him according to the *Brahmamedha* rites which are accorded only to the brāhmaṇas. Rāmānuja was embarrassed by the radical length to which his preceptor Mahā Pūrṇa went in flagrantly violating caste codes. He protested to Mahā Pūrṇa, worried about the social implications of such an act. There was a significant exchange between Mahā Pūrṇa and Rāmānuja in which the latter expressed the anxiety that while he was trying to keep the fence in shape and maintain the social order, Mahā Pūrṇa was doing away with the cultural fabric of the society.

Mahā Pūrṇa stressed on transcending the barriers of caste. He said he was not for half-measures. He reminded Rāmānuja of the impressive line of exceptions in the Hindu epics and Puranic literature. 'Am I superior to Rāma, the Hero of the Ikṣvāku race? Is Māranēr inferior to the bird Jatayu, for whom Rāma performed the *brahmamedha*? Am I greater than Dharmaputra? Is Māranēr lower than Vidura to whom the same *saṃskāra* were administered?'[49]

Thus, one can conclude that the theme of caste and its treatment was, in many ways, a response to the context of that time. As stated in section two, in the post-Rāmānuja period, the social milieu underwent a transformation. The rise of a non-brāhmaṇa landed class, the emergence of merchants and the migration of Telugu warriors and landed magnates to the Tamil region led to the evolution of a distinct Śrīvaiṣṇava non-brāhmaṇa identity. Since these groups were powerful and influential, they emerged as major benefactors of temples and sectarian leaders. A network of redistribution and exchange between non-brāhmaṇa and brāhmaṇa elite groups developed that brought the former into the temple arena and provided a regular channel for patronage to the latter. Hence, caste affiliations were interwoven with the community-class paradigm. Srivaisnavism became the integrative factor between the brāhmaṇa and the non-brāhmaṇas, when powerful sections of both the caste groups joined in an interactive/productive relationship. The presence of non-brāhmaṇas in the community influenced the Śrīvaiṣṇava discourse on society. New concepts like *ubhaya-vedānta* and *prapatti* were evolved, which were all-inclusive. Tamil came to be emphasized along with Sanskrit. Some of the Brahmanical religious leaders like the Kandadais and Periya Jiyar at Tirupati had non-brāhmaṇas as their disciples. Referred to as *ekākīs*, *ekaṅgīs* and *śāttada Śrīvaiṣṇavas*, these non-Brahmanical groups figured prominently as recipients of several shares in temple offerings.

Thus, the representation of a past through the biographical delineation of Rāmānuja in the *guru-paramparā* texts influenced the religious attitudes of the Śrīvaiṣṇava community for whom

Rāmānuja was the most revered *ācārya.* The *guru-paramparās*, developing as scriptures of the community despite their sectarian affiliations of Vaṭakalai and Teṉkalai, reiterated the normative notion of a single, homogeneous, uniform community in the charismatic portrayal of Rāmānuja. Uniformity became the dominant theme in all sectarian hagiographies that provided the respective sects with a lineage. The origin of the lineage, in most of the cases, was traced to Rāmānuja. In this manner, each sect with its lineage claimed to represent the uniform Śrīvaiṣṇava community. The projection of a uniform community became important for establishing claims in the competitive spheres of resource control in the temples. It represented an integrative framework, whereby devotees could be from any section of the society. Therefore, the concept of uniformity made caste ascription secondary to that of community.

The representation of caste and a radical social past associated with Rāmānuja had an impact that went beyond community boundaries. This image became so popular that various religious communities from the thirteenth to the seventeenth centuries considered Rāmānuja as their founder and the most revered saint. In this context, he has been considered the preceptor of Ramanand, who, in turn, was supposed to be the guru of Kabir. Rāmānuja is also considered to be the founder of yet another sect called the Ramanujis who rose to prominence in the nineteenth century. Both the Ramanandis and the Ramanujis located in Vrindavan in the Braj region have a large following from the marginalized sections of the caste hierarchy. Interestingly, both these communities do not regard Rāmānuja as a philosopher but as a saint who disregarded caste barriers and made access to god and attainment of salvation possible for everybody, an image that was already prominently portrayed in Śrīvaiṣṇava hagiographies from the thirteenth century onwards.

This catholic representation of Rāmānuja endures till today. Swami Vivekananda in his paper, 'The Historical Evolution of India', pointed out that:

> . . . The movement of Shankara forced its way through its high intellectuality, but it could be of little service to the masses, because of its adherence to

strict caste laws, very small scope for ordinary emotion and making Sanskrit the only vehicle of communication. Rāmānuja, on the other hand, with a most practical philosophy, a great appeal to the emotions, an entire denial of birthrights before spiritual attainments and appeals through popular tongue, completely succeeded in bringing the masses back to the Vedic religion.[50]

Such a hagiographical delineation has also influenced modern-day history writing:

Rāmānuja was not as brilliant metaphysician as Shankara, but Indian religion perhaps owes even more to him than to his predecessor. In the centuries immediately following his death his ideas spread all over India, and were the starting point of the devotional sects of later times.[51]

The transition from the sacred/religious realm of the hagiographies to a secular domain in such a perception can be seen and needs to be analysed but is currently beyond the scope of this paper. It should be noted that the hagiographical accounts do enter into the realm of history writing blurring the line between the sacred and the secular.

NOTES

1. Here the word 'saint' is used largely for the religious figures of the Śrīvaiṣṇava community, the Ā̱lvārs and *ācāryas*.
2. The *Nālāyira Divya Prabandham* is a corpus of 4,000 hymns composed by the Ā̱lvārs. The Ā̱lvārs were the early Vaiṣṇava saints of south India who existed between the fifth and eighth centuries. Their hymns to Viṣṇū form a seminal part of the popular devotional literature of their times.
3. Garuḍa Vāhana Panḍita, *Divyasūricaritam*, with Hindi Rendering and ed. Pandita Madhvacharya, T.A. Sampathakumaracharya and K.K.A. Venkatachari, Bombay: Anantacharya Research Institute, 1978, Chapter 16, pp. 333-6.
4. Alfred Kroeber, 'Introduction' in Milton Singer, ed., 'Introduction', *Traditional India: Structure and Change*, Jaipur: Rawat Publications, 1975, p. xii.
5. Eric Hobsbawm, 'Introduction: Inventing Traditions', in Eric Hobsbawm and Terence Ranger, eds., *The Invention of Tradition*, Cambridge, Cambridge University Press, 1983.
6. For details, see K.K.A. Venkatachari, *The Manipravala Literature of the Śrīvaiṣṇava Acharyas*, Bombay: Anantacharya Indological Research Institute, 1978.

7. A.K. Rāmānujan 'Three Hundred *Rāmāyaṇas*: Five Examples and Three Thoughts on Translation', in Paula Richman, ed., *Many Rāmāyaṇas: The Diversity of a Narrative Tradition in South Asia*, Delhi: Oxford University Press, 1994, pp. 22-49.
8. S. Anantachari, ed., *Teṉkalai Muāyirappaṭi Guruparamparāprabhāvam*, Tiruvellikeni, 1964; Shri Tirukrishnaswami Aiyangar, ed., *Pinbalagiya Perumāḷjīyararuḷiya Ārayirappaṭi Guruparamparāprabhāvam*, Tirucci: Puttur Agraharam, 1979; *Muāyirappaṭi Guruparamparāprabhāvam of Tritiya Brahmatantra Parkālasvāmi*, Madras: Lifco, 1968; Arangasvami Mudaliyar, ed., *Panniāyirappaṭi Guruparamparāprabhāvam*, Madras, Śrī Viśiṣṭādvaita Prachārini Sabha, 1952.
9. R. Rajamani, ed., *Śrī Rāmānujadivyasīricaritam of Pillai Lokajīya*, Tirucci: Puttur Agraharam, 1975; V.V. Rāmānuja, ed., *Sri Pillailoka-charya Jiyar's Yatindra-pravaṇaprabhāva*, Madras: Tiruvellikeni, 1992.
10. K.A. Nilkantha Sastri, *The Cōḷas*, vol. II, Madras: University of Madras, 1975, rpt., pp. 479-80.
11. The discourse against caste and the messianic notion of the community that included devotees from diverse backgrounds has led many scholars to conclude that the bhakti of the Āḻvārs was a radical protest against conservative social norms. Undoubtedly, the elements of protest were present but they should not be over-stressed. In fact, the religion of the hymnists, influenced by the contemporary socio-political environment, evolved a conservative attitude that became synonymous with the dominant ideology of the subsequent period, the ninth to the twelfth century. For details, see R. Campakalakshmi, 'From Devotion and Dissent to Dominance: The *Bhakti* of the Tamil Āḷvārs and Nayanars', in R. Champakalakshmi and S. Gopal, eds., *Tradition, Dissent and Ideology: Essays in Honour of Romila Thapar*, Delhi: Oxford University Press, 1996, pp. 135-63.
12. For a detailed understanding of the Viśiṣṭadvaita philosophy, see John Braisted Carman, *The Theology of* Rāmānuja*: An Essay in Interreligious Understanding*, Bombay: Anantacharya Indological Research Institute, 1981 (Indian rpt.).
13. R. Champakalakshmi, 1996, op. cit., p. 151.
14. Ibid., p. 161.
15. Ibid., p. 147.
16. Friedhelm Hardy, *Viraha-Bhakti: The Early History of Krsna Devotion in South India*, Delhi: Oxford University Press, 1983, p. 441; R. Champakalakshmi, 1996, op. cit., pp. 140-1.
17. Arjun Appadorai, 'Kings, Sects and Temples in South India, AD 1350-1700', in Burton Stein, ed., *South Indian Temples: An Analytical Reconsiderartion*, Delhi: Vikas, 1978, pp. 11-46; Noboru Karashima, *Towards*

a New Formation: South Indian Society Under Vijayanagar Rule, Delhi: Oxford University Press, 1976, pp. 43-125.

18. Mattison Mines, *The Warrior Merchants: Textiles, Trade and Territory in South India*, Cambridge: Cambridge University Press, 1984; Vijaya Ramaswami, *Textiles and Weavers in Medieval South India*, Delhi: Oxford University Press, 1985.
19. Burton Stein, 'Vijayanagara and Transition of Patrimonial System', in Anna Dallapicola, ed., *Vijayanagar-City and Empire: New Currents of Research*, Weisbaden: Franz Steiner Verlag, 1985, pp. 2-23; Burton Stein, *Vijayanagar: The New Cambridge History of India*, Cambridge: Cambridge University Press, 1988, pp. 14-38.
20. The Śrīvaiṣṇava textual tradition is complex and more than an agglomeration of certain thematic texts which are extremely difficult to classify. This is due to the fact that there is a considerable amount of overlap, repetition and inter-linkage between these texts. However, one can roughly divide them into six categories, viz., the hymnal tradition; the *sampradaya*—the theological and philosophical tradition; the commentatorial tradition; the hagiographical tradition; the liturgical tradition, and finally, the pilgrimage (textual) tradition as represented in the genre of texts called the *sthalapurāṇas*. Of these, the *sthalapurāṇas* do not necessarily form a part of the canonical tradition.
21. Indira Parthasarathy, *Rāmānujar: The Life and Ideas of Rāmānuja*, tr. from Tamil by T. Sriraman. Critical Introduction and Commentary by C.T. Indra, Delhi: Oxford University Press, 2008, p. xiv.
22. Ibid.,Vaali, *Rāmānuja Kavyam*, Chennai: Vanathi Publishers, 2003.
23. *Divyasūricaritam*, 1978, op. cit., Chapter 17, pp. 354-7.
24. The Smārta brāhmaṇas usually follow the Advaita tradition of Śaṅkara. They abo worship five deities—Viṣṇu, Śiva, Pārvatī, Gaṇeśa and Sūrya.
25. *Divyasūricaritam*, verses 11 and 12, pp. 357-8.
26. *Divyasūricaritam*, Chapter 17, verses 17-31, pp. 359-64. This is an approximate translation done by me.
27. Hagiographies inform us that the *utsavamurti* of the deity at Melukote was with a Muslim princess of the north, who had already started considering the idol as her husband. So strong was her devotion that when Rāmānuja recovered the idol and brought it to Melukote, she came along. Later, she was deified as Talukka Nacciyar or Bibi Nacciyar and placed next to the deity. For details, see Ranjeeta Dutta, 'Politics of Religious Identity: A Muslim Goddess in the Shrivaishnava Community of South India', *Studies in History*, 19, 2, 2003, pp. 157-84.
28. *Ārayirappaṭi Guruparamparāprabhāvam*, pp. 150-4.
29. The *Yatirāja Vaibhava* differs in this context. The text designates Periya Nambī (Mahā Pūrṇa) as the only guru of Rāmānuja: 'At that

place, he (Mahā Pūrṇa) gave to Rāmānujācārya the marks with conch and discus, the sectarian mark, the method of worship, the *mantras* together with their meaning, the great *mantra* and also other *mantras*. He (Mahā Pūrṇa) who was (then) much pleased taught him (Rāmānuja) the three thousand hymns (of the Āḻvārs) and the meaning of *sūtras* of Vyāsa (*Brahmasūtra*). Rāmānuja too worshipped the preceptor and his wife by leading a desirable (worthy) way of life.' See for details, V.V. Varadacharia, ed. and tr., *Yatirāja Vaibhava of Andhra Pūrṇa (Vaṭuka Nambī)* [in Sanskrit with Sanskrit translation], Madras: M.C. Krishnan, 1978, *shlokas* 44-7.

30. The *Ōrān* tradition comprised Viṣṇu as the *paramācārya* who passed on his teachings to Sri. From Sri, it was disseminated to Vishvakasena, then to Nammāḻvār, to Nāthamuni and finally to Yāmuna who had five disciples.
31. See the *Yatirāja Vaibhavam*, *shlokas* 107-10, 113. According to the tradition, after Rāmānuja became an ascetic, he established his own *maṭha* at Kāñcīpuram near the Varadarājasvāmī temple.
32. *Yatirāja Vaibhava*, op. cit., *shloka* 108.
33. These four main persons were Kurattāḻvān, Nadadūr Āḻvān, Kiḍāmbi Accan and Mudaliyāṇḍan. All of them belonged to the Vaṭakalai lineage.
34. It is not possible to give the names of all the seventy-four here. The hagiographical texts provide the list, the contents of which vary from one to the other.
35. In inscriptions, the term *acharyapurusha* is used in a generic sense as the recipient of some honours in temples, along with other Śrīvaiṣṇava groups.
36. In the late nineteenth century, a court case was filed by an *acharyapurusha* against the head of a *maṭha* at Kanchi, for the latter had appropriated the rights of initiation and was performing the *pancha-samskara*.
37. This information was made available to me personally by the present *jiyar* of the *maṭha* at Tirukkovalur.
38. Probably this title of *siṃhāsanapati* was used to enhance the prestige of the institution of the *ācāryapuruṣas*. Most of the hagiographies composed after the thirteenth century referred to the seventy-four in detail. Probably such a focus emerged to ascribe an impressive network of organization to either Rāmānuja or to one of his successors. In the thirteenth-fourteenth centuries, one comes across the seventy-two; i.e. *bahattara-niyoga*, in temples of the Telugu country. According to a legend, when Kumara Kampana, the Vijayanagara chief, conquered the southern regions, he or one of the chief *nāyakas* established the institution of the seventy-two *nāyakas*. This would perhaps be the political prototype of the seventy-four religious heads in Srivaisnavism.

According to N. Jagadeesan, Rāmānuja was probably inspired in this move by the examples of the Jainas who had seventy-two religious *samasthānas*. However, Jagadeesan does not provide the reference. According to him, the Śaiva canon, which speaks of the sixty-three *nayanars* is a precedent for the sixty-three Jaina *ācāryas*. See for details, N. Jagadeesan, *History of Shrivaishnavism in the Tamil Country (Post Rāmānuja)*, Madurai: Koodal Publishers, 1977, p. 47.

39. The *adhyayanotsava* festival involves the recitation of the Sanskrit Vedas as well as the *Nālāyira Divya Prabandham* in the presence of the god, Āḻvārs and *ācāryas*, thereby symbolically involving the entire community.
40. V.N. Hari Rao, ed. and tr., *Koil Oḷūgu*: *The Chronicle of the Srirangam Temple with Historical Notes*, Madras: Rockhouse and Sons, 1975, pp. 41-112.
41. Ibid., p. 43.
42. Ibid., p. 142.
43. The numbers of disciples vary in various hagiographical texts. However, this variation is minor and of no consequence.
44. The *Koil Olugu,* p. 46.
45. John Braisted Carman, 1981, op. cit., p. 37.
46. For instance, see N. Jagadeesan, 1977, op. cit.; K.K.A. Venkatachari, 1978, op. cit.
47. K.K.A. Venkatacari, 1978, op. cit.; Robert C. Lester, 'Rāmānuja and Srivaishnavism: The Concept of *Prapatti* or *Sarnagati*', in *History of Religion*, 5, 2, 1966, pp. 266-82.
48. C.T. Indra, 'Hagiography Revisited', in Indira Pathasarathy, 2008, op. cit., pp. xlii-xliii.
49. Ibid., pp. xxxix-xl. Here the author cites Alakondavilli Govindacharya, *Sri Rāmānujacharya: The Exponent of the Viśiṣṭadvaita Philosophy*, Chennai: Sri Nrisimhapriya Trust, 2004, rpt., p. 144.
50. As quoted in Swami Ramakrishnananda, *Life of Sri Rāmānuja*, Madras: Sri Ramakrishna Math, 1986, 4th edn., Preface, p. i.
51. A.L. Basham, *The Wonder That was India*, London: Picador, 2004, 3rd rev. edn., p. 335, as quoted in C.T. Indra, 2008, op. cit., p. xxxvii.

FOUR

Culture Under Interpretative Stress

Bankim Chandra and the Re-Formulation of '*Dharma*' in Colonial Bengal

Amiya P. Sen

Speaking of the Western-educated Hindu intelligentsia in nineteenth-century Bengal, it is important not to lose sight of the hermeneutical tasks that this class created for itself and subsequently performed with some measure of finesse and conviction. In hindsight, it would be reasonable to claim that this overt cultural enterprise arose from a pressing need to critically re-formulate certain indigenous categories of thought and modes of self-expression. The late Nirad C. Chaudhuri has observed that the growing dissemination of English education introduced new words into the Bengali lexicon. Words such as *adarshaparayanata* (idealism), *kartavyaparayanata* (dutiful) and *neetiparayanata* (moral sensitivity) are, in his understanding, good examples of this lexical innovation.[1] It is thus that the educated Bengali now began to make a sharper distinction between say, lying and making incorrect/inexact statements. Such changes, one might argue, emanated from the view, often articulated in the contemporary Bengali press, that it was really colonial rule and the contact with the modern West that first threw a moral and intellectual challenge before the Hindu.[2] Nirad Chaudhuri himself recounts how, in his days, Bengali gentlemen would feel less offended if they were called *mithyabadi* (which somewhat blurred the distinction between inexactness and untruth) than they would upon being called a 'liar'.[3] Importantly enough, the same sources deny that comparable changes had at all arisen under nearly 600 years of Indo-Muslim rule.[4]

The hermeneutical enterprise in Bengal, as I shall argue in this paper, though responding to some unique challenges, put greater faith on investing traditional idioms or categories of thought with somewhat atypical meanings, rather than creating or popularizing altogether new modes of cultural self-expression. This, it would be important to add, was the practice even with those Hindu thinkers of the late nineteenth century such as the novelist and civil-servant, Bankim Chandra Chattopadhyay (1838-94) who maintained that translation from one language to another did not also mean a translation of ideas as well.[5] The semantic horizons of language, in other words, had to be suitably stretched or expanded in order to facilitate communication between two languages or cultures. There is some reason to doubt therefore, if, as alleged by some critics and scholars, that men like Bankim so radically altered the accepted meaning of terms like *Dharma* that what remained in place hereafter was more a similarity of forms than of content. In an essay that he wrote over thirty years ago, the German Indologist, Paul Hacker (1913-79), found rethinking around the term *Dharma* to be perhaps the 'most instructive instance of the re-interpretation of Hindu modernism'.[6] Hacker tried to clinch his argument by especially citing the work *Dharmatattva* (May 1888) of Bankim Chandra which quite uninhibitedly and copiously drew upon European authors. Admittedly, this work targeted the Western-educated Bengali for, at many places, the author deliberately left reproductions from the original English-language sources un-translated.[7] It is true that by the 'educated', Bankim essentially meant the English educated. On the other hand, Hacker overlooks the tendency, quite transparent in Bankim, of locating the roots of ideas occurring in European writings to older sources in the Hindu tradition. The ideas of the Positivist scholar, August Comte, for instance, are said to be anticipated in the works of Hindu scholars and sages. The *Dharmatattva* is also structured in the manner of an indigenous text of philosophical/theological disputation wherein there is a *purvapaksha* pitted against an *uttarapaksha*—one putting forth a thesis and the other critically negating it. In this particular instance, it cannot be simply fortuitous that the actors engaged in the dialogue are a traditional *guru* and his Western-educated pupil. One of the underlying arguments of this paper is that it is Bankim's uneasiness or reservations about some Western social theories that produced incipient conflicts of argument within the narrative structure of a work like the *Dharmatattva*. Operatively, both Utilitarianism and Positivism, two of the most important intellectual influences upon Bankim, were often qualified in the light of 'native' insights or experiences. Almost 10 years before he began to write his *Dharmatattva*, Bankim had claimed that 'Truth' could be as much a matter of inference (*anumana*) as direct sense-perception (*pratyaksha*) and quite palpably, the supernatural and miraculous events abound in his immensely popular Bengali novels.[8] If indeed he had stuck to a single mode of self-expression, Bankim might well have been less self-conflicted as an author. This paper also argues, perhaps more emphatically than ever, that the term *Dharma* was under interpretative stress well before Bankim and that some of these ideas may well have shaped the ideological grid of the *Dharmatattva.*

THE CONCEPT OF *DHARMA* IN THE HINDU-BRAHMANICAL TRADITION: GENERAL OBSERVATIONS

In his celebrated work, *Indian Philosophy*, Sarvepalli Radhakrishnan observes that after 'Reality', the concept of *Dharma* was the most important one to have been created within the Hindu tradition.[9] This appears to uphold the view expressed in certain quarters that the Brahmanical tradition preferred 'good life' to 'moral life'; transcendental freedom to social and moral realism. The Bengali mystic, Sri Ramakrishna Paramhamsa (1836-86), who could be justifiably identified with this tradition, understood moral virtues to merely prepare an individual for 'higher' spiritual goals. It produced *chittashuddhi*—the cleansing of the heart that was preparing to meet God.[10] For Bankim, too, while activism and ethical responsibility were desirable qualities in men, no social organization could be made to rest on a moral theory alone.[11]

Within Hindu thinkers of the nineteenth century, perhaps the sole exception to this position occurs in the speeches or writings of Swami Vivekananda (1863-1902) for whom Karma Yoga (moral activism) could be dissociated or disengaged from any belief in god and religion.[12]

Prima facie it appears quite intriguing that the Hindu-Brahmanical mind attached comparable significance to terms as far removed in their social and metaphysical import as 'Reality' and *Dharma*. Whether in the Buddhist, Jain or Brahmanical tradition, *Dharma* was not necessarily located within the framework of metaphysical thought. Ironically enough, in so far as the Brahmanical tradition was concerned, the philosophical school to first raise definitional questions about *Dharma* (*atho dharma jigyasa*) was Purva-Mimamsa which many take to be atheistic in its orientation. Strongly rooted in praxis and actualization, Purva-Mimamsa treats *Dharma* as an injunction which, when dutifully followed, gave meaning and order to the universe. Even where the category 'Reality' was born of metaphysical speculation (the Uttara-Mimamsa School or Vedanta raises the question *atho brahma jigyasa*), *Dharma* was always tied to concrete, this-worldly contexts. *Dharma*, for instance, speaks not of the self but the self in relation to others. The quest for spiritual liberation required the isolation of the self (*kaivalya*), the distancing of the self from the world and worldly processes. *Dharma*, on the contrary, presumed the very opposite. As the late A.K. Ramanujan had once perceptively pointed out, *Dharma* always remained bound to contexts whereas *moksha* (liberation/salvation) meant going beyond all contexts.[13]

Broadly speaking, the Brahmanical tradition offers three distinct, though at times overlapping perspectives on the category of *Dharma*. These are respectively, that emanating from the Nyaya philosophy, the Purva-Mimamsa and the Dharmashastras. Nyaya defined *Dharma* as *adheya padartha*, an innate quality that can be associated with various objects, as, for instance, heat with fire.[14] Purva-Mimamsa, as we have already noted, speaks of moral imperatives (the 'ought'). Significantly enough, this view, when conjoined to that of the Naiyayikas (practitioners of Nyaya) suggests that there could well be a general or universal quality (*samnayadharma*) in men. Scholars like P.V. Kane have suggested that *ahimsa* (non-violence/non-injury) may be one such defining quality.[15] By comparison, the view taken by the Dharmashastras assigns variable conduct to things rather than treat *Dharma* as an omnibus category. Thus, *ahimsa* could be a general and universally valid virtue but it was a virtue specific to human beings, not animals. Operatively therefore, the Dharmashastra view breaks down *samanya* or *sadharana dharma* into specificities of group behaviour (*vishesha dharma*). *Svadharma* falls into this category for it is a variable associated with specific jatis or varnas. All jatis or varnas were to adhere to *svadharma* but that assigned to one could not be replicated in another. As the well-known dictum of the *Gita* goes, abandoning one's *Dharma* for the sake of another's was fraught with disaster.[16]

Predictably, such multiple perspectives on a socially and culturally operative category create as much ground for conflict as for positive sharing. In the work *Dharmatattva*, for example, Bankim creatively borrows from all the three perspectives to suggest that *Dharma* could be taken to be both a normative category (a conclusion that his Western critics find unacceptable) and as one that could be applied to specific social groups. Thus, there is something like *manavadharma*—the quality of being human transcending divisions of time and space but also *stridharma* or the ideal conduct to be followed by women. However, problems may be located even within this argumentative structure. Thus, if varna-based collectivities determined the *Dharma* of individual members, was this compatible with the quest for *moksha* which surely lay outside such determinants?[17] Again, while consuming flesh or liquor may be generally barred for a brahmana, an exception had to be allowed in the case of he who was a follower of the Agama.[18] In the *Mahabharata*, the warrior Arjuna was clearly torn between *svadharma* and *samanyadharma,* not knowing whether to annihilate the enemy and thereby fulfil the duties of a kshatriya or else bemoan the wanton killing and bloodshed that was bound to follow a fratricidal war.

THE RE-FORMULATION OF THE TERM *DHARMA* IN NINETEENTH-CENTURY BENGAL

In modern Bengal, apparently, fresh thinking around the term *Dharma* was born of a perceptible and profound paradigm shift from autology to anthropology. From raising questions such as 'Who am I?', Western-educated Bengalis also began to investigate the social and moral identity of man. The former represented the search for individuality and subjecthood, the latter a discursive effort at aggregating and objectifying man. In the traditional Hindu conception, both man and this world (*samsara*) defied any definitive understanding for they were eternally subject to either some inscrutable divine play (*lila*) or else, the inexorable working of the laws of *karma.*[19] On the contrary, the Victorian conception of man, widely disseminated in modern Bengal, postulated that man could not possibly understand what he did not create through his works. From this it followed that man had to constantly work and re-work his nature and, through that process alone, begin to grasp the inner or intrinsic purpose of human life.

A further point that needs to be adequately stressed is that the reinterpretation of the term *Dharma* in the nineteenth century was a part of the larger effort to wrest the moral autonomy of human action in this world. In an underlying sense, discursive definitions of this term are deeply related to the questions of forging the social collective and that of a nascent nationhood. In the nineteenth century, Raja Rammohun Roy (1774-1833) anticipates Bankim in suggesting that *karma* (in the more general sense of action) ought to be read as acts of moral merit rather than the practice of abiding by social or ritual observances.[20] Here it is important to recall that in his philosophical orientation, the Raja was both a Vedantin and a follower of Tantra, both of which may be said to significantly depart from the mechanistic ritualism of the orthodox tradition. However, what Rammohun did not attempt (and perhaps deliberately so) was the joining of altruism or the belief in man's common source in God to any serious critique of the Hindu social organization. For all his radicalism related to social or religious questions, Rammohun Roy never renounced his sacred thread as a brahmana, not even in England, where such an act might have passed off with practically no opposition and might have been even valorized. In Bankim's time, emerging thoughts on the collective had forced Hindu thinkers to at least notionally tone down the oppressive and offensive hierarchies built into the jati structure. Bankim himself was willing to confer 'Brahminhood' on the non-brahmana social reformer, Keshab Chandra Sen (1838-84).[21] Also, contrary to what has sometimes been claimed,[22] the tendency to equate *Dharma* with 'religion' antedates Bankim. Alberuni himself is said to have read *Dharma* as religion.[23] And we gather from Sanskrit inscriptions of early medieval India that Mecca and Medina were known as *Dharmasthanams* (religious sites).[24] Closer to Bankim's time, the spiritual successors of Rammohun used the term to indicate religion and a sense of the religiously-defined community. This would be quite apparent from the name that Maharshi Debendranath Tagore (1817-1905), father of Rabindranath, chose to give to a source-book he compiled for the Brahmos by the early 1850s. The work, importantly, was called *Brahmodharmagrantha*.

A survey of Bengali periodicals of the nineteenth century reveals that between 1840 and 1890, there were at least 13 periodicals with the term *Dharma* either prefixed or suffixed to their names. On 6 April 1822, a letter from a traditional Hindu scholar by the name of Pandit Kashinath Tarkapanchanan, writing under the pseudonym of *dharmasthapanarthi* or one keen to re-establish *Dharma*, appeared in the journal *Samachar Darpan*, accusing the likes of Rammohun of violating the rules of conduct laid down for the brahmanas. In this instance, however, the term *Dharma* was also used in the sense of religion since the Pandit feared that by openly consorting with non-Hindus, upper caste men like Rammohun would radically depart from their ancestral faith.[25] That the category *Dharma* was cogitating in the minds of many Hindus even before Bankim Chandra is apparent from the writings of Chandranath Basu (1844-1910), a prominent writer and literary critic who increasingly identified himself with the conservative camp. Chandranath, like Bankim, was originally drawn towards the Positivist conception of religion proffered by August Comte and his followers, especially for its tendency to see religion as some kind of regulatory mechanism with which to strengthen the social organization. On the other hand, both men were quick to renounce their faith in Positivism for its failure to accommodate the construct of a theistic god. It may surprise some to hear that Bankim Chandra's tendency to use *Dharma* in a normative sense (as in *manushatya*) is anticipated by the arch-conservative scholar, Pandit Shashadhar Tarkachudamani (1851-1928), a man with whose conception of Hindu social and religious life, he had serious differences. Pandit Shashadhar is credited with the birth of the pseudo-scientific variety of neo-Hinduism; it was he who also instigated middle-class homes in Calcutta and its neighbourhood to a state of near-rebellion over the proposed amendments to the age of Consent Bill in 1890-1. Notwithstanding such conservative credentials, two of the Pandit's works, *Dharmavyakhya* (1884) and an essay titled 'Dharma ebong Dharmer Anusthata' (Dharma and its Practitioners,1885) argued, well before Bankim himself did in the *Dharmatattva*, that *manushatya* was the dharmic property of man. The category, in Pandit Shashadhar's understanding, comprised introspection, intelligence, discrimination, forgiveness and respect for fellowmen. Pandit Shashadhar also anticipates Bankim in arguing that nationalities could be solidly founded on public adherence to *Dharma* or dharmic conduct. With Shashadhar, however, this commonwealth is not so much about a moral awareness of the other as the common pursuit of prescriptive habits, rites and customs. Compared to Bankim Chandra, the Pandit was also less prepared to grant the idea of a historically evolving Hinduism. Rather, his attention was riveted on the timeless and the immutable (*sanatana*).[26] For Chandranath Basu, Pandit Shashadhar and the Brahman educationist, Bhudeb Mukhopadhyay (1827-94), the Hindu commonwealth depended on the observance of *shauch*, *achar* and *upasana*, that is, rules of hygiene, daily rites and usages, and the adoration of god.[27] On the other hand, whether in the *Dharmatattva* or elsewhere, Bankim does not have any scruples about taboos of food or drink. In an essay authored roughly around the same time, he offers the shocking argument that having reached an exalted state of body and mind, even a Vaishnava would not have any reservations about eating fowl-curry![28]

DHARMATATTVA: THE HUMAN PURSUIT OF HAPPINESS

Some of the key ideas occurring in the *Dharmatattva* go back to Bankim Chandra's writings in the 1870s. In the year 1877, at a time when he was strongly influenced by Utilitarianism, Bankim contributed two essays for the journal *Bangadarshan* titled *Bahubal O Bakyabal* (The Pen and the Sword) and *Manushatya Kee?* (What is it to be human?) The common thread running through these essays is how an individual may advance in life only by curtailing or giving up the pursuit of certain goals commonly valued in society. The pursuit of wealth, though a natural propensity in man, was not the prime objective of human life.[29] This again has an interesting though somewhat surprising overlap with the preaching of Sri Ramakrishna who consistently warned his devotees against the lures of wealth and female sexuality (*kamini-kanchan*). This is surprising because on the day he met the saint, Bankim reportedly defined the objectives of human life as nothing beyond 'eating, drinking and sex-life'. The convergence of thought is also surprising considering the disparaging remarks Sri Ramakrishna made about altruism and man's attempts at constructively changing the *status quo*.[30]

In another essay written in the early 1880s, *Bhalobashar Atyachar* (The Tyranny of Love), Bankim also goes on to make a seminal point about *Dharma* and selflessness. For him, both moved along the same moral trajectories towards the fulfilment of certain social obligations. That which was founded on love for the other attained fullness in *Dharma* and conversely, the fulsome pursuit of dharmic life found its exalted state in selflessness and universal love.[31] In three other essays contributed elsewhere, Bankim Chandra makes another point of some significance. He rejects attempts to sharply differentiate matters concerning the self from that of the other as quite arbitrary and purely synthetic.

The social good, he argues, must include individual welfare and no public cause can be taken forward by inflicting undue hardship or suffering upon oneself.[32] The political subjugation of India followed from the failure on the part of Indians to take enough interest in themselves. Ironically, enough, Bankim attributes this to the Hindu's penchant for *nishkam dharma* (unmotivated action). This is ironical given the fact that this itself was to be one of the vital operative principles in the work *Dharmatattva*. In this instance, evidently, *nishkam dharma* becomes the moral and social edifice of the nascent nationhood.

The *Dharmatattva* opens with an important though often debated question in nineteenth-century Bengal. Was the pursuit of happiness not the prime objective in human life and if so, how was this to be sufficiently advanced? Poverty, ailment, sorrow or suffering, we are given to understand, follow from *adharma* or negating the rules of righteous conduct.[33] In this work, although Bankim consistently tries to play down karmic theories about causal linkages between deeds performed in some past life and experiences undergone in the present one, this is a rather naïve theory to arrive at. For one, poverty or suffering have also to be understood in material terms and not simply as states of mind as an idealist is likely to do. Compared to some of his other writings of the 1870s like the *Samya* (Egalitarianism), the *Dharmatattva* also reveals greater conservatism with regard to both caste and man-woman relationships. Whereas in the *Samya*, the brahmana is among the perpetrators of social injustice, the *Dharmatattva* ascribes the social and intellectual growth in early India to the respect shown to the brahmana. In later life, Bankim refused to reprint certain portions of the *Samya,* as, for instance, the section dealing with gender-equality, but the *Dharmatattva* makes this back-tracking even more explicit. Here, Bankim is quite upset at egalitarian ideas being imposed on Hindu society and the resulting subversion of certain social values. Allegedly, there was now a visible decline in the respect that a son once showed towards his father, or, for that matter, the wife to her husband. In Bankim's view then, disturbing changes had begun to occur within Hindu domestic life. The wife who once venerated her husband now saw him only as a friend or companion and, at times, even her servant![34] It now occurs to Bankim that the inequality between sexes was not so unnatural or unjust after all, for this was founded on some natural and biological differences between man and woman. Arguably, Bankim is not too rigid with his categories. It was quite possible, he grants, that the woman, too, could serve her country on the battlefield. A closer look, however, suggests that such arguments are clothed in considerable sarcasm. 'Each of us should be able to cultivate our inherent powers', he argues at another place. 'If it be in the woman's powers to fight, let her by all means fight and if it be in a man's power to breast-feed the child, let him do that.'[35] Bankim himself would have known that this bordered on the ridiculous. Apparently, equality between sexes is a legal fiction with him, not a matter of social preference. Weakening social values, Bankim argued, could be effectively strengthened only with an innovative application of traditional paradigms themselves. In the *Dharmatattva*, bhakti, for instance, is not merely the pious adoration of god but a socially relevant gospel that can be made to restore prescribed social and cultural hierarchies.

In the *Dharmatattva*, one also discerns an underlying political argument, albeit fairly guarded and subtle in character. Soon after he wrote the patriotic novel *Anandamath* (1882), the civil servant, Bankim Chandra was, summoned before the Bengal Secretariat to answer charges of sedition. Understandably, therefore, Bankim appears quite reluctant to push his political sentiments beyond a point. He was clearly offended by the Arms Act in 1878, which, by disallowing Indians to carry arms on their person, cast doubts upon their 'unquestionable' loyalty. Within the project of self-disciplining, he also assigned an important place to developing physical prowess as this was vital for self-defence, the defence of one's family and even the larger collective of the nation.[36] From this it may be inferred, and certainly so in the case of Bengal, that Bankim was not averse to the idea of individual armed resistance, if not a popular and violent rebellion against British rule, though he would have been very reluctant to actually express this.

However, with Bankim Chandra, individual self-disciplining was not an end in itself but a means for realizing the social good and here, the paradigm of *nishkam karma* becomes operatively valuable. Arguably, Bankim derived this from the *Gita* (on which he was also to produce an unfinished commentary), which would, in itself, indicate a perceptible shift in orientations and context. *Dharma* in the *Gita* is essentially the category of *svadharma* and human activism, too, is ultimately directed to the realization of certain spiritual ends by surrendering the consequences thereof to god. For Bankim, on the other hand, patriotism is the highest form of *Dharma*—this is precisely the note on which the *Dharmatattva* concludes.[37] However, applying the paradigm of *nishkam karma* to even somewhat covert political ends also placed Bankim in some logical difficulty. For one, if selfless or unmotivated action required foregoing the results thereof, what was the patriot to look forward to? In Bankim's days, there was an apocryphal story in circulation about the patriot who lost all interest in freedom upon realizing that this would not come about in his own lifetime. In the *Dharmatattva*, Bankim seems to be vaguely aware of this problem and a resolution is offered only in a later work, the unfinished commentary on the *Gita*. It was never the intention of the *Gita*, he argues, that *nishkam karma* be utterly devoid of expectations or at least in all cases. Service rendered to the nation was *ipso facto nishkam* for it was for the sake of the collective, not the individual self.[38]

Scholars and critics have taken *Dharmatattva* to represent a conservative back-tracking on the part of Bankim even though, quite paradoxically, this is also considered to be work almost entirely modelled on the writings of Western authors. Neither of these propositions, I would argue, can be accepted unqualifiedly. Admittedly, didacticism and conservative sentiments are evident in the later writings of Bankim Chandra. On the other hand, a critical approach to the Hindu tradition never deserted him. He was, for instance, one of the earliest to claim that rather than be lost in abstract metaphysical speculation, the Hindu mind was quite capable of dwelling on the common pleasures of life. The *Dharmatattva* includes an entire chapter on the linkages between Hindu art, aesthetics and dharmic life.[39] On the question of identifying the intellectual sources of the *Dharmatattva*, Bankim's critics, I find, are themselves self-conflicted. Thus, the American scholar, Rachel van Baumer, one of the earliest to comment on the subject, found the work to carry a Spencerian flavour but to also bear a great likeness to Vaishnava theology.[40] Intellectual indebtedness to the West is never really concealed in the *Dharmatattva* and appended to this work are excerpts from a host of European writers including Kant, Schliermacher (the anthropologist), Tylor, Fichte, Seeley, John Stuart Mill and Herbert Spencer.[41] There are, at the same time, an overwhelming number of citations from classical religious and philosophical texts of the Hindus. The list includes the *Bhagavad-Gita*, *Bhagavat Purana*, *Vishnu Purana*, *Vajsaneyisamhitopanishad* (*Ishopanishad*), *Chandogya Upanishad*, *Shandilya Bhakti Sutra* (together with Svapnesvar's commentary), the *Mahabharata, Vrihad Gautamiya Samhita, Manu Samhita* (with Kulluka Bhatta's commentary), and the fifteenth-century Vedantic work, *Vedantasara* of Sadananada. This is a very learned and eclectic mix of *shruti*, *smriti*, *itihasa* and *purana*. Of particular interest here is the way in which Bankim locates a correspondence between himself and scriptural authority. In Chapter 26 of the *Dharmatattva,* for instance, he cites the commentary of Kulluka Bhatta (on Manu) to contend that rational considerations cannot be overridden by a blind faith in scriptural authority. So far as one can see, this is a double-edged argument for here Bankim implies that a tradition can be internally self-critical.

It is not unlikely that in the course of writing the *Dharmatattva,* Bankim realized the immodesty underlying some of his claims. Perhaps it dawned on him that the capacity for self-improvement he had come to expect in men was grossly unrealistic and utopian. Hence, for Bankim, an ideal dharmic life is located in god, not man. From this perspective, the *Dharmatattva* really has to be read together with Bankim's *magnum opus*, the *Krishnacharitra.* In modern Indian literature, this is possibly the first work attempting to rescue the historical Krishna from the multiple layers of myths and legends surrounding him. For Bankim, Krishna was the exemplar of all human virtues, a historical figure whose life and exploits reinforced and set new standards of dharmic conduct.[42] Importantly again, though Krishna was a god who descended on earth (*avatar*), he lived out his life on earth as an ordinary mortal, doing only that which was humanly possible and never invoking the omnipotence or the supernatural powers of god. It is thus that in the entire galaxy of Hindu *avatars*, it was Krishna whose life and activities constituted an ideal that was entirely intelligible and worthy of human emulation.

Arguably, there might have been another reason why *Dharma* and its operative principles had to be ideally located in god. While activity was endemic to human life, argues Bankim, men often lacked the acuteness to pick right from wrong.[43] For a man who valued utilitarian considerations and yet did not believe that society could be run on moral principles alone, this was indeed a problem. If Bankim is to be believed, even truthfulness could not be always morally defended; its value, in other words, depended much on its situational context. Here Bankim comments on the well-known incident from the epic *Ramayana*, arguing that it would have been more prudent of King Dasharatha not to honour the vow given to his queen that meant sending his eldest son and heir to the throne, Rama, to long years of exile. In this instance, the king may have been truthful and morally virtuous from a commonplace perspective but this truthfulness was tragically oblivious of the larger good. Individual moral failings, in other words, could be more than compensated by a concern for public welfare, suggests Bankim.[44] Rather than trust man's actions or judgement, therefore, he prefers to go by 'historical feats' performed by a god.

Here it is useful to remember that Bankim's god (Krishna) is conceptually very different from that of the Deists for he is possessed of human qualities and fully implicated in his creation. Bankim's Krishna can acquire anthropomorphic form, exhibit human sentiments and passion, and inspire the same in his devotees. This conception of god clearly separated Bankim from the reformist camp within the neo-Hindus (as, for example, the more iconoclastic Brahmos) who adhered to the idea of a god who was *nirakar* (formless), if not also fully *nirguna* (not endowed with human qualities). For Bankim, on the other hand, god was a being to whom one could very emotionally relate even though it was his rational acts that man needed to focus on and emulate.[45]

Notwithstanding his growing dissatisfaction with it, Bankim seems to repeatedly fall back on the notion of utility. Utility had its limitations but it was not *adharmic*. Again, notwithstanding all limitations, he found this to be a moral tool that could be constructively wedded to the paradigm of *nishkam karma*. In the *Dharmatattva*, while Bankim often returns to the importance of self-preservation, his inherent tendency is to somehow harmonize the good of the individual with that of the community. It is thus that he argues that among the many natural qualities or dispositions in man, some had to be developed more than others. Piety, love and compassion (*bhakti*, *preeti* and *daya*) were qualities that certainly needed to be cultivated more than anger, avarice and erotic desire. Uncontrolled anger could come in the way of exhibiting love and compassion; on the other hand, feelings of love when sufficiently developed, could keep anger in check.[46] It is important to note though that for Bankim, while certain feelings or sentiments had to be controlled or reined in, none of these could be wholly exterminated. Anger, though otherwise an impediment to the growth of human character, could prove useful as a part of rightful aggression and self-defence. Similarly, though one ought not to over-indulge in erotic desire, its universal suppression would result in the extermination of the human race.[47] Hence, the harmonious integration of the various faculties of body and mind had to be suitably tempered with the virtues of moderation. This was immensely useful as it also helped to overcome the self-other dichotomy. When nobler feelings in man were adequately developed, they became better equipped to handle social differences and conflict. Also, under these conditions, the pursuit of the social good became more compatible with individual self-interest, up to a rationally pre-determined point. In this manner, love of the self and love for mankind could be made to more closely approach one another. Holding the self to be an integral part of the universe, argues Bankim, was true egalitarianism.[48]

In the *Dharmatattva*, Bankim Chandra also ponders over the question of whether or not the category of *sukha* (happiness) could be understood even outside the framework of dharmic conduct. Perhaps this became necessary in view of the fact that, at one level, happiness and unhappiness (*sukha* and *duhkha*) were also tied to Hindu-Brahmanical theories of *karma*, karmic bondage and redemption. In the *Dharmatattva*, surprisingly, Bankim admits to a belief in the after-life and believes that one could offer ample proof in support of this.[49] Effectively then, Bankim takes happiness to be important both in this life and the next. At the same time, his more pragmatic side to him persuaded him to argue that *Dharma* was not quite contingent on a belief in the after-life, and that any attempt to induce dharmic feelings by playing upon the fears and anxieties of people would be plainly unjust.[50] On the whole, though, he appears to draw some consolation from the thought that ultimately *Dharma* and dharmic life could be acceptable and meaningful to everybody. He who rebutted the idea of a life after death could be comforted by the knowledge that righteous conduct could turn worldly life itself into a paradise. On the other hand, people who did believe in the after-life would be happy upon learning that merit accrued through good work in one life could be carried over to the next.[51] Apparently, with such thoughts in mind, Bankim Chandra put concluding touches to an older argument. In this life, *Dharma* enabled us to realize our true worth and meet our pressing social obligations. In the life beyond, the happiness we had created for others would bring us unbounded joy.

Bankim Chandra believed that everybody had the right to be happy and disagreed with the depressing pessimism that ran through certain schools of Hindu and Buddhist thought. On the other hand, as far as one can see, the quest for *Dharma* did not necessarily end with the coming of happiness, whether for the individual or community. In its more meaningful form, *Dharma* was not simply about *sukha* but *sadhana*, an intense personal quest for realizing the truth.[52] *Sukha* was but a fleeting moment of happiness, *sadhana* an enduring reality. In the *Dharmatattva*, the *guru* who so painstakingly explains to his pupil the basic principles of *Dharma* admits that his own understanding had come only after a lifetime of sustained self-questioning.

NOTES

1. Nirad C. Chaudhuri, 'Bankim Chandra', in Nirad C. Chaudhuri, ed., *Nirbachito Probondho* (Select Essays), Calcutta: Ananda, 2001, p. 117.
2. On this see Amiya P. Sen, 'Looking at the Coloniser: Hindu Hermeneutics and the Politics of Self-representation in Nineteenth Century Bengal', in Beate Eschment and Hans Harder, eds., *Looking at the Coloniser*, Warzburg: Ergon Verlag, 2004.
3. Nirad C. Chaudhuri, *Scholar Extraordinary: The Life of Rt. Hon'ble Max Müller*, Delhi, 1974, p. 309.
4. Amiya P. Sen, 2004, in Beate Eschment and Hand Harder, eds., op. cit.
5. On the question of how a classical text had to be re-interpreted and re-validated in the light of contemporary needs, see Bankim Chandra Chattopadhyay, *Srimadbhagavatgita* (Preface) in *Bankim Rachanavali*, hereafter *BR* (*Collected Works of Bankim Chandra*), vol. II, ed. J.C. Bagal, Calcutta: Sahitya Samsad, 5th rpt., 1973, p. 680.
6. Wilhelm Halbfass, ed., *Philology and Confrontation: Paul Hacker on Traditional and Modern Vedanta*, New York: State University of New York Press, 1995, pp. 237-8.
7. Bankim Chandra Chattopadhyay, *Dharma Dharmatattwa*, ed. Brojendranath Bandopadhyay and Sajani Kanta Das, Calcutta: Bangiya Sahitya Parishad, 3rd rpt., 1965, Appendix B. See especially Bankim's footnote to page 146.
8. This is palpable in his novel *Rajani,* written in the late 1870s. For details on recurring holy men, the supernatural and the miraculous in his works of fiction, see: Amiya P. Sen, *Bankim Chandra Chattopadhyay: An Intellectual Biography*, Delhi: Oxford University Press, 2008.
9. S. Radhakrishnan, *Indian Philosophy*, vol. I, Delhi: Oxford University Press, 2003, p. 52.
10. On this, see Amiya P. Sen, *Three Essays on Sri Ramakrishna and His Times*, Shimla: Indian Institute of Advanced Study, 2001, Essay III, pp. 89-152.
11. *BR*, II: 478 (FN).
12. Swami Vivekananda, *Karma Yoga*: *The Complete Works of Swami Vivekananda*, vol. I, Calcutta: Advaita Ashrama, 14th edn., Calcutta, 1972, pp. 25-118.
13. A.K. Ramanujan, 'Is there an Indian way of thinking? An Informal Essay', in *Contributions to Indian Sociology* (NS), 23.1 (1989), pp. 41-58.
14. P.T. Raju, 'Activism in Indian Thought', in *Annals of the Bhandarkar Oriental Institute*: 39, 3-4, July-October 1958, p. 284.

15. P.V. Kane, *History of the Dharmashastras*, vol. II, part I, Poona: Bhandarkar Oriental Research Institute, 1974, pp. 2-3.
16. *Gita*, III, p. 35.
17. This is aptly posed in J.C. Heesterman, *The Inner Conflict of Tradition: Essays on Indian Ritual Kingship and Society*, Chicago: University of Chicago Press, 1985, pp. 198-9.
18. A point once made by Rammohun Roy when responding to his critics. See *Rammohun Rachanavali* (*The Collected Works of Rammohun in Bengali*, hereafter *RR*), ed. Ajit Kumar Ghosh, Calcutta: Haraf Prakshani, 1973, pp. 250-9.
19. A.K. Saran, 'The Traditional View of Man', in Ramchandra Gandhi, ed., *Language, Tradition and Modern Civilization,* Pune: PQ Publishers, 1983, pp. 21-3, 26.
20. Rammohun Roy, 'A Second Defence of Monotheistic Worship . . .', in Kalidas Nag and Devjyoti Burman, eds., *The English Works of Rammohun Roy*, vol. II, Calcutta: Sadharan Brahmo Samaj, 1946, p. 117.
21. Bankim Chandra Chattopadhyay, *Dharmatattva*, op. cit., p. 58. Possibly as a result of the conservative backlash in the 1890s, Bankim went back on this question in the second edition to this work in 1894.
22. See, for instance, Wilhelm Halbfass, *India and Europe: An Essay in Understanding*, New York: State University of New York Press, Albany, 1988, p. 340.
23. R.D. Karmakar, 'Indian Philosophical Literature Known to Alberuni', *Annals of the Bhandarkar Oriental Institute*, 38 (1957), p. 245.
24. B.D. Chattopadhyay, *Representing the Other? Sanskrit Sources and the Muslims, 8th to 14th Centuries*, Delhi: Manohar, 1988, pp. 74, 90.
25. *RR*: 643.
26. Shashadhar Tarkachudamani, 'Dharma Ebong Dharmer Anusthata', in *Nabajeebon*, 1885-6; *Sri Dharmavyakhya*, Kasimbazar, 1910, p. 4.
27. Ibid. Brajendranath Bandopadhyay, 'Chandranath Basu', in *Sahitya Sadhak Charitramala*, no. 83, Calcutta: Bangiya Sahitya Parishad, 1963, pp. 15-17. For Bhudeb, see his *Samajik Probondho* and the *Achar Probondho* (Essays on the Society, Essays on Hindu Rites and Customs) both included in Promothonath Bishi, ed., *Bhudeb Rachanasambhar*, (*Collected Works of Bhudeb Mukhopadhaya*), Calcutta: Mitra and Ghosh, 1968.
28. Bankim Chandra Chattopadhyay, 'Gourdas Babajir Bhikshar Jhuli', *BR*: II: 268-9.
29. *Dharmatattva*, Chapter 1.
30. See *Three Essays on Sri Ramakrishna*, op. cit., Essay II, pp. 60-88.

31. Bankim Chandra Chattopadhyay, 'Bhalobashar Atyachar', in *BR*: II, 213f.
32. These essays were written for the journal *Prochar* and titled *Kam* (July 1885); *Dharma O Sahitya* (December 1885-January 1886) and *Chittashuddhi* (February-March 1886).
33. *Dharmatattva*, op. cit., Chapter 1.
34. Ibid., Chapter 10.
35. Ibid., p. 122, translation mine.
36. *Dharmatattva*, op. cit., Chapter 8.
37. Ibid., p. 141.
38. Bankim Chandra Chattopadhyay, *Srimadbhagavadgita* (Commentary), *BR*: II, p. 775.
39. *Dharmatattva*, op. cit., Chapter 24.
40. Rachel van Baumer, 'The Reinterpretation of *Dharma* in Nineteenth Century Bengal: Religious Conduct for Man in the Modern World', in Rachel van Baumer, ed., *Aspects of Bengali History and Society*, Delhi: Vikas, 1976, p. 74.
41. *Dharmatattva*, op. cit., Appendix B.
42. Bankim Chandra Chatopadhyay, *Krishnacharitra*, *BR*: II, 407f. On this also see Sudipta Kaviraj, 'The Myth of the Praxis: The Construction of the Figure Krishna in the Krishnacharitra', Delhi: Nehru Memorial Museum & Library, Occasional Papers on History and Society, no. L, 1987. This is also available as a monograph.
43. *Dharmatattva*, op. cit., p. 26.
44. 'Bhalobashar Atyachar', op. cit.; Bimal Krishna Matilal tells us that this was an argument offered to Dasharatha at the time by the sage Jabala. See B.K. Matilal, '*Dharma* and Rationality', in Shlomo Biderman and Ben Ami Scrafstein, eds., *Rationality in Question: Eastern and Western Views of Rationality*, Leiden: E.J. Brill, 1989.
45. For statements to this effect, see *BR* II: Preface, p. 24.
46. *Dharmatattva*, op. cit., p. 52.
47. Ibid., pp. 24-5.
48. Ibid., p. 116.
49. Ibid., p. 33.
50. Ibid., p. 31.
51. Ibid., pp. 33-4.
52. Ibid., p. 29.

PART II

Divinity and the Feminine: Representations of Gender and Gender Relations

FIVE

A Home for the Goddess

Structural Shrines for Independent Female Deities in Early Medieval Tamiḻakam, *c.* CE 600-1300

R. Mahalakshmi

There have been many studies of divine pantheons that reveal how closely the relationships between gods and goddesses are modelled on specific regional kinship and marriage patterns that structure the lives of men and women in that context.[1] In fact, there have been misplaced interpretations of the conspicuous presence of goddesses within the Brahmanical religion as revealing a more liberating space for women in those historical contexts which produced them.[2] A number of Indological studies have focused on religious texts, particularly myths, or practices to elucidate this point. However, the doyen of early Indian history, R.S. Sharma had pointed out that religious texts encoded myths in such a manner as to make existing social practices seem more acceptable, or they attempted to legitimize newer codes of conduct.[3] In my research on the evolution of goddess worship within the Tamil Śaiva traditions in early medieval Tamiḻakam, I have focused on a variety of sources that indicated the nature of transformations of local and regional religious cults and practices, and located them in historical contexts when, in general, there was a transition from a largely tribal material milieu to a highly-evolved agrarian society.[4] This transition saw the displacement or marginalization of the religio-cultural mores of the tribal people and the evocation of Brahmanical Puranic deities and rituals by newly-emerging socio-political elites. However, what is most striking from the point of view of its gender implications is that the independent traditions of worship of goddesses were sought to be appropriated by the patriarchal Brahmanical sectarian traditions, where, invariably, the goddess was married off to Śiva and transformed into a benevolent consort.

In this paper, I focus on the construction of structural shrines for independent goddesses in the Tamil region during the early medieval period (*c.* CE 600-1300), whose worship I would trace to earlier cults and traditions in the region. Even a cursory survey of the inscriptions related to goddesses in early medieval Tamiḻakam reveals instances where the goddess was being accommodated spatially within the Śaiva pantheon, through the building of a shrine for her in the precincts of the Śiva temple. However, the names of the goddesses and the fact that they are not identified as the spouse of Śiva in inscriptions reveals their status as independent deities organically linked to localities and communities, which can perhaps be traced to earlier tribal cults and belief systems. I have closely examined the evidence to map out the presence of the goddesses in terms of shrines built in their honour.

The paper is divided into three sections. In the first, a brief survey of the literature related to temple-building in the Tamil region is undertaken. The construction of structural shrines using non-perishable material was a phenomenon of the early medieval period. What the implications of temple-building were as a cultural activity in the Tamil region and in what way did it establish the influence of the Brahmanical religious tradition are some of the questions explored here.

In the second section, a chronological survey of the goddess shrines known to us from inscriptions and field investigations has been undertaken. The focus is on a topographical plotting of shrines dedicated to independent goddesses, and the numerical strength of the latter is examined. In the third section, the connection between deities and localities is explored to understand whether these goddesses were indigenous deities or belonged to the Brahmanical Puranic pantheon of female deities. We wish to locate the impetus for the building of shrines for the independent goddess and understand the possible reasons for patronage to them. Also, a premise that historians generally adopt while looking at processes of accommodation and assimilation within the Brahmanical religion is that it is irreversible—the goddess permanently loses her independent institutional status once she is housed in structures built according to Brahmanical prescription. Is this premise borne out in our sources? Also, does the importance of these female deities diminish once they are appropriated and assimilated within the Brahmanical tradition? These are some of the questions addressed here.

I

It has been argued that beyond the abstract spiritual level, bhakti can be examined at the functional level as closely interlinked with the Brahmanical temple.[5] 'It is implied that elements of temple propaganda and Brahmanical missionary enthusiasm were inseparable components of the movement. Bhakti not only started from the temple, but it connected one temple to another . . . and this led to the proliferation of temples.'[6] It is believed that 'the Puranic ideology of bhakti appears to have percolated to the South through the temple-centred brāhmaṇa [*sic*] settlements'.[7] The proponents of this view go so far as to argue that the process of transformation of Brahmanism into Hinduism, already completed in the north, occurred in south India due to the rise of temple-centred bhakti.[8]

R. Champakalakshmi has expressed a similar opinion. She sees the institutions of the *brahmadeya* or brāhmaṇa settlements and the temple as products of the Vedic and Puranic religion.[9] She has focused in great detail on the integrative character of the temple, especially from the ninth century onwards, in linking regions, social groups and economic resources.[10] The centrality of the temple as an ideological tool of validation is also emphasized in her work.[11]

The Sangam and post-Sangam works refer to structures that may have housed a deity.[12] The most common terms that we find in literature are *kōṭṭam*, *nagaram*, *paḷḷi* and *kōyil*.[13] However, they appear in the latest cluster of poems (the first to the third centuries and the fourth to the sixth centuries for the Sangam and post-Sangam, respectively) and are used with reference to the five *tiṇai* deities, the Buddhist and Jaina places of worship, and the deities of the Brahmanical religious tradition.[14] We may, therefore, conclude that this was a later development that may have been influenced by the northern Sanskritic traditions. However, the use of perishable materials for these structures meant that there were no archaeological remains and we can only conjecture about the kinds of structures these were.

K.R. Srinivasan's conclusion that the early Tamil people did not use stone for building temples, even when they had developed a more complex notion of the sacred by the early centuries of the Christian era, is understandable given the earlier association of stone with memorials to the dead.[15] N. Venkataramanayya demonstrates that the dolmen can be seen as the earliest precursor to the structural temple, at least in form. However, it is also clear that there were various stages in the development of the formal shrine, which culminated in the structural temple of the early medieval period in peninsular India. The first stage was the excavation of natural rock surfaces, which resulted in the development of cave-temple architecture. This was, in the Tamil region, a difficult task as the natural rocks were of hard granite, unlike in the western Deccan where sandstone provided an easier medium for architects.

The earliest stone structures that we have in Tamiḻakam belong to the beginnings of the early medieval period (sixth century). The reign of the Pallava king, Mahendra (*c.* CE 580-630), saw the chiselling of the natural rock face in northern Tamil Nadu to create pillared halls, with a cell at one end housing images of Brahmā, Viṣṇu and Śiva. The back walls of the cells have revealed a coating of lime plaster and paint, indicating that rather than stone images, the earliest shrines may have housed paintings or stuccoes of deities.[16] Half a century later, cave-temples exhibited certain innovations in terms of size and decoration. The main cells now began to contain, on their back walls, the depiction of panels of Śiva, Umā and Muṟukaṉ (Skanda of the Puranic tradition) seated together, representing the composite icon called Somāskanda.[17]

Towards the middle of the seventh century, during the time of Narasimhavarman (*c.* CE 630-68), the monolithic rock-cut shrine—*ratha*—was developed as a new form in temple architecture in the region. The Pāṇḍyas in the southern Tamil region also began to build cave-temples around *c.* CE 650. In fact, there are many more cave-temples that can be attributed to them than to the Pallavas in the first half of the early medieval period.[18] It is from the time of the Pallava king, Rājasimha (*c.* CE 700-28), that structural stone temples came to be built in the Tamil region.[19]

It has been argued by various scholars that the socio-political elite patronized the Brahmanical religion and its institutions, and received non-religious and extra-religious benefits, in addition to enhancing their status as great and 'ideal' followers of the tradition.[20] In the Tamil region, this is very apparent as numerous temples began to dot the landscape over the seven centuries of the early medieval period. The construction of temples according to Brahmanical prescription, the bringing in of ritual specialists to conduct worship, and the movement of service personnel to meet the daily requirements of the temple were all acts designed to make the people aware of and participate in the religious and cultural tradition of which the custodians were the brāhmaṇas. Kings proclaimed their status as great protectors of the faith through such acts of construction and maintenance, and this enhanced their legitimate claims to power. The forms of deities depicted in temple iconography, and the development of narrative traditions in literature and art in the region based on Brahmanical mythology, reveals the anxiety of patrons and custodians to transmit motifs and symbols so that the local populace could become familiar with what was essentially an alien religion.

The importance of the bhakti hymnists, who wandered from place to place singing in praise of gods manifested at particular sites, was also significant in this regard. Appar, a Śaiva saint (*nāyanār*), sang of the *to<u>r</u><u>r</u>tum kōyil* or the temple that was conceived of, and the *tō<u>n</u><u>r</u>iya kōyil* or the existing temple at Tirumiyachur.[21] This was seen to correspond with the *Bṛhat Saṃhitā's* distinction between the *pratiṣṭhā* and the *adhivāsa* of the deity in a temple. The first was the permanent or fixed abode, while the latter was the temporary and preliminary placement of the deity. In Tamil, the terms *maṭakkōyil* and *ilaṅkōyil* were used to denote these two categories.

It was not a coincidence that these *pāṭalpeṟṟa talaṅkal* (sites sung of by the bhakti hymnists) had structural stone temples erected under the aegis of the Pallavas, Pāṇḍyas and the Cōḷas in the early medieval period, which underscores the connection between the spread of these institutions and their patronage by royalty through the mediation of bhakti.[22] It can be shown that some important pre-Brahmanical goddess cult centres were now associated with the high gods of the Puranic religion—Viṣṇu and Śiva—which perhaps led to a shift even in the site where the deity was originally conceived of as being housed. For instance, Tiruvālangāḍu, as we know from local legends and Sangam and bhakti sources, was considered the home of the goddess Nīlī who was depicted as vengeful goddess.[23] However, the bhakti hymnists, while singing of this site, either ignored her or relegated her to the background. They also suggested a difference in status accorded to temples by referring to some as *peruṅkōyil* or great temples. It is not clear if this was on the basis of size or some other parameters. Another term that appears is *kaṟakōyil* (stone temple), implying that the practice of using perishable material to build temples was still in vogue.[24]

The Śaiva saints, the *nāyanār*, in the course of their peregrinations, also conceived of associations among the sacred sites of Śiva. These were intrinsically linked to the mythology of this deity and drew heavily on Puranic themes even while integrating local influences.[25] Thus, these saints developed three concepts. The first was of the *vīraṭṭānam* (eight sites associated with the heroic exploits of Śiva).[26] The second was the *pañcapūta talam* (five sites in which Śiva in the form of the *liṅga* was associated with the five elements).[27] The third was the *sapta viṭaṅka kṣētram* (seven sites associated with the deity Tyāgarāja), and so on.[28]

This study of goddess shrines in the Tamil region attempts to trace the appearance of structural shrines for the goddess in the beginning of the early medieval period, and their importance as evinced by patronage and donations to them. The primary concern is to document evidence of the existence of shrines for independent goddesses within the Śaiva tradition and we have included, for our purpose, even those cases where no standing structure exists today. This survey focuses on temples to those female deities who may be considered independent goddesses in the sense that they are not intrinsically connected to Śiva as consorts, even though their shrines were sometimes physically located within the Śiva temple complexes.

II

A historical geography of the Tamil region reveals the classification of the larger Tamil macro-region into five broad sub-regions: the Cōḷamaṇḍalam, Toṇḍaimaṇḍalam, Pāṇḍimaṇḍalam, Naḍuvilnāḍu and Kongumaṇḍalam. The Cōḷamaṇḍalam consists of the modern districts of Tanjavur and Tiruchirapalli, and was the political core of the Cōḷas, a dynasty that rose to power in the middle of the ninth century in the region and dominated regional politics until the thirteenth century CE. The Tanjavur district has now been sub-divided into three districts—Nagapattinam, Tiruvarur and Tañjāvūr. The Tiruchirapalli district is now separated into the following districts—Tiruchirapalli, Perambalūr and Karūr. Toṇḍaimaṇḍalam was considered the traditional heartland of the Pallavas, an early medieval dynasty that, in the fourth century, was visible in the contiguous region of southern Andhra. By the sixth century, it was the major power in the northern Tamil region until it was eclipsed by the Cōḷas in the ninth century. The Pallava region consisted of the modern Chengalpet district, the Union Territory of Pondicherry, and parts of the modern Chitoor and Nellore districts in Andhra Pradesh. By the time of Rājarāja I (CE 985-1014), this region was more or less under the control of the Cōḷas and remained so until the time of Rājarāja III (*c.* CE 1245).

The Pāṇḍimaṇḍalam was the stronghold of the Pāṇḍya lineage from the early historic period up until the end of the early medieval period (*c.* CE 1300). Broadly, it comprised the regions in the southern extremity of the peninsula such as modern Tirunelveli, Nagarkoyil, Kanyakumari, Ramanathapuram and Madurai districts, with its epicenter at Madurai. The Naḍuvilnāḍu was the intermediate zone of Cōḷa control, which was constituted in this form during the period of Cōḷa ascendancy in the region.[29] It comprised the territories between the Peṉṉai and northern Veḷḷarū rivers between the Cōḷa and Pallava core regions (Cōḷamaṇḍalam and Toṇḍaimaṇḍalam, respectively). There were traditionally eight chieftaincies that were ruling in this region in the early medieval period. Some of them were Vanakoppadi in Tiruvaṇṇāmalai taluk, Singapuranāḍu in Jinjee taluk, Oymanāḍu in Tindivanam taluk and Malaiyamān in Tirukkoyilūr taluk.[30] In its fullest extent, however, the region was not integrated as Naḍuvilnāḍu until the time of Kulōttuṅga I (*c.* CE 1070-1125).[31] It broadly comprised the modern colonial districts of North and South Arcot. Kongumaṇḍalam comprised the north-west of modern Tamil Nadu and included a part of southern Karnataka. The Kongu region appears to have had chiefdoms, which were overrun by Aditya I (*c.* CE 871-907), the Cōḷa ḵing.[32] We have extended our survey along these traditional divisions to indicate the topographical pattern of distribution of goddess shrines in the early medieval period given the political geography of the region.

CŌḶAMAṆḌALAM

The earliest epigraphical reference to a goddess shrine appears in Sendalai (Tanjavur), where the temple is referred to as Mākālattu Piṭāri (the goddess at Makalam) at Nemam (Niyamam).[33] This temple is known from the eighth century inscriptions found in a Śiva temple and, as is evident, is not extant. The name *Piṭāri* used in this early inscription and in others is interesting. Mylai S. Venkatasamy has suggested that the term Piṭāri (Paṭāri/Paṭṭāraki/Paṭāraki) refers to one who mitigates all suffering.[34] Subrahmanya Aiyer sees this as the feminine form of *Paṭṭārar*.[35] The Sanskrit form of this term is *Bhaṭṭārikā* (masculine *Bhaṭṭāraka*, 'great lord', 'venerable or worshipful person'),[36] and it appears to be a generic term used for local goddesses in different regional contexts.[37] Early twentieth-century ethnographic evidence also indicates the existence of village deities who are worshipped by this name.[38]

At Alambakkam, the Piṭāri temple that is the Selliyamman temple in current usage can also be dated to the eighth-ninth centuries.[39] The interesting fact is that a Saptamātṛkā shrine is mentioned in an inscription from this temple. It appears that this temple was either originally a Saptamātṛkā shrine or was converted into one by the end of the ninth century.[40] An extant temple, referred to by the locals as the Selliyamman temple, in Nangavaram has a foundation inscription of Parāntaka I (*c.* CE 907-55), wherein the goddess is addressed as Cāttanūr Naṅkai[41] and as Kāla Paṭāri.[42] The name Selliyamman denotes the goddess who was the younger sister. This may be a resonance from the Saptamātṛkā tradition of the seven mother goddesses, wherein one goddess began to attract greater ritual worship and attention. Or it may be a reference to the Puranic tradition of the goddess Durgā, where she is often referred to as the sister of Viṣṇu. The term *naṅkai* with reference to the inscriptional name appears to have been derived from *nal* meaning good, and from *naṅku* meaning that which is good, in abundance, beauty, health, stability and happiness.[43] Here, the former goddess was the good goddess of the settlement, Sattanūr.

NAḌUVILNĀḌU

There is again a Saptamātṛkā temple at Kappalūr, which can be dated to the ninth century on the basis of the paleography of its inscription.[44] The latter refers to the Piṭāri and the Kāṭukāl kōṭṭam. It is not possible for us to identify which of the two is the shrine with the inscription. There is a mid-tenth-century inscription referring to a Piṭāri temple in Vasukur.[45] The interesting fact is that this belongs to the reign of the Rāṣṭrakūṭa king, Kannaradeva III (*c.* CE 953), and is not a foundation record of the temple. This suggests that the temple had been constructed before the Rāṣṭrakūṭa ruler's incursions into the region. Second, the temple boasts of three inscriptions of Rājarāja I's time.[46] Here, the deity is referred to as Ūruṭaiya Cunaimēnaṅkai, or the good goddess on the village hill. A tenth-century inscription on a slab in Cōḷapuram refers to a Piṭāri temple, which has been identified with the Kāliyamman temple where the slab has been found.[47]

In Kilachur, the Selliyamman temple has a foundation inscription of the middle of the tenth century.[48] The goddess here is called Vaṭapālamāṇṭaḷ—the goddess of the northern quarter.[49] An inscription from Karikal of the last quarter of the tenth century records the building of a Piṭāri temple. This is currently referred to as the Poṉṉi Amman temple and appears to have been rebuilt at a later date.[50] At Ukkal, a Piṭāri temple is referred to as the only place where betel leaves were to be sold.[51] Any transgression of this injunction would result in the levying of a fine by the tank committee. Interestingly, this reference to the goddess temple is found in the temple of the male deity, Mahāśāstā. At Viriñjipuram, lands of the goddesses Durgā and Piṭāri are mentioned in an early eleventh-century record, but it is uncertain whether this meant that temples of these goddesses also existed, or whether this was a reference to images in some temple.[52] However, the Śiva temple in the same place has a mid-eleventh-century record that mentions a Durgā temple in the village, which may be used to substantiate the evidence from the previous record, at least with regard to one of the goddesses mentioned.[53] In Pallikonda, a record of the last quarter of the tenth century in the Selliyamman temple refers to the Paṭāriyār of the village, which presumably refers to the Saptamātṛkā.[54] At Tiruppanamur, inscriptions in the Śiva temple mention Mūkkārai Naṅkai in the mid-tenth century CE.[55] This temple also has a record regarding the Saptamātṛkā, Durgā, and other deities situated in the *tiruvannāḷikai* (*-māḷikai*) or *prākāra* of the temple.[56] The Śiva temple at Brahmadesam mentions the Saptamātṛkā of the village in the mid-eleventh century, suggesting its existence even earlier.[57]

At Aruvahur, modern Tondur, a rock carries an early ninth-century inscription referring to the goddess(es) as Ēṟṟukuṉṟanar[58] Paṭāri.[59] At Manalurpet, there exists the ruins of a temple, which locals call the Kāka Nācciyār *maṇḍapam* (hall of the 'crow' goddess), that belongs to the mid-ninth century period.[60] However, if the name is an indicator, this may have been a temple in honour of Jyeṣṭhā Devī who had a crow as her banner. A mid-tenth-century inscription at Karadi records the existence of the Piṭāri Iṭaimalai[61] Naṅkai temple, which has been identified with the present Selliyamman temple there.[62] At Elvanasur, a record of *c.* CE 1153 in the local Śiva temple speaks of the shrines of Durgā and Piṭāriyār.[63] The Chidambaram Nataraja temple attests, in a tenth-century record, that a temple of Piṭāri Tiruccirrampala Mākālī stood outside the temple precincts.[64]

TOṆḌAIMAṆḌALAM

The seventh-century cave-temples dedicated to goddesses in Māmallapuram, the Koṭikkal *maṇḍapam* and the Draupadi *ratha,* are the earliest independent shrines dedicated to goddesses, perhaps in the entire Tamil region.[65] At Sirrambākkam, a late seventh-century inscription recording the building of a Piṭāri temple found on a slab at the entrance to the Saptamātṛkā shrine of the Celliyamman temple suggests the antiquity of the shrine where the record was found.[66] The latter may have been built over the ruins of the original shrine at this site. Similarly, at Pudupakkam, the slabs containing an inscription referring to a Paṭāri temple are found in the Celliyamman temple there.[67] At Selai, the goddess temple is called the Bhadra Mahākālī in the tenth century.[68] The Durgā shrine in the Kachisvara temple at little Kanchipuram is called Aiñcaṇṭi Durgā Paṭṭāri in the late tenth-century.[69] It is difficult to decide whether this was originally an independent shrine that came within the Śiva temple complex or whether it arose as a *parivāram* shrine.[70] The Draupadiyamman temple, also in Kancipuram, contains a tenth-century inscription.[71] At the Mādari Amman temple in Uttaramērūr, the deities are referred to as Piṭārimār, which we consider as an allusion to the group of seven goddesses.[72] One of the records, in fact, describes them as Kaṇṇiyāpaṭāri or virgin goddesses.[73] The present Kakkattamma temple at Iluppuru has a tenth-century record in its compound, referring to the Ēri Naṅkai temple in the village, which is perhaps the same temple renovated later, or an earlier shrine at the same site.[74] A tenth-century inscription from the Selliyamman temple at Velicheri, a Saptamātṛkā shrine, refers to the goddess as Kāla Pāṭāri.[75] We infer from this that either the earlier shrine to a single goddess was later converted into a shrine for the entire group, or the deity mentioned in the inscription is actually Cāmuṇḍā of the Saptamātṛkā group.[76] The latter is more likely as there is a late tenth-century record referring to this as the site of the Saptamātṛkā temple.[77] The Viṣṇu temple in Uttaramallūr refers to the temple of Turkai Paṭṭārakiyār in the village.[78] The same Viṣṇu temple mentions another goddess shrine for Kōnērinaṅkai in Kumanpadi in another context.[79] The existence of a Kāṭukāḷ temple in Kalakkattūr is known from the Śiva temple in Manamadi.[80] A Durgā Paṭāraki temple was in existence in or around Pulaḷḷūr in the late tenth to early eleventh century CE.[81] At Sattarai, there existed a Saptamātṛkā temple of the mid-eleventh century.[82] An inscription from Neyyadipakkam mentions a Piṭāri temple in the late eleventh century.[83] The same site records the building of a stone temple to the same goddess, hinting at an earlier brick structure.[84] At Tribhuvani, the Viṣṇu temple records the presence of the Ēmalattu Turkaiyār Ōmkāra Cuntari temple in the eastern hamlet of this settlement.[85]

KONGUMAṆḌALAM

Two thirteenth-century inscriptions from the Piṭāri temple at Dalavayanapattanam attest to its importance as the abode of Nānāteca Naṅkai.[86] This appears to be the presiding deity of the mercantile group called Nanadesi or the Ticai Āyirattu Ainūṟṟuvar (the merchants of different places, or the 500 merchants from thousand directions). The reference to Cāmuṇḍā in a record at Devarmukkulam indicates the presence of a Saptamātṛkā temple in the vicinity of the Viṣṇu temple where the inscription was found.[87] The Kunjamma temple in Sinnakkottur was in existence in the mid-eleventh century.[88] The Mariyamman temple in Dharmapuri was perhaps built on an earlier foundation of an eighth-ninth-century Piṭāri temple.[89] An early thirteenth-century inscription from Arumbavur mentions the shrines of Durgā and Piṭāri amongst others in this village while enumerating the *devadāna* lands of these temples.[90] There is evidence that the Durgā temple at Sinnamanur was built at least by the early eleventh century.[91]

PĀṆḌIMAṆḌALAM

At Tirupparankuṉṟam, the Durgā temple is said to have been built by the Pāṇḍya queen in *c.* CE 771, making it the second earliest shrine to an independent goddess known from inscriptions in the Tamil region after Sendalai.[92] An inscription reminiscent of the patron goddess of the merchants in the Kongu region is available from Narttamalai, where the goddess is called Caṅku Parameśvarī, or the great goddess of the conch.[93] Again, this could be a reference to the sister of Viṣṇu, the wielder of the conch, or to the patron of merchants who used shells as a medium of exchange. The Kanyakumari Kaṇṇikā Parameśvarī temple has an early tenth-century inscription (*c.* CE 916), and it is the only example of a shrine to a goddess clearly associated as a consort-to-be of Śiva in the pre-twelfth-century period.[94]

PERIPHERAL AREAS

The Kolaramma temple, dedicated to the Saptamātṛkā, was in existence by *c.* CE 997, as the donative records of Rājarāja I dated in that year are found here.[95] The importance of this shrine can be seen from the fact that there are ten records of the Cōḷas here, spanning the reigns of Rājarāja I to Kulōttuṅga I.[96] At Mālur, a Durga temple was in existence by *c.* CE 1015.[97]

Table 5.1: Independent Goddess Shrines in Tamil Inscriptions

Place	Goddess	Year	Details
1. Alambakkam–Cōḷamaṇḍalam	Piṭāri (Selliyamman)	8th-9th centuries CE	Saptamātṛkā
2. Nangavaram–Cōḷamaṇḍalam	Cāttanūr Naṅkai/ Kāla Paṭāri	Parāntaka I (*c.* CE 907-55)	(Selliyamman)
3. Makalam/Nemam–Cōḷamaṇḍalam	Mākālattu Piṭāri	*c.* 8th century CE	(Sendalai Śiva temple)
4. Kappalur–Naḍuvilnāḍu	Piṭāri + Kāṭukāl Koṭṭam	*c.* 8th century CE	Saptamātṛkā
5. Vasukur–Naḍuvilnāḍu	Piṭāri	*c.* 953 CE	Ūruṭaiya Cunaimēn Naṅkai (Rajaraja I)
6. Cōḷapuram–Naḍuvilnāḍu	Piṭāri	*c.* 10th century CE	(Kaliyamman temple)
7. Kilachur–Naḍuvilnāḍu	Vaṭapālamāṇṭāl	*c.* CE 956	(Selliyamman)
8. Karikal–Naḍuvilnāḍu	Piṭāri	*c.* CE 975	Ponni Amman
9. Ukkal–Naḍuvilnāḍu	Piṭāri (Mahāśāsta)	*c.* CE 1002	Sale of betel leaves
10. Viriñjipuram–Naḍuvilnāḍu	Piṭāri + Durgā	*c.* CE 1013	(Śiva temple)
11. Pallikonda–Naḍuvilnāḍu	Paṭāriyār	last quarter of 10th century	(Selliyamman)
12. Tiruppanamur–Naḍuvilnāḍu	Mūkkārai Naṅkai	late 10th century CE	(Śiva temple)
12a. Tiruppanamur–Naḍuvilnāḍu	Saptamātṛkā + Durgā (*parivāra*)	*c.* CE 1008	(Śiva temple)
12b. Sembakkam (Vellore)–Naḍuvilnāḍu	Piṭāri	Mid-11th century CE	(Rajendra Choleshvara temple)
13. Brahmadesam–Naḍuvilnāḍu	Saptamātṛkā	*c.* CE 1044	(Śiva temple)
14. Aruvahur/Toṇḍūr–Naḍuvilnāḍu	Ē<u>r</u>ruku<u>n</u>ranar Paṭāri	*c.* CE 801	(rock)

15. Karadi–Naḍuvilnāḍu	Piṭāri Iṭaimalai Naṅkai	*c.* CE 959	(Selliyamman temple)
16. Elvanasur–Naḍuvilnāḍu	Durgā + Piṭāriyar	*c.* CE 1153	(rock)
17. Cidamabram–Naḍuvilnāḍu	Piṭāri Tirucir̲r̲ampala Mākālī	*c.* 13th century CE	(Śiva temple)
18. Māmallapuram–Toṇḍaimaṇḍalam	Koṭikal Maṇṭapam	*c.* 7th century CE	
19. Māmallapuram–Toṇḍaimaṇḍalam	Draupadi Ratha	*c.* 7th century CE	
20. Sirrambakkam–Toṇḍaimaṇḍalam	Piṭāri	Mid-7th century CE	Saptamātṛkā (Selliyamman)
21. Pudupakkam–Toṇḍaimaṇḍalam	Paṭāri	??	(Selliyamman)
22. Selai–Toṇḍaimaṇḍalam	Bhadra Mahākālī	*c.* 10th century CE	
23. Little Kāñcīpuram–Toṇḍaimaṇḍalam	Aiñcaṇḍī Durgā Paṭṭāri	*c.* late 10th century	(Kacchisvara temple)
24. Kāñcīpuram–Toṇḍaimaṇḍalam	Piṭāri	*c.* 10th century CE	(Draupadiyamman)
25. Uttaramērūr–Toṇḍaimaṇḍalam	Piṭārimār (Saptamātṛkā)	*c.* 10th century CE	(Madari Amman)
26. Iluppuru–Toṇḍaimaṇḍalam	Ēri Naṅkai	c. 10th century CE	(Kakkatamma)
27. Velicheri–Toṇḍaimaṇḍalam	Kāla Paṭāri (Sapta-mātṛkā)	*c.* 10th century CE	(Selliyamman)
28. Uttaramallur–Toṇḍaimaṇḍalam	Durgai Paṭṭārakiyār	*c.* 10th century CE	(Viṣṇu temple)
29. Kumanpadi (Uttaramallur)–Toṇḍaimaṇḍalam	Kōnēri Naṅkai	*c.* 10th century CE	(Viṣṇu temple)
30. Kaḷakkatūr (Manamadi)–Toṇḍaimaṇḍalam	Kāṭukāl	*c.* 10th century CE	(Śiva temple)
31. Pullalur –Toṇḍaimaṇḍalam	Durgā Paṭṭāraki	*c.* late 10th, early 11th century	(Viṣṇu temple)

(Contd.)

Table 5.1 (Contd.)

Place	Goddess	Year	Details
32. Sattarai–Toṇḍaimaṇḍalam	(Saptamātṛkā)	*c.* 11th century CE	
33. Neyyadipakkam–Toṇḍaimaṇḍalam	Piṭāri	*c.* 11th century CE	(brick, later stone)
34. Tribhuvani–Toṇḍaimaṇḍalam	Ēmalattu Durgaiyar Ōmkāra Sundari	n.d.	(Viṣṇu temple)
35. Dalavayanapattanam–Kongumaṇḍalam	Nānādeśa Naṅkai	*c.* 13th century CE	(Piṭāriyamman temple)
36. Devarmukkulam–Kongumaṇḍalam	Cāmuṇḍeśvarī	*c.* 10th century	(Viṣṇu temple)
37. Sinnakottur–Kongumaṇḍalam	Piṭāri	*c.* CE 1073	(Kunjamma temple)
38. Dharmapuri–Kongumaṇḍalam	Piṭāri	*c.* 8th-9th century	(Mariyamman)
39. Arumbavur–Kongumaṇḍalam	Durgā + Piṭāri	*c.* 13th century	(Śiva temple)
40. Sinnamanur–Kongumaṇḍalam	Durgā	*c.* 11th century	(Śiva temple)
41. Tirupparankuṇṛam–Pāṇḍiamaṇḍalam	Durgā devī	*c.* CE 771	(Subrahmanya cave-temple)
42. Narttamalai–Pāṇḍiamaṇḍalam	Caṅku Parameśvarī	*c.* 1056	(Tirumalaikkadambar temple)
43. Kanyakumari–Pāṇḍiamaṇḍalam	n.d.	*c.* CE 916	(Kannika Parameśvarī)
44. Kolar–Karnataka	Piṭāriyar (Saptamātṛkā)	*c.* CE 997	(Kolaramma)
45. Mālur–Karnataka	Durgaiyār	*c.* CE 1015	(Śiva temple)

III

Our survey leads us to a discussion of the concept of Saptamātṛkā itself, and its association and institutionalization within the Śaiva temple complex by the ninth century. The Saptamātṛkā refers to a group of the seven deities, associated with seven male deities as their *śaktis,* and are known by the names of Brahmāṇī, Vaiṣṇavī, Maheśvarī, Indrāṇī, Kaumārī, Vārāhī and Cāmuṇḍā/ Yamī.[98] According to the Puranic tradition, these deities represented the seven evil qualities of pride, greed, anger, jealousy, illusion, envy and slandering.[99] J.N. Banerjea, on the basis of the commentary of Utpala on Varāhamihira's *Bṛhat Saṃhitā,* points out that eight goddesses are mentioned in this text.[100] In the early Cōḷa temples, with the introduction of the *aṣṭa-parivāradevatā* shrines as a regular feature within the Śaiva temples, the Saptamātṛkā were a group given a defined space within the sacred complex.[101] These temples had only single *prākāras*, enclosed by a wall with an entrance gateway. Inside the enclosure were eight sub-shrines, which were located around the main shrine but were not attached to it.[102] These were normally dedicated to Sūrya, Saptamātṛkā, Gaṇeśa, Subrahmaṇya, Jyēṣṭhā, Candra, Caṇḍeśvara and Durgā.[103] In the lists provided in the prescriptive texts *Kāśyapa Śilpa* and *Mayamata,* Vṛṣabha, Gaṇeśa, Saptamātṛkā and Subrahmaṇya are common. In addition, the former mentions Agni, Durgā, Jyēṣṭhā and Viṣṇu/Kātyāyinī/ Sūrya, and the latter enumerates Brahmā, Āryan, Acyuta and Caṇḍeśa.

D.D. Kosambi examines the conceptualization of the Mothers or the *Aṭṭakas* (*Aṣṭakas*), and suggests their origins in a pre-agrarian, hunting-gathering society, with a consanguineous family structure.[104] Here, the assumption is that in the hunting-gathering societies, power was conceptualized as dangerous and unharnessed. 'The food gatherer worshipped a goddess, while the god first appeared on the scene with pastoral life. The marriage of these mother goddesses is a phenomenon of the later conjoint society. . . .'[105] To begin with, the goddesses were unmarried mothers because no father seemed necessary to the society in which they originated. In other myths related to funerary rites and the male deity, Skanda's six mothers, Kosambi reiterates this position that the earliest conceptualization of the sacred was as feminine and dangerous, and very often as a collectivity of divine 'mothers'.[106]

According to K.V. Soundararajan, the concept of the subsidiary shrine was a pre-Agamic, early Pāṇḍya innovation.[107] There are numerous examples of the ninth and early tenth-century shrines to substantiate this assumption. In some cases, the evidence is assumed on the basis of the sculptures available.[108] It is to be kept in mind that this is the region that is sung of in the Sangam text, *Patiṟṟupattu*, as the home of the goddess of war and victory.[109] Was this tradition amalgamated into the worship of the seven sisters, known from the Puranic pantheon? It is extremely significant that our evidence for the Saptamātṛkā within the Śaiva temple does not appear in the post-eleventh-century period, while there are about twenty references to them in the period before this. This is striking given that the tradition already seems to have been in existence, as seen from the early Pāṇḍya temples, and as, subsequently, the Āgamas themselves recommend the construction of these shrines. It may imply the complete marginalization of the tradition of worshipping these mother goddesses, either due to the transference of their protective and maternal attributes to the consort of Śiva, who was now provided space within the temple, or because the Brahmanical religion had made sufficient inroads into the Tamil cultural landscape so that it became unnecessary for it to continue to try to accommodate local cults and deities by associating them with the seven mothers known in the Puranic tradition.

The names of the goddesses who are mentioned as consecrated in structural shrines are significant here. The name that recurs most often is Piṭāri, which we read as an epithet for the local, independent goddess. While it is among the village goddesses that we come across this name today,[110] it is uncertain whether all these deities referred to as Piṭāri necessarily had an early origin.[111] We are also not in agreement with the epigraphist, K.G. Krishnan's view that the term referred to Pārvatī.[112] From the evidence, it appears that across the Tañjāvūr, Tiruchirapalli and Chengalpet regions, Piṭāri/Kāla-Paṭāriyār was used either for an independent goddess or for the Saptamātṛkā.[113] It is our contention that these independent, local goddesses were gradually subsumed under the category of the spouse goddess, Umā-Pārvatī, which explains their absence from inscriptional records from the middle of the eleventh century CE. In other words, while Piṭāri is not an indigenous descriptive term, it is a generic Sanskrit descriptive category used in early medieval inscriptions to signify a variety of local goddesses encountered in the course of their accommodation within the Brahmanical religion.

Interestingly, the secondary meanings of Piṭāri denote a snake charmer/catcher (indicating their association with Śiva perhaps), and a member of the Kurava tribe, who were said to live in hilly regions (*kuriñci tiṇai*) in the *Sangam* literature.[114] Keeping these meanings as well, the clear indication is that this was a goddess (or various goddesses) who may have been associated with snake worship, and/or as the patron of the Kurava tribe.[115] What is equally essential to note is that, at the village level today, these goddesses are treated primarily as independent deities, and their marriage myths clearly indicate an attempt at subjugation, which is repulsed by the goddess herself.[116]

There are two goddesses referred to as Ēṟṟukuṉṟanar Paṭāri and Piṭāri Iṭaimalai Naṅkai, respectively. The first term indicates, literally, the 'taking on' by the goddess of perhaps the welfare of the local populace. The second shows two usages for local goddesses being clubbed together. The goddesses variously referred to as Naṅkai, also indicate local cultic importance. The epithet, in our opinion, seems to refer to a conceptualization of a beneficent indigenous goddess, whose propitiation ensured fertility of the land and abundance of water, both necessary ingredients for the prosperity of a settlement. This explains why many of them are Ēri Naṅkai, Ūruṭaiya Cuṉaimēn Naṅkai or Malai Naṅkai, suggesting that she overlooked the settlement from her abode near water bodies and on top of hills. The reference to Kōnērinaṅkai—the benevolent goddess of the tank/lake, with the *kō* prefix, hints at a royal connection with the water source. The term *cuṉai* is conventionally understood as referring to a mountain pool or spring, a tank, reservoir or a pasture ground with tanks and shady trees.[117] This name Cuṉaimēn Naṅkai, thus, appears to refer to a benevolent goddess, propitiated for water and agriculture.

We have references to Mūkkārai Naṅkai and Cāttanūr Naṅkai, associating the goddess with a community or place. *Mūkkārai* may refer to a place where a wild botanical species called hogweed is found.[118] There is also the derivation *Mūkkar*, which means low, vulgar people, according to the Tamil lexicon.[119] Could this be a reference to the goddess of a pastoral community whose animals fed on a pasture of hogweed? Pastoralism may have been looked down upon with the gradual spread of an agrarian society and, hence, the allusion to low and vulgar people in common usage. The term Piṭāri Iṭaimalai Naṅkai is very significant as it suggests that the goddess was the patron of the hills, which were the pasturelands of the shepherds (*iṭaiyar*). The South Arcot district was primarily a dry-wet zone and hence, pastoralism would have been an important occupation in this region.[120]

From the evidence gathered here, we observe that about fifty shrines were dedicated to independent goddesses during the early medieval period (the sixth to the thirteenth centuries). Our evidence also clearly shows that more than 80 per cent of them belonged to the first five centuries of the early medieval period (the sixth to tenth centuries). Another striking feature is that the generic epithets, Piṭāri or Naṅkai, are used in about 90 per cent of cases. These independent goddess shrines can further be classified as those to a single deity and those to group of goddesses, the 'seven mothers'. Durgā is often followed by the epithet Piṭāri, and there is no doubt that she was associated with Śiva, both in her mythology and by her inclusion in the iconographic plan of the Śaiva temple.[121] However, the early conceptualizations of this deity show a strong connection with Viṣṇu as well, and this is seen in her retention in the visual imagery of the conch and discus—the attributes of Viṣṇu. The Saptamātṛkā were clearly conceived of as mother goddesses, but our inscriptional evidence also clearly points to their veneration as independent deities.

This study is significant on two counts. It shows a clear periodization in the construction of shrines to independent goddesses. These were built from the seventh-century onwards even as shrines to the great gods of the Puranic sectarian traditions were constructed. However, this temple-building activity for independent goddesses appeared to have lost momentum in the later Cōḷa period. Second, there was considerable royal initiative in the building and maintenance of these shrines, and many boast of extensive and uninterrupted gifts.[122] It appears that goddesses associated with localities and communities were already accommodated, symbolically, in the Brahmanical structure because they were mostly represented as one of the mothers in the Saptamātṛkā group. As far as temple style is concerned, goddess temples to the Piṭāri and Saptamātṛkā may have originally resembled the hut-shaped and wagon-roofed *rathas*, respectively. The latter was convenient to accommodate the seven figures of the mother goddesses.[123] The significant feature of these temples is that the Saptamātṛkā, even when incorporated within the Śiva temple, were given a *separate structural space*.

In the final analysis, it appears that early small structural temples to independent goddesses were incorporated through the innovation of architectural structures such as subsidiary shrines within Śiva temples in a period characterized by the growth of state power. The goddesses were accommodated from the Brahmanical viewpoint, but there is enough ethnographic evidence to show that they retained their own space symbolically and ritually in the cultural life of the Tamil people, as seen from their continued worship at local and regional levels. This accommodation can be seen in political terms as reflecting the attempts of the state to absorb local and regional elements in the course of its expansion in the Pallava-Pāṇḍya and Cōḷa periods. In cultural terms, it reflects the spread of Brahmanical religious ideas and practices into different parts of the Tamil region. In social and religious terms, such an accommodation suggests assertions made by Brahmanical patriarchy that independent female deities needed to be brought within the protective environs of the Śiva temple, projecting the subservient status of these cults to that of Śiva.

NOTES

1. See John Stratton Hawley, 'Preface', in John Stratton Hawley and Donna Marie Wulff, eds., *The Divine Consort Radha and the Goddesses of India*, Delhi: Motilal Banarsidass, 1984, pp. xiv-xv.

2. See R. Mahalakshmi, 'Scrutinizing Goddesses, Interrogating Religious Traditions: Some Methodological Issues', in *University of Kelaniya Journal of Humanities and Social Sciences*, forthcoming.
3. R.S. Sharma, *Perspectives in Social and Economic History*, Delhi: Munshiram Manoharlal, 1995 (1983), p. 25.
4. R. Mahalakshmi, 'The Making of the Goddess Koṟṟavai-Durgā in the Tamil Śaiva Tradition, *c.* 300 BC to AD 1300', unpublished PhD thesis, Delhi: Centre for Historical Studies, Jawaharlal Nehru University, 2006.
5. M.G.S. Narayanan and Kesavan Veluthat, 'Bhakti Movement in South India', in S.C. Malik, ed., *Indian Movements: Some Aspects of Dissent, Protest and Reform*, Shimla: Indian Institute of Advanced Study, 1978, pp. 45-6.
6. Ibid., p. 46.
7. Ibid., p. 40.
8. Ibid., p. 41.
9. R. Champakalakshmi, *Trade, Ideology and Urbanization South India 300 BC to AD 1300*, Delhi: Oxford University Press, 1996, p. 38.
10. R. Champakalakshmi, 'State and Economy: South India, Circa AD 400-1300', in Romila Thapar, ed., *Recent Perspectives of Early Indian History*, Bombay: Popular Prakashan, 1996, pp. 281-3.
11. Ibid., pp. 296-301.
12. Sangam literature refers to a collection of texts that, according to legendary accounts, were composed by a fantastic number of gods, sages and poets. Historical linguistic studies have revealed that some of these texts were most likely to have been compiled between *c.*300 BCE and CE 300, while others in this corpus can be dated to a later period termed post-Sangam (*c.* CE 300-800). See Kamil V. Zvelebil, *Tamil Literature*, Leiden: E.J. Brill, 1973.
13. K.R. Srinivasan, *Temples of South India*, Delhi: National Book Trust, 1972, p. 17.
14. The *tiṇai* was a term used to denote physiographic zones in the Tamil region. There were five such eco-zones: the sea shore (*neital*), hills (*kuṟiñci*), river valleys (*marutam*), brushland (*mullai*) and dry, arid tracts (*pālai*). The last was apparently formed due to the scorching of the hills and brushlands.
15. K.R. Srinivasan, *Some Aspects of Religion as Revealed by Early Monuments and Literature of the South*, Madras: University of Madras, 1960, pp. 5-6.
16. Srinivasan, op. cit., 1972, pp. 33-8.
17. This is an important symbol of the nature of integration and syncretism evident in the Tamil region. As I have tried to show, the association of Koṟṟavai with Umā and of Muṟukaṉ with Skanda was occurring

simultaneously in the hymns of the bhakti saints, while Koṟṟavai was herself known as the mother of Muṟukaṉ in later Sangam texts. R. Mahalakshmi, op. cit., 2006, Chapter one.

18. Ibid., pp. 45-6.
19. Ibid., pp. 98-9.
20. See Cynthia Talbot, *Precolonial India in Practice: Society, Region and Identity in Medieval Andhra*, Delhi: Oxford University Press, 2001, Chapters 2-4; Burton Stein, *Peasant State and Society*, Delhi: Oxford University Press, 1994 (1980), pp. 63-5; and James Heitzman, *Gifts of Power*, Delhi: Oxford University Press, 1997, pp. 121-2, 139-40.
21. Cited in S.R. Balasubrahmanyam, *Early Chola Temples*, Madras: Mudgala Trust, 1971, p. 261.
22. George W. Spencer, 'The Sacred Geography of the Tamil Shaivite Hymns', in *Numen*, 17, 1970, pp. 232-44.
23. See R. Mahalakshmi, 'Outside the Norm, Within the Tradition: Kāraikkāl Ammaiyār and the Ideology of Tamil *Bhakti*', in *Studies in History*, vol. 16, no. 1, pp. 33-5.
24. S.R. Balasubrahmanyam, *Later Chola Temples*, Chennai: Mudgala Trust, 1979, p. 119.
25. See for example, the myths around the Śvētarānyēsvarar temple in Tiruvenkadu (Tj), which sees the destruction of the *asura* Maruttuvan by Śiva in the form of Aghoreśvara. See S.R. Balasubrahmanyam, *Later Chola Temples* (Supplement), Chennai: Mudgala Trust, 1979, p. 414. Also, for many such examples see David Dean Shulman, *Tamil Temple Myths, Sacrifice and Divine Marriage in the South Indian Saiva Tradition*, Princeton: Princeton University Press, 1980.
26. Heroic Exploits of Siva:

Place	Exploit	Details
1. Tiruvadigai	*Tripurāntakam*	Destruction of the three flying forts of the three *asura* brothers
2. Tirukkaṇḍiyūr	*Brahmakapālam*	Cutting off the fifth head of Brahma for lying
3. Tirupariyalur	*Dakṣavadham*	Cutting off the head of Dakṣa, after destroying his sacrifice
4. Tiruvirkkudi	*Jālandharavadham*	The overthrow of the demon Jālandhara
5. Valuvur	*Gajāsuravadham*	The overthrow of Gajāsura, the demon who took the form of an elephant
6. Tirukkoyilūr	*Andhakāsuravadham*	The overthrow of Andhakāsura
7. Tirukkuruhai	*Kāmāntakam*	The burning of Kāma
8. Tirukkaḍavūr	*Kālāntakam*	The overthrow of Yama

27. The *pañcapūta talam* were those where the *liṅga* was associated with the five elements: Kalahasti with *vāyu* or wind; Chidambaram with *ākāśa* or sky; Tiruvannamalai with *agni* or fire; Tiruvanmiyur with *āpu* or water; and Tiruvarur with *pṛthvī* or earth.
28. The *sapta viṭaṅka kṣētram* referred to those sites associated with Śiva as Tyāgarajā: Tiruvarur, Tirunagaikaronam, Tirukkaravasal, Tirukkuvalai, Vedaranyam, Tirunallaru and Tiruvaymur. See, Rajeshwari Ghose, *The Lord of Ārūr: The Tyāgarājā Cult in Tamilnādu*, Delhi: Motilal Banarsidass, 1996), p. 57.
29. Y. Subbarayulu, *Political Geography of the Cōḷa Country*, Madras: Tamilnadu State Department of Archaeology, 1973, p. 83. Burton Stein, op. cit., 1994 (1980), pp. 91-2.
30. Ibid.; James Heitzman, op. cit., 1997, pp. 29, 98.
31. Ibid., p. 87.
32. Nilakanta Sastri, *The Cōḷas*, 2 vols., Madras: University of Madras, 1935 and 1937, pp. 114-15.
33. *Epigraphia Indica*, vol. 13, no. 10, Calcutta/Delhi: Government Publications, pp. 134-49. Also see *Annual Report on Epigraphy* (hereafter, *ARE*), Madras: Government Publications, 1899, nos. 10, 11, 12, 13, 16, p. 23; paras 16, 17, 22, pp. 4-6.
34. See K.G. Krishnan, 'The Muttaraiyar', in *Studies in South Indian History and Epigraphy*, Madras: New Era Publishers, 1981, p. 154, fn. 58. Krishnan disagrees with him and sees this as merely a Sanskritized form of Bhaṭṭārakī [*sic*], an epithet used for the spouse of Śiva.
35. K.V. Subrahmanya Aiyer, 'Sendalai Pillar Inscriptions', in *Epigraphia Indica*, vol. 13, no. 10, p. 135.
36. M. Monier-Williams, *Sanskrit English Dictionary*, Delhi: Munshiram Manoharlal, 1999 (1872), p. 745: 'Bhaṭṭārikā: noble lady, tutelary deity, N. of Durgā'.
37. See, for example, Ranjan Anand, 'Social and Cultural History of Uttarākhaṇḍa (Kumaon and Garhwal), From *c.* AD 600-1300', unpublished PhD thesis, Delhi: Centre for Historical Studies, Jawaharlal Nehru University, 1997, p. 42: A goddess is referred to as 'Durgā Bhattārikā of Harṣapura'.
38. Rev. Henry Whitehead, *The Village Gods of South India*, Delhi: Asian Educational Services, 1999 (1930), pp. 91, 94, 103, 108 and so on.
39. *ARE* (1910), no. 704; *ARE* (1909), no. 705; *ARE* (1909), no. 706.
40. *ARE* (1909), no. 706.
41. *ARE* (1903), no. 345.
42. *ARE* (1903), no. 345; *ARE* (1903), no. 346; *ARE* (1903), no. 347.

43. See T. Burrow and M.B. Emeneau, *Dravidian Etymological Dictionary* (from now onwards *DED*), 2nd edn., Oxford: Clarendon Press, 1984, 3610.
44. *ARE* (1938-9), no. 287.
45. *ARE* (1941-2), no. 86; *ARE* (1941-2), part ii, para 23.
46. *ARE* (1941-2), no. 87; *ARE* (1941-2), no. 85; *ARE* (1941-2), no. 84.
47. *ARE* (1902), no. 426.
48. *ARE* (1938-9), no. 238; *ARE* (1938-9), part ii, para 20.
49. The significance of this name will be discussed later in the context of sacred spaces prescribed for different deities.
50. *ARE* (1896), no. 12. This is because the foundation inscription slab has been built into the roof and not the base, as is normally the case.
51. *ARE* (1893), no. 23.
52. *South Indian Inscriptions*, Madras: Archaeological Survey of India, 1890, vol. 1, no. 64.
53. *ARE* (1887), no. 56; *ARE* (1939-40), no. 208.
54. *ARE* (1925-6), no. 477. Paṭāriyār is the plural or honorific of Paṭāri/Piṭāri.
55. *ARE* (1939-40), no. 155.
56. *ARE* (1939-40), no. 154.
57. *ARE* (1915), no. 249.
58. We are not sure if this is an honorific or is in the plural as there is no other corroborative evidence. In either case, our purpose is to document the existence of shrines for independent goddesses here.
59. *ARE* (1916), no. 283.
60. Ibid., part ii, paras 23, 87, *ARE* (1937-8), no. 469.
61. See James Heitzman (1997), op. cit., p. 34 for an association of the South Arcot region with pastoralism.
62. S.R. Balasubrahmanyam (1971), op. cit., p. 82.
63. *ARE* (1906), no. 177.
64. *ARE* (1913), no. 312.
65. See R. Mahalakshmi, 2006, op. cit., Chapter Five, pp. 495-504.
66. *ARE* (1947-8), no. 83.
67. *ARE* (1923), no. 60; *ARE* (1923), no. 61; *ARE* (1923), no. 62.
68. *ARE* (1944-5), no. 25.
69. *ARE* (1921), no. 79.
70. The *parivāram* shrines were a group of eight that, according to architectural texts, had to be placed around the main shrine.
71. *ARE* (1955-6), no. 283.
72. *ARE* (1898), no. 58; *ARE* (1898), no. 59; *ARE* (1898), no. 60.
73. *ARE* (1898), no. 60.

74. *ARE* (1942-3), no. 174.
75. *ARE* (1911), no. 317.
76. See, for instance, the Kolar grants of the Cōḷas in Karnataka, which refers to both Cāmuṇḍā and Piṭāriyār. *Epigraphia Carnatica*, X (hereafter *EC*), Bangalore, 1905), KC 106b; KC 106a, 112; KC 112a, 111.
77. *ARE* (1911), no. 316.
78. *South Indian Inscriptions*, vol. 3, part iii, no. 159.
79. This is reminiscent of the goddess at Ilupuru, Ēri Naṅkai. See, *South Indian Inscriptions*, vol. 3, parts iii and iv, no. 172.
80. *ARE* (1931), no. 220.
81. See, *ARE* (1923), no. 51.
82. *ARE* (1947-8), no. 80; *ARE* (1947-8), no. 81.
83. *ARE* (1947-8), no. 81.
84. *ARE* (1922), no. 262.
85. *ARE* (1919), no. 207.
86. T.V. Mahalingam, ed., *A Topographical List of Inscriptions in the Tamil Nadu and Kerala States* (hereafter *TLI*), Delhi: ICHR, 1985, Cb-343; *ARE* (1920), no. 158.
87. *ARE* (1926), no. 481.
88. *TLI*, Dh-218.
89. *ARE* (1901), no. 348.
90. *ARE* (1913), no. 5.
91. *ARE* (1907), no. 439; *ARE* (1907), no. 432.
92. *ARE* (1908), no. 37.
93. *ARE* (1904), no. 359.
94. *ARE* (1896), no. 108.
95. *EC*, X, KC, 106 b.
96. *EC*, X, KC, 106 b, 106 a, 112, 112 a, 111, 115, 109 a, 112 b, 107; *ARE* (1892), no. 131.
97. *EC* IV, CN 88, 83, 84.
98. T.A. Gopinatha Rao, *Elements of Hindu Iconography*, Delhi: Motilal Banarsidass, 1968 (1914), vol. 1, part 2, pp. 380-1.
99. Ibid., p. 381.
100. J.N. Banerjea, *The Development of Hindu Iconography*, Delhi: Munshiram Manoharlal, 1984, p. 504.
101. Balasubrahmanyam, 1971, op. cit., pp. 327-9.
102. Ibid., p. 327.
103. Ibid., pp. 328-9.
104. The term 'consanguine family' is used in the sense developed by Morgan, as cited in Engels. See, Frederick Engels, 'The Origin of the

Family, Private Property and the State', in Karl Marx and Frederick Engels, *Selected Works*, Moscow: Progress Publishers, 1969-70, vol. 3, p. 216.

105. D.D. Kosambi, *Myth and Reality*, Delhi: Popular Prakashan, 1994 (1962), p. 86.
106. Ibid., Chapter 3: 'At the Crossroad: A Study of Mother-Goddess Cult Site', pp. 87-109.
107. K.V. Soundararajan, 'Early Pandya, Muttarayar and Irukkuvel Architecture', in Pramod Chandra, ed., *Studies in Indian Temple Architecture*, American Institute of Indian Studies, 1975, pp. 252, 259, 278-81.
108. See, the Pallava Kailāśanātha temple in Kāñcīpuram, the Virattanesvara temple at Tiruttani, the Muttarayar Bhumishvara temple at Viralur (Tiruchirapalli), the Othanavanesvarar temple at Tirusatturai (Tañjāvūr), the late Pāṇḍya temples of Nelliapparcuvamin at Tirunelveli, the Śiva temple at Tirukkattalai (Tiruchirapalli), the early Cōḷa Śiva temple in Tiruppalaturai (Tiruchirapalli district), and the Mucukuṇḍeśvaram temple at Koḍumbāḷūr (Tiruchirapalli).
109. R. Mahalakshmi, 2006, op. cit., Chapter One.
110. See *Madras Tamil Lexicon*, Madras: University of Madras, 1924-1930, vol. 5, p. 2652: *piṭāri*—a village goddess.
111. The case of Maleramma from the Bangalore region, the protector against malaria, is well known in south India.
112. Krishnan, 1981, op. cit., p. 154, fn. 58.
113. Subrahmanya Aiyer, the editor of an early Tamil inscription where this term occurs, sees Piṭāri as being used indiscriminately for Aryan and village deities. See *Epigraphia Indica*, vol. 13, no. 10, p. 135.
114. See, *Madras Tamil Lexicon, 1924-1930*, op. cit., vol. 5, p. 2652, '*piṭāran*'—(1) snake-catcher; (2) doctor; (3) man of the Kurava caste. For *kuravan*, see *Madras Tamil Lexicon*, op. cit., vol. 2, p. 1046.
115. While the goddess Ko<u>r</u>ravai was associated with tribes in the *pālai* region, we have to keep in mind that *pālai* was not considered a natural physiographic zone. It was formed when the *kuriñci* and *mullai* tracts experienced a severe drought.
116. Rev. Henry Whitehead, op. cit., pp. 103, 104, 108. Also see the chapter on folklore in this book for myths relating to local goddesses in pp. 112-38.
117. *DED*, 2717. See also *Madras Tamil Lexicon*, op. cit., vol. 3, p. 1554: *cunai* (3)—mountain pool or spring, tank, reservoir, pasture ground with shady trees.
118. See, *Madras Tamil Lexicon, 1924-1930*, op. cit., vol. 6, p. 3312: *mūkkirattai* = *mūkku* + *irattai*—spreading hogweed.

119. See ibid., p. 3311.
120. See Heitzman, 1997, op. cit., p. 34.
121. The Āgamas accord her the northern quarter in the temple layout. See R. Mahalakshmi, 2006, op. cit., p. 463. In this context, the reference to *Vaṭapālam Āṇṭāḷ*, mentioned earlier, is significant.
122. See ibid., Chapter 3, Section II, pp. 235-65.
123. K.V. Soundararajan, 1924-30, op. cit., pp. 252-8.

SIX

Rādhā and Radhaism
Neutralizing Gender in *Brajmaya* Krsnaism of Medieval Braj

Farhat Nasreen

> The nature of ladies is quite unstable and the mind of ladies cannot be read properly by *yogīs*, *siddhas*, *tapasvīs* who have controlled their senses and anger. A woman is the cause of illusion and a bundle of passions. Brahma had in earlier times created her to establish victory over Kāmadeva. She happens to be the door to *mokṣa* and an obstruction in the adoration of the Lord . . . her life is a vase of nectar with poison plastered on the neck of it.
>
> *Brahmavaivartta Purāṇa*[1]

In the context of *Brajmaya* Krsnaism, a study of Radhaism is exigent. In the midst of the medieval Krsnaite revolution in the Braj region, Rādhā's theology gained approval, and it is Radhaism and the popularity of Rādhā which makes Kṛṣṇa worship of this region unique. The Braj region is an area of 84 leagues which, according to conventional persuasion, was called Braj Mandal. Its centre was Mathura, which was also called Surasena Pradesh in early times. A medieval text, *Braj Bhakti Vilās*, states that the Braj region's eastern boundary is along Hasyavan, i.e. Barhad village in Aligarh, western, along Uphārvan, i.e. Gurgaon in Haryana, southern, Jambhuvan, i.e. Batesar village near Agra and northern, Bhuvanvan/Bhushanvan, in Shergarh, in Mathura. Radhaism is the defining characteristic of *Brajmaya* Krsnaism.

Phenotypically, Rādhā, the goddess, and Radhaism, the attitude, can be branched as distinguishable abstractions. *Brajmaya*

Krsnaism celebrates love as its guiding principle and, within this, feminine emotionalism could not have been better underlined. Rādhā is perceived of as a soul in love with Kṛṣṇa and the imagery used to convey the idea is typically defiant of established social principles. In fact, this defiance is overplayed by some sects of *Brajmaya* Krsnaism. But Radhaism is not as self-willed. There is a conscious attempt to ensure that the model of Rādhā as a *parakīyā* (unmarried or wed to another—not being one's lover's wife) is not to be emulated in real life. In keeping with pre-Rādhā traditions, advocates of Radhaism prescribe punishments for adulterers. Even though Rādhā is pictured as powerful enough to dominate Kṛṣṇa, her superiority does not translate easily into an equalization of gender among her devotees. In Radhaism, *bhaktas* may mentally act like *gopīs*, *sakhīs* or *mañjarīs* but their outlook towards gender issues in everyday life is another matter. Rādhā may appear aberrant and maverick, but attempts at maintaining the *status quo* are inbuilt in Radhaism. This work attempts to capture the growth of Rādhā, the goddess, and Radhaism, which, despite worshipping her passionately, tries to contain the influence of her panache in real life. An attempt is also made to analyse the philosophical interpretations and practical implications of the growth of Radhaism.

I

The Hindu attitude towards adultery varied from age to age and from place to place but, in general, lawgivers held it to be an offence. Manu tried to ensure the subservience of women. Many ancient legends preserve details of a polygamous society. The wife of Sage Dirghatamas is said to have had extra-marital relationships. Uddalaka, we learn, explained to his son, Śvetaketu, that the sharing of women was an ancient custom. In another context, however, Uddalaka insisted that a wife should not have a secret lover. The *Mahābhārata* relates that Pāṇḍu, due to a curse, asked his wife to seek another man for the sake of obtaining progeny. There are references to women having a *jara* or paramour, confirming the fact that illicit love was by no means unusual.[2] Kauṭilya's *Arthaśāstra* permitted wives to contract temporary unions in the event of the prolonged absence of their husbands. Muladeva, the authority on *Kāmaśāstra*, wrote an entire treatise on the art of stealing other men's wives. The *Kāmasūtra* of Vātsyāyana has a section on the technique of seducing married women.[3] However, according to Manu, the punishment for an adulterous pair was death by torture. He ordained that a woman guilty of adultery be sentenced to be devoured by dogs, and death in some form was the prescribed punishment, to be executed by the husband. If he did not choose this extreme step, her head was to be shaved and she was to be made to ride through the streets mounted on a donkey, with her face turned towards the tail, or she had to stand up in a public place with a basket of ordure on her head. In some cases, her nose and ears were to be cut-off and she was to be subsequently banished from the village.[4] The Purāṇas also took a similar type of stance. For an adulteress, the punishment after death was the insertion of a heated iron cylinder in her vagina. In life, her punishment was that her hair was to be shorn off, her nose and ears cut, and she was to be driven out of the locality. She was further excommunicated from her *gotra*.[5] The *Liṅga Purāṇa* condemns sex with another's wife.[6] The *Brahma Purāṇa* says that sex with another's wife renders a man blind. Utathya drank up all the water on the surface of the earth to punish Varuṇa who had abducted his wife, Bhadra. Later on, Utathya's blind son, Dīrghatamas, was betrayed by his wife, Pradveśī, and he ordained that every woman was to be subject to her husband and should have only one husband, dead or alive. Śvetaketu, son of Uddālaka, is also said to have advocated the rule of the wife's unconditional fidelity to her husband. In a ritual, the wife was required to publicly confess the names of her lovers and, if she lied, Varuṇa was to punish her.[7]

In the Krsnaite legend, Yayāti married Devayāṇī, who later became the mother of Yadu, the ancestor of the Yadava tribe. Yayāti fell to the charms of Śarmiṣṭhā, a friend of Devayāṇī, and was cursed by his father-in-law that he would age prematurely. However, his youngest son, Puru, exchanged his youth with his father's old age. After a thousand years, Yayāti realized the futility of physical pleasures and died by voluntary starvation after returning his son's youth. If this tradition is analysed in the context of the social conjecture on adultery, the man, Yayāti, is punished for his adulterous relationship. So, finally, *Kāma* (sexual desire) did lose the race to austerity and denunciation.[8]

One of the fundamental scriptures of *Brajmaya* Krsnaism is the *Bhāgavata Purāṇa*. In the *Rāspañcādhyāyī* of the *Bhāgavata*, one finds an imagery of the *gopīs* leaving their husbands and families for the sake of meeting Kṛṣṇa.[9] Interestingly, the act is glorified as a religious action. This theme constitutes the ideological configuration of many *Brajmaya* Krsnaite sects.[10] However, medieval presentations of the *Rāspañcādhyāyī* were imbibed with a new inspiration which came from the growth of Radhaism. Pica Maria Pauwels has made insightful observations about the deliberate portrayal of Rādhā and the *gopīs* as figures boldly defying social norms. Hari Ram, the author of the *Rāspañcādhyāyī*, applauds the *gopīs*' act of leaving their husbands and children to join Kṛṣṇa in the *Rās*. For example, he says: 'Boiling milk was not taken off, cooked porridge was flung in the hearth, men were left in the midst of their meals. Children taken down from the breast and abandoned; care for the husband was totally neglected and their own food left aside untouched. Forgotten were their oil massages and toilet. Yet fortunate women they were; they had found the essence of life. One should sing in praise of the lovers of the round dance'.[11] The male relatives of *gopīs*' are called givers of sorrow.[12] In fact, if the *Rāspañcādhyāyī* of Hari Ram is compared to the works of Vallabhacharya and Nandadas on the same theme, one would find that Hari Ram treats the subject most boldly.[13] In the *Bhāgavata*, Kṛṣṇa flattered the *gopīs* by calling them *sumadhyamah* and *mahābhāgya*. It is ironic because married women keeping a tryst are being called lucky and the 'luck' of the women lies in coming to meet Kṛṣṇa.[14] At the same time, in the *Bhāgavata*, there are questions and answers between Rājā Parīkṣit and Sukadeva which justify the *gopīs*' actions in the conventional contexts.[15] Vallabhacharya, too, emphasizes the supramundane character of the *gopīs*' love.[16] The *Bhāgavata* does voice social reservations in the form of King Parīkṣit's bewilderment at the behaviour of the *gopīs* and, as a justification, Kṛṣṇa is compared to the *puruṣa* (God) and the *gopīs* to his *śakti* (energy).[17] Further, it is insisted that the *gopīs* gave up their carnal bodies in order to unite with the spiritual self. In fact, the *gopīs* who did not manage to leave their houses to meet Kṛṣṇa had to be content with an embrace in meditation. Meditation was acknowledged, as religious means in the early imagery of *Rās* and *Mahārās*. In fact, *Rāslīlā* was compared to a child's play with a mirror, implying whereby that the *gopīs* and Kṛṣṇa are ultimately one.[18] Hari Ram, in his *Rāspañcādhyāyī*, underplays metaphors and ignores theological justifications to highlight the illegitimate behaviour of the *gopīs* from the orthodox point of view. He repeatedly emphasizes their renunciation of social values to participate in the *rās*.[19] There is a proud stress on their defiance. For instance, in a verse, Hari Ram states that the *gopīs* threw porridge in the oven. This was a deliberate act of destruction.[20] However, the *gopīs* in the *Bhāgavata* simply forgot to take it off the fire. They even offended their relations and neglected the family honour.[21] The choice exercised by the *gopīs* was not just between god and society but between god and family. The example of a breast-fed child being left aside is a notable one.[22] Ironically, Hari Ram compares the *gopīs*' love for Kṛṣṇa with a wife's love for her husband. He has mentioned mothers among the people looking for the *gopīs*.[23] The *Bhāgavata* also mentions them but the emphasis on the emotions becomes pronounced later. [24] Instead of begging Kṛṣṇa to pay heed, as they did in the *Bhāgavata*, the *gopīs* of the *Rāspañcādhyāyī* demand his attention. There is no clear account of Rādhā in the *Bhāgavata*, but, in the later *Rāspañcādhyāyī*, she dominates the *Mahārās* and *Raslīlā*.[25] In the *Bhāgavata* Kṛṣṇa shares his chewed betel leaves with the *gopīs*.[26] But, in Hari Ram's version, only Rādhā and Kṛṣṇa savour each other's chewed betel.[27] The *gopīs* of the *Bhāgavata* merely left their houses but those of Hari Ram came despite opposition from their family.[28]

It is important to note that despite drawing an imagery that is antithetical to the usual socio-cultural norms, Hari Ram had also not completely done away with the classical role model of a wife as suggested in the *Bhāgavata*. He repeated that husbands should not be deserted whatsoever and infidelity on the part of the wife would certainly drag her into hell.[29] The *gopīs' viraha* (separation), and Kṛṣṇa's *aiśvarya* (royal attributes) are replaced with *mādhurya* (love).[30] Yet in spite of their power over Kṛṣṇa, the *gopīs* call themselves weak women, lacking in wit just as they did in the *Bhāgavata*.[31] In the same manner, in some other works of *Brajmaya* Krsnaism, a perfect bhakta is compared to a perfect wife.[32]

In the Purāṇas, a married woman is ordained to serve her husband faithfully. Bathing with the water touched by the foot of the husband is supposedly equivalent to bathing in holy waters. In the *Brahmavaivartta Purāṇa*, the wife is advised to drink the water touched by the feet of her husband. She is also ordained to eat the food that remains after her husband has partaken of it. The husband is Brahma, Viṣṇu, Maheśa and *Nirguṇādhār Brahmarūp*. For a woman, her husband is *guru* and *devatā*, and no relation is dearer than him. Women who do not serve their husbands cannot earn any merit.[33] Those women who are rude to their husbands are thrown in a hell where huge snakes bite them day and night; they have to eat and drink excreta, blood and urine, and rods are inserted in their mouth. At another place, the text divides women into three categories, i.e. *uttama* (best), *madhyama* (medium) and *adharma* (worst). The first one is a bhakta of her husband and loyal to him of her own will. The second is loyal because elders and the society guard her, and the third is rude and has the tendency of fighting. She is disloyal and disrespectful towards her husband.[34] While speaking of the duties of a good wife, Kṛṣṇa is made to say that a beautiful woman gazing upon a good husband, regarding him as equal to nectar and greeting him early with a smile and affectionate devotion, is a chaste woman and redeems a thousand ancestors. The husband of a devoted wife is freed from all sins. The spouses of chaste women have not to endure the suffering of *karma* and with their wives, free of *karma*, they rejoice in the abode of Hari. The dust of the feet of chaste women at once purifies the earth. A man bowing to a loyal wife is released from sin. Gopal Bhatt Goswami in *Hari Bhakti Vilās* praises a *pativratā* woman who is devoted and loyal to her husband.[35] The

Brahmavaivartta says that a man who has an illicit relationship with a woman goes to *raurav* and *kumbhipāk* hell for innumerable years, thereafter he is born as a worm in the vagina of a diseased woman, then as an animal, followed by a birth as a *mallecha* and *śūdra*, until finally he gets purified. Adulterous woman, after staying in *raurav* hell for a long time, is born for seven lives as a *vidhvā* (widow), *asparśa* (untouchable), *jātihīna* (casteless) and *nakti* (noseless).[36] To maintain a rigid stand on social propriety in sexual matters, the Purāṇa states that a man who stares at a woman's neck, breast and face in a sensual manner would, in his next birth, be blind and impotent. Gopal Bhatt in *Hari Bhakti Vilās* affirms this view by saying that a man who falls in love with another's woman dies an early death and suffers in hell. In his next life, he is born as a boneless insect. An adulteress's love is destructive in both the *lokas* and so, wise men should be loyal to their wives. A go-between woman in an adulterous relationship stays for a hundred years in *kālasūtra* hell and, thereafter, is born as a lizard, deer, buffalo, bear, hippopotamus and fox. The same text says that a good wife should serve her husband with *bhakti bhāva*, should not argue with him, and should never get angry, she should give him well-cooked and clean food, and more love than what she would have given to a thousand sons. In fact, the importance of a *pativratā* is so much that she is said to be born only in those houses where men had been earning merit for a hundred years.[37]

In the *Brahmavaivartta* runs a thread of narrative that gives mythological, religious, and philosophical justification for the so-called 'amorous dalliance' of Kṛṣṇa with Rādhā and the *gopīs*. For example, the women who participated in the *rasmaṇḍal* were supposedly wives of the *saptarṣis* who were cursed to be born as humans because another *devatā* touched their bodies by mistake. They cried and pleaded their innocence. However, it was finally decreed that Śrī Hari by his *yogamāyā* (power of delusion) would make *chāyā mūrtis* (shadow images) of them, which would stay in the houses of some men in Braj. These apparently would be their husbands. After the blessing of Kṛṣṇa, they would come to Golok (Krsnaite heaven; a replica of Braj region) with him and join their real husbands. A comparable logic is formulated to justify the *cīrharaṇ līlā* of Kṛṣṇa.[38] Thus, it is obvious that despite an apparently permissible philosophy at the religious end, it was not meant to have any direct bearing on the practical lifestyle of the common man or the *bhaktas*. As illustrated, the *Brahmavaivartta*, one of the extensive canons of Radhaism, maintains the *status quo*. Yet, despite the favourable position granted to the husband, the Purāṇa also speaks in favour of the equality of husband and wife, which, it says, brings prosperity and peace and gives meaning to their life.[39]

A major medieval sect, the Gauḍīya Vaiṣṇavas, consider Rādhā a *parakīyā* (unmarried or wed to another) and they argue that *swakīyā* (legally married) or conjugal love is not intense enough. Rupa Goswami writes in the *Bhakti Rasamrita Sindhu* that *kāmānuga* (transcendental lust) is the highest path to bhakti. He has also specified that this love should be free of lust. Rādhā, the *gopīs* and the *sakhīs* did not desire physical sense gratification. In *Hari Bhakti Vilās*, it is stated that the chemistry of male-female attraction was only to be used as a paradigm to understand attraction, as a phenomenon to be applied to the relationship between divinity and the human soul. A prayer in this work is as follows: 'Just as a female is attracted to a male and a male to a female so may I feel attracted towards you (Kṛṣṇa)'.[40]

Notions of the Puṣṭī Mārgīs also seem to be the same. For example, in the *Haridās Khawas Sanodiya kī Vārtā*, the Goswami warns Haridas against two things; the misappropriation of funds and talking to another's woman in seclusion. In yet another case, when a *virakta* (ascetic) Vaiṣṇava became friendly with a woman and was getting defamed for it, Viṭhalnāth is reported to have made efforts to detach him from her. Thus, social defamation on account of adultery was unacceptable.[41] In the *Chaurāsī Pada* of Hit Harivanśa, the meeting of the *gopīs* with Kṛṣṇa is said to have destroyed lust rather than increasing it.[42]

In a work based on oral discussions held between scholars of Radhaism and Brajiya Krsnaism at Jai Singh ka Ghera in Vrindavan, the *parakīyā* issue was discussed. In the context of the practical implications of this philosophy, Shri Vatsa Goswami said:

. . . But what is the *parakīyā bhāv*? Some historians have argued that the Goswamis were having a high time in Vrindavan with their *parakīyā nāyīkās* and to justify that they had to float a theory. . . . But in itself if you see and if you go back into the history of the whole thing and of this relationship, the model presented to us is the model of Rādhā and Kṛṣṇa, it is a totally unorthodox model. Rādhā is *parākiyā*, *prauḍhā* and *paraudha* at the same time. . . . We have a very strange *nāyīkā* . . . *parakīyā bhāv* . . . here is a feeling, which may not fit into the conventional aesthetic categories established, by the *rāsa* theorists of the great Indian tradition or even the *Dharma-Śāstra* or the *Mokṣa-Śāstra*, traditions. But the question is of a feeling, a very authentic, very rich and very life-giving feeling. And that is the way I see the whole *bhakti* movement and also *bhakti* philosophy.[43]

I do agree with Shri Vatsa Goswami that the *parakīyā bhāv*, or the theories of *rāsmaṇḍal* or *rāslīlā,* could not have rested on the personal fancies of any individual Goswami; they were part of a larger ideological growth in the region and are revered till today by almost all sects of *Brajmaya* Krsnaism in one way or another. Besides, the theory of *nāyak-nāyīkā* relations was definitely not new because it dates back at lcast to the *Bhāgavata*, which itself clearly stated that the purpose of *rāslīlā* was the redemption of souls and not sexual gratification.[44] When Rādhā is conceived of as a symbol of the human soul, the question of her marital status is significant because her love serves as a model for all men, but when she is regarded as a goddess, this question, in some ways, becomes less crucial because goddesses are too exalted to be role models. Some theologians of Brajiya Krsnaism tried to divide the theory of Rādhā and the practise of Radhaism into neat compartments. The goddess may be a defiant divine, but her *bhaktas* were expected to confirm to the usual social regulations in their daily lives.

II

In medieval Braj, at least three major sects were set to experience the emotions of the *gopīs* and *sakhīs* towards Kṛṣṇa and Rādhā in order to achieve true bhakti. In an account of Mirabai in the *Bhaktamata* and *Bhakti Rās Bodhīni Ṭīkā*, it is stated that during her visit to Vrindavan, Jiva Goswami refused to meet her on the pretext that she was a woman, but when she sent word to him, saying that she had thought that Kṛṣṇa was the only 'man' in the Braj region and all the rest were females (*Vrindavan ki swāminī Śrī Rādhā sukumārī param puruṣa Śrī Kṛṣṇa ek aur sakal hain nārī*), the Goswami granted her an audience.[45] It is to be noted that Jiva Goswami belonged to a sect in which *Rāgānuga bhakti*, and *Mañjarī Bhāv* were held in great esteem.[46] In *Bhaktirasamritsindhu*, Rupa Goswami states that the highest level of bhakti is *kāmānuga*, which is the path of the *gopīs* and this topmost path is facilitated by those in *mañjarī bhāv* (*mañjarī bhāv* is feeling like a teenage friend and associate of Rādhā).[47] The Gaudiya school of Rupa and Jiva wanted to limit this imitation of feminity to the meditative level, thus the *Rāgānuga bhakti* did not require bhaktas to physically dress up as women. Nevertheless, there emerged groups of Prakaṭya Sahajiyas who were keen on making a physical show of the psychological phenomenon of bhakti.[48] In the *Bhakti Sandarbh*, Jiva had indirectly mentioned such groups while speaking of the distinction in types of *rāgānuga bhakti*/*bhaktas* and said that it was the *gurus*' call to ascertain a disciple's *siddha rūpa*, i.e. his perfected form in the spiritual world.[49] The mental *sādhanā* of *Rāgānuga bhakti* chiefly involves a meditative technique called *līlā smaraṇa*, i.e. remembering/ visualizing a *līlā*. June McDaniel, in her work wrote that the Vaiṣṇava *gurus* specialize in teaching such visualization.[50] Dr. Srinivas of the Guval Foundation, Vrindavan, affirmed that diagrams of *līlā smaraṇa* were, in fact, maintained, in which humans were personified as petals of flowers, usually lotuses.[51] The innermost core had Rādhā and Kṛṣṇa, whom the bhakta was supposed to visualize as the centre of his being and also the centre of the universe. The petals were then named. Closest to the core were the eight *sakhīs* and eight *sakhās*, and so on and so forth, and the disciple was allotted a position in the flower diagram. Speaking in the same context, Srinivas said that, in this kind of meditation, he 'acted' as a *gopī*, a female, but he or the members of his institute did not copy the physical ways of females. In fact, the subject of Gaudiya Vaiṣṇavas dressing up as *gopīs* was laid to rest by Visvanath Chakravarti in the seventeenth century. He defeated the ideas of Rupa Kaviraj, saying that the 'practitioner body' should behave as an ascetic (male), while the internal 'meditative body' may emulate a *mañjarī*.[52] Yet the Caitanyaite traditions record the accounts of one 'Jangal Priya' or 'Jangali', a bhakta whose sexual identity could not be deciphered. It is stated in the *Premvilās* that Sita Thakurani, wife of Advaita, had a woman disciple called Jangali. She engaged in solitary meditation in a jungle. The legend is that, on one occasion, the Shah of Bengal, hunting in the region, attempted to rape her but was shocked to find that she transformed into a man. The astonished king asked her whether she was a man or a woman. She answered cryptically, 'women see woman, and men see man, but at no time ever have I been a man'. Some scholars are of the opinion that Jangali or Jangal Priya was, in fact, a male disciple, who acted as a woman (*gopī*) after initiation. His last unambiguous statement that 'at no time have I ever been a man' could be nothing more than the firm conviction of the possession of an eternal feminine identity in relation to the eternal male Kṛṣṇa.[53]

The assumption of feminity by bhaktas in Braj did not end with the meditative devices of the *rāgānuga bhakti* of the Gauḍīyas. In medieval times, the Hit Harivanśas, the Nimbarkas and to a limited extent, the Vallabhas, also showed interest in the subject. The supreme goal of the *sakhī bhāvas*, an off-shoot of the Radhavallabhas, was to become a *sakhī* of Rādhā. Accordingly, for *seva*, the members not only assumed female thoughts, manners and dress, but went to the extent of imitating having the monthly, periodic, menstrual cycles of women.[54] Some Puṣṭī Mārgī bhaktas replaced *Vātsalya Rās*, which propagated motherly bhakti, with *Mādhurīya Rās*. The impact of this philosophy of assumed feminity for salvation can be gauged by a supposed correspondence between Nandadas, an Aṣṭachāp poet, and his brother, Tulsidas, a Ram bhakta, where the former is replying to a query of the latter as to why he has become a Kṛṣṇa bhakta. Nandadas says:

> Śrī Rām had only one wife (*ek patni vrata hai*), so how will he take care of another wife? Even one wife he could not look after properly, Rāvaṇa

abducted her. Śrī Kṛṣṇa is the Lord of innumerable females, and his wives have nothing to fear. He can give pleasure and protection to endless number of wives. That is why I have chosen Śrī Kṛṣṇa to be my husband.[55]

It is essential to remember that the male bhaktas were imitating aspects of feminity, which were, at times, abhorred by earlier traditions. *Brajmaya* bhaktas were proud of it. Although I did not interview any members of the Sakhī Bhāv sect, yet it was confirmed by Srinivas that they acted feminine to the extent of secluding themselves in small apartments during their three days of supposed menstruation! John Stratton Hawley says that the male bhaktas of Rādhā-Kṛṣṇa underwent voluntary social devaluation by acting as uneducated females.[56] According to tantric beliefs, Rādhā, as the divine feminine, is manifest in all female beings and Kṛṣṇa in all male beings. Hence, as *gopīs*, *sakhīs* and *mañjarīs*, men were psychologically defying their physical gender.[57]

The recognition of female sexuality in the Brajiya Kṛṣṇa cults is explicit. It features prominently in the descriptions of the love sports of the divine couple, and forms the very basis of the religious theme of some of the sects like the Hit Harivanśas and the Haridasis.[58] A work on the goddess in world mythology describes Rādhā's attributes as luck, love and sexuality, and her name's meaning as success, achievement or the beloved one.[59] Yet another definition describes her as 'cow-elephant', the *śakti* of Kṛṣṇa. According to the *Kāmasūtra*, the elephant represented maximum sexual capacity and unflagging desire.[60] In the *Bhāgavata*, Kṛṣṇa and the 'special' *gopī* have been compared to elephants.[61] In some of the works of medieval Braj, this theme reappears, as in the following passage:

. . . the Lord's walk is that of a king elephant, Vrasbhanu's daughter (Rādhā) has the gait of an elephant queen.

Or

. . . like an elephant in rut that tramples the shores, he played in the water together with the women. . . .[62]

Some scholars trace this sensual element in the worship of Kṛṣṇa to the Abhiras, a nomadic pastoral tribe.[63] Though Kṛṣṇa-worship developed in diverse formats, a novel one was that of the *rasiks* who focused mainly on the love sports of the divine couple. They were the Hari triumvirate, i.e. Hari Rām Vyās, Hit Harivanśa and Swami Haridas.[64] In fact, the assertion of female sexuality in some of the scriptures of sects such as Sakhi Sampradāya is remarkable. Patriarchal religions disapprove of sexuality in feminine nature. For example, in the *Mārkaṇḍeya Purāṇa*, we learn that sex, described as the cause of death in the world, is also the direct result of the passionate nature of women. The *Mahābhārata* links the origin of evil to the sexual passion of women and the *Manusmṛti* provides the famous saying that women are intuitively promiscuous, fickle-minded and were possessed of an indiscriminate sexual desire.

In the *Mahābhārata*, however, the question of female sexuality is dealt with in both a negative and positive way. For example, Bhangashvana produced a hundred children as a man and hundred as a woman. Later, after the death of all her/his children, he asked Indra to bring back to life the children she/he produced as a woman and not as a man on the grounds that the love of a woman is greater than the love of a man. When asked to choose a sex, Bhangashvana chose to be a woman on the grounds that women experience greater pleasure in sex than men.[65] The negative side is brought forth in a story narrated by Bhīṣma.[66] Related to the concept of eroticism in ancient world history is the cult of Eros, where sexuality was worshipped as a powerful medium of procreation. Gradually, though, sexual allurement became a great danger because ancient ethics of asceticism preached the detachment of the mind from all worldly desires.[67] The power to arouse desire was equated with the power to delude. Yet *Brajmaya* Krsnaism celebrated it. The most prominent *bhakti bhāva* (devotional emotion) propagated in Braj was *Mādhurya*, i.e. bhakti with the kind of affection one feels for one's beloved. The erotic dalliance of Rādhā and the *gopīs* with Kṛṣṇa was the theme of at least two prominent sects of the region. An example of their religious texts is as follows:

> O beloved, your body is like nectarous mud, (my) eyes are stuck in it; my (mind) went to extricate them, but remained in the soft cavity where your breasts meet. There are many means to rescue them, but they do not work. Haridas' sovereign Śyāma Kuñjabihārī says, may it remain so.[68]

In fact, the veneration of the feminine rose to such an extent that the roles between the divine couple were exchanged:

Having rubbed (her) limbs with musk, holding a flute, wearing a yellow, sash, she says: Rādhā, I am Śyāma. The youth having decorated himself with saffron wears a *sārī*, bracelets, ear studs, puts Śyāma's black color in his eyes. (She) takes (his) arm, come let us go, to the bower; he sees (her) face and smiles, it is as if she were Śhyāma.[69]

The divine couple did not want to be separated, even temporarily, by festive crowds of friends on Holi.[70] The *Caurāsī Padas* of Hit Harivanśa describe Rādhā in the following words:

You are drunk with the essence of Mohanlala . . . your broken string of pearls dangles down, your bosom, is marked with the crescent moon of finger nails, your bimba fruit lips are split, your cheeks decorated with collyrium, and you walk unsteadily.[71]

In ancient cultures, where the female principle was accorded freedom and honour, as in Egypt, men were counselled never to be rude to a mistress or a wife, nor try to order her about.[72] In the Indian context as well, the tantric identification of the sexual bliss of the goddess and god who continually engender life in the universe was a philosophy of gender equalization.[73] In a similar context, as the *Hlādinī Śakti* of Kṛṣṇa, Rādhā was empowered to such an extent that Kṛṣṇa was even conceived of as pressing her feet.[74] It is believed that, traditionally, India saw more in sex than mere physical pleasure.[75] Thus, it is no wonder that a mystical and a poetic view of female sexuality developed with Radhaism. It goes to the credit of the philosophers of Radhaism who tried to understand and emulate feminine love, even though, culturally, they might have been trained not to pay attention to women. The philosophy of the interdependence of the divine couple on one another must have counter-balanced, at some level, the destructiveness of a totally male-dominant society. In the philosophies of *Brajmaya* Krsnaism, feminine sexuality borders most closely on the more complex psycho-sexual area of its being, which contains a heady mixture of many intense and yet delicate human facets like devotion, patience and so on. *Kāma*, who denotes sexual desire, is either subordinated to the divine couple or overawed by their love:

. . . Collyrium enhance, the beauty of your (Rādhā's) eyes, so that seeing them, the God of love (Kāma) himself is afraid. The flute of Madan Gopāl is an enchantress—Hear me to Rādhikā, as one hears her sweetness, she destroys the anguish of *Kāma*.[76]

Thus, the descriptions clearly indicate that the meditation of the divine couple would not incite *Kāma* but destroy it. The couple is never dominated by *Kāma*. The mutual interdependence of the couple seems like a celebration of the equalization of gender. Rādhā's *Mān Līlā* sequences are occasions when Kṛṣṇa loses to Rādhā and says that he will die if she does not leave her anger behind:

Even inadvertently do not sulk O Beloved, when I see your eyebrows frowning, no life remains in my body; I sacrifice (my) life for you, O Beloved. Why are you silent? says the cloud dark one (Kṛṣṇa). How could I have peace, now, when I see you like this O treasure of my life . . . ?[77]

In the celebrated plays of Rupa Goswami, Kṛṣṇa declares that he cannot live without Rādhā, and calls her a life-giving herb.[78] Due to his craving for her, he sees her in all directions, so much so that, at one point, Kṛṣṇa is shown rushing headlong to meet her, and Madhumangala, Kṛṣṇa's friend, asserts that he has been maddened by some magical spell uttered by the *gopīs*. Rādhā, too, expresses her inability to live without him and goes to the extent of contemplating suicide.[79] *Brajmaya* Krsnaism recognized the strong emotional content in the female system and the power that it could exercise over male psychology; but for those who did not have the right kind of attitude, women could still prove to be a cause of *kāma*. So even while Rādhā was being worshipped with all her sensuality and charm, the dicta for ordinary mortals were to be aware of these very qualities in females.[80]

III

To someone making the sound 'rā' I trembling grant him the highest devotion. Through my desire to listen I go after him, who makes the sound 'dhā'. Those who serve me, offering the sixteen ingredients of worship for a lifetime, arouse delight in me. Greater is my delight in hearing the sound: 'Rādhā'.[81]

Rādhā is depicted as a consort par excellence. She is considered not only equal but sometimes even greater than Kṛṣṇa, when he is conceived of as pressing her feet or even her placing her foot on his head.[82] In one imagery, a few words from her have life-giving powers for Kṛṣṇa.[83] Her relationship with Kṛṣṇa is so unique that theologians are still debating the structural background against which it should be conceived. From the ambiguity of her origin to the development of various theories around her, Rādhā remains beyond a structure. She dominates Kṛṣṇa and is dominated by him.

Her journey from a non-descript cowherd girl to the mother goddess is a long one. In the Radhaism of medieval Braj, she assumes complete divinity and, thereafter, her position in the theological equations stabilizes. Even as she changes many forms, she almost never confirms to the traditional role models specified for women, not even as a mother. The account of her motherhood in *Brahmavaivartta Purāṇa* says that she was angry with the egg that she gave birth to and kicked it with her foot. This annoyed Kṛṣṇa who cursed her of barrenness—

> O Damsel you are heartless and filled with rage, you have disowned your progeny, and therefore henceforth you will always remain childless. . . .

Since they were born from Rādhā and Mula Prakriti, both Lakṣmī and Saraswatī had no issue.[84] The first extended accounts of the Krsnaite legend were found in the *Harivaṁśa Purāṇa* (second to fifth century AD) but Rādhā does not feature here. This is followed by the *Viṣṇu Purāṇa* (third to sixth century AD). Next is the *Bhāgavata Purāṇa* (sixth to ninth century AD). In this Purāṇa, the frenzied devotion of the *gopīs* towards Kṛṣṇa is depicted. When Kṛṣṇa vanishes from amidst them, they see the footprints of one woman with him. The *gopī's* name is not mentioned, and there is no direct reference to Rādhā, only the word—*aradhika* appears. The footprints of the 'special' *gopī* suddenly vanish and the others fear that Kṛṣṇa might have lifted her onto his shoulders. But, in fact, Kṛṣṇa had abandoned her because, due to her self-conceit, she had asked him to lift her.[85]

It is believed by some scholars that the earliest reference to Rādhā can be traced to the *Gāthāśaptaśatī* or *Gahasattasai* attributed to Hala (first century AD).[86] The seventh-century writer, Bāṇa Bhaṭṭa, alludes to the *Gāthāśaptaśatī*, but B. Majumdar points out that there were several additions to the latter and that some post-seventh-century materials are included in it.[87] However, by the eighth-century, references to Rādhā become obvious.[88] The *Veṇīsaṃhāra* of Nārāyaṇa Bhaṭṭa, an eighth-century work, mentions Rādhā.[89] With reference to the same work B. Majumdar states that it mentions Rādhā and Kṛṣṇa in its opening benedictory verse, and yet some scholars think that though Kṛṣṇa is definitely regarded as a divinity, Rādhā may only be considered his lady love.[90] In the *Dhvanyālokālochanā* of Abhinavagupta, an early tenth-century work, Rādhā weeps pitifully when Kṛṣṇa leaves her.[91] In Kṣemendra's *Daśāvatāracarita*, a eleventh-century work, she is barely able to speak when Kṛṣṇa leaves for Mathura.[92] Her love for Kṛṣṇa turned into a legend with the *Gīta Govinda* of Jayadeva, which refers to her first meeting with Kṛṣṇa as follows: 'Clouds thicken the sky, Tamala trees darken the forest. The night frightens him. Rādhā, you take him home! They leave in thickets on their way, until secret passions of Rādhā and Mādhava, triumph on the Jamuna river banks.'[93]

The passage apparently portrays her as someone elder to Kṛṣṇa. The *Brahmavaivartta Purāṇa,* too, refers to a similar theme. In the later work, after Rādhā is married to Kṛṣṇa, he changes his form to a small fearful child whom Nanda had given to Rādhā and whom she hands over to Yaśodā, knowing full well that all this is the illusion of *Māyāpati* Kṛṣṇa. This might be a case of the addition of the mythology of Rādhā to the simple poetry of Jayadeva. The whole relationship of Rādhā and Kṛṣṇa is duly legitimized in the *Brahmavaivartta*, with Brahma performing their marriage rites. Later, an *ākāśavāṇī* (divine pronouncement) takes place which instructs Rādhā to leave her shadow at home and come to the grooves everyday to be with Kṛṣṇa.[94] However, it is possible that the incident of Nanda being caught in the rain storm, handing over baby Kṛṣṇa to Rādhā who happened to pass by, and his (Kṛṣṇa's) sudden disappearance from her lap and then returning as a young man in a magically constructed *Rāsmaṇḍal* where he was married to Rādhā by Brahma, were all mentioned in some older version of the *Brahmavaivartta*, which had actually inspired Jayadeva and not vice versa.[95] Some scholars suggest that both Jayadeva and the author of the *Brahmavaivartta* relied on some older unknown sources but two essential points on which the versions differ are that, in the *Brahmavaivartta*, Rādhā is definitely treated as a divinity with great emphasis, while in the *Gīta Govinda*, her treatment is more human.[96] Second, in the *Brahmavaivartta*, she is married to Kṛṣṇa, and, by many other references, established as his eternal consort. The *Gīta Govinda* is silent on this issue. Once the worship of Rādhā was established, her portrayal without the addition of divine attributes would have been impossible, so the version of the extant *Brahmavaivartta* seems to have been composed after the *Gīta Govinda*.

Due to the sensual portrayal of Rādhā in the *Gīta Govinda*, A.K. Majumdar feels that she acquired a divine status after the twelfth century. Indeed, for lack of affirmative evidence, it may be taken that Rādhā was not worshipped even at the end of the twelfth century.[97] However, the fact remains that some medieval works on Radhaism depicted her in a sensual manner despite her divine status. Some scholars feel that the emergence of Rādhā can be traced to the *jyotiṣaśāstra*, where Kṛṣṇa was the sun and Rādhā, the personification of a planet named Viśākha. Later on, her planetary aspect was forgotten and only her human personification remained. Gopāl Bhaṭṭ in *Haribhakti Vilās* compares Kṛṣṇa to the moon and says that one who respects planets like Aświn, Rohiṇī, Punarvasu, Anurādhā, Śravaṇa and so on is blessed with a son. He further advises that one should not urinate while looking at the stars, sun, moon or planets.[98]

Yet others believe that Rādhā might have been the love goddess of the Abhiras and later, when the identity of Bāl Kṛṣṇa merged with that of Vāsudeva Kṛṣṇa, Rādhā emerged.[99] Another school traces her origin to the Vajrayāni school of thought amongst the Buddhist.[100] However, Nimbārka, usually assigned to the twelfth century, offers praise to Brasbhanu's daughter, Rādhā, whom he refers to as *devī*. He says that she shines with delight on Kṛṣṇa's left side.[101] Nimbarka vaguely suggests that Rādhā originated from Kṛṣṇa's left side but no concrete theory is built-up by him.

In fact, *prakriti* for Nimbarka is merely a primal matter and not yet identified with Rādhā.[102] She seems to have developed initially in a *parakiya*-type format. Even though the *Gīta Govinda* does not define her marital status, some scholars say that she was Kṛṣṇa's beloved because the secrecy of the relationship was an underlying theme in this work. Rādhā's love for Kṛṣṇa is the central theme of Vidyapati's (thirteenth to fourteenth century) and Chandidas's poetry (fourteenth to fifteenth century). In both these works, she is bold and rebellious. Her perceived rebelliousness can be gauged from the following lines:

I throw ashes to all laws, made by man or God, I am born alone, with no companion, what is the worth of your vile laws that failed me; In love, and left me with a fool, a dumb skull (Ayana). My wretched fate is so designed that he is absent, for whom I long, I will set fire to this house and go away.[103]

Thereafter, Rādhā's love for Kṛṣṇa was portrayed in such strong terms that it gradually became a metaphor for devotion. The legitimacy of an allegedly illicit relationship as a metaphor of religious devotion became a subject of debate. In fact, the evolution of Kṛṣṇa as a devotee of Rādhā herself could be traced back as early as Kṣemendra's *Daśāvatāracarita* (1066) and Hemachandra's *Siddhanemaśabdānusāna* (1088-1172). The devotion in the latter text reads as follows: 'Though Hari sees every person with full regard still his glance goes wherever Rādhā is—who can arrest eyes ensnared by love?'[104]

Kṛṣṇa's submission to Rādhā is found in the *Gīta Govinda* as well. It was believed that Jayadeva wrote the following climax only after Kṛṣṇa wrote the couplet in the poet's guise: 'Place your foot on my head—a sublime flower, destroying poison of love, let your foot quell the harsh sun, burning its fiery form in me, to torment love.'[105]

Some medieval works give arguments to justify the omission of Rādhā's name in the *Bhāgavata*. Hari Ram Vyās says:

Rādhā's name is the greatest treasure. Śyām plays that name on his flute, remembering it constantly. She is the thread in every fabric, each *yantra*, and *tantra*, each *Veda* . . . , Śukadeva (the author of *Bhāgavata*) knew this secret of secrets, but decided it best stays unrevealed. Kṛṣṇa takes numerous forms to pursue it, still its depth eludes him. But I Vyāsdeva, now shout it out openly, throwing all caution to the winds.[106]

In a modern retrospective speculation, Śrīvatsa Goswāmī maintains that Śukadeva's silence on Rādhā was deliberate:

His was an intentional silence, for Rādhā as the quintessence of *rasa*, the supreme aesthetic experience is the most valuable jewel in the treasure house of love. Only a chosen few who know the code of love have access to this highest wealth. Outsiders such as intellect and will are carefully kept away.[107]

In her journey from being *aradhika* of the *Bhāgavata* to *prakriti*, the mother goddess of the *Brahmavaivartta*, Rādhā took the fastest and longest steps in medieval Braj.[108] The *Brahmavaivartta* traces Rādhā's origin to the left of Kṛṣṇa's body and proclaims her as *Prakriti*, the mother goddess.[109] The *Ṛgveda* also spoke of a male creator who gave birth to the mother of creation and then impregnated her to bring forth the world.[110] The *Brahmavaivartta* repeatedly rubs in the fact that she is not only born of him but equal to him.[111] Her ability to interchange even an apparent manifestation of roles has been stressed upon so much that, at one point, it establishes the indeterminability of the gender of the ultimate reality itself.[112] Despite being born out of/created by Kṛṣṇa, Rādhā goes on to become his *hlādinī* or *icchā śakti*.[113] Besides this, she is the *mūla prakriti* who is *saguṇa* and *nirguṇa*. She became fivefold, and her five forms are Durgā, Rādhā, Lakṣmī, Saraswatī and Sāvitrī. At many places, it is said that Rādhā is Durgā and Durgā is Rādhā, and sometimes Durgā is subordinated to her.[114] The varying description of the evolution of gods in the different *khaṇḍas* of the *Brahmavaivartta* shows the gradual development of Radhaism. In the *Brahma Khaṇḍa*, probably the oldest portion, the gods are said to have emanated from Kṛṣṇa.[115] In a later version, Goddess Lakṣmī is said to have emanated from *Prakriti* who is Rādhā.[116] In yet another version, Saraswatī is also said to have emanated from Rādhā's tongue-tip.[117]

The idea of difference in non-difference, *bheda-abheda* was located in Rādhā and Kṛṣṇa.[118] *Bheda-abheda* emerged repeatedly in prominent, sectarian works of medieval Braj, either consciously or unconsciously. Its presence in the works of Swāmī Haridas is apparent.[119] It is also found in the Puṣṭīmārgī Sūrdās:

> You become Rādhā and I will become Mādhava, truly Mādhava; This is the reversal which I shall produce, I will braid your hair and will put your crown upon my head. Sūrdās says thus the Lord becomes Rādhā and Rādhā the son of Nanda.[120]

This exchange of roles was not a mere game but the manifestation of a complex philosophy. In the process, a totally new dimension was added to the theology of *Brajmaya* Krsnaism, the combination of the maternal and the amorous. The *Brahmavaivartta* says that Rādhā, impregnated by Kṛṣṇa, gave birth to a golden egg but, for some unexplained reason, she cast the egg angrily in the cosmic waters, created by her perspiration. Kṛṣṇa, angry over this act, cursed her to be forever barren. Out of this egg emerged the *Mahāvirāṭ/Mahāviṣṇu* who was the sixteenth part of Kṛṣṇa. Later, the other deities and the whole universe emerged.[121] In the foregoing account, four ancient notions of cosmology have been taken over and assimilated in the theme of Rādhā's role in the original act of creation. The four older notions are related to the primordial androgyny, the golden egg, the cosmic elements (water and wind) and Brahma's creative activity.[122] The *Brahmavaivartta* itself has an earlier version of the creation of the world where Rādhā is absent, thus the version in which she does feature is a later interpolation and proof of her growing popularity.

In the *Brahmavaivartta*, Rādhā's role in creation is emphasized:

> The syllable *Rā* signifies Mahāviṣṇu, in whose hair pores the worlds exist. The syllable *dhā* means creation or wet nurse (*dhātrī*) in the sense of mother, in the worlds containing all creatures. I am the wet nurse, the mother of all these, I am the Goddess *Mula Prakriti*.[123]

In her maternal capacity, she has been given names like—'Mahāviṣṇor Mātṛ', 'Mahāviṣṇudhātrī' 'Mahāviṣṇov Jananī'. Trailokyamātṛ, Jaganmātā, Jagatam Mātṛ.[124] The Purāṇa lists fifteen other names besides Rādhā:

1. Rasikeśwarī—Because she is the consort of Rasikeśwar.
2. Rasvāsinī—She resides in the *rās maṇḍala.*
3. Rasikeśwarī Rānī—She is the prime goddess among all the *rasik* goddesses.
4. Kṛṣṇa Prāṇādhikā—More beloved to Kṛṣṇa than his life.
5. Kṛṣṇa Priyā—Beloved of Kṛṣṇa.

6. Kṛṣṇa Swarupiṇī—Close in likeness to Kṛṣṇa.
7. Kṛṣṇa Vānsambhutta—Born out of the body of Kṛṣṇa.
8. Paramānandarūpiṇī—She is the quality of Paramānanda.
9. Kṛṣṇa—The giver of *mokṣa*.
10. Vrindavani—Owner of Vrindavan.
11. Vṛndā— As *Tulasī* she has many *sakhīs* with her.
12. Vrindavinodini—She loves to be in Vrindavan.
13. Candrāvalī—She has the beauty of many moons in her face.
14. Candrakāntā—Her light is comparable to the cool light of the moon.
15. Śarad Candra Prabhānan—Her face has the shine of the sarad moon.[125]

The very purpose of the Kṛṣṇa *avatār* is said to be Kṛṣṇa's desire to accompany her to earth, where she would go due to a curse, to be born as *mānavayoni* (human form).[126]

IV

On Holi, the day Kṛṣṇa drenched
Vrindavan in colour
A widow died.
No man, *paṇḍā* or priest
Was willing to carry her body,
For burial
To the river side,
On that day four women became pallbearers,
To cremate another woman,
As her body, touched flame,
Vrindavan burnt,
Kṛṣṇa died.[127]

I learned of the presence of two 'Miras' in contemporary Braj and was compelled to look into the persona of Mirabai, in relation to *Brajmaya* Krsnaism.[128]

In the *Bhaktamālā* and *Bhaktiras Bodhinī Ṭīkā*, Mirabai is described as a popular female bhakta. A temple at Vrindavan is dedicated to the memory of her supposed meeting with Jiva Goswami.[129] Two more accounts of her meetings with Kṛṣṇa bhaktas from Braj feature in the Vārtā literature. In one case, Mirabai supposedly asked a Puṣṭī Mārgī bhakta, Ramdas, to sing something else, while he was singing praises of Vallabhacharya. He was very annoyed about this and pledged to never see her face again. Another account is of her meeting with Krisandas Adhikari, who went to her house but he refused to accept anything from her, saying that she was not a '*sevak* of *Mahāprabhu*'. Thus, Krisandas had, according to a sectarian text, 'cut to size' all those religious leaders and *swāmīs* who had came for donations. He, a '*śūdra*' follower of Vallabhacharya, would not accept anything out of his own will. Thus, the other saints would think that if the disciple is so scrupulous, then how scrupulous his *guru* must be.[130] It is possible that women bhaktas were not readily accepted and, therefore, Mirabai was not associated with any sect of Braj. Though different sects claimed bhaktas like Surdas and Raskhan to increase their popular appeal, interestingly enough, no sect tried to claim Mirabai.[131]

The contribution of the Caitanyaite movement towards the incorporation of female bhaktas seemed to be positive, and it manifested itself in the ecclesiastic leadership of Janhava Devī, wife of Nityānanda.[132] However, it is reported that the early *kīrtanas* of Caitanya in the house of Srinivas Pandit were not open to women.[133] Later too, he did not really encourage association with women. Nevertheless, there are two instances in the *Caitanya Caritamrita* which speak of a rather tolerant attitude of Caitanya towards female devotees. The first instance was when he was impressed by a female singing the *Gīta Govinda* and the second was when he appreciated a woman's enthusiasm for seeing Jagannath.[134] Hemlata Thakurani, daughter of Srinivas Acharya, initiated many disciples into the sect, while his second wife, Gaurang Priya, also initiated some.[135]

Krishnapriya and Vishnupriya were daughters of Narottam Das's disciple, Ganga Narayana Chakravarti. They are believed to have lived at Rādhā Kund for some time. According to the *Narottam Vilās* of Narahari, Krishnapriya took a number of disciples but disowned one of them, Rupa Kaviraj. This is because Kaviraj took sides with those who felt that her sex restricted her role in certain public religious acts. In particular, he objected to her presence in the assembly of men at the reading of the *Bhāgavata* and, as a result of his offensive behaviour, was forced to leave Vrindavan and return to Orissa.[136] It is also reported that Srinivas Acarya's daughter, Hemlata Thakurani, tore his *tulasi* beads necklace.[137] A modern researcher notes that during her fieldwork, she was not able to find any Vaiṣṇava holy women to interview.[138] While in a book on a family of Vrindavan Goswamis, the author, Margaret Case, writes that the mother of *Mahārājajī* was the acknowledged leader of women's devotional singing. In the context of the same lady, she says that all decisions were taken only after consulting her. Her opinions on many matters were said to have overruled *Mahārājajī's* opinion. Yet, while writing about the celebration of birthdays in the family, Case says that she never observed any celebration of the birthdays of the women of the household.[139] If we look at the status of women as portrayed in the *Caurāsī Vaiṣṇavoṅ ki Vārtā* (84VKV) and *Do Sau Bāvan Vaiṣṇavoṅ kī Vārtā* (252VKV), the Mirabai-Krishnadas Adhikari episode needs to be reconsidered.[140] If we look at the other episodes related to Krishnadas Adhikari, for example, his role in the eviction of Bengalis from a temple, or his dispute with Viṭhalnath and the banning of his entry inside the Srinath temple for some time, or his supposedly aggressive conversation with Rupa and Sanatana Goswami, his arrogant attitude towards Mira does not seem like a case of deliberate discrimination against a female bhakta.[141] The same man is also shown as being instrumental in the 'liberation' of a prostitute.[142] Thus, while dealing with Mirabai, Krishnadas displayed the same pride, arrogance and rigidity which he showed towards others. In the same manner, the attitude of Ramadas showed more of a rigid sectarianism than a particular hatred towards Mira.[143] In fact, both these works do not exhibit any contempt for women *bhaktas*. Many of them are praised in these works. Some of them are Tulsā, Pārvatī, Rjo kṣatrāṇī, Amma kṣatrāṇī and a female from Mahāban.[144] In *Govind Dās Bhalla kī Vārtā*, when Govind Dās reported that he was unable to do *sevā* because his wife was a hindrance, he was advised to leave his wife but also give her one-fourth of his property for her sustenance.[145] The 252 VKV also cites many instances of female bhaktas like Kanhabai Satyabhama, Jaimal's sister and daughter of one Haridas, and Birbal's daughter and Mirabai's sister-in-law, Ajab Kunwar Bai.[146] This text also mentions one Ganga Bai kṣatrāṇī who was physically attracted to Goswami Viṭhalnath and so, her entry into Gokul was banned for twelve years.[147] There are instances that say that females attending sessions of discourses on the *Bhāgavata* were condemned. In one case, neighbours of a bhakta named Premnidhi reported to Akbar that the *Bhāgavata kathā* should be stopped in his house because women came to attend it.[148] In yet another instance, a man supposedly suspected his wife's intentions while she was doing *Bhāgavata vārtā* with a male Vaiṣṇava.[149] However, by and large, a favourable attitude towards female bhaktas was displayed.[150] Women were accepted as temple *kīrtanīyas*. Bhāgwat Mudit gives an account of two orphan sisters from Mahāban who were initiated into Kṛṣṇa bhakti by Hit Harivanśa.[151] The *Vārtā* literature applauds the actions of a Rajput queen who danced uninhibitedly before Kṛṣṇa.[152] *Vārtās* report instances of queens who wanted to have a *darśan* of Srinathji in an exclusive manner because they observed purdah.[153]

I read an account of the contemporary Miras of Braj by Nancy M. Martin and tried to find them during my trips to Braj.[154] One of them is now called Bansidhari Mirabai. The most interesting thing about her is that she does not dress up like the medieval Mira at all but as Kṛṣṇa, a male, always carries a *bansī* (flute) with her! It is too obvious a question to ask as to why does she dresses up like Kṛṣṇa and not as Rādhā/the *gopīs*/Mirabai? Her reply was the following couplet:

Prāṇ bhaye Kānhā maye
Ye na jān sakun, main hun
Ke prāṇ hain, ke Kṛṣṇa Kānhā hai

This implies that she sees and feels Kṛṣṇa within herself and cannot make out whether it is the soul or Kṛṣṇa himself. She says that she carries a *bansī* because that was the lifeline of the *gopīs*. She dresses up as *Ācāryajī*/*Mahārājajī* or *Bansīdhārī* like *Rās Bihārī* Kṛṣṇa and has no male disciples.

The other female *bhakta* whom I met near the Bāṅke Bihārī temple was called Yamunā *sakhī.* She was blind and aged about seventy years. The second 'Mira' whom I met resides in Rādhā Kṛṣṇa Dham at Pani Ghat, Vrindavan. A board outside her house reads *Mīrā Dāsī Braj Mādhurī* (maid of Mira, the sweetness of Braj). It is interesting that she, too, like the first 'Mira', assumes masculinity and is called 'Mahārājajī', a male rubric. So, in Radhaism, we have female *bhaktas* trying to manipulate the *puruṣ* Kṛṣṇa within them, while male *bhaktas* are to feel like the *gopīs* and *mañjarīs*.

In the context of the neutralization of genders in Rādhā and Radhaism, understanding beyond explanations is essential. Explaining them against a rationale or an objective standard of truth that lies outside the world-view of the phenomenons themselves would be futile. All attempts at explanation are bound to be reductionist in that they assume that the phenomenons being explored are not valid within themselves. Thus, we need to take a mixture of processual and structural views to understand the impact of the *Brajmaya* movement on women. The structural view may be useful for illuminating those aspects of the social structure which are not easily apparent. However, putting the structural view to this exercise would need keen observation, selection and interpretation. The processual view is crucial in order to understand the philosophical logistics behind a particular social pattern. The pattern may be observed at a collective or personal level. Radhaism probably gave rise to ideas which, in some ways, confuted orthodox viewpoints at the theological level, but no socially unaccepted behavioural patterns were admitted practically. Rādhā and Radhaism are a subtle interplay of freedom and commitment, unpremediation and design. If we envision these poles as opposite ends of a continuum of a common cultural understanding of gender equations, we may place Kṛṣṇa nearer to the freedom end and Rādhā nearer to the commitment because Kṛṣṇa had thousands of *gopīs* but Rādhā had only Kṛṣṇa. Those logotypes, which could have a direct bearing on the moral and social conduct of men and women, were never explained or understood in a literal way.

Thus, with feminity holding a pivotal position in *Brajmaya* Krsnaism, genders may have been neutralized at some time, somewhere, but the society did not become entirely free of pre-sentimentalism. I wish to conclude with the remarks of Swāmī Haridas, a devoted *bhakta* of Rādhā:

> You make the false appear true. O clever Hari, Day and night (you) keep on weaving and unravelling the ocean of illusion. (You) have formed the woman but she is shrewder than the *puruṣa*. Listen, says Haridas, I know this with my heart, it is like awareness in sleep.[155]

NOTES

1. *Brahmavaivartta Purāṇa* (*BVP*), ed. Acharya Ramesh Chaturvedi, tr. Shanti Lal Nagar, Delhi: Parimal Publications, 2001, vol. I, Ganesh Khanda 6: 55, 57-8 ab, 59, 60, p. 533. The *BVP* is an important document for studying the Krsnaite revolution and Radhaism. It is suggested by scholars that the *BVP* was probably an older Purāṇa, which was re-written in medieval Braj. The re-worked Purāṇa accommodated new notions about Rādhā.
2. *Manusmriti*, 9.2-3, ed. and tr. Prof. Surendra Kumar, Delhi: Arsh Sahitya Prachar Trust, 1985, pp. 738-9; A.S. Altekar, *The Position of Women in Hindu Civilization*, Banaras: Motilal Banarsidass,1956; J.J. Meyer, *Sexual Life in Ancient India: A Study in the Comparative History of Indian Culture*, London: Routledge and Kegan Paul, 1930, p. 114; Benjamin Walker, *Hindu World: An Encyclopedic Survey of Hinduism*, Delhi: Harper and Collins, 1995, pp. 3-4. See *Mahābhārata*, ed. & tr., Pt. Ram Narayana Dutt Shastri, Gorakhpur: Gita Press, 1997, *Sambhav Parv*, pp. 356-9; S.C. Sarkar, *Some Aspects of the Earliest Social History of India*, London: Oxford University Press, 1928, p. 85.
3. Cf. S.A. Dange, *Encyclopedia of Puranic Beliefs and Practices*, Delhi: Navrang Publications, 1986, p. 2.
4. *Manusmriti*: 8: 371, p. 723; 8: 369-70, p. 721; 4: 133-4, p. 365.
5. *Śiva Purāṇa Māhātmyam* III.39 and *Skanda Purāṇa* III.3.22.68, cf. Dange, op. cit., p. 2; *Skanda Purāṇa* III.3.19.51 cf. Dange, op. cit., pp. 2-3.
6. *Liṅga Purāṇa* II.6.67-69, cf. Dange, op. cit., p. 1279.
7. *Brahma Purāṇa* 225.49-52, 16.496 and 16d, cf. Dange, op. cit., p. 1281; J.J. Meyer, op. cit., p. 114; B. Walker, op. cit., p. 538, p. 527; P.V. Kane, *The History of Dharmasastra*, Poona: Bhandarkar Oriental Research Institute, 1941, Chapter 31, pp. 1091-1106, cf. Samjukta Gombrich

Gupta, 'The Goddess, Women and their Rituals in Hinduism', in Mandakranta Bose, ed., *Faces of the Feminine in Ancient, Medieval and Modern India*, Delhi: Oxford University Press, 2000, p. 91.

8. For Yayāti, see the *Mahābhārata*, Narayana Dutt, op. cit., pp. 243-78 (*sambhava parva*).
9. Hanuman Prasad Poddar, ed., *Shri Mad Bhāgavata Purāṇa*, Gorakhpur Gita Press, 10: 32: 16, p. 318. 'For me (Kṛṣṇa), you (*gopīs*) have broken the bondage of those household duties which are difficult to leave even for the biggest of *mahātmas*. This spiritual meeting is clean and without any fault' *Bhāgavata Purāṇa*, 10: 3: 22, p. 323.
10. 'Mohana plays the flute and with this sound he calls the women, on hearing the sound of his reed pipe, the women of Vraja come, dismissing all thought of husbands and kinsmen; a vision of the captivating Madan Gopala checks the anguish of desire.'
    Hit Harivanśa, '*Chaurāsīpada*' 63(ii) cf. Rupert Snell, *The Eighty-Four Hymns of Hita Harivamsa*, Delhi: Motilal Banarsidass, 1991, p. 241.
11. Hari Ram Vyas, *Rāspañcādhyāyī*, 3: 2-3: 4, cf. *Kṛṣṇa's Round Dance Reconsidered*; Hari Ram Vyas, Hindi *Rāspañcadhyāyī*; H. Rica Maria Pauwels, *London Studies on South Asia*, no. 12, London: Curzon Press, 1996, p. 83. All references of Hari Ram Vyas' *Rāspañcādhyāyī* have been cited from Pauwels.
12. 'Husband and son, guru and brothers, nothing but sorrow they bring' *Rāspañcādhyāyī*, Hari Ram Vyas, 11: 2, p. 101.
13. James D. Redington, *Vallabhacarya on the Love Games of Kṛṣṇa*, Delhi: Motilal Banarsidass, 1983; McGregor Ronald Stuart, *The Round Dance of Krishna and Uddava's Message*, London: Luzac, 1973.
14. *Bhāgavata Purāṇa* 10: 29: 19, 10: 29: 18; *Rāspañcādhyāyī*, Vyas, 6: 4a-b, p. 90.
15. *Bhāgavata Purāṇa,* 10: 29: 12-16.
16. McGregor, op. cit., pp. 67-8.
17. *Bhāgavata Purāṇa,* 10: 33: 28-29, p. 328; 10: 32: 10, p. 320.
18. Ibid., 10: 29: 10-11, p. 301; 10: 29: 8-9, p. 301; 10: 29: 35, p. 305; 10: 3: 176, p. 200.
19. Vyas, *Rāspañcādhyāyī*, 28.2; pp. 152-3, 27: 3-4; p. 151, 28: 3; p. 155, 29: 1-4; p. 157.
20. Ibid., 3: 1-4; p. 83, 4: 3-4; p. 85, 7: 1-4; p. 93, 3: 2; p. 83.
21. *BgP.* 10: 29.5; p. 300. Vyas, *Rāspañcādhyāyī*, 5: C, p. 87; 12: 16, pp. 102-3.
22. Ibid., 3: 2-3, p. 83.

23. Ibid., 4: 3, p. 85; 5: 1a, p. 86.
24. *Bhāgavata Purāṇa*, 10: 29: 8, p. 300; 10: 29: 19-20, p. 303; 10: 31: 6, p. 316; 10: 29: 38, p. 306. The tone of conversation of the *gopīs* with Kṛṣṇa is such that it clearly implies they are talking to a divine person and they refer to him often as Viṣṇu, in the context of his wife Lakṣmī; 10: 29: 36-37, p. 306. They say that he is the redeemer of poor and sad people and they have come here for their redemption; 10: 29: 41, p. 307.
25. Vyas, *Rāspañcādhyāyī*, 9: 4, pp. 96-7. It is believed that Rādhā was that nameless, special *gopī* who asked Kṛṣṇa to carry her on his shoulders and he deserted her and vanished to reprimand her for her arrogance.
26. *Bhāgavata Purāṇa*, 10: 33: 13, p. 325 and 10: 32: 5-6, p. 320.
27. Vyas, *Rāspañcādhyāyī*, 27: 3, pp. 150-1. The exchange of betel leaves between Rādhā and Kṛṣṇa was a popular theme in works of sixteenth-seventeenth-century Braj; see Swāmī Haridās, *Kelimal* 32, in Ludmila L. Rosenstein, *The Devotional Poetry of Swami Haridas*, Groningen Oriental Studies, Netherlands: Royal Netherlands Academy, 1997, p. 134.
28. *Bhāgavata Purāṇa*, 10: 29: 38a, p. 300. Vyas, *Rāspañcādhyāyī*, 10: 3, p. 99 and 12: 16, p. 103.
29. In the *Bhāgavata Purāṇa*, Kṛṣṇa says to the *gopīs*: It is the duty of the wives to serve their husbands and his relatives and bring up children. Those women who wanted to attain heaven should not desert any kind of husband, be he short-tempered, old, foolish, sick, poor or unfortunate. Serving another man is bad for any chaste woman, this ruins their future, they do not get heaven and in this world they are defamed. This misdeed is absolutely mean and momentary (in pleasure) and it can fill one's present also with pain; this drags one into hell', 10: 29: 23-26, p. 303. The *gopīs* also agree with him, saying: 'you are the knower of the depth of all religions, and your saying that we should serve our husbands, sons and relatives is literally true, but according to this sermon we should serve you only because you are the ultimate end; you are the absolute God. 10: 29: 31-2, pp. 304-5.

    Whether the husband be old and hapless, foolish or diseased, the wife should not leave him, only a sinner is to be spurned. If she abandons her husband and indulges in a lover, such a woman cannot be noble, without a shred of honour, she will fall into hell'. Vyas, *Rāspañcādhyāyī*, 8: 1-2, p. 95 and 7: 3-4, p. 93.
30. *Bhāgavata Purāṇa*, 10: 30: 3-4, p. 309; 10: 32: 17-19, pp. 318-19; 10: 31: 13, p. 317; 10: 29: 41, p. 307; 10: 29: 36-7, p. 306.
31. Vyas, *Rāspañcādhyāyī*, 11: 1, pp. 100-1. *Bhāgavata Purāṇa*, 10: 29: 41, p. 307 and 10: 31: 6, p. 316.

32. 'People go astray, well let them do so, but you rosary bearer do not stray, to leave your Lord and to love others is to be like a prostitute among wives.' Swami Haridas, *Aṣṭadassiddhānt*, 16, cf. L. Rosenstein, op. cit., p. 199. In the *BVP*, too, disloyal women are compared to prostitutes, *BVP*, Prakriti Khanda (Pk.Kh.) 16: 58-79, vol.1, pp. 234-5.
33. *Padma Purāṇa, Bhumi Khanda*; 16: 41-15-16, cf. Dange, op. cit., p. 287 & 16: 10-13, p. 287. *BVP*, vol. II, Kṛṣṇa Janma Khanda (Kj. Kh.), 57-20-21, p. 411. *BVP*, H.P. Poddar, tr. and ed.; C.L. Goswami & S.K.R. Agarwal, Gorakhpur: Gita Press, 1996, pp. 540, 392-3.
34. Ibid., p. 541.
35. *BVP*, V-II, Kj.Kh, 83: 120-6, pp. 534-53.
    It states that a man, whose wife is easily controlled, well behaved and chaste, attains the happiness of heaven in this world and *dharma* and *mokṣa* in the next . . . and the husband of an unchaste woman is like the dead Kj.Kh 83: 127-37, p. 535 & Pk.Kh 6.66-7, p. 173. A man without a wife is impure to perform rites for the Gods or manes and his daily rites are fruitless. A house in which there is no chaste lady speaking sweet words, one should leave that house and retire to the forest because for him the forest and the house would be alike. He whose beloved wife is abducted by someone, should retire to the forest because for him the house and the forest would be the same—Pk.Kh. 59: 9-15, pp. 471-2. See *Hari Bhakti Vilas (HBV)*, ed. & tr. Haridas Shastri, Vrindavan: Shri Gadadhar Gaur Hari Press, 1986, Ch. 1; 194, p. 36. '. . . when duty is lost chaos overwhelms the family, in overwhelming chaos Kṛṣṇa, women of the family are corrupted and when women are corrupted disorder is born in society.' Barbara Stoler Miller, *Bhagvad-Gita*, 1.40-1, New York: Bantam Classics, 1986, p. 3.
36. *BVP*, Poddar, pp. 546-8.
37. Ibid. Also *HBV*, Ch. 12: 169-74, vol. 2, pp. 539-40, 547, 651.
38. Ibid., pp. 403, 438-44.
39. Ibid., p. 513.
40. Rupa Goswami, *Bhakti Rasamrita Sindhu* (*BRS*), 1.2: 290, cf. B. Steven J. Rosen, 'Raganuga Bhakti Bringing out the Inner Woman in Gaudiya Vaishnava Sadhana', in S.J. Rosen (ed.), *Vaishnavi, Women and the Worship of Kṛṣṇa*, Delhi: Motilal Banarsidass, 1996, p. 119.
    Rupa Goswami, *BRS*, 1.2.285, cf. A.C. Bhaktivedanta Swami Prabhupada, *Teachings of Lord Chaitanya*, Los Angeles: Bhakti Vedanta Press, 1974, pp. 331-2 and *HBV*, Ch. 8: 436, p. 461.
41. Goswami Harirai, *Do Sau Bāvan Vaiṣṇavoṅ kī Vārtā* (252VKV), Dwarka Das Parikh, ed., Mathura: Shri Bajrang Pustakalaya, 1970, pp. 165-6 and '*Ek Virakt ki Varta*', pp. 154-6.

42. Hit Harivansha, *Chaurasi Pada*, 63(ii) in Rupert Snell, p. 241.
43. Shri Vatsa Goswami is associated with the Govinddeva temple at Vrindavan. See Margaret Case, *Seeing Krishna: The Religious World of a Brahman Family in Vrindaban*, Delhi: Oxford University Press, 2000, Daya Krishna, Mukund Lath and Francine E. Krishna, *Bhakti: A Contemporary Discussion*, Delhi: Indian Council of Philosophical Research, 2000, pp. 113-14.
44. The purpose of the *līlā* was that a contact may be established between Kṛṣṇa and the *gopīs*. It is important to have *sambandha* with the *bhakta* be it of sex, anger, fear, love or compassion. Once any of these feelings are associated with the divine, they, too, become divine. The purpose and the end of *līlā* is the redemption of mankind. *Bhāgavata Purāṇa*, 10: 29: 14-15, p. 302.
45. Nabhadas calls Mīrā 'a visible *gopī* of Kaliyuga' who left the fear of society and family for Giridhar Nabhadas, *Bhaktamālā*, Lucknow: Tej Kumar Press, 1977, verse no. 115, p. 290. For her meeting with Jiva, see Priyadas, *Bhaktirasbodhini*, Lucknow: Tej Kumar Press, 1977, verse no. 479, p. 292.
46. The *Mañjarīs* were supposed to be young beautiful *gopīs* who helped in the sports of Rādhā and Kṛṣṇa.
47. Cf. B. Steven J. Rosen, 'Raganuga Bhakti: Bringing out the Inner Woman in Gaudiya Vaishnava Sadhna', in *Vaishnavi*, pp. 119-21.
48. For *Parakiya-Sahajiya* groups, see Suhotra Swami, 'Deviant Vaishnava Sects' in *Back to Godhead*, vol. 25, nos. 3-6, June-November 1991.
49. Rupa Goswami, *BRS*, Tridandi Swami Bon Maharaj, Calcutta: Institute of Philosophy, 1965, p. 125.
50. June McDaniel, *The Madness of the Saints: Ecstatic Religion in Bengal,* Chicago: University of Chicago Press, 1989, p. 49.
51. Dr. Srinivas Acharya is the founder President of GVALA (Gauranga Vedanta Art and Life Academy, Vrindavan). He is promoting the concept of *go-seva* (service of cows) in India and abroad.
52. David Haberman, 'Imitating the Masters: Problems in Congruity', in *Journal of the American Academy of Religion*, 53, no. 1 (March 1985), pp. 41-9, Neal Del Monico, 'Trouble in Paradise: A 17th C. Conflict in the Chaitanyai Vaishnava Tradition', Proceedings of 21st Conference of Bengali Studies, Oshkosh: America, May 1987; cf. *Vaishnavi*, p. 131.
53. Haridas Das, ed., *Gauḍiya Vaiṣṇava Abhidhān*, Nabdwip: Haribolkutir, 1964, p. 471. Cf. Jan Brzezinski, 'Women Saints in Gaudiya Vaishnavism', in *Vaishnavi*, p. 83.
54. R.G. Bhandarkar, *Vaisnavism, Saivism, and Minor Religious Systems,* Delhi: Munshiram Manoharlal, 2001, pp. 86-7.

55. 252 VKV, Goswami Harirai, p. 40.
56. J.S. Hawley 'Images of Gender in the Poetry of Krishna', in Walker Bynum, Steven Harrell and Paula Richman, eds., *Gender and Religion: On the Complexity of Symbols*, Boston: Beacon Press, 1986, pp. 231-302.
57. *BVP*, vol. I, Pk.Kh. Ch. 12: 17, p. 216.
58. See Haridas, *Kelimal*, Vrindavan: Haridas Press, 1987. Hit Harivansha, *Hit Chaurāsī* and *Sphut Vānī*, with commentary of Shri Lalithacharan Goswami, Vrindavan, Harinaam Sankirtan Mandal, 1991.
59. 'There are several women in Hindu religion with this name. One is said to be the lover or wife of Krishna. In tantricism her infinite love is the essence of Krishna and she presides over life and its energies. The Rādhā who is the wife of Adhiratha became the foster mother of Karna when he was rescued from the Ganges river. (Rādhā is also) A form of Lakshmi and an alternate form of Parvati.' Martha Ann and Dorthy Myers Imel, *Goddesses in World Mythology*, California: ABC-CLIO Inc., 1993, p. 293.
60. Barbara G. Walker, *The Woman's Encyclopedia of Myths and Secrets*, New York: Harper One, 1983, p. 839; P. Rawson, *The Art of Tantra*, London: Thames and Hudson, 1978, p. 99.
61. The state of the *gopīs* after Kṛṣṇa left them is compared to the female elephants who are restless when *Gajraaj* (the king of elephants) is not with them. *Bhāgavata Purāṇa*, 29: 30; 1, p. 309. When the *gopīs* see the footprints of Rādhā with Kṛṣṇa, they say that the footprints look like those of a female elephant, walking with her beloved *Gajraaj*. *Bhāgavata Purāṇa*, 10: 30: 27, p. 312. In the *BVP*, her style of walking has been compared to that of an elephant. *BVP*, vol. II, Kj.Kh, Ch. 84: 72, p. 541.
62. Hit Harivansha, *Chaurāsī Pada*, verse no. 9, cf. Rupert Snell, op. cit., pp. 190-1.Vyas, *Rāspañcādhyāyī*, verse no. 29.2, p. 157.
63. Thakur Harendra Dayal, *The Vishnu Purāṇa: Social, Economic and Religious Aspects*, Delhi: Sandeep Prakashan, 1983, pp. 20-8. Campbell says that in the erotic poem song of the cowherd, the God was incarnated as Kṛṣṇa and the Goddess spouse as his sexually insatiable consort, Rādhā; 'she elephant'. Campbell Joseph, *The Masks of God: Oriental Mythology*, Delhi: Arkana, 1968, p. 352.
64. Swami Haridas, *Kelimal*, p. 2.
65. It was Indra himself who had caused the change in Bhangaśvana's sex and later, the death of her children because he was angry with him/her. *Mahābhārata*, XIII. 12. Cf. G.L. Simon, *Sex and Superstitions*, New York: Barnes and Noble Books, 1973, p. 119.

66. *Mahābhārata*, XIII-19, 20, p. 93.
67. Eros was a bisexual Greek deity of erotic love; close in resemblance to the Indian Kāmadeva. Some ancient cults believed that Eros was the first God to emerge from the womb of the primal creator, Mother Night. Plato said that Eros was the oldest of deities, the most worthy of honour, the one who gave souls strength to ascend to the heaven after death, he was a kind of saviour before cults of asceticism began to replace the older worship of sexuality as a primary life force. See Walker, op. cit., p. 283.
68. Swami Haridas, *Kelimal*, verse no. 7, p. 208. The same kind of theme can be observed in verse nos. 8, 20, 21, pp. 209, 221 and 222, respectively.
69. Ibid. verse no. 56, p. 258. In verse no. 70, p. 272, Kṛṣṇa is portrayed as combing Rādhā's hair and dressing her up, usually a feminine role: Does anyone know how to braid hair, as I do? I swear to you, with white yellow and red flowers in the middle, who else can do this? I swear to you, O friend, sitting the connoisseur, does her hair with the comb of his gentle hands. Kuñjbihārī with his finger nails applies collyruim to the eyes of Haridas', sovereign Śyāma.
70. Ibid., verse nos. 100, 101 and 105, pp. 302, 303 and 307, respectively.
71. Hit Harivanśa, *Chaurāsīpada*, verse no. 20, p. 201. Also verse nos. 21, 23, 32, 3, 82 and 15; pp. 202, 203, 212, 186, 259 and 197, respectively.
72. J. William Fielding, *Strange Customs of Courtship and Marriage*, New York: Perma Books, 1942, pp. 145-6. C. Gasquoine Hartley, *The Truths About Woman*, New York: Dodd Mead, 1913, p. 196.
73. Arther Avalon, *Shakti and Shakta*, New York: Dover Books, 1978, p. 912.
74. 'Come O Friend, Let us meet Kuñjbihārī and look attentively at his beloved (see how) the beautiful woman plays with the handsome man, and indeed how she sings. Unexpectedly the *sakhi* came there; Rādhā was letting her beloved massage her feet; she was lying together with Haridās's sovereign Śyāma and sporting with mind and body', Haridas, *Kelimal*, verse no. 104, Rosenstein, p. 306. In fact, some ancient beliefs portrayed Parvati, too, in the same kind of sexual context. See Allen Edwardes, *The Jewel in the Lotus: A Historical Survey of the Sexual Culture of the East*, New York: Julian Press, 1965, p. 52.
75. Philip Rawson, op. cit., p. 78.
76. Haridas, *Kelimal*, verse no. 50, p. 252. Hit Harivanśa, *Chaurāsī Pada*, verse no. 26, p. 205. Verse no. 36, p. 215 is as follows: Skilful of gesture and with eyes overhung by curls, her eyebrows have set Kāma dancing; seizing a new rhythm with *tata thei tat thei*, she has delighted her husband, the Lord of Vraja.

77. Haridas, *Kelimal*, verse no. 10, p. 211. The following verses of *Kelimal* also have the same theme: 17, p. 125; 22, p. 223; 59, p. 261; 80, p. 282; 57, p. 259; 51, p. 253; 76, p. 278; 79, p. 281.
78. Rūpa Goswāmī, ed. and tr., *Vidagdha Mādhava* (*VM*), Vrindavan: Vaishnavadasanudas Shri Shyam Das Harinaam Sankirtan Mandal, 1998, Ch. 3: 69, p. 30 & Ch. 5: 167, p. 50. Ibid., 3: 128; p. 32. Ibid., 3: 58, p. 29.
79. His friend, Madhmangala, says to the *gopīs* that Kṛṣṇa cannot sleep because of his love for Rādhā and meditates on her like a *Yogendra: VM*, Ch. 3: 26, pp. 27-8. Ibid., Ch. 2: 142, 146, 148, p. 23. When Rādhā's *sakhī*, Viśākhā, informs her that Kṛṣṇa is unable to meet her, she wants to end her life by merging into the Yamunā. *VM*, Ch. 2: 148, p. 23.
80. *BVP*, vol.II, Kj.Kh., 86: 92-4, pp. 564-5 & 86: 81-2, p. 564.
81. Shri Krishna, in *BVP*, vol. II, Kj.Kh.15: 70-74, p. 111.
82. Swami Haridas, *Kelimal*, verse no. 104, pp. 177-8. See Jayadeva, *Gīta Govinda* in J.S. Hawley, *The Divine Consort*, Delhi: Motilal Banarsidass, 1995, p. 24. For more on *mān līlā,* see *Kelimal*, verse no. 39, p. 241; no. 22, p. 223; no. 59, p. 261; no. 80, p. 282; no. 57, p. 259; no. 51, p. 253; no. 76, p. 278; no. 79, p. 281. In *VM*, Kṛṣṇa's friend, Madhumangala, is made to say to Mukhara that he swears on his sacred thread, *yajñopavīt*, that he has seen Kṛṣṇa prostrating before Rādhā. Ch. 4: 181, p. 43. In another sequence on Lalita's advice, Kṛṣṇa offers to comb Rādhā's hair to please her, Ch. 3: 141-3, 33.
83. Leave anger O Rādhā O Rādhā! The more you hold back the more I am hurt. I constantly show you deep devotion. It nourishes my life to hear even a few words from you. *Kelimal*, verse no. 17, p. 125.
84. *BVP*, vol. I, Pk.Kh, 2: 53, 60-1, p. 152.
85. *Bhāgavata Purāṇa*, 10: 30: 45-7, p. 308; 10: 30: 28, p. 312; 10: 30: 26, p. 312;10: 30: 30-1, p. 313 & 10: 30: 35-8, p. 314.
86. Cf. S.S. Mehta, *A Monograph on Mirabai: The Saint of Mewar*, Bombay: Bhatwadi Girgaon, p. 100. A.K. Majumdar suggests that Hala may have lived in the second century AD. See A.K. Majumdar, 'A Note on the Development of the Rādhā Cult', in *Annals of the Bhandarkar Oriental Research Institute,* XXXVI, p. 234.
87. B. Behari Majumdar, *Krishna in History and Legend*, Calcutta: Calcutta University Press, 1969, p. 166.
88. S.M. Pandey and Norman Zidi, 'Surdas and his Kṛṣṇa Bhakti', in Milton and Singer, eds., *Krishna Myths, Rites and Attitudes*, Chicago: University of Chicago Press, 1968, p. 182, and B. Majumdar, op. cit., p. 170.
89. Barbara S. Miller, *Love Song of the Dark Lord: Jayadeva's Gita Govinda*, New York: Columbia University Press, 1977, p. 29.

90. B. Majumdar, op. cit., p. 170.
91. Miller, op. cit., p. 30.
92. Ibid., p. 34.
93. *Gita Govinda* 1: 1 cf. Barbara Stoler Miller, 'Radha: The Divine Duality of Radha and Krishna', in *The Divine Consort*, p. 3.
94. Ibid. & *BVP*, Poddar, p. 383.
95. B. Majumdar, op. cit., p. 195.
96. Sushil Kumar De opines that it is possible that Jayadeva derived and developed erotic mysticism from the same source as Nimbārka and, to the same obscure source, the writer of the later portion of the *BVP*, was also indebted for his treatment of the Radha legend. S.K. De, *Early History of the Vaishnava Faith and Movement in Bengal from Sanskrit and Bengali Sources*, Calcutta: Mukhopadhyay, 1961, pp. 9-10.
97. A.K. Majumdar, op. cit., p. 241. Lucy L. Rosenstein calls the *Gīta Govinda* 'another Sanskrit religious work', in L.L. Rosentein, op. cit., p. 2.
In the *Krishna Bhatt ki Vārtā*, while putting forth the point that Rādhā was to be pleased before Kṛṣṇa, if a *bhakta* wanted to earn merits, the instructor first quoted *Gīta Govinda* and then Nandadās, thus treating it as religious work. *Do Sau Bāvan Vaiṣṇavoṅ kī Vārtā*, p. 56. An eighteenth-century work of Maddupalani in Telugu portrays Rādhā in an extremely erotic manner. See Muddupalani, *Rādhāsantwanam*, in Susie Tharu and K. Lalita, *Women Writing in India: 600 BC to The Present*, New York: Feminist Press, 1993, p. 120.
98. Shri Yogesh Chandra Rai's remarks in *Bhāratvarṣa Patrika*, Magh, 7, 340; cf. Kalyanmal Lodha, ed., *Bhāratīya Sāhitya Mein Rādhā*, Delhi: Raj Kamal Prakashan, 1988, p. 9.
99. Hazari Prasad Dwivedi, *Sur Sāhitya*, pp. 16-17, cf. Lodha, op. cit., p. 8.
100. Lodha, op. cit., p. 9.
101. Nimbārka, 'Dashshloki', no. 5, cf. C. Mackenzie Brown, *God as Mother*, Hartford: Claude & Stark, 1974, pp. 146-7.
102. Mackenzie Brown, *God as a Mother*, p. 154. For a theory of her emergence due to the influence of the *Samkhya Śāstra*, where Kṛṣṇa was the male *shakti* and Rādhā had to accompany him as *prakriti*, see Lodha, op. cit., p. 8. Roma Chaudhri, 'The Nimbarka School of Vedanta', in the *Cultural Heritage of India*, Calcutta: 1953, rev. edn., vol. III, p. 3.
103. See Edward Dimock Jr. and Denise Levertov, tr., *In Praise of Krishna: Songs from the Bengali*, New York: Anchor, 1967, p. 51 and Deben Bhattacharya, tr., *Love Songs of Vidyapati*, Delhi: Motilal Banarsidass, 1987, p. 135; Deben Bhattacharya, tr., *Love Songs of Chandidas*, p. 67, cf. Kinsley, op. cit., p. 88. It is suggested that the name 'Rayan'

used for Rādhā's shadow husband in the *BVP* was picked up from the Bengali 'Ayana'.

104. Cf. Barbara S. Miller, 1977, p. 33; ibid., p. 35.
105. Barbara S. Miller, in *The Divine Consort*, p. 24. The *Nāradīya Pāñcarātra* acknowledges the absence of Rādhā's account in the earlier sources and yet grants her the supreme position saying: 'The previously unknown story of Rādhā is secret and hard to obtain. It gives *mukti* at once, is pure, the essence of Vedas, bestowing merit.' *Nāradīya Pāñcarātra*, II. 3.50 ff., cf. Mackenzie Brown, op. cit., p. 164.
106. Basudeva Goswami, 'Hari Rām Vyās', in Prabhu Dayal Mital, ed., *Bhakta Kavi Vyas ji*, Mathura: Pavan Prakashan, 1952, p. 199.
107. Shrivatsa Goswami, 'Radha the Play and Perfection of Rasa', in *The Divine Consort*, p. 88.
108. 'Whoever first pronounces 'Rādhā' and afterwards 'Kṛṣṇa' the supreme, he indeed is learned Yogin and goes easily to Golok. A great sinner in reversing the order, commits (as it were) the murder of a brāhmaṇa. You, Rādhā, are the mother of the world, the supreme self, Hari the father. The Guru of the father is the mother, to be worshipped and honored as supreme' *BVP*, 12.4.9, cf. Mackenzie Brown, op. cit., p. 118.
109. Since birth-giving was the only true work of divinity in primitive belief, the first God to claim any kind of supremacy had to claim also the ability to give birth. In fact, usurpation of the feminine power of giving birth seems to have been the distinguishing mark of the earliest Gods. Lacking vaginas, many Gods gave birth from the mouths. See Wendy Doniger O'Flaherty, *Hindu Myths*, England: Penguin, 1975, pp. 32-3, 297.
110. Cf. Larousse, *Encyclopedia of Mythology*, London: P. Aldington & D. Ames, Paul Hamyln, 1968, p. 345 and Wendy O'Flaherty, op. cit., p. 26. In fact, the idea of a male giving birth to a female who later procreated is not limited to Hinduism alone. Some works trace the idea of the magic birth-giving rib of Adam to the legend of the Hittite God, Kumarbi, who had become pregnant by eating his rival's penis, or the Sumerian childbirth Goddess' Nin-ti' 'Lady of the rib' since 'ti' meant, both 'rib' and 'life', she made infants bones *in litero* from their mother's ribs, which is why biblical writers thought that ribs possessed the magic of maternity. See S.H. Hooke, *Middle Eastern Mythology*, England: Penguin Books, 1963, p. 115. In fact, Gnostic Gospels said that Adam came into being from the virgin Earth, who was no other than Eve. See Elaine Pagels, *The Gnostic Gospels*, New York: Vintage Books, 1979, p. 53.

111. 'You have arisen from the left half of Kṛṣṇa's body, equal to Kṛṣṇa in all ways. Is that Śrī Kṛṣṇa you Rādhā? Or are you Rādhā Hari himself? This matter has not been determined by me in the Vedas? By who can it be ascertained? . . . by whom can it be determined, whether you are a portion of him or he is a portion of you?' *BVP*, vol. II, Kj.Kh. 15.101, 102, 104-15, pp. 113-14.
112. 'Kṛṣṇa was bearing the form of Rādhā, his wife bore the form of Kṛṣṇa, Brahma was unable to realize, whether the supreme has the form of a woman or the form of a man.' *BVP*, vol. I, Pk.Kh., 11-110-11, 2001, vol. I, p. 214.
113. *BVP*, vol. II, Kj.Kh. 43: 58-60, p. 353.
114. *BVP*, vol. I, Pk.Kh. 55: 70-72, p. 453. *BVP*, vol. I, Pk.Kh. 1: 11-13, pp. 143. & 1: 59-61, p. 141. Ibid., Pk.Kh. 55: 50-6, p. 451; Kj.Kh. 129: 94-5, p. 755; Pk.Kh. 65: 26-7, p. 507. *Padma Purāṇa*, 82-53-6, cf. Mackenzie Brown, op. cit., p. 166.
115. *BVP*, vol. I, *Brahma Khanda*, 3: 1-52, pp. 8-11. Here the 'self-born lord' is not only Kṛṣṇa but the image that is projected is of the form of Kṛṣṇa popular in medieval Braj, i.e. of a cowherd, and a link with his older folk name 'Vāsudeva' is also established as Dharma calls him—'Kṛṣṇa, Vāsudeva, Paramātmā, Īśvara, Govinda. . . . Lord of the cowherds, protector of the cows, . . . Lord of the cows . . . one who resides in the home of a cow. *BVP*, vol. I, Br.Kh. 3: 45-6, p. 11.
116. *BVP*, vol. I, Pk.Kh 35: 4-13, pp. 344-5 & 48: 26-9, pp. 412-13.
117. (i) For emanation of Saraswatī from Rādhā's tongue tip see *BVP*, Pk.Kh. 2: 53-4, p. 152. (ii) for Saraswatī merging in the tongue-tip of Kṛṣṇa, see *BVP*, Pk.Kh. 34. 61-8, p. 341. (iii) For Savitrī emerging out of the tongue-tip of Kṛṣṇa, see *BVP*, Br.Kh. 4: 1-3, p. 14 & 3: 56-9, p. 12.
118. The *Rādhā Tapani Upaniṣad* and *Radhopaniṣad* say that Rādhā and Kṛṣṇa are one. See Lodha, op. cit., p. 39. 'Soul is my reflection, this is admitted by all. *Prakriti* is my deformed form, and I alone happen to be the form of *Prakriti*. O king, as the whiteness cannot be separated from milk and the coolness of water cannot be separated from it, the instinct of burning cannot be separated from fire, the sound cannot be separated from the sky, the fragrance cannot be separated from the Earth, lustre cannot be separated from the Sun or Moon, the soul cannot be separated from the great soul, since there is no difference between them. Similarly Rādhā and myself are inseparable' *BVP*, vol. II, Kj.kh. 73: 47-50, p. 484, also see Pk.Kh. 55: 80-2, p. 453.
119. 'Having rubbed (her) limbs with musk, holding a flute, wearing a yellow sash she says: Rādhā, I am Śyāma. The youth (Kṛṣṇa) having

decorated himself with ear stud, puts Śyāma's black colour in his eyes'. Haridas, *Kelimal*, verse no. 56, p. 258.

120. Sūrdās cf. Srivatsa Goswami in *The Divine Consort*, p. 86.
121. *BVP*, vol. I, Pk.Kh. 2: 28-50, pp. 151-2 & 3.47-48, p. 158.
122. Some earliest reference to the egg are in the *Ṛgveda* X. 121.1 ff, cf. Deussen Paul, *The Philosophy of the Upanishads*, tr. A.S. Geden, New York: Dover, 1966, p. 182. In *Śatapatha Brāhmaṇa*, the Prajapati having created the primeval waters enters them as an egg.; Paul, op. cit., p. 183 and Larousse, op. cit., p. 346. Egg as the mythical symbol of the creator was, popular in oriental world history as well. For example, Egyptians's sign for the world egg was the same as for an embryo in a woman's womb. In Egypt, the mother of the world egg was Hathor in the guise of the Nile goose, later mythologized as the goose who laid the golden egg; Barbara G. Walker, op. cit., p. 107. Orphic said that the Great Goddess of darkness first brought forth the world egg, which was identified with the moon; heaven and earth were made of the eggshell and the first deity to emerge was the bisexual Eros. Jack Lindsay, *The Orgins of Astrology,* New York: Muller, 1971, p. 116. A Greek carving showed the God Apollo sitting on a pile of eggs, trying to copy the life-giving magic of his mother Leto or Lalona, who gave birth to the world egg and hatched it; Richard Payne Knight, *The Symbolical Language of Ancient Art and Mythology*, New York: J.W. Bouton, 1892, p. 147.
123. *Bhāgavata Purāṇa*, III.10.5-6 in Mackenzie Brown, op. cit., 175. 'Ra' was also the name of Egypt's Sun God, just like Rādhā, mystery surrounds this God as well. Priests say—'his image is not spread out, in books—he is too mysterious that his glory should be revealed, too great that men should question concerning him . . . too powerful that he should be known . . . whose name is hidden for that he is a mystery'; Adolf Erman, *The Literature of the Ancient Egyptian*, New York: Dover, 1971, pp. 296, 299-300. Same kind of explanation is given for the absence of Rādhā's name in the *Bhāgavata Purāṇa*; *BVP*, vol. I, Pk.Kh. 55: 80, p. 453.
124. *BVP*, vol. II, Kj.Kh. III. 57-58a, p. 674; Pk.Kh. 55: 79, p. 45; Kj.Kh. 92: 71, 124: 83; Pk.Kh. 55: 18-20, p. 449; Pk.Kh. 56: 43, p. 458; Kj.Kh. 124: 2-3, pp. 724-5; Kj.Kh. 124.3, vol. II, p. 725; Kj.Kh. 124: 11, p. 725. Here it is said that the one who recites the name of Rādhā and then of Kṛṣṇa surely goes to Goloka if the order is reversed, one earns the sin of *Brahmahatyā*.
125. Ibid., Poddar, pp. 397-8.
126. Ibid., Poddar, p. 331 & *BVP* 2001, vol. II, Kj.Kh. 4: 77-117, pp. 15-18.
127. Pawan Verma, *Widows of Vrindavan: A Poetic Monograph*, Delhi: Penguin, 2002.

128. Nancy M. Martin, 'Mirabai, Inscribed in Text, Embodied in Life', in *Vaishnavi*.
129. *Bhaktamāla*, Nabhadas, verse no. 115, p. 290, and *Bhakti Ras Bodhinī*, Priyadas, verse nos. 471-80, pp. 290-3.
130. Goswami Harirai, *Chaurāsī Vaiṣṇavoṅ kī Vārtā*, pp. 189-90 and *Kṛṣṇadas kī Vārtā*, Bombay: Pushti Prakashan, 1976, p. 314.
131. Maura Corcoran, 'Life and Poetry of Ras Khan', in Monika Thiel Horstman, *Bhakti in Current Research*, Berlin: Dietrich Reimer Verlag, 1983, pp. 78-9.
Also see J.S. Hawley, 'The Sectarian Logic of the *Sur Das ki Vaarta*', in the same work, pp. 157-68.
132. Ram Kanta Chakravarti, *Vaishnavism in Bengal*, Calcutta: Bengal Press, 1985, p. 174.
133. Vrindavan Das, *Caitanya Bhāgavata*, ii-16. 1-18, cf. Jan Brzeziginski, 'Women Saints in Gandiya Vaishnavism', in *Vaishnavi*, p. 65.
134. Rādhā Govinda Nath, ed., *Caitanya Caritamrita*; *Antya Khanda,* Calcutta, 3rd edn., 1973, p. 89. cf. Renukanath, *Notable Mughal and Hindu Women in the 16th-17th Century AD*, Delhi: South Asia Books, 1988, p. 201. Also see Brzezinski, op. cit., pp. 60-1.
135. Sukumar Sen, *Bangla Sahitya Itihas*, Delhi: Sahitya Akademi, 2003, p. 409.
136. *Narottam Vilās* 204, cf. Edward C. Dimock, *Place of the Hidden Moon*, Chicago: University of Chicago Press, 1966, pp. 100-1.
137. Cf. Brzezinski, op. cit., p. 73.
138. June McDavid, op. cit., p. 192.
139. Margaret Case, *Seeing* Kṛṣṇa*: The Religious World of a Brahman Family in Vrindaban*, Delhi: Oxford University Press, 2000, pp. 43-53.
140. R.K. Barz, 'Krishnadas Adhikari: An Irascible Devotee's Approach to the Divine', in Bailey and Watson, eds., *Bhakti Studies*, New Delhi: Sterling, 1991, p. 238.
141. *Chaurāsī Vaiṣṇavoṅ kī Vārtā*, pp. 314, 318 and 330.
142. Ibid., p. 324.
143. Ibid., pp. 189-90.
144. Ibid., pp. 42-9 & 74-6. For more see pp. 57, 134.
145. Ibid., p. 71. For more female *bhaktas*, see pp. 175-6, 180, 182-5, 211, 213, 224, 234, 243-4, 286-7.
146. *Do Sau Bāvan Vaiṣṇavoṅ kī Vārtā*, pp. 17-19, 72-8, 131.
147. Ibid., p. 138. For more female *bhaktas*, see pp. 143-4, 188-9, 212, 240, 284, 320, 311, 309, 300-2, 303, 322, 344, 350, 360, 394, 396, 449, 456, 462-3, 471-8.
148. Ibid., p. 172.
149. Ibid., p. 125.
150. Ibid., p. 251.

151. Bhagwat Mudit, *Rasik Ananyamal*, cf. P.D. Mittal, *Braj ka Sānskṛtik Itihās*, Mathura: Shri Hari, 1948, p. 483. There are many instances of prostitutes being converted to *Kṛṣṇabhakti*, and then performing for the deity. For example in *Do Sau Bāvan Vaiṣṇavoṅ kī Vārtā,* pp. 264-5, 252, *Caurāsī Vaiṣṇavoṅ kī Vārtā*, p. 324.
152. *Do Sau Bāvan Vaiṣṇavoṅ kī Vārtā*, pp. 449-56.
153. *Caurāsī Vaiṣṇavoṅ kī Vārtā*, pp. 286-7 and *Do Sau Bāvan Vaiṣṇavoṅ kī Vārtā*, p. 101.
154. Nancy M. Martin in *Vaishnavi*.
155. Swami Haridas, *Aṣṭasiddhānta*, no. 14, cf. Rosenstein, op. cit., p. 197.

PART III

Religious Identities: Negotiating Conflict and Accommodation

SEVEN

Understanding Sufi-Sant Interaction in Medieval India

Rameshwar Prasad Bahuguna

INTRODUCTION

Modern historical writings on the religious history of medieval India are mostly the histories of either Sufism or bhakti devotionalism. These two histories—one based on Persian sources and the other on regional literary sources—have, however, followed their own independent trajectories and progressed largely in isolation from each other. Research on medieval Indian Sufi orders is usually viewed as an integral part of the larger project of constructing the history of Islam in India. Similarly, most of the scholarship on the medieval bhakti 'movement' perceives itself as being engaged in the study of 'medieval Hinduism' or 'bhakti Hinduism'.[1] It is convenient to seek an explanation for this long-lasting historiographical division of labour in the difficulties involved in the combined use of two entirely different genres of history sources—one requiring expertise in Persian sources and the other in regional literary materials. More importantly, what lies at the root of this divisive historiographical practice is the assumption that all religious beliefs, practices and experiences in pre-colonial times can be neatly classified into two universal and well-demarcated categories of Hinduism and Islam.

In all fairness to some of the practitioners of these largely insular histories, they do incorporate the theme of the interaction between Sufism and bhakti devotionalism in their studies. As we shall see in the following pages, historians of all ideological affiliations—from Hindu communalists and Muslim separatists to syncretic nationalists and Western Orientalists—have, over the decades, reflected upon the extent to which medieval Sufism and bhakti devotionalism have directly or indirectly influenced each other. However, since most of the studies of the relationship between the two religious phenomena get submerged in the grand narratives of the encounter between Hinduism and Islam, the possibilities of exploring the full range of this complex and diverse interaction become severely restricted. Neither Sufism nor bhakti represented monolithic entities and the existence of multiple tendencies, conflicts, claims and counter-claims within each one of them must be recognized. It should also be noted that both Sufism and bhakti devotionalism spread virtually in all parts of the country during the medieval centuries and the interaction between them acquired different regional characteristics.

This paper seeks to study the various patterns of interaction between the Sufis and sants in northern India during the period between the thirteenth and seventeenth centuries. The relationship between Sufis and Vaiṣṇava bhaktas constitutes a separate area of investigation and does not form part of this paper. There is a general consensus among scholars that *nirguni* monotheistic sants like Kabir, Nanak and Dadu were much closer to the Sufis in ideological and theological terms than the *saguni* Vaiṣṇava bhaktas who believed in divine incarnations and image worship. It has been argued in this paper that neither the Hindu-Muslim conflictual model nor the syncretic model is of much value in explaining and understanding the complex process of interactions between the Sufis and sants, and more importantly, between their respective followers. Mutual accommodation, tolerance and appropriations defined this interaction as much as did the conflicts, rivalries and denunciations.

HISTORIOGRAPHY

One of the important features of twentieth-century nationalist historical writings on religious movements in medieval India is the nationalization and secularization of the connections and parallels between the Sufi and sant movements. The interaction between the two movements is seen as an important building block in the making of India's 'national composite culture'. In the words of Tarachand, Kabir's was the 'first attempt to reconcile Hinduism and Islam. . . . He was the first to come forward boldly to proclaim a religion of the centre, a middle path. . . .'[2] In Tarachand's opinion, Sufism and santic bhakti evolved a synthesis of the two religions by developing emotional piety and disregarding the ritualistic and sectarian sides of religion. The resulting synthesis was, in his words, 'so complete that they virtually lost themselves in one another'.[3] Scholars like M. Mujeeb,[4] Yusuf Husain,[5] K.A. Nizami[6] and S.A.A. Rizvi[7] have also, in one way or the other, stressed the ways in which medieval sants and Sufis transcended the barriers of Hinduism and Islam to prepare a common meeting ground for the followers of the two religions. An important passage in K.A. Nizami's celebrated work on the religious history of thirteenth-century India may be cited here as illustrative of the nationalist historiographic practice:

> The quintessence of mystic teachings in the thirteenth century was the unity of Godhead and the brotherhood of man. The extent to which the Hindu mind was moved by these principles may be gauged from an analysis of the Hindu religious movements of the subsequent centuries. The fact that the religious leadership of the Bhakti movements in the fourteenth and fifteenth centuries came from the lower strata of Hindu society—a section which had been deeply influenced by the Muslim mystics and their khanqah life—is too significant to be ignored. Probably never before in the long history of Hinduism had religious leaders sprung from those strata of society to which Chaitanya, Kabir, Nanak, Dhanna, Dadu and others belonged. There was hardly a saint of the Bhakti school who had not passed some of his time in a khanqah.[8]

It may be difficult to prove the existence of direct links between the Sufis and leading bhakti sants of the time and, therefore, the last part of Nizami's statement may be a sweeping generalization. Moreover, the age of leading Sufi saints of the thirteenth-fourteenth centuries was long over before the advent of Kabir and other bhakti sants in the fifteenth-sixteenth centuries on the historical scene.

Satish Chandra has argued that the period between the eleventh to the fifteenth century is characterized by the growing interaction between Sufis and non-conformist Nāthpanthī *yogīs* and *siddhas* who mostly belonged to non-Brahmanical sections of society. The influence of the Nāthpanthī *yogīs* began to decline in the subsequent period and the lower caste groups began to be attracted to the sant movement led by Kabir and Nanak.[9] Like Tarachand, Satish Chandra also believes that sants were influenced by Islam and Sufism. He stresses the commonalities and 'amalgam' between the two groups of preachers in particular, and between Hinduism and Islam in general:

> The Sufis, the nath-panthi jogis, and the nirgun sants among whom Nanak may be included, formed separate but overlapping concentric circles, with the overlap varying in each case. What is significant is not the attempt of a merger of the two religions—something never seriously attempted by anyone, but the emergence of a long measure of understanding and harmony between the two religions in which the Sufis, the jogis and the nirguna saints played a definite role.[10]

The above-cited statement is a classic example of how empirically sound accounts of interaction between various devotional and mystical orders are ultimately turned into cannon fodder for demonstrating the existence of harmonious relations between 'the two religions' in medieval India. The two-way exchange of mystical ideas and practices between the Sufis of different *silsilahs* and the Nāthpanthī *yogīs* is an established fact of medieval Indian religious history.[11] The appropriation of Nāthpanthī symbols and images was a popular practice among Sufi authors of Hindavi romances such as *Cāndāyan*, *Mṛgāvatī*, *Padmāvat* and *Madhumālatī*.[12] It is also not difficult to come across instances of Sufi saints embracing many Vaiṣṇava bhakti themes and practices.[13] The secular-nationalist history writing, however, characteristically yokes all these exchanges and mutual appropriations between the Sufis and non-Muslim devotees of various categories to its core ideas of 'understanding and harmony between the two religions' (that is Hinduism and Islam).

The emphasis in the liberal and secular nationalist historiography on composite culture and syncretism serves the purpose of presenting Islam as the 'domesticated element of everyday popular life.[14] The concept of syncretism has come under the close scrutiny of historians and other scholars who argue that it assumes the prior and readymade existence of two fixed and tightly bounded religions into which all the sections of the populace could be classified.[15] Not only does it overlook conflict between the two religions, and heterogeneity and plurality within each one, it also privileges these religions by erasing from historical discourse multiple forms of religious beliefs and practices that could neither be characterized as Hindu or Muslim.

In any case, the portrayal of santic figures like Kabir and Nanak as the advocates of reconciliation between Hinduism and Islam is neither based on facts nor does it offer us insights into the actual contestatory and resistive character of non-Brahmanical, lower class religious culture in medieval India.

Satish Chandra has reaffirmed the earlier assumption prevalent among liberal nationalist historians that Kabir and Nanak were indebted to medieval Indian Sufis for many of their ideas.[16] Among medieval bhakti preachers, the *nirguni* sants form a group that is highly critical of both Vaiṣṇaya and Sufi practices. It is virtually impossible to establish the existence of any mutual influence or accommodation between sants and Sufis in the same way as we can attempt in the case of Sufis and Vaiṣṇava bhaktas or Sufis and Nāthpanthī *yogīs*. Although strong and uncompromising faith in a formless god was upheld by both the sants and Sufis, it appears that there was hardly any common meeting ground between the two groups of devotees in other crucial aspects. It was a miracle of nationalist historiography to establish a unity of purpose between Sufis—who were firmly rooted in the Islamic system of belief and practice—and sants who completely rejected that system along with the Brahmanical one. Yet, when we turn to hagiographic materials about the sants and Sufis, an altogether different world emerges before us—a world in which their followers were competing with each other and with myriad other religious groups for spiritual and material influence. During the course of the sixteenth and seventeenth centuries, the respective followers of the sants and Sufis established a pattern of relationship that contained elements of both competition and triumphal assertions of superiority on the one hand, and mutual appropriations and accommodation on the other.

The liberal nationalist tradition of history writing emerged as a counterweight to the colonial and Orientalist portrayal of perpetual antagonism between the 'foreign' Islamic civilization, imposed through conquest on Indian soil, and the 'native' Hindu civilization. Wholeheartedly embracing this perspective, many Indian historians depicted the medieval *nirguni* sants and Vaiṣṇava bhakti preachers as Hindu reformers whose main objective was to defend Hinduism in the face of the Islamic challenge.[17] On the other hand, scholars who came under the influence of Muslim separatism in the twentieth century either argued that attempts by the bhakti preachers and Sufis to find a common meeting ground between Hinduism and Islam were never strong enough and ultimately failed, or asserted, like the Hindu communalists, that rivalry rather than accommodation defined the relations between the two groups of devotees. Thus, in Aziz Ahmad's words, 'In fourteenth and fifteenth centuries as Sufism penetrated into the masses of converts and semi-converts from Hinduism, the Bhakti movements rose as a popular Hindu counter-challenge to the proselytizing pull of Sufi humanism.'[18]

Some Western writings of more recent origin have also expressed skepticism about the transformative potential of the interaction between the Muslim Sufis and 'Hindu' sants. W.H. McLeod, for instance, rejects the idea that Islam influenced Guru Nanak's religious thought in any significant way.[19] Charlotte Vaudeville argues that 'there is nothing in Kabir's verses to suggest more than a casual acquaintance with the Shaykhs and Pirs of his times'. She would rather have us believe that the Nāthpanthī beliefs and practices had a major role in shaping Kabir's religion, followed by Vaiṣṇava influences.[20] Bruce Lawrence thinks that Sufism did not have much influence on the sant movement, and that direct links between the Sufis and leading sants cannot be proved. Accounts such as the Janamsākhīs, which show frequent meetings between the sants and Sufis, are 'fictionalized in their content' and 'only serve legitimating function for followers of a particular sant figure'. Lawrence, however, does explore the possibility of indirect connections between Sufism and santism by analysing the technical terms and literary techniques employed by the sants and, more importantly, by drawing our attention to references to Sufis in various genres of santic literature.[21] Another eminent scholar on medieval santism, David Lorenzen, would rather use the utterances of medieval sants to show the existence or an anti-Islamic Hindu identity in pre-colonial period.[22]

SOCIAL BACKGROUNDS AND ATTITUDES OF SUFIS AND SANTS

The foregoing analysis of historical writings on the relations between the medieval sants and Sufis makes it clear that there are two dominant historiographical trends—one focusing on mutual accommodation and harmony between the two, and the other portraying them as rivals. Undoubtedly, apart from a common belief in monotheism and a formless god, there were many other striking similarities between their ideological and religious doctrines (e.g. *zikr-jap*, *virah-dard*, *prem-ishq*, *tawhid-nirgun*, etc.). However, there existed striking differences between their social backgrounds, social perceptions and many religious aspects. To begin with, most of the Sufi leaders, particularly of the established orders, belonged to the Persian-speaking higher classes, while the sants of the formative period were, by and large, from lower and lowest castes, were illiterate peasants and crafts-makers, and composed their verses in the vernacular. Most of the Sufis were firmly rooted in the system of Islamic belief and practice. Serious disagreements prevailed between them and the *ulema* over many ritualistic aspects of religion and among the Sufis themselves, but no Sufi ever questioned the basic principles of the Islamic faith. Mohammad Habib has observed that Sufism 'is a post-graduate creed' in Islam.[23] Thus, for instance, Shaikh Nizamuddin Auliya's Sufi ideas were characterized by a high degree of knowledge of Islam in all its aspects. He was both a Sufi as well as a scholar, and did not accept the false distinction between Sufism and theological sciences. His differences with the *ulema* were not the differences of Sufism *versus* theology but were caused by the worldliness and empty externalism of the latter. He placed considerable emphasis on knowledge.[24] He was an accomplished scholar of the Koran and commentaries on it, of *hadith* and *fiq* (jurisprudence).[25] He was conversant with all literature on judicial, theological and mystical topics. Mohammad Habib has rightly pointed out that as far as Islamic knowledge was concerned, the *ulema* and Sufis were the product of the same system of education (*darsiyāt*).[26] Shaikh Nizamuddin Auliya was aware of Ali Hujviri's famous treaties on Sufism called *Kashf-u'l-Mahjub* (The Unveiling of What Has Been Hidden)[27] and another work *'Awarif-u'l-Ma'arif* (Insights From Men of Discernment) written by Shaykh Shihabuddin Suhrawardi.[28] It was because of his emphasis on knowledge that he decided that Maulana Akhi Siraj, who was otherwise eligible, could not become his successor because he lacked necessary academic knowledge.[29] He also made a distinction between various types of prayers and their virtues.[30] Sufis of most established orders combined the knowledge of Islamic scriptures with Sufi ideology and practices.

On the whole, as preachers of Islam and Islamic mysticism, Sufi shaikhs of the leading orders were an integral part of the Persian-speaking Muslim elites in India. Some of them (e.g. the Chishti saints of the early period) kept aloof from the state and court but their activities, ideas and popularity were not bereft of significant political implications, particularly in terms of their role in legitimizing the state, its authority and hierarchy.[31] One could try in vain to look for evidence of the Sufis' opposition to the hierarchical structure of medieval Indian society in the entire corpus of Sufi literature. Thus, although Shaikh Nizamuddin Auliya praised the acts of manumitting a slave, he was not opposed to the system of slavery itself.[32] It is true that the leading Chishti saints of the early period lived on *futuh* (unasked charity) and led an austere and simple life. But, as I.A. Zilli has observed, there was a paradox between what the Chishti Sufis preached and what they practised—they accepted *futuh* from those they otherwise criticized.[33] Many Sufis of the Chishti order and also of other *silsilahs* were known for their liberalism, and for their willingness to adopt local customs, practices and dialects. Yet, as Zilli pointed out, their faith in *tawakkul* (resignation to divine will) implied rejection of the means and occupations to earn one's livelihood. The Sufis adopted a passive attitude to work and very few of the eminent ones were engaged in manual work.[34] Large numbers of the disciples of Shaikh Nizamuddin Auliya belonged to the class of nobility and government servants.[35] Many Sufi saints were patronized by the rulers and other elites for their charisma (*baraka*), and their blessings were sought by contemporary rulers to perpetuate their rule. Both during his lifetime and after his death, the Sufi shaikh was regarded as an intercessor between God and his followers.[36]

On the other hand, the sants mostly belonged to lower castes and subordinate social groups. Namdev was a fourteenth-century calico printer (*chhīnpā* or *rangrez*) from Maharashtra and Kabir was a late fifteenth- early sixteenth-century weaver (*julāhā*) from Banaras. Raidas or Ravidas was a tanner or cobbler belonging to the *camār* caste and a contemporary of Kabir from the same city. Sen was a barber (*nāī*) and Dhanna was a jāṭ peasant from Rajasthan. That both Kabir and Raidas lived in Banaras is interesting because Banaras (or Kashi) was a citadel of Brahmanical orthodoxy and ritual. It was a city where brāhmaṇa ideologues most vigorously and assiduously practised and legitimized the inequalities of their socio-religious order.

Most of the sants led the lives of householders.[37] Far from isolating themselves form the society (like the Nāthpanthīs), they led a family life and pursued their hereditary occupations. Kabir and Ravidas were petty commodity producers using their own and their families' labour. Most of them were neither slaves nor serfs. They were free artisans in the sense that they had full control over the means of production and the labour process. They were not alienated form the work they did. They were small-scale producers with the ability to conceptualize their work and do it as well. Such a thinking-doing method of work enabled them to develop a language of work which we come across repeatedly in their utterances. Since work was a hereditary occupation for them, knowledge about work and craft was transmitted from one generation to the other, developing a cultural continuity that is so important for the technological innovations that mark human labour.

Most of these artisan-sants were proud of their professions and mention them repeatedly in their verses, particularly in the signature lines. Most of the early paintings of Kabir depict him as pursuing his craft and preaching at the same time. Various legends about Kabir and Raidas narrate the encounters of these sants with their adversaries in the market-places where they used to go to sell their products.[38] Asceticism is rejected but the accumulation of wealth, greed and Brahmanical system of *dāna* are also denounced.

The sants can hardly be called 'Hindu', and were harshly critical of both Islam and Brahmanism. Kabir did not accept either the Brahmanical theory of 'avatār' or the Islamic prophetology. There is hardly any criticism of the caste hierarchy in medieval Sufi literature but santic utterances abound in the denunciation of birth-based social distinctions. In fact, there is a clear association of the Brahmanic and Islamic religions in Kabir's poetry with the interests of the contemporary ruling elites of Turks and Rajputs. In the case of the relationship between santism and Sufism, we come across a more complex scenario. There are references to certain Sufi saints, and Sufi beliefs and practices in santic poetry. Here the attitude is clearly sarcastic and denunciatory. There are many verses in the Kabir corpus which are critical of the Sufis. One may cite here the following utterance which shows Kabir's clear disapproval of them:

> Through Manikpur, Kabir has passed,
> There he heard of the fame of Shaykh Taqqi
> At the place which they call Jaunpur,
> And at Jhusi heard the names of many pirs:
> There are written the names of the twenty-one pirs,
> People read the Khatma and sing the Prophet's praise.
> Hearing that talk, I could not restrain myself,
> Seeing those graves, I was bewildered:
> The works prescribed by that friend of God and that prophet,
> And all their commands—all that is unlawful.[39]

This verse clearly demonstrates that Kabir had gained some knowledge of the activities of the Sufi saints whose *khanqahs* were located in various parts of eastern Uttar Pradesh. He may have even visited some of the *khanqahs* and *dargahs*. However, what is remarkable is that he expresses his disapproval of Sufi saint-cults and also rejects the idea of prophethood. In the following verse, he advises two Sufi saints to listen to his words:

> O Shaykh Aqardi, O Shaykh Saqaardi,
> Listen to my words
> With open eyes, consider
> the beginning and the end
> and the succession of ages.[40]

As is well known, Kabir was opposed to the ritual of pilgrimage that was prevalent both among Hindus and Muslims. Nor did he support the practice of ritualistic sacrifices:

> If the sheikh be denied of patience
> of what use is that Kaba pilgrimage
> How can he whose soul is not firm
> ever hope to reach God?[41]
> Allah, the Eternal—is the protector of the Poor
> He never ordered violence
> Tell me, you Murshid and you Pir
> Where did they come from?[42]

In the case of Guru Nanak, W.H. McLeod is of the strong opinion that the affinities between his religious thought and Sufism are not the product of any Sufi influence on him.[43] J.S. Grewal also draws our attention to certain verses of Guru Nanak in which clear disapproval of the dependence of Sufi establishments on royal patronage has been expressed.[44] The sants rejected the caste hierarchy and the dominance of brāhmaṇas and *qāzīs*. They clearly dissociated themselves from the Brahmanical and Islamic religions. The *sant-vāṇīs* reflect the santic attitude of ridicule towards and disapproval of the medieval religious and ruling elites. The following verse of Raidas indicates the santic idea of a casteless egalitarian social order:

> Begampur is the name of the place,
>   without suffering or distress.
> Without anxiety, taxes or property,
>   without fear of failure or fear of loss.

I have found a good home in my own land.
    O my brother, there is everlasting well-being there.
Its everlasting sovereignty is firm and stable,
    there none is third or second, all are one.
Flourishing and ever famous,
    the wealthy dwell in that town.
They wander around wherever they please,
    they stroll through places unchallenged,
Says Ravidas the liberated Chamar,
    whoever is my fellow citizen, is my friend.[45]

SUFI-SANT INTERCATION IN HISTORY AND HAGIOGRAPHY

K.A. Nizami's assertion that there was 'hardly a saint of the Bhakti school who had not passed some of his time in a *khanqah*' may appear to be the expression of the modern secular nationalist sentiment of Hindu-Muslim unity. But while there is very little evidence of bhakti sants frequently visiting Sufi *khanqahs* in large numbers, we do have instances of interaction between the non-Brahmanical Nāthpanthī *yogīs* and some of the leading Sufi shaikhs of the thirteenth and fourteenth centuries. There are references to Shaikh Nizamuddin Auliya's conversations with the Nāthpanthī *yogīs* in which he has shown his approval of the religious path followed by them.[46] In an anecdote, the Shaikh refers to the victory of a Sufi over a Nāthpanthī *yogī* in the performance of miracles. The basic idea behind the anecdote was to prove the superiority of Islam over the path followed by the *yogīs*.[47] The Sufi romance narratives of the medieval period, such as Malik Muhammad Jaisi's *Padmāvat*, Qutbans's *Mṛgāvatī* and Manjhan's *Madhumālatī,* contain reverential references to the founder of the Nāthpanthī religion, Gorakhnath.[48] There existed a two-way interaction. There were mutual borrowings but also clear religious disagreements. The later Nāthpanthī texts, e.g. *Gorakh-Muhammad Goṣṭhī*, testify to a relationship of conflict and assimilation between the two. Moreover, the popularity of ambivalent religious personalities such as Guga Pir among the lower classes also indicates a process of mutual appropriation between the Nāthpanthīs and Sufis.

Sufi hagiography from the seventeenth century and Kabīrpanthī legendary materials of a much later period contain accounts of Kabir's encounters with Sufis of different *silsilāhs*. Similarly, the *janamsākhī* hagiography includes many narratives of Guru Nanak's meetings with the Sufis of Punjab, including Shaikh Fariduddin Masud Ganj-i-Shakar. Since the dates of Shaikh Farid and Guru Nanak are separated by more than two centuries, scholars have rightly rejected the possibility of any such encounter. However, it does appear that Guru Nanak visited Multan and met the lineage head (*sajjādanashīn*) of Shaikh Farid's shrine. The inclusion of the utterances attributed to Shaikh Farid in the Sikh scripture, *Ādi Granth*, clearly testifies to the existence of a certain degree of interaction between the Sufis or Sufi followers and the early Sikh *gurus*.[49]

There are Sufi hagiographic texts like Shaikh Abdul Rahman Chisti's *Mirāt-ul Asrār* (mid-seventeenth century) and Shaikh Abdu'llah Khweshgi's *M'ariju'l-wilayat*, which narrate Kabir's interaction with the medieval Sufis.[50] The biographical and hagiographical literature on medieval Indian Sufis began to present him first as a *muwahhid* (monotheist) and then as a Sufi, albeit of a different kind. If one has to look for interactions and encounters between santism and Sufism, one must move beyond great Sufis and sants and focus on the concerns, anxieties and aspirations of their followers during the course of sixteenth, seventeenth and eighteenth centuries. The vibrant religious culture in later medieval India was characterized by the efflorescence of a large number of religious fraternities, communities and saint-cults. The followers of the sants, Sufis, Nāthpanthīs, Śāktas and Vaiṣṇavas faced each other in a relationship of conflict and mutual appropriation. At the lower level of the society, there was much competition among various religious groups for followers. This process begins with the writing of biographical dictionaries on medieval Sufis, the composition of the *bhaktamāls* and *janamsākhīs*, the *samvāds*, *parachaīs* and *goṣṭhī* literature, and, finally, the hagiographic accounts of the lives of medieval Sufis. These are the areas where one has to look for the multiple processes of encounters, negotiations and frequent boundary-crossings among the Sufi followers and sant-followers. These literary texts indicate all kinds of rivalries and reconciliations between the sants, between sants and Sufis, between Sufis, between sants and Nāthpanthīs, between sants and Vaiṣṇavas, between sants and Shaktas, between Sufis and Vaiṣṇavas, between Sufis and Nāthpanthīs, etc. The picture that one gets is not just that of Turk-Hindu conflict at the elite level but a fierce religious competition among the new religious communities for followers, resources, and patronage.

One can see this happening from the end of the sixteenth century. Abdul Haqq Muhaddis Dahlawi wrote the biographical details of the major Sufi shaikhs of medieval Hindustan in his *Akhbār al akhyar.* In this work, Kabir is represented as neither Hindu nor Muslim but as a monotheist (*muwahhid*).[51] By the middle of the seventeenth century, the Chishti Sufi tradition in Awadh began to look upon Kabir as a *muwahhid* and as a Sufi. The image of Kabir as it emerges in Shaikh Abdul Rahman Shisti's *Mir āt ul Asrār* is very interesting:

> Makhdum Shaikh Bhikh who lies buried at Bilahri, four *kos* from Awadh, was a leading disciple of Shaikh Jamal Gujar. . . . One of the eminent *khalifas* of Makhdum Shaikh Bhikh was Kabir *malamati.* At the beginning of his mystic career, Kabir was a disciple of Shaikh Taqi bin Shaikh Ramazan Ha'ik (a weaver). Suhrawardi. Shaikh Taqi's grave is in Jhusi near Allahabad. Later Kabir *malamati* became a disciple of Ramanand Bairagi and did hard ascetic exercises. The predominance of Tawhid in his mystic preception caused him to ignore the externalists ('ulama) and he began to express mystic thoughts without any inhibition. The externalists condemned him as having turned into an infidel, but gnostics and experts in esoteric knowledge considered him a frank *muwahhid.* He lived like *malamatiyya* ecstatics. Finally he obtained the Firdausiya *khirqa* from Shaikh Bhikh and found spiritual comfort in *sulh-i kul* (universal concord). His tomb at Maghar in Gorakhpur is visited by a large number of people.[52]

This hagiographic narrative imparts multiple identities to Kabir—ranging from a Rāmānandī Bairāgī and a *malāmatī* Sufi to a follower of the Firdausiya order of Sufis. Another hagiographer, Shaikh 'Abdu'llah Khweshgi, the author of the *M'ariju'l-wilayat,* wrote:

> Shaikh Kabir Jolaha (weaver) is the disciple of Shaikh Taqi. Kabir was one of the perfect *awliya* (Sufis) and the most famous Gnostic of his age but

he chose for himself the Sufic path of the *malamatiyya.* This technique he adopted in order to remain unknown. His Hindi poetry is sublime and is a proof of the eminence of the author. If his poetry is carefully examined it is found full of ideas of unification (*wisal*), with little mention of separation. He was a pioneer in expressing spiritual truth and gnosis through the medium of Hindi. He wrote a great variety of Hindi poetry, and his *Bishnupads* and *sakhis* are very famous. Those who do proper justice to Kabir's poetry are convinced that no other poetry can match it in expressing Divine secrets and spiritual truth. Muhaqqiq-i Hindi (Ja'isi) imitated the style of Kabir, but he chose the medium of Soratha, and dohas through which to express his thoughts. Kabir's spiritual eminence attracted both Muslims and Hindus to his discipleship. Each religious group considered him to be a member of its own religion, but in reality he transcended all religious distinctions.[53]

These hagiographic accounts seek to represent Kabir as a Sufi but, at the same time, his image of a religious figure who transcended existing Hindi-Muslim distinctions is kept intact. On the other hand, if we take into consideration the santic hagiographic narratives, as contained in the *vānīs* of later sants and also in texts such as Raghodas's *Bhaktamāl,* many medieval Sufis are treated as devotees of God, along with Puranic figures like Dhruv and Prahlad, and historical figures like Kabir, Raidas and Dadu. Some of the important Sufi saints like Rabiya, Mansur al-Hallaj and Shaikh Farid are accorded a high status in santic hagiography.[54] From the beginning of the seventeenth century, the followers of Dadu began to glorify the lives and deeds of great santic heroes of the past, particularly Kabir. What is, however, remarkable is that great Muslim Sufis of the remote past are frequently named among the devotees of God in the works of Dādūpanthī hagiographers and poets. Rajjab, a seventeenth-century follower of Dadu, mentions Mansur-al Hallaj as one of the leading bhaktas.[55] As is evident from Raghodas's early eighteenth-century *Bhaktamāl*, many Sufis, including Mansur, Rabia and Shaikh Farid, came to be regarded as an integral part of the sant movement in the same way as Prahlad, Dhruv, Kabir and Dadu were.[56]

To sum up, sant-Sufi interactions occurred more in hagiography then in actual reality. But hagiographic accounts of both the Sufis and sants express the concerns and agenda of their followers. It is evident that the popularity of both the leading sants and Sufis of the period could not be overlooked by the two groups of followers, who were engaged in a process of mutual interaction. It is this two-way interaction based on mutual appropriations and negotiations that made it possible for the followers of Sufis and sants to see them as part of the same religious universe.

NOTES

1. Among the recent studies that seek to question and transcend the dominant tendency among modern historians to understand the religious history of medieval India in terms of Hindu-Muslim categories, mention may be made of essays in David Gilmartin and Bruce B. Lawrence, eds., *Beyond Turk and Hindu: Religious Identities in Islamicate South Asia*, Gainesville: University Press of Florida, 2000. Although written from an altogether different perspective and focusing on both socio-economic and ideological factors, Irfan Habib's 'Kabir: The Historical Setting', in Irfan Habib, ed., *Religion in Indian History,* Delhi: Tulika, 2007, pp. 142-57 is also an attempt to view Kabir and other *nirguni* sants as religious figures who were neither Hindus nor Muslims and who rejected both the religions.
2. Tara Chand, *Influence of Islam on Indian Culture*, 2nd edn. (1st pub. 1922), Allahabad: The Indian Press Publication, 1963, p. 165.
3. Tara Chand, *Society and State in the Mughal Period*, Patel Memorial Lectures, Delhi: Publications Division, pp. 39-40.
4. M. Mujeeb, *The Indian Muslims*, London: George Allen and Unwin Ltd., 1967, pp. 283-315.
5. Yusuf Husain, *Glimpses of Medieval Indian Culture*, 2nd edn., Bombay: Asia Publishing House, 1959.
6. K.A. Nizami, *Religion and Politics in India during the Thirteenth Century*, Delhi: Oxford University Press, 2002 (1st pub. 1961), pp. 186-280.
7. S.A.A. Rizvi, *A History of Sufism in India*, vol. I, Delhi: Munshiram Manoharlal, pp. 322-96.
8. K.A. Nizami, *Religion and Politics in India*, op. cit., p. 280.
9. Satish Chandra, *State, Pluralism and the Indian Historical Tradition,* Delhi: Oxford University Press, 2008, Ch. 9, pp. 148-64. See also his 'Historical Background to the Rise of Bhakti Movement in Northern India', in idem, *Historiography, Religion and State in Medieval India*, Delhi: Har-Anand Publication, 1996, pp. 110-31.
10. Satish Chandra, *State, Pluralism*, op. cit., p. 157. See also another recent publication in the same mould: Shahabuddin Iraqi, *Bhakti Movement*

in Medieval India: Social and Political Perspectives, Delhi: Manohar, 2009, pp. 241-57.

11. For a detailed account of the accommodation and encounter between Chisti Sufis and the Nāthpanthī *yogīs*, see K.A. Nizami, *The Life and Times of Shaikh Nizam-ud-din Auliya*, new edition, Delhi: Oxford University Press, 2007, pp. 135-41, and S.A.A. Rizvi, *A History of Sufism in India*, vol. 1, op. cit., pp. 322-69.
12. For Hindavi Sufi romances, see Malik Muhammad Jaisi's *Padmāvat*: see Vasudev Sharan Agrawal, *Padmāvat Malik Muhammad Jaisi Kṛt Mahākāvya* (Hindi), Allahabad: Lokbharati Prakashan, 2005; Srinivas Batra, *Hindi Aur Pharsi Sufi Kāvya Kā Tulnātmak Adhyayan* (Hindi), Varanasi: Nagari Pracharini Sabha, vs 2027 (AD 1970); Aditya Behl and Simon Weightman, tr., *Madhumalati: An Indian Sufi Romance*, Oxford: Oxford University Press, 2000; and Shyam Manohar Pandeya, *Madhya Yugīn Premākhyān* (Hindi), 2nd rev. edn., Allahabad, 1992.
13. See, for instance, Muzaffar Alam, 'Assimilation from a Distance: Confrontation and Sufi Accommodation in Awadh Society', in R. Champakalakshmi and S. Gopal, eds., *Tradition, Dissent and Ideology: Essays in Honour of Romila Thapar*, Delhi: Oxford University Press, 1996, pp. 164-91.
14. Partha Chatterjee has used this expression in his *The Nation and Its Fragments: Colonial and Postcolonial Histories*, Delhi: Oxford University Press, 1994, p. 115. He argues that modern histories of medieval Islamic encounter with India have constructed a binary image of Islam by either projecting its history as the history of foreign conquest or by narrating the story of accommodation between the Muslims and Hindus. In both cases, according to him, Islam came to be looked upon as a religion that was already formed before it reached India and was, therefore, extraneous to the country.
15. For a criticism of religious syncretism in medieval India, see the editorial introduction in Gilmartin and Lawrence, eds., *Beyond Turk and Hindu*, op. cit. Barbara Metcalf, 'Preface' and 'Introduction: A Historical Overview of Islam in South Asia', in idem, ed., *Islam in South Asia in Practice*, Ranikhet: Permanent Black, 2009, pp. xvii-xxv 1-17; and Raziuddin Aquil, ed., *Sufism and Society in Medieval India*, Delhi: Oxford University Press, 2010.
16. Satish Chandra, *State, Pluralism*, op. cit., p. 156.
17. See, for example, R.C. Majumdar, 'Religion: General Review', in idem, ed., *The History and Culture of Indian People:* vol. VI, *The Delhi Sultanate*, Bombay: Bharatiya Vidya Bhavan, 1960, pp. 554-5, and A.L. Srivastava, *The Sultanate Delhi*, Agra: Shivlal Agarwal and Co., 1977, p. 331.

18. Aziz Ahmad, *Studies in Islamic Culture in the Indian Environment*, Delhi: Oxford University Press, 1966, pp. 1369.
19. W.H. Mcleod, *Guru Nanak and the Sikh Religion*, Delhi: Oxford University Press, 1996 (rpt.), pp. 158-63.
20. Charlotte Vaudeville, *A Weaver Named Kabir*, Delhi: Oxford University Press, 1993, p. 82. See also Ch. 3.
21. Bruce B. Lawrence, 'The Sant Movement and North Indian Sufis', in Karine Schomer and W.H. McLeod, eds., *The Sants: Studies in a Devotional Tradition of India*, Delhi: Motilal Banarsidas, 1987, pp. 359-73.
22. David N. Lorenzen, *Who Invented Hinduism? Essays on Religion in History*, Delhi: Yoda Press, 2006, pp. 27-32.
23. Mohammad Habib, 'Early Muslim Mysticism', in K.A. Nizami, ed., *Politics and Society during the Early Medieval Period: Collected Works of Professor Mohammad Habib*, vol. I, Delhi: People's Publishing House, p. 277.
24. Amir Hasan Sijzi, *Fawa'd al-Fu'ad* (*Morals for the Heart*), tr. and annotated by Bruce B. Lawrence, New York: Paulist Press, 1992, pp. 160-2, 325-7.
25. Ibid., pp. 206, 341-2.
26. Mohammad Habib, 'Early Muslim Mysticism', op. cit., p. 277.
27. *Fawa'd al-Fu'ad*, p. 132.
28. Ibid., p. 167.
29. Mohammad Habib, 'Early Muslim Mysticism', op. cit., p. 177.
30. *Fawa'd al-Fu'ad*, pp. 112, 133, 142, 152, 162, 181-2, 189, 196, 340-1, etc.
31. See, for instance, Simon Digby, 'The Sufi Shaykh as a Source of Authority in Medieval India', in Richard M. Eaton, ed., *India's Islamic Traditions, 711-1750*, Delhi: Oxford University Press, 2003, pp. 234-62.
32. *Fawa'd al-Fu'ad*, pp. 83-4, 306-7, 361. See also Irfan Habib, 'Economic History of the Delhi Sultanate—An Essay in Interpretation', *Indian Historical Review*, vol. 4 (1978), pp. 287-303. According to Irfan Habib, Nizamud-din Auliya's attitude 'no more sanctioned the flight of slave than the praise of charity sanctioned theft', fn. 8.
33. I.A. Zilli, 'Precepts and Paradox: The Chishti Attitude Towards Social Labour', *Proceedings of the Indian History Congress*, 47th Session (Srinagar), 1986, pp. 281-9.
34. Ibid., p. 284.
35. Ibid., p. 286.
36. For all these aspects, see R.M. Eaton, *Sufis of Bijapur Social Roles of Sufis in Medieval India*, Princeton, NJ: Princeton University Press,

1978. See also Metcalf, ed., *Islam in South Asia*, op. cit., first two sections.

37. For recent studies on medieval sants, Karine Schomer and W.H. McLeod, eds., *The Sants: Studies in Devotional Tradition of India*, Delhi: Motilal Banasidas, 1987 is the most influential and comprehensive study of medieval sants by Western experts. Other major works published in recent times include Charlotte Vaudeville, *Kabir*, Oxford: Clarendon Press, 1974, later published in a revised form under a new title, *A Weaver Named Kabir*, Delhi: Oxford University Press, 1993; *The Bijak of Kabir*, tr. Linda Hess and Shukdev Singh, Essays and Notes by Linda Hess, Delhi: Motilal Banarsidas, 1986; Winand M. Callewaert, ed. and tr., *The Hindi Biography of Dadu Dayal* (a critical edition and English translation of Jan Gopal's *Dadu Janma Lila Parchi*), Delhi: Motilal Banarsidass, 1988; Winand M. Callewaert and Op de Beeck, eds., *Nirgun Bhakti Sagar: Devotional Hindi Literature*, 2 vols., Delhi: Manohar, 1991; Winand M. Callewaert, ed., *The Sarvangi of Gopaldas: A 17th Century Anthology of Bhakti Literature*, Delhi: Manohar, 1993; Winand M. Callewaert and Peter G. Fiendlander, *The Life and Works of Raidas*, Delhi: Manohar, 1992; Daniel Gold, *The Lord as Guru: Hindi Sants in the North Indian Tradition*, Delhi: Oxford University Press, 1987, and 'The Dadu-Panth: A Religious Order in Rajasthan Context', in Karine Schomer et al., eds., *The Idea of Rajasthan: Explorations in Regional Identity*, vol. II, Delhi: Manohar, 1994, pp. 242-64, David N. Lorenzen, ed. and tr., *Kabir Legends and Anantadas's Parachai*, Albany: State University of New York Press, 1991; David N. Lorenzen, ed., *Bhakti Religion in North India: Community Identity and Political Action*, Delhi: Manohar, 1996; David N. Lorenzen, ed., *Religious Movements in South Asia 600-1800*, Delhi: Oxford University Press, 2004; David N. Lorenzen, *Who Invented Hinduism? Essays on Religion in History*, Delhi: Yoda Press, 2006, R.S. McGregor, ed., *Devotional Literature in South Asia: Current Research, 1985-1988*, Cambridge: Cambridge University Press, 1992; Alan W. Entwistle and Francoise Mallison, eds., *Studies in South Asian Devotional Literature: Research Papers, 1988-91*, Delhi: Manohar, 1994; Winand M. Callewaert in collaboration with Dr. Swapna Sharma, *The Hagiographies of Anantadas: The Bhakti Poets of North India*, Richmond, Surrey: Curzon Press, 2000; Monika Horstmann, ed., *Images of Kabir*, Delhi: Manohar, 2002; Winand M. Callewaert and Dieter Taillieu, eds., *Devotional Literature in South Asia, Current Research 1997-2000*, Delhi: Manohar, 2002; Mariola Offredi, ed., *The Banyan Tree: Essays on Early Literature in New Indo-Aryan Languages*, 2 vols, Delhi: Manohar, 2000; John Stratton Hawley and Mark Juergensmeyer, *Songs of the Saints of India*,

Delhi: Oxford University Press, 2004 (originally published in 1988), and John Stratton Hawley, *Three Bhakti Voices: Mirabai, Surdas and Kabir in their Times and Ours*, Delhi: Oxford University Press, 2005.

38. For legends about Kabir, see David N. Lorenzen, ed. and tr., *Kabir Legends and Anantadas's Parachai*, Albany: State University of New York Press, 1991. For the hagiography of Raidas and other sants, see Winand M. Callewaert in collaboration with Dr. Swapna Sharma, *The Hagiographies of Anantadas: The Bhakti Poets of North India*, Richmond, Surrey: Curzon Press, 2000.
39. Vaudeville, *A Weaver Named Kabir*, verse 8, p. 152.
40. Ibid.
41. Ibid., verse 6, p. 200.
42. Ibid., verse 13, p. 229.
43. W.H. McLeod, *Guru Nanak and the Sikh Religion*, pp. 158-9.
44. J.S. Grewal, *Guru Nanak in History*, Chandigarh: Panjab University 1998 (rpt.), 231-3.
45. Winand M. Callewaert and Peter G. Friedlander, *The Life and Works of Raidas*, verse 36 AG, p. 126. The socio-political implications of this verse have been stressed in recent works on medieval sants. These studies include Rameshwar Prasad Bahuguna, 'Symbols of Resistance: Non-Brahmanical Sants as Religious Heroes in Late Medieval India', in Biswamoy Pati et al., eds., *Negotiating India's Past: Essays in Memory of Partha Sarathi Gupta*, Delhi: Tulika, 2003, pp. 222-3; Eugenia Vanina, *Urban Crafts and Craftsmen in Medieval India (Thirteenth-Eighteenth Centuries)*, Delhi: Munshiram Manoharlal, 2004, pp. 149-50, and Gail Omvedt, *Seeking Begumpura: The Social Vision of Anti-caste Intellectuals*, Delhi: Navayana, 2008, pp. 103-7.
46. *Fawa'd al-Fu'ad*, op. cit., p. 178. The meeting between Nizamuddin Auliya and the *yogīs* took place in Ajodhan at the *khanqah* of Shaikh Fariduddin Masud Ganj-i Shakr. The *khanqah* was frequented by the Nāthpanthī *yogīs*.
47. Ibid., p. 138. For the interaction and encounters between the Sufis and *jogis*, see also S.A.A. Rizvi, *History of Sufism in India*, vol. I, pp. 322-96, and vol. II, pp. 390-432.
48. S.A.A. Rizvi, *History of Sufism in India*, vol. I, pp. 364-70.
49. For the anecdotes of encounter between Sufis and Guru Nanak, see W.H. McLeod, *Exploring Sikhism*, Delhi: Oxford University Press, 2000, pp. 1-18; W.H. McLeod, *Essays in Sikh History, Tradition and Society*, Delhi: Oxford University Press, 2007, p. 44; and J.S. Grewal, *Lectures on History, Society and Culture of the Punjab*, Patiala: Publication Bureau, Punjab University, 2007, pp. 178-79. For various aspects relating to the inclusion of Shaikh Farid's *vani* in the *Adi Granth*, see Pashaura Singh,

The Bhagats of the Guru Granth Sahib: Sikh Self Definition and the Bhagat Bani, Delhi: Oxford University Press, 2003, pp. 42-80.

50. See S.A.A. Rizvi, *History of Sufism in India*, vol. II, pp. 411-13 for Kabir's interaction with Sufi saints.
51. For this reference, see M. Athar Ali, 'Encounter and Efflorescence: Genesis of the Medieval Civilization', *Social Scientist,* 2000-01; 1990, p. 25.
52. For this reference, see S.A.A. Rizvi, *History of Sufism in India*, vol. II, p. 412.
53. Ibid., p. 413.
54. For these and other related aspects, see Rameshwar Prasad Bahuguna, 'Symbols of Resistance: Non-Brahmanical Sants as Religious Heroes in Late Medieval India', in Biswamoy Pati et al., eds., op. cit., pp. 233-4.
55. Narayan Das, *Shri Rajjab Vani*, Ajmer: Prakashnalaya, 1967, pp. 172, 685, 1353.
56. Agarchand Nahata, ed., *Raghavadaskrit Bhaktamal*, Granthank 78, Jodhpur: Rajasthan Oriental Research Institute, 1965, p. 256.

EIGHT

Saiyid Ahmad Barelvi, Altaf Husain Hali and the Formation of Muslim Identity in the Nineteenth Century

N.R. Farooqi

The publication of James Mill's *magnum opus History of British India* in 1817 was a defining moment in Indian history. The book that sought to split Indian history into Hindu, Muslim and British periods sowed the seeds of the Hindu-Muslim divide, and contributed substantially to the construction of the religio-cultural identity of Hindus and Muslims in the country. It separated the 'Hindu past' of India from her 'Muslim past' and, in the process, laid the foundation of the religious or communal interpretation of Indian history.[1] The emergence of the 'two-nation' theory in the second quarter of the twentieth century bolstered the communal divide and reinforced Hindu-Muslim identity and animosity in political, religious and cultural terms. The Partition of the country into Hindu-majority India and Muslim-majority Pakistan was the direct result of this clash of identities. However, the Partition failed to douse the communal fire and India continued to be plagued by the communal virus. A sordid manifestation of the identity conflict and the imagined consciousness of the past that it generated is the unwarranted destruction of the Babri Masjid on 6 December 1992.

What exactly prompted Mill to write a book on India and why did he took such a narrow and sectarian view of India's pre-colonial past is hard to ascertain. Mill, it is argued, was an admirer of Jeremy Bentham and wrote the book to propagate the utilitarian doctrine of his friend, philosopher and guide. He was dismayed, we are told, to find that the knowledge required for handling the problems faced by British administrators in India, as well as the information needed to formulate a pragmatic policy towards India, were nowhere available. To fill this gap in the extant literature on India, Mill wrote his *History*.[2] Whatever may have motivated Mill to undertake a task of such magnitude, it is well known that he was not fully equipped to do so. He had never visited India and did not even have a working knowledge of Sanskrit and Persian—so vital for the reconstruction of India's past. What is more intriguing is that while writing his book, he ignored the works of William Jones, Charles Wilkins, Henry Colebrook and others on India and preferred to rely on the testimonies of Christian missionaries, whose assessment of India has never been beyond reproach, and on sources of dubious merit and authenticity. Mill even ridiculed William Jones for having adopted 'the hypothesis of a high state of civilization in the principal countries of Asia'.[3] He selected his evidence carefully and is said to have utilized only those sources that substantiated his view of India and Indians. His failure to take note of the Parliamentary Report on India (1813), for instance, has been noted both by his admirers as well as by detractors.[4] Above all, Mill's harsh and largely unfair appraisal of ancient Indian civilization indicates that notwithstanding his claim to have written the *History* to collect information 'requisite for attaining an adequate conception of that great Indian scene of British action', his own knowledge of India was woefully inadequate. He was particularly dismissive of the achievements of the ancient Indians in science and mathematics. Their laws and institutions,' observes Mill,

> are adapted to the very state of society which those who visit them now behold, such as could neither begin, nor exist, under any other than one of the rudest and weakest states of the human mind. As the manners, the arts and sciences of the ancient Hindus are entirely correspondent with the state of their laws and institutions, everything we *know* of the ancient state of Hindustan conspires to prove that it was rude.[5]

Mill's assessment of the Muslim civilization in India, though slightly more positive, was far from flattering. The establishment of Muslim rule in India, he believed, led to the mere transfer of political power from the Hindus to the Muslims. It brought practically no change in the state of affairs and left the country much the same. 'The conquest of Hindustan, effected by the Mahommedan nations,' writes Mill,

> was to no extraordinary degree sanguinary or destructive. It substituted sovereigns of one race to sovereigns of another—but it altered not the texture of the society; it altered not the language of the country; the original inhabitants remained the occupants of the soil; they continued to be governed by their own laws and institutions; nay, the whole detail of administration—remained invariably in the hands of the native magistrates and officers.[6]

Six centuries of Muslim rule in India, implied Mill, brought no material and intellectual progress to the country, which remained in the throes of backwardness. The situation was therefore tailor-made, as far as Mill was concerned, for the British takeover of India and the enactment of the British civilizing mission: to take India out of the abyss of backwardness and lead her on the path of progress and modernization. Needless to say, this defense of the British conquest of India was Mill's primary motive for writing his *History*.

Despite its obvious blemishes, Mill's *History* left a favourable impression on his fellow Britishers. Sixteen years after its publication, Macaulay hailed it as the 'greatest historical work which has appeared in our language since that of Gibbon'.[7] As many as five editions of the book appeared in the next four decades. Haileybury College of London, where new recruits to the East India Company's civil service were trained, adopted the *History* as its basic textbook on Indian history. Indian colleges and universities prescribed it as the standard history of India for well over a century. Mill's influence on British policy makers and Indian students can, therefore, hardly be over emphasized.

Mill's impact on Indian historiography was equally longlasting. His division of Indian history into Hindu and Muslim periods was adopted by all subsequent historians, without a proper investigation of its validity and implications, so much so that the history of India began to be seen (and continues to be seen) 'through a series of stereotypes rooted in religious identity'.[8] The reconstruction and interpretation of India's past came to be increasingly dominated by contemporary political concerns. British historical writing on India, appearing in the later half of the nineteenth century, naturally displayed a distinct impress of Mill's views on the character of Indian civilization. Though a few civil servants-turned-historians like Mountstuart Elphinstone, Grant Duff, John Briggs and Alfred Lyall, were broadly sympathetic in their appraisal of the political, intellectual and cultural attainments of the Indians, most British historians wrote with a definite agenda. Denigrating India's past and justifying their colonial rule over India was their primary concern. They assumed the role of what R.G. Bhandarkar called the prosecuting counsel while writing Indian history. By the selective use of evidence that tended to support their line of thinking, they presented, in the words of a modern scholar, 'a peculiarly jaundiced view of India's past'.[9] Instead of describing the past as it actually was and ignoring the Rankean dictum that the 'strict presentation of facts is the supreme law of historical writing', most British historians preferred to pass moral judgement on Indian history.

A devoted follower of the Mill tradition in his writing on Indian history was Sir H.M. Elliot. A member of the East India Company's Bengal civil service, Elliot chose the medieval period of Indian history for special interest and investigation. He spent a lot of time and money in collecting Arabic and mainly Persian manuscripts concerned with the history of Muslim rule in India. Excerpts from these chronicles were translated, later corrected and edited by Professor John Dowson of London University, and published under the title *The History of India as told by its own Historians* in eight volumes between 1867 and 1877. While due credit should be given to Elliot for bringing to light and preserving for posterity many rare and invaluable medieval chronicles, his assessment of Muslim rule in India leaves much to be desired. The preface he wrote for the first volume of his collection of extracts, the only piece of Elliot's original writing available to us, betrays his mindset. Commenting on the relative merit of European and Indian historical literature, he hailed the former as 'useful repositories of knowledge' but he had nothing but contempt for the latter. He dismissed the medieval Indian chronicles as mere collections of 'fairy tales and fictions' that 'comprise for the most part nothing but a mere dry narration of events, conducted with reference to chronological sequence, never grouped philosophically according to their relations. Without speculation on causes or effects—without any observations calculated to interrupt the monotony of successive conspiracies—so common in Asiatic monarchies, and to which India unhappily forms no exception'.[10] He concludes that 'it is almost a misnomer to style them histories'.[11] In the same vein, Elliot discarded the medieval historians as 'dull, prejudiced, ignorant, and superficial' and observed that 'If the artificial definition of Dionysius be correct, that History be philosophy teaching by example, then there is no Native Indian Historian'.[12]

However, if medieval Indian historians and histories scarcely deserved the name, why did Elliot take the trouble of preparing such a massive collection of extracts from them? His preface supplies the answer to this riddle as well. Drawing the attention of Indians to the mildness and equity of the British government in contrast to the tyranny of the preceding regime, and justifying British rule in India, was the *raison d'être* of this exercise. One way of accomplishing this was to include in the collection of extracts only those passages that showed Muslim rulers and governments in a poor light, and ignore those which tended to highlight the positive achievements of the medieval period. Elliot used this ploy with telling effect. An alternative approach was to underscore the benefits accruing to the Indians under British rule. Elliot managed to do this also with great success. 'Notwithstanding a civil policy and an uncongenial climate,' writes Elliot,

> which forbid our making this country a permanent home—notwithstanding the many defects necessarily inherent in a system of foreign administration—we have already, within half a century of our domination, done more for the substantial benefit of the people than our predecessors, in the country of their own adoption, were able to accomplish in more than ten times that period.[13]

Elliot may or may not have succeeded in convincing his audience of the mildness and equity of British rule but he certainly showed his Indian subjects the ways and means of using the past for political benefits. Henceforth, the past became a tool in the hands of those who knew how to exploit it for mundane gains.

After the withdrawal of the British from India, the use of the past became a fine art in the hands of diverse political outfits who nonchalantly abused it for mobilizing public opinion in their favour, endangering, in the process, the very existence of the secular-democratic polity of India. A more sinister weapon in Elliot's armoury was to accentuate the alleged tyranny perpetrated by the Muslim rulers on their Hindu subjects. 'The few glimpses we have,' writes Elliot,

> even among the short Extracts in this single volume, of Hindus slain for disputing with Muhammadans, of general prohibitions against processions, worship, and ablutions, and of other intolerant measures, of idols mutilated, of temples razed, of forcible conversions and marriages, of proscriptions and confiscations, of murders and massacres, and of the sensuality and drunkenness of the tyrants who enjoined them, show us that this picture is not overcharged.[14]

It would not be an exaggeration to suggest that such grave pronouncements contributed immensely in popularizing the 'sword of Islam' motif in the construction of India's medieval past. The trend of tracing pre-colonial Indian history 'as a sort of religious genealogy of India's present-day Muslims', and the formation of the stereotypical image of Muslims marauding over the fertile plains of India with a sword in one hand and the Quran in the other, slaughtering harmless Hindus, plundering their temples and carrying away Hindu women as trophies of their triumph, may well have begun from this period.[15] This hackneyed image of the Muslims also inflicted considerable damage to the psyche of the Hindus and their Muslim compatriots. 'The Hindu feels it his duty,' writes a modern scholar, 'to dislike those whom he has been taught to consider the enemies of his religion and his ancestors; the Mussalman, *lured into the false belief that he was once a member of a ruling race*, feels insufferably wronged by being relegated to the status of a minority community.'[16]

II

Before long, the theme of Muslim tyranny and Hindu suffering made its appearance in history textbooks and popular vernacular literature. History textbooks, written and published under the aegis of the governments of Punjab and the North-Western Provinces in the nineteenth century, reflected the ideological predilections of their authors. A book written by a Muslim official posted in Lahore, for instance, dealt with the 'Hindu past' in an extremely sketchy and cavalier fashion. Another authored by a Hindu functionary stationed in Banaras, on the other hand, focused on the oppression, villainy and misgovernment of the medieval Muslim monarchs.[17] Another distinguished resident of Banaras, the poet-scholar Bhartendu Harishchandra, gave vent to his 'Hindu consciousness' by accusing Muslim foreigners, in one of his oft-quoted couplets, of divesting the Hindus of their faith, women and wealth.[18] At about the same time, Bankim Chandra Chatterji, the doyen of the Bengali literati, was articulating, in his widely-read historical fiction, 'the stereotypical recollection of Muslim conquest and its effect on a Hindu India'. Thus, by the end of the nineteenth century, thanks to the popular perception of an imagined past propagated by British bureaucrats and their Indian camp followers, Hindus and Muslims were drifting into opposite camps, 'each trying to create its own icons and golden epochs in constructing the past accordingly'.[19]

Damage control exercises soon began in right earnest. Driven by a nationalistic and patriotic fervour, a new generation of indigenous historians embarked upon a campaign to write a new history of India. The defense of Indian heritage against the European onslaught and a pragmatic appraisal of India's past was the main intent of this brand of historians. Before long, this campaign blossomed into a full-fledged trend of historical writing: the nationalist historiography. The nationalist historians made sincere efforts to blunt the 'sword of Islam' motif in the writing of Indian history. Precisely for this purpose, the theory of Hindu-Muslim unity and the composite nature of medieval Indian culture were underscored. Neither was the Muslim rule in India, they stressed, a foreign rule nor was the medieval era a period of Hindu-Muslim conflict. However, in their zeal to deconstruct the colonial historiography and set the record of the ancient Indian civilization straight, many nationalist historians went to the other extreme of the spectrum and claimed that India had already achieved in the age of the epics what Europe accomplished in the nineteenth century, even in the sphere of science and technology.[20] Inspiration for this theory of a 'golden age' of Hindu society had obviously come from the Orientalists who had postulated the hypothesis of a high level of civilizational excellence achieved by the Hindus before the arrival of political Islam in India. Needless to say, the nationalist approach to the study of Indian history came to be plagued by practically the same defects and was weighed down by the same lack of objectivity that had characterized colonial historiography on India.

The nationalist historians may not have cared to observe the established canons of historiography in their treatment of India's ancient past but they did provide the Hindu intelligentsia of their time something to ponder upon and boast about. The writings of the Hindu revivalists of the nineteenth century and their communal successors of the twentieth century harp upon the theme of an idyllic Hindu past repeatedly. An explanation for the subsequent decline of the Hindus was eagerly sought and readily found in the advent of Muslim rule in the country. Atrocities perpetrated by the Muslims on the Hindus, it was argued, demoralized them and adversely affected their intellectual vitality. The Muslims were, therefore, held responsible for all the ills of Hindu society. Even the stagnation of traditional Indian medical science, the Ayurveda, was traced to the establishment of a new political order by 'forces from outside' and 'external enemies' in the thirteenth century.[21] In this discourse of the past, each and every Muslim was labelled as the enemy—an 'outsider' who was not a part of the Hindu past and, hence, stood outside the 'Hindu nation', which was freely identified with the Indian nation.[22]

Muslims were not only deprecated as 'outsiders' and 'foreign aggressors' by their Hindu compatriots in the nineteenth century, but their British masters were equally ill at ease with their role and place in Indian history. They had snatched political power from the hands of the Muslims and were naturally wary of their political aspirations and expectations. The Muslims, on the other hand, were afflicted by diverse ills and tribulations. The loss of political power, coupled with their failure to adjust to the new realities and exigencies of the time, had left a deep impact on their psyche.

While the Hindus had taken advantage of new opportunities in education and employment offered by British rule and had surged ahead in the race of progress, the Muslims had remained wedded to their old lifestyle and world-view and had suffered consequently. Although the Muslims continued to dominate the East India Company's subordinate revenue and judicial services in the north-western provinces in the 1850s, their influence in society was on the wane.[23] Higher positions in these services were the exclusive preserve of British officers and were consequently denied to them. The abolition of Persian as the official language of the government in 1837 and the consequent emphasis on the knowledge of English as a prerequisite for recruitment in government services meant further erosion in the once-dominant position held by Muslims in the Indian bureaucracy. By the end of the first half of the nineteenth century, these changes had ensured that the Muslims 'would not be subordinate partners of the British, but merely subordinates'.[24]

The revolt of 1857, which most British officers blamed squarely on the Muslims, and its aftermath, further added to their woes. British retribution fell heavily upon the Muslims. The Mughal Emperor was exiled to Burma and as many as 27 male members of his family were executed on charges of treason. Centres of Muslim education and places of worship were closed down or razed to the ground. Anyone suspected of having abetted the rebels was put to the gallows. 'Here there is a vast ocean of blood before me,' wrote the renowned Urdu poet, Asadullah Khan Ghalib (d. 1869), 'God alone knows what more I shall have to behold.'[25] Muslim landlords, pension-holders, and *mu'afidars* (holders of revenue-free lands) also bore the brunt of British vengeance. Although some loyal Muslims were rewarded, a large number residing in the major centres of revolt were forced to forfeit their estates. W.W. Hunter's remark, made 14 years after the revolt, that 'the Musalmans in all respects—are a race ruined under British rule' does not seem to be very far off the mark.[26]

Much has been written about the Muslim response to the British presence in India but their view of the past, as well as their mode of using the past for the sake of the community, has surprisingly eluded the interest of scholars so far.[27] The available evidences indicate that the Muslim attitude to the past in the nineteenth century was distinctly different from that of their Hindu compatriots. Unlike the majority of Hindus who tended to accuse the Muslim 'outsider' for the decline and loss of indigenous civilizational attainments, the nineteenth-century Muslims did not put the blame on the other. They blamed themselves for the decay and degeneration of their community. Recent studies have also shown that 1857 and its aftermath brought about a definite change in the Muslim response to British rule. Before 1857, they had not fully realized the implications of the British presence in India. The British, they believed, were the advisors and subordinates of the Mughal Emperor, and could be removed from the scene like the Afghans and Marathas who had earlier performed these functions. They sneered at British culture and language and found nothing worthy of emulation in them. 1857 changed all this. The sordid reality of the passing away of the Mughal Empire and the birth of a new regime dawned upon them belatedly. The culture that they had consistently ignored so far had come to stay and had to be taken seriously. For the majority of Indian Muslims, 1857, therefore, came as 'a divine punishment, if not for sin then for ignorance'.

The change in the Muslim response to the British presence also transformed their attitude to the past and obliged some of them to utilize their past for constructing a new identity for their community. This is clearly reflected in the words and deeds of two distinguished representatives of the nineteenth-century Indian Muslims, Saiyid Ahmad Barelvi (1786-1831) and Altaf Husain Hali (1837-1914), who flourished before and after the revolt, respectively. Both are crucial to a proper understanding of the process of identity formation among Indian Muslims in the nineteenth century. The former was a native of Rae Bareli in the kingdom of Awadh that, though technically under Muslim rule at the time, had suffered from increasing British intervention in its affairs. Saiyid Ahmad and his fellow Muslims of Rae Bareli were direct victims of British influence in Awadh and had sufficient grounds to foster anti-British sentiments. The latter lived in the historic town of Panipat, the venue of three major battles that had played a vital role in the establishment and consolidation of Mughal rule in India, and was an eye-witness to the British atrocities on Muslims after 1857. The response of these two gentlemen to Muslim sufferings at the hands of the British and their methods of utilizing the past for the amelioration of their co-religionists was, however, not the same. Their impact on their contemporaries was, in the same manner, different. These issues will be addressed below.

III

Saiyid Ahmad was born in 1786 in Rae Bareli (in modern Uttar Pradesh) to the family of an eminent seventeenth-century Naqshbandi saint, Sheikh 'Alamullah (d. 1684). At the age of four, he was sent to school but showed little interest in studies. Lack of interest in formal education, however, was adequately compensated for by his passion for sports. He soon became adept at wrestling and swimming. His Urdu biographers would have us believe that the zeal for *jihad* (holy war) had taken firm root in the young Saiyid's heart at this very stage of his life, and that his interest in such 'manly' sports was but a symbol of and preparation for his future career as a warrior of Islam.[28] At the age of 18, he went to Lucknow in search of suitable employment. Having failed in this endeavour, he moved to Delhi and joined the *madrasa* (seminary) of Shah 'Abdul 'Aziz (1746-1824), the son and successor of a leading Indian Muslim scholar of the eighteenth century, Shah Waliullah (d. 1763). The Shah placed him under the educational and spiritual tutelage of his younger brother, Shah 'Abdul Qadir (d. 1814). During his sojourn in Delhi, Saiyid Ahmad met the eminent '*ulama* (scholars) of his time. He acquired elementary knowledge of Arabic grammar and the *hadith* (Traditions of the Prophet) but his training in Islamic sciences remained far from complete. He, however, showed unmistakable signs of advancement on the path of spiritual knowledge. At this time, writes Sir Saiyid Ahmad Khan (d. 1898), his 'power of concentration was stronger than that of even orthodox recluse mystics'.[29] Impressed by the Saiyid's progress in the mystic way, Shah 'Abdul 'Aziz formally initiated him into the Chishti, Qadiri and Naqshbandi *silsilas* in 1807. Subsequently, he claimed to be an *Uwaysi* (one who receives initiation directly from Prophet Muhammad without the mediation of a guide). In a series of visions, he declared he saw the Prophet, Ali, Fatima and, finally, god himself.[30]

In 1812, Saiyid Ahmad joined as an ordinary trooper in the army of the Afghan adventurer, Amir Khan (1768-1834), later the *nawab* of Tonk. Ghulam Rasul Mehr asserts that the Saiyid's entry into Amir Khan's service was motivated by his desire to utilize the Khan's military prowess for the revival of Muslim political power in India.[31] Other admirers of the Saiyid claim that the decision to join the Khan's army was inspired by god and that it was a necessary concomitant in the fulfilment of the former's mission.[32] Not much is known about Saiyid Ahmad's activities in Amir Khan's camp. We are told that he participated in the Khan's military operations in Rajasthan and, in the process, gained ample experience in warfare. A parting of ways between the two, however, came in 1817 when Amir Khan decided, much to the chagrin and sustained opposition of the Saiyid, to enter into an alliance with the English East India Company.[33]

The break with Amir Khan proved to be a blessing in disguise for Saiyid Ahmad. It relieved him of his mundane liabilities and enabled him to return to Delhi (1818) where he began the most crucial phase of his life, embarking on a career of a Sufi guide, reformer and warrior in the way of god. Around this time, he developed a Sufi order of his own and named it Tariqa-i Muhammadiyya (the way of Prophet Muhammad). Inspiration for the establishment of this order, he claimed, had come directly from god and Prophet Muhammad.[34] Saiyid Ahmad asserted that his *tariqa* differed from existing orders in one essential aspect: whereas the other Sufi orders emphasized the esoteric dimension of the teachings of the Prophet, the Tariqa-i Muhammadiyya 'emphasized strict conformity to religious law, and subordinated all activity of the individual Muslim to the devotion and service of god'.[35]

Before long, stories of the Saiyid's spiritual prowess and charisma began to circulate far and wide, and people began to flock to the Akbarabadi mosque, where he was residing at that time, to join his order. Saiyid Ahmad's mission got a shot in the arm when two leading *'ulama* of the time, Shah Muhammad Isma'il (d. 1831) and Maulana 'Abdul Hayy (d. 1828), nephew and son-in-law, respectively, of Shah 'Abdul 'Aziz, offered allegiance to him. Shah Isma'il was well known for his opposition to the evils and innovations that had permeated Indian Islam and had already published (*c.* 1798) a treatise on the subject, *Radd al-ishrak.*[36] He shared Saiyid Ahmad's view that, for the rehabilitation of Muslim society, a sustained campaign of socio-religious reform was the need of the hour.

Saiyid Ahmad made strenuous efforts to revive three major *sunna* (practice or precept) of Prophet Muhammad that that had long fallen into desuetude by the Indian Muslims: widow remarriage, *hajj* and *jihad*. He began by setting a personal example: he married the widow of his elder brother. Saiyid Ahmad, thus, became perhaps the first Indian reformer to focus attention on the plight of widows and to take effective practical steps to eradicate a long-established evil. He was, likewise, distressed to learn that north Indian Muslims had long neglected, in contravention to Quranic injunctions, the observance of pilgrimage to Makkah. Because of the hazards of the voyage to Makkah, he was told, *hajj* had ceased to be obligatory for Indian Muslims. A *fatwa* to this effect had also been issued.[37] Even Shah 'Abdul 'Aziz's decree questioning the *fatwa* did not have the desired effect. Saiyid Ahmad decided to settle the controversy by once again setting a personal example. He invited all his friends and supporters to accompany him on the journey for the *hajj*, and promised to pay their expenses from his own pocket. In July 1821, he left Rae Bareli (where he had been staying since 1819) with a large number of volunteers for Calcutta, from where the party was to set sail for Makkah. Many more joined on the way. The Saiyid's party comprising as many as 752 pilgrims reached their destination in May 1822. They stayed in the holy land for eight months, performed the *hajj* and returned to Rae Bareli in April 1824.[38] Saiyid Ahmad, thus, again proved by word and deed that the Quranic injunction in favour of *hajj* was perfectly feasible in practice.

Saiyid Ahmad was deeply conscious of the glorious past of the Indian Muslims. The might and grandeur of the Mughals, who once reigned supreme from Kashmir to Cape Comorin, loomed large in his thought. Like all thinking Muslims of his day, he sorrowed at the gradual but steady decline of Muslim political power and the rise of British paramountcy in India. On the micro level, he attributed the economic decline of his hometown, Rae Bareli, and the consequent financial distress of the Muslims of the region to increasing British involvement in the affairs of the kingdom of Awadh.[39] Farther from home, the Sikhs' occupation of Punjab and their atrocities on their Muslim subjects were causing him great mental and emotional anguish.[40]

Ahmad was also painfully conscious of the corruption and laxity that prevailed in the Muslim society of his day. The moral turpitude of Muslim religious and intellectual elites hung heavier on his soul than it did on the average Muslim who seemed content to let things happen and had apparently no inclination to introspection or historical reasoning. He held them responsible for letting the rot take root in Muslim society in the interest of their petty, mundane benefits. Muslims, he lamented, have forsaken the commands of god and the teachings of the Prophet. Their fall from the grace of god and the consequent breakdown of their political power was, therefore, inevitable. Ahmad was convinced that like the *hajj*, the Indian Muslims have long neglected the obligation of *jihad* and the consequences of this neglect were before them. The revival of Muslim political power was incumbent on the revival of the spirit of *jihad*. He also claimed that god had inspired him to wage *jihad* against the enemies of Islam, and that 'he was invested with a heavenly mission to restore the rule and the glory of Islam in India'.[41]

In 1818-19, Saiyid Ahmad, accompanied by Shah Isma'il and a host of other disciples, went on extensive tours of the western and eastern districts of modern Uttar Pradesh. He met a cross-section of Muslims on these tours and addressed large gatherings of sympathizers and opponents. The past greatness of the

Muslims, and their present decline and consequent loss of Muslim pride and identity, was the main theme of his discourses. The Muslim political elites, he said, were steeped in moral corruption and the people should expect nothing from them. For reclaiming their glorious past and restoring of their missing pride and identity, he reminded his audience again and again that the revival of the long-lost spirit of *jihad* was imperative. Un-Islamic and heterodox practices, the undue veneration of Sufi saints and shrines, and customs and ceremonies of Hindu and Shi'i origin were also vehemently attacked. Muslim women, the custodian of future generations of Muslims, were urged to refrain from *shirk* (polytheism) and *bida't* (undesirable innovation in religion).[42] Efforts were also made to build an organizational structure, in the places visited by the Saiyid, to keep up the campaign for politico-religious revival. Trained disciples were deputed to provide much-needed guidance to the people.[43] The Saiyid also sent his trusted lieutenants to diverse towns and cities of the country to create Muslim public opinion in favour of the impending *jihad*. On his homeward journey from Makkah, he had halted at Patna and arranged for the establishment of a central organization for the supply of men and money in the event of an armed struggle.[44]

In January 1826, Saiyid Ahmad decided to wage a *jihad* against the Sikhs. He believed that they were a softer target than the British who commanded more territory and military power. The north-west frontier was also technically *Darul Islam* and, thus, eminently suitable for conducting the *jihad* against them. Moreover, Saiyid Ahmad expected support for his cause from the tribal chieftains of the north-west who had suffered at the hands of the Sikhs.

In December 1826, military operations against the Sikhs began. Saiyid Ahmad and his band of warriors tasted success in initial encounters but, after that, their luck ran out. The Saiyid perhaps did not realize that he was fighting in an unknown, inhospitable and difficult terrain. What is more surprising is that he had undertaken a venture of such magnitude without adequate planning and groundwork. The Sikhs were a less formidable foe than the British but were still powerful enough to deal effectively with the *mujahiddin* (holy warriors). The Saiyid had neither the wherewithal nor enough experience of warfare to lead a sustained military campaign against the Sikhs. He was also handicapped by the misplaced religious enthusiasm of his key subordinates who were determined to enforce the *Sharia't* (Islamic law) on the Afghan tribesmen, entirely unmindful of the fact that neither the sociology nor the economics of the latter were conducive to the changes they were hurriedly propagating in the name of Islam. They failed to comprehend that, in a traditional society, a revolution in the minds and hearts of the people should precede a revolution in action. They had neither the time nor patience to bring about such a revolution. 'The tribal people,' writes a modern historian, 'were ready to die for the faith but were not prepared to live according to it.'[45] Saiyid Ahmad realized rather belatedly that the time for total change had not yet come and that a war cannot be won by religious zeal alone. Unable to muster the required number of men and armaments for conducting the *jihad*, and betrayed by the tribal chieftains whose support he had taken for granted, Saiyid Ahmad was defeated and slain along with his 700 followers in the battle of Balakot on 8 May 1831.[46]

Saiyid Ahmad's endeavours to mobilize the Muslims through the instrumentality of the past did not yield the desired result. His mission to salvage Muslim pride and construct a new political identity for them by restoring Muslim power in the 'occupied territories' suffered a similar fate. He was perhaps the first Indian Muslim to use the past for political gains. His efforts were, however, not designed to fulfil a personal agenda. Time and again, he declared that the revival of Islam and not the acquisition of political power for himself was his primary aim. In a letter addressed to the Sikh general, Budh Singh, he observed that neither wealth nor territory but the glory of the Din-i Muhammadi (Islam) was his goal and that for the fulfilment of this objective he was ready to sacrifice everything.[47] Even a few days before the battle of Balakot, he told his fellow *mujahiddin* that the strengthening of Islam and the removal of non-Muslim rule from Muslim territories was his sole objective.[48] His was also a maiden attempt to unite Indian Muslims on the plank of *jihad*. He succeeded in projecting *jihad* as the lifeblood of Muslims. The spirit of *jihad*, he believed, had made the Muslims invincible in the past and its abandonment in the present had made them weak and rudderless.[49] Reclaiming this spirit is, therefore essential, if the Muslims had to regain their former dignity and develop a new identity of their own.

Recent studies have shown that the *jihad* propagated by Saiyid Ahmad was not characterized by communal overtones. In his correspondence, anti-Hindu sentiments are nowhere discernible. On the contrary, extant evidences demonstrate that his movement enjoyed the sympathy and, at times, active support of the Hindus.[50] Saiyid Ahmad's correspondence also indicates that although the *jihad* was originally directed against the Sikhs, the British were the ultimate and eventual target.[51] The anti-British feeling aroused by the movement did not die with the passing away of the Saiyid. A band of dedicated followers centred in Bihar and Bengal and labelled as Wahhabis took active part in the events of 1857. Even in the post-1857 era, they continued to fight the British until they were finally suppressed, tried and convicted in 1871. Small wonder then that British scholars writing in the later half of the nineteenth century saw the revolt as the culmination of a Muslim conspiracy initiated by Saiyid Ahmad.

IV

Six years after the demise of Saiyid Ahmad was born Altaf Husain Hali to a respectable Muslim family of Panipat (in modern Haryana). His ancestor, Khwaja Malik 'Ali, had migrated from Herat in the mid-thirteenth century and had settled in Panipat, where the ruling prince, Sultan Ghiyasuddin Balban (r. 1266-86), bestowed upon him a substantial *jagir* (estate) and the office of the *qazi* (judge) of the town. Panipat subsequently emerged as an important centre of Islamic learning and mysticism, both of which had a bearing on Altaf Husain's upbringing. He received the conventional education given to the Muslim gentry of his day and learnt Arabic, Persian and the Quran. At the age of 17, he moved to Delhi and joined the *madrasa* of Husain Bakhsh situated near the city's grand mosque. Although Delhi had lost its old glory and was a shadow of its former self, it was still the country's intellectual capital. Great Urdu poets of yesteryears, Sheikh Ibrahim Zauq (d. 1854) and Hakim Momin Khan Momin (d. 1852), were already dead, but the greatest of all, Ghalib, still graced the city and, inspired by his name and fame, many a young men tried their hand at poetry. In keeping with the current tradition of composing poetry under the tutelage of an established poet, Altaf Husain approached Ghalib for guidance. The great poet, we are told, was impressed by young Altaf's poetic potential and made the now-famous remark: 'If you don't write poetry, you will be doing great injustice to your temperament.'[52] He adopted the pen-name *khasta* (the exhausted or the heart-broken), which was subsequently changed to *Hali* (the contemporary, the modern).

In 1855, Hali returned to Panipat, responding to his family's call for sharing the burden of his household. Shortly afterwards, he joined the East India Company's service in nearby Hissar. The events of 1857 traumatized the young poet. The sorry plight of Muslim women, many of whom had been left homeless, destitute and widowed, especially troubled him. He wrote two moving poems, *Munajat-i bewa* (Supplication of the Widows) and *Chup ki dad* (Homage to the Silent) to publicize the sufferings of Muslim widows. The events of 1857 also left Hali jobless. Unable to find suitable employment, he began to tutor the son of the famous Urdu poet and landlord, Nawab Mustafa Khan Shefta (d. 1869). In the Nawab's company, Hali found an opportunity to fine-tune his poetic skills. 'Mirza's [Ghalib's] advice', he later wrote, 'did not help me. What helped was the company of the Nawab Sahib.'[53]

In 1874, Hali got the job he had been looking for—a teaching assignment at the Anglo-Arabic School in Delhi. It was in Delhi that he met his future friend and mentor, Sir Saiyid Ahmad Khan. This meeting became a watershed in Hali's life and thought. Sir Saiyid was the first protagonist of the policy of Muslim-British rapprochement. Early in his life, he had realized that the British were here to stay for several years to come and that the survival of the Muslim community was primarily dependent on their pleasure. He believed that 1857 was an exercise in futility. The best course for Indian Muslims, he urged, was to take advantage, like their fellow Hindus, of the opportunities offered by the British system. This would require a radical change in the Muslim mindset, a new philosophy of life, a pride in its past and a new identity.[54]

The formation of the Muslim identity, according to Sir Saiyid, was incumbent upon the rediscovery and retrieval of the glorious Muslim past. He was hurt by the negative portrayal of Islam in European writings and endeavoured hard to show that Islam was not incompatible with progress, reason and science. More than that, he desired to make Indian Muslims aware of the glorious achievements of their co-religionists in the past. He wished to awaken his fellow Muslims from their slumber and make them conscious of their present predicament. Precisely for this reason, he requested Hali to compose a poem depicting the splendid past and dreadful present of the Muslim community. 'Put your poetic skills at the service of the community and write something like *Marsiya-i Andalus* (Elegy of Spain)', Sir Saiyid is reported to have told him.[55] Responding to his mentor's call, Hali composed his famous poem *Musaddas-i Hali* or *Madd-o jazr-i-Islam* (The Flow and Ebb of Islam). Sir Saiyid was thrilled when the poem was published. 'Yes, it was I', Sir Saiyid wrote to Hali, 'who urged you to write it, and I rank this so high among my stock of good deeds that when (on Judgement Day) God will ask me, "What have you brought here?" I will say, "I have brought the *Musaddas*, which I got Hali to write: nothing more." '[56]

Written in 1879 and consisting of 294 stanzas of six lines each, the *musaddas* (literally, six or a verse of six lines) presents a nostalgic narrative of the glorious Muslim past followed by a poignant account of its nineteenth-century decline. The poem begins with a *rubai* (quatrain) that sets forth the context and content of what is to follow: the decline of Islam and its failure to regroup itself and march ahead in the race of progress. Anyone who sees the way Islam declined (after its rise), says the poet, will forget that the tide flows after every ebb. The malaise afflicting the Muslim community and its inability or complacency to diagnose its ills is described in the opening verses, followed by a vivid description of pre-Islamic Arab society, characterized by idol worship, internecine tribal conflicts and social evils. The birth of

Prophet Muhammad and the social revolution brought by him in the 'land of darkness' are then described in verses of great power and eloquence. The wonder that Islam became in subsequent centuries and its splendid manifestations in Umayyad Spain, and Abbasid Iraq, and Muslim attainments in science, medicine, mathematics, art and literature, are enumerated one by one.

A recent study has shown that 'the poem is in part structured around a series of contrasts or oppositions. The main opposition in the poem is between decline and progress, and Hali's vision of broad historical movements in the *Musaddas* is to a large extent based on this opposition.'[57] In keeping with this basic format, a narrative of decline follows the account of Muslim progress. How the garden of knowledge and wisdom planted by the Prophet and nurtured by his worthy successors was, in course of time, transformed once again into a barren landscape is described in verse after verse. 'With my unskilled hands', writes Hali in the preface to the first edition of the *Musaddas*, 'I have built a house of mirrors for my people in which they can see their faces and realize who they were and what they have become.'[58]

Hali holds the Muslims responsible for their ignoble present. No one escapes from the acerbity of his facile pen. He chides all and sundry for their acts of omission and commission: the rich for their haughtiness and insensitivity to the plight of the poor, the poor for their repugnance to earn their livelihood through hard work and their aversion to trade and craft, the Sufis for selling the reputation of their great ancestors and 'robbing their disciples', the theologians for their bigotry and divisive activities, and the poets for their mediocrity and failure to use poetry for the good of the community.[59] The Muslims, Hali laments, have become bereft of wisdom, knowledge and wealth, and one who is deprived of these blessings of god is as good as dead. He implores his co-religionists to wake up from their slumber, dissolve their differences and put their house in order before it was too late.[60]

Hali explained the loss of the golden past of the Muslims in terms of the loss of the pristine purity of Islam. He writes:[61]

So long as the clear honey remained unpolluted by filth, the might of Islam remained unchallenged and its standard continued to fly proudly in all directions. However, as soon as the 'spring of purity became muddied', all hell was let loose. The commands of God were forsaken and the teachings of the Prophet forgotten. The 'shadow of the phoenix was removed' from the heads of the Muslims. Their wealth, their arts, sciences and above all their prestige vanished one by one. Ultimately, neither religion nor Islam was left. Only the name of Islam was left.

This sordid narrative of decline, Hali says, is devoid of any melody of diction or sweetness of artifice and, hence, may not be relished by the readers. 'However, the poem has not been composed,' he avers, 'to please the reader and elicit the applause of the audience. Its intent is to make my friends and fellows feel a sense of outrage and shame.'[62]

Hali, thus, uses his constructive genius to create a historical consciousness among the Muslims of their past greatness. By juxtaposing the civilizational excellence of classical Islam with its nineteenth-century degradation, he wanted to give a shock treatment to his contemporaries and to remind them that 'what were you yesterday, and what have you become today'. The Muslims, Hali implied, had a past, and an identity based on that past which they have lost because of their own wrongdoings in the present. This identity was inexorably linked with the power of Islam, which was inherent in its purity. The rehabilitation of the present was, therefore, dependent upon the retrieval of the lost identity. For this, the reclamation of the past as well as the purity of the past was imperative. Hali's clarion call to his brethren to mend their ways and reform them must be seen in this context. Reform is not possible without re-assertion of the pristine purity of Islam. Hence, Hali's plea to return to the golden past and draw inspiration from it to make their mark on the sands of time once more. A sense of confidence among them as a community and the feeling of a distinct identity would automatically follow. The composition of *Musaddas* was, therefore, an exercise in identity formation.

The *Musaddas* touched the heart of every Indian Muslim, educated and uneducated alike, and became an instant hit. It was read, sung and staged in every nook and corner of India. Students recited it in schools, courtesans sang it in public and private gatherings, and preachers read it in religious assemblies. Schools included it in their curriculum and *imams* (prayer leaders) made it a part of their discourses. The elegy of the Muslim community filled many an eye with tears. Many more were forced to introspect and take recourse to appropriate measures. 'No other book sold out as fast; no other book appeared in as many editions in such quick succession.'[63] The *Musaddas* mania, as a recent study puts it, took the Muslims by storm and broke all records of popular reception and publication.[64] Hali was also surprised at the unprecedented adulation received by his poem. 'The popularity and renown which the poem has won in all parts of India', Hali wrote in 1886, 'is truly astonishing—The poem has nevertheless spread in this quite brief period to all corners of the country and has already gone through seven or eight editions in various districts of northern India—After reading it, most people are unable to stop themselves weeping and shedding tears.'[65]

The *Musaddas*, writes a modern scholar, changed the destiny of millions of people and deserves a place among the few most outstanding poems of world literature.[66] It provided a collective memory to the Indian Muslims and endeavoured to unite them on the plank of a common past and a set of common concerns.[67] It gave them a new sense of identity and, by recreating their glorious past, offered them something to cheer about and cherish.[68] The *Musaddas* also set the tone of subsequent Urdu historiography and poetry. Its echo can be found in the equally celebrated poems *Shikwa* (1911) and *Jawab-i Shikwa* (1913), penned by the greatest Urdu poet of modern times, Sir Muhammad Iqbal (d. 1938).

CONCLUSION

The *jihad* of Saiyid Ahmad Barelvi and the writings of Altaf Husain Hali, two major representatives of nineteenth-century Indian Islam, have received the adequate attention of modern scholars. Their perception of the past and their endeavours to use the past for the benefit of their community have, however, been largely ignored. The foregoing accounts of their activities suggest that their view of the past and the strategies adopted by them to use it was governed by the contemporary situation. Their strategies were different but their aim was one and the same: the regeneration of the Muslim community and the restoration of their lost prestige in society. The former used the past for political mobilization and adopted violent means to accomplish his objectives. The latter, on the other hand, utilized the past to construct an identity for his co-religionists in a non-violent and peaceful manner. While Saiyid Ahmad failed in his objectives and died for his cause, Hali succeeded in his mission, given the unprecedented response his poem received from all classes and categories of Muslims, and lived long enough to reap the reward of his trials and tribulations. In many ways, Hali's *Musaddas* continues to be popular among large sections of Indian Muslims. Given their present predicament in view of the rise of right-wing fundamentalist forces in India, the *Musaddas* can still capture their prevailing mood. To that extent, the message of Hali and *Musaddas-i Hali* is still relevant.

NOTES

1. Romila Thapar, 'Communalism and the Writing of Ancient Indian History', in Romila Thapar, Harbans Mukhia and Bipin Chandra, *Communalism and the Writing of Indian History*, Delhi: People's Publishing House, 1969, p. 4. Also see Brajdulal Chattopadhyaya, *Representing the Other? Sanskrit Sources and the Muslims (Eight to Fourteenth Century)*, Delhi: Manohar, 1998, pp. 14-21.
2. C.H. Philips, 'James Mill, Mountstuart Elphinstone, and the History of India', in C.H. Philips, ed., *Historians of India, Pakistan and Ceylon*, London: Oxford Univesity Press, 1962, pp. 219-20.
3. James Mill, *The History of British India*, vol. I, Delhi: Low Price Publications, rpt. 1990, p. 478.
4. C.H. Philips, 'James Mill, Mountstuart Elphinstone, and the History of India', in C.H. Philips, ed., op. cit., pp. 220-1.
5. James Mill, op. cit., p. 461; Also see R.C. Majumdar, 'Nationalist Historians', in C.H. Philips, ed., op. cit., p. 417; R.C. Majumdar, *Historiography in Modern India*, Bombay: Asia Publishing House, 1970, pp. 8-15; Amartya Sen, 'History and the Enterprise of Knowledge', Inaugural Address, 61st Annual Session of the Indian History Congress (Calcutta, 2001), *Social Scientist*, vol. 30, nos. 1-2, January-February 2001, pp. 10-11.
6. James Mill, op. cit., p. 461.

7. Macaulay made this statement in the House of Commons in the course of the debate on the Charter Act of 1833. See G.P. Gooch, *History and Historians of the Nineteenth Century*, London: Longmans, Green and Co., 1913, p. 306.
8. K.N. Panikkar, 'Outsider as Enemy: Politics of Rewriting History in India', in his *An Agenda For Cultural Action and other Essays*, Delhi: Three Essays, 2002, p. 53. I am grateful to my colleague, Dr. Lalit Joshi, for drawing my attention to this article.
9. Carl W. Ernst, *Eternal Gardens: Mysticism, History, and Politics at a South Asian Sufi Center*, Albany: Suny, 1992, p. 19. For R.G. Bhandarkar's views on British historians of India, see A.L. Basham, 'Modern Historians of Ancient India', in C.H. Philips, ed., op. cit., p. 281.
10. H.M. Elliot, 'Original Preface', *The History of India as Told by its Own Historians: The Muhammadan Period*, vol. I, Delhi: Low Price Publications, 8 vols., rpt., 1996, p. xix.
11. Ibid., xviii.
12. Ibid., xix.
13. Ibid., xxvii.
14. Ibid., xxi.
15. Shahid Amin, 'On Retelling the Muslim Conquest of North India', in Partha Chatterjee and Anjan Ghosh, eds., *History and The Present*, Delhi: Permanent Black 2002, pp. 24-9.
16. K.A. Nizami, ed., *Politics and Society During the Early Medieval Period: Collected Works of Professor Mohammad Habib*, vol. I, Delhi: People's Publishing House, 1974, p. 12.
17. Avril A. Powell, 'History Textbooks and the Transmission of the Pre-colonial Past in North-western India in the 1860s and 1870s', in Daud Ali, ed., *Invoking the Past: The Uses of History in South Asia*, Delhi: Oxford Uniersity Press, 1999, pp. 91-133. The books in question were *Waqi'at-i Hind* (1863) and *Itihas timir-nasak* (1864), and were written by Maulvi Karimuddin and Raja Shiv Prasad, respectively. I am grateful to Dr. Badri Narain Tiwari for drawing my attention to Daud Ali's book.
18. Shahid Amin, op. cit., p. 26. The couplet was composed in 1888.
19. Mushirul Hasan, 'Textbooks and Imagined History: The BJP's Intellectual Agenda', in *India International Centre Quarterly*, Delhi: India International Centre, 2002, p. 79. I am grateful to Dr. Lalit Joshi for bringing this article to my notice.
20. R.C. Majumdar, op. cit., pp. 420-5. For a recent critique of nationalist historiography in the African context, see Mamadou Diouf, *Historians and Histories: What For?, African Historiography Between the State*

and the Communities, Kolkata: Centre for Studies in Social Sciences, 2003, pp. 1-5.

21. Kavita Sivaramakrishnan, 'The Use of the Past in a Public Campaign: Ayurvedic *Prachar* in the Writings of Bhai Mohan Singh Vaid', in Daud Ali, ed., op. cit., pp. 178-91.
22. For an incisive analysis of the use of labels in pre-colonial historiography, see Romila Thapar, 'The Tyranny of Labels', IX Zakir Husain Memorial Lecture, Zakir Husain College, New Delhi, 1996, pp. 1-24.
23. Avril A. Powell, *Muslims and Missionaries in Pre-Mutiny India*, London: Curzon Press, 1993, pp. 54-5; Peter Hardy, *The Muslims of British India*, Cambridge: Cambridge University Press, 1972, p. 38.
24. Ibid., p. 37.
25. Ibid., p. 70.
26. W.W. Hunter, *The Indian Musalmans: Are They Bound in Conscience to Rebel Against the Queen?*, London, 1871, p. 149.
27. For the Muslim response to British rule, see, for instance, Mushirul Haqq, 'Indian Muslims' Attitude to the British in the Early Nineteenth Century: A Case Study of Shah 'Abdul 'Aziz', unpublished Ph.D. thesis, McGill University, 1964; and F.A. Nizami, 'Madrasahs, Scholars, and Saints: Muslim Response to the British Presence in Delhi and the Upper Doab, 1803-1857', unpublished D.Phil thesis, Oxford University, 1983. Also see Peter Hardy, op. cit., pp. 92-115.
28. Ghulam Rasul Mehr, *Saiyid Ahmad Shahid*, vol. I, Lahore, 1952, pp. 59-60.
29. Saiyid Ahmad Khan, *Asarus-Sanadid*, n.d., part IV, p. 26, quoted by Aslam Siddiqi, 'Syed Ahmad Shahid', *Islamic Culture*, vol. XIX, no. 2, 1945, p. 125.
30. Marc Gaborieau, 'Sufism in the First Indian Wahabi Manifesto: Siratu'l mustaqim by Isma'il Shahid and 'Abdul Hayy', in Muzaffar Alam, François Nalini Delvoye and Marc Gaborieau, eds., *The Making of Indo-Persian Culture: Indian and French Studies*, Delhi: Manohar and Centre de Sciences Humaines, 2000, pp. 154-5. In the Indo-Muslim Sufi tradition, particularly in the Naqshbandi order, instances of Sufis claiming direct initiation from god or the Prophet are common. Mirza Mazhar Jan-i Janan (d. 1781) and Shah Ghulam 'Ali (d. 1824) claimed this distinction. Sheikh Ahmad Sirhindi (d. 1624) also claimed to be an *Uwaysi.* See Y. Friedman, *Shaykh Ahmad Sirhindi: An Outline of His Thought and a Study of His Image in the Eyes of Posterity*, Montreal: McGill Queen's University Press, 1971, p. 28.
31. Mehr, op. cit., p. 89; Saiyid Abul Hasan 'Ali Nadavi, *Sirat-i Saiyid Ahmad Shahid*, Lucknow, 1939, p. 75.

32. S. Moinul Haq, *Islamic Thought and Movements in the Subcontinent (711-1947)*, Karachi: Historical Society, Pakistan History Society Publilcation, no. 69, 1979, p. 436.
33. Peter Hardy has suggested that the theory that Saiyid Ahmad advised Amir Khan not to make peace with the British was a later addition to the saga of the Saiyid and is, therefore, apocryphal. See Peter Hardy, op. cit., p. 51.
34. Gaborieau, op. cit., pp. 154-5.
35. Aziz Ahmad, *Studies in Islamic Culture in the Indian Environment*, Delhi: Oxford University Press, rpt., 2000, p. 211; Mehr, *Saiyid Ahmad*, vol. I, op. cit., pp. 130-1; Mohiuddin Ahmad, *Sayyid Ahmad Shahid: His Life and Mission*, Lucknow: Academy of Islamic Research and Publications, 1975, pp. 59-60.
36. Gaborieau, op. cit., p. 149.
37. Qeyamuddin Ahmad, *The Wahhabi Movement in India*, Delhi: Manohar, rpt., 1994, p. 69, n. 29. There were precedents for such *fatwas* in Indo-Muslim history. During the reign of Akbar, Mulla 'Abdullah Sultanpuri has decreed that since the pilgrims going for *hajj* from India by the sea route had to face the Portuguese aggression and while those proceeding by the land route had to sustain Safavid tyranny, *hajj* is not obligatory for Indian Muslims. See N.R. Farooqi, *Mughal-Ottoman Relations: A Study of Political and Diplomatic Relations between Mughal India and the Ottoman Empire 1556-1748*, Delhi: Idarah-i-Adabiyat-i-Delhi, 1989, p. 148.
38. Mehr, vol. I, op. cit., pp. 178-241; Saiyid Abul Hasan 'Ali Nadavi, *Sirat*, op. cit., pp. 104-19.
39. For a succinct account of the financial hardship faced by Rae Bareli Muslims in the early nineteenth century, see J.R.I. Cole, *Roots of North Indian Shi'ism in Iran and Iraq: Religion and State in Awadh, 1772-1859*, Delhi: Oxford University Press, 1989, p. 235.
40. For Sikh atrocities on the Muslims of Punjab, see Aslam Siddiqi, 'Syed Ahmad Shahid', in *Islamic Culture*, vol. XIX, no. 2, 1945, p. 128.
41. Marc Gaborieau, 'The *Jihad* of Saiyid Ahmad Barelwi on the North West Frontier: The Last Echo of the Middle Ages? Or a Prefiguration of Modern South Asia?', paper presented at the International Seminar on Culture, Economy and Social Change, 12th-18th Centuries, Aligarh, 5-7 January 2002, p. 14.
42. Mehr, vol. I, op. cit., p. 175.
43. Mohiuddin Ahmad, op. cit., p. 65.
44. Qeyamuddin Ahmad, op. cit., pp. 47-8.
45. K.A. Nizami, 'Socio-Religious Movements in Indian Islam 1763-1898', *Islamic Culture*, vol. XLIV, no. 2, 1970, p. 137; Also see Muhammad

Baqir, 'A Warrior Scholar of the Nineteenth Century', in 'Abdullah Butt, ed., *Aspects of Shah Isma'il Shahid: Essays on His Literary, Political and Religious Activities*, Lahore: Quami Kutub Khana, 1943, pp. 56-7. I am grateful to my friend, Dr. Javed Ali Khan, for bringing this book to my notice.

46. Mehr, op. cit., vol. I, pp. 282-439; vol. II, pp. 35-385; Abul Hasan Ali Nadavi, op. cit., pp. 120-203; and Qeyamuddin Ahmad, op. cit., pp. 48-67.
47. Mehr, op. cit., vol. I, 386-7.
48. Ibid., vol. II, p. 358.
49. Ibid., vol. I, p. 248.
50. Aziz Ahmad, op. cit., p. 213; Mohiuddin Ahmad, op. cit., p. 387.
51. Marc Gaborieau, op. cit., p. 9.
52. Cited in Syeda Saiyidain Hameed, tr., *Hali's Musaddas: A Story in Verse of the Ebb and Tide of Islam*, Delhi: HarperCollins India, 2003, p. 27.
53. Ibid., p. 29.
54. A.B.M. Habibullah, 'Historical Writing in Urdu: A Survey of Tendencies', in C.H. Philips, op. cit., p. 484.
55. Syeda Saiyidain Hameed, op. cit., p. 30.
56. Cited in Ralph Russell, *The Pursuit of Urdu Literature: A Select History*, London: Zed Books, 1992, p. 127. The letter is dated 10 June 1879. See *Maktubat-i Sir Saiyid*, ed., *Sheikh Muhammad Ismail Panipati*, Lahore, p. 54 1959, p. 312. I am grateful to my brother, Professor S.R. Faruqi, for permitting me to use his copy of Russell's book.
57. Christopher Shackle and Javed Majeed, *Hali's Musaddas: The Flow and Ebb of Islam*, translated, and with a critical introduction, Delhi: Oxford University Press, 1997, p. 49. I am grateful to Professor S.R. Faruqi for permitting me to use his personal copy of this book.
58. Altaf Husain Hali, *Madd-o-Jazr-i-Islam,* Kanpur: Nami Press, 1909, p. 10.
59. Ibid., pp. 53-77.
60. Ibid., pp. 103-8.
61. Ibid., pp. 52-3; Christopher Shackle and Javed Majeed, *Hali's Musaddas*, op. cit., p. 143.
62. Altaf Husain Hali, op. cit., pp. 10-11; Christopher Shackle and Javed Majeed, op. cit., p. 10.
63. Syeda Saiyidain Hameed, op. cit., p. 32.
64. Christopher Shackle and Javed Majeed, op. cit., p. 37.
65. Second Introduction to *Madd-o-jazr-i-Islam,* Karachi, 1999, pp. 46-7. The English translation has been taken from Christopher Shackle and Javed Majeed, op. cit., p. 99.

66. S. M. Ikram, *Mauj-i Kausar*, Delhi: Adabi Dunya, rpt., 1991, p. 126.
67. Shardul Chaturvedi, '*Musaddas*: The Historical Poem of Maulana Altaf Husain Hali', *Think India*, vol. 5, no. 4, 2002, p. 73.
68. Saiyid Suleiman Nadavi, 'Musaddas-i Hali', in *Madd-o-jazr-i-Islam*, Karachi, 1999, p. 14.

NINE

Exclusive Resources and Inclusive Objectives

Islam in the Making of Indian Nationalism: 1857-1922

Rizwan Qaiser

In recent times, Islam and its philosophical resources have been under an academic and sometimes quasi-academic scanner. In either case, sociological and cultural resources have largely been ignored, while undue importance has been attached to political resources, with special reference to its suitability and adaptability in the global context of the formation of nation states and the vocabulary associated with those processes. The impression that is sought to be given is that, 'in most Muslim countries Islam is still the ultimate criterion of group identity and loyalty. It is Islam which distinguishes between self and other, between insider and outsider, between brother and stranger.'[1] Immediately after making this statement, a contrast is drawn between the Islamic or, shall we say, Muslims' self-perception, with the West: 'We in the Western world have become accustomed to other criteria of classification, by nation, by country and by subdivisions of these.'[2] It is interesting to observe the mechanical contrasting of the two diverse historical experiences: of the Muslims, who mostly inhabit the Asian and African continents, with that of the people in the Western world, who have followed an entirely different historical trajectory. Yet, in a historical manner, the contrast is considered necessary, which, in a way, also seems like a subtle attempt to place the Western world on a higher pedestal. In this perspective it is further argued that,

> in the course of the nineteenth century, the word *watan* with derivatives for 'patriot' and 'patriotism' passed into common use as part of the new nationalist terminology, and a number of older terms, part of the political language of Islam, began to acquire new meanings. The ideological influences coming from Europe after the French Revolution suggested new concepts of political identity and authority, based not on communal loyalty and dynastic allegiance but on country or nation.[3]

In other words, Bernard Lewis would like us to believe that loyalty to the country or the nation was possible only because of the fact that Islamic societies came under the ideological influence of the West. Conversely, it is also possible to argue that had these Muslim societies not come under the influence of the West, then the notion of the nation or loyalty to one's country among these societies would not have been possible.

Lewis's arguments would be considered theoretical since no particular Muslim society is subjected to rigorous empirical enquiry. Therefore, a mere theoretical construction is likely to miss out on the diverse historical experience of Muslims in equally diverse historical settings, whether they constitute the majority or minority. However, there are historians who have studied Muslims' history in their specific historical setting. In this context, it is relevant to examine the work of an eminent historian, Francis Robinson, who has closely studied the history of Muslims of India. He does not seem to be anywhere close to Lewis's formulation that the Muslim world-view of allegiance to one's nation or country was due to the impact of the West. On the contrary, he seems to argue that separatism seems to be inherent among Muslims, wherever they are in a minority. He argues, 'In the development of Muslim separatism many Muslim leaders had been constrained by political ideas derived from the Islamic culture, indeed on occasions they had been constrained by religious belief itself.'[4] Robinson seems to have maintained a certain consistency while formulating this position. In one of his essays, he argues that it is rather surprising that the *ulemas* of Jamiatul-Ulema-i-Hind were able to strike a conciliation with nationalism, considering that 'separatism in Islam is inherent'.[5]

It would be interesting to examine historical developments with special reference to the role of Islam and its philosophical resources invoked by the Muslims in the wake of India's struggle for freedom. In the process, an attempt shall be made to establish that the historical experience of Indian Muslims does not conform to the theoretical formulation of Lewis nor does it sustain the formulations of Robinson. Contrary to these articulations, Indian Muslims did not necessarily borrow the notion of either *watan* or 'patriotism' or nationalism from the West. They derived the notion of *Hubbul watani* (love for the motherland) from their internal resources, including Islam, and organized their political energies to challenge the colonial domination in diverse hues. Similarly, while they were doing so, they were not necessarily charting out a separate path from the rest of the people, as they strove hard to align themselves with others in order to put up a joint struggle. It is another issue that this kept on changing its character from anti-colonialism to a mature phase of Indian nationalism.

It is true that in many ways, Muslims, like other religious communities such as the Hindus, were invoking religion in their fight against British colonial domination, particularly in the context of the Rebellion of 1857. However, we are concerned with Muslims mobilizing all possible resources, including Islam. Therefore, it is pertinent to underline the fact that Muslims did not necessarily rely on religion in all cases, as they drew upon other sources of political energy. In several cases, the immediate historical experiences of subjugation, exploitation and humiliation, too, played an important role in igniting the fire of resistance to the British. This happened at the level of individual efforts made by some. In other cases, similar endeavours were more organized.

I

Begum Hazrat Mahal, one of the wives of the deposed Nawab of Awadh, resisted the British in Lucknow and other parts of Awadh with great élan. In the entire course of her resistance, she did not rely on mobilizing Islamic resources, as she was more engaged in organizing those rajas, zamindars and taluqdars who had once been loyal to the Nawab of Awadh. In the entire region, she was the rallying force. It is a well-known fact that after Wajid Ali Shah was deposed in February 1856, Awadh had come under the direct control of the British East India Company, which was widely resented by the elites as well as the masses. Hence, discontent was simmering. The Rebellion in Lucknow broke out on 30 May 1857 and its command fell into the hands of Begum Hazrat Mahal. However, as a part of her strategy, she chose to reclaim the lost Nawabi of Awadh in the name of her young son, Birjis Qadar, being well aware of the fact that she alone would have to provide the required leadership. Qadar was coronated on 5 July 1857. This was widely accepted by all notables of the region who gave gifts to the new ruler, since he was treated as the true heir to the throne of Awadh Nawabi.[6] A pronouncement was made in his name:

> *Khalq Khuda ki Mulk Badshah Delhi ka, Hukm Mirza Birjis Qadar Bahadur ka. Har khas aur aam ko ittela di jati hai ki Us Pak Parwardigar ne jo hum sab ka Khaliq hai, usne hamari hukumat lauta di hai. Ab jabki hukumat ka Nizam hamare hathe mein hai, Hukm diya jata hai ki koi shakhs fasad ya loot nahi karega. Khilafwarzi karne wale hakim Shara ki ru se saza ke mustahaq honge.*[7]

Throughout the rebellious campaign, she ensured that despite occasional appeals to Islam in order to mobilize the Muslims of the region, no attempt was made to give these the colour of *jihad* or Islamic victory. There were many occasions when she resisted the attempts of a rebel, Maulvi Ahmadullah Shah, to give the rebellion a religious colour, as she was keen to maintain unity among the ranks of rebels, irrespective of religious distinctions.[8]

With the passage of time, as she started losing to the British, instead of surrendering or accepting any offer of reconciliation, she chose to remain steadfast to the cause and decided to escape to Nepal. While she was retreating, for a while she was stationed at a place called Bondi, in the present-day district of Bahraich in Uttar Pradesh. It was around that time (in November 1858) that Queen Victoria issued a royal proclamation by which the governance of India was brought under the direct control of the British Crown instead of the East India Company. The tone of the proclamation was highly patronizing but reconciliatory.[9] There was a near-total silence, with regard to this proclamation all over the subcontinent. However, Begum Hazrat Mahal responded to it by issuing a rejoinder, published in Persian as well as the Nagari script. It clearly exhorted Indians not to believe in what was said in the proclamation. She went on to recount the manner in which Indian states were deprived by deceit and fraud of their independent existence. In such a situation, the only option Indians were left with was to take up arms against the British.[10]

Similarly, there was another lady called Azizan, who took an active part in the Rebellion of 1857. She was a dancer by profession and had very little connection with the native rulers. Yet she showed exemplary courage in the course of the rebellion. She chose to dress herself as a soldier and moved about on horse-back, exhorting people to take part in the rebellion. She organized a contingent of women, which looked after the injured in battlefronts and also arranged for provisions for soldiers. Azizan enthusiastically participated in a victory procession after Nana Dhodhupant became the ruler of Bithur.[11] However, after she was captured by the British soldiers, an offer of pardon was made to her by the officer-in-charge because he was quite taken in by her beauty. She declined the offer and chose to be shot dead.[12]

Azizan and many like her were not inspired by the call of *jihad* or any similar exhortation by the theologians of the time. They were guided more by the circumstances of history. For instance, Azizan had lost many of her close relatives in the wake of the rebellion in places like Itawah and Kanpur, which filled her with a strong sense of revenge against the British.[13] It is generally believed that she had played a crucial role in the Bibi Ghar massacre in which about 150 women and children were put to death.[14]

Apart from these two women who showed exemplary courage in the Rebellion of 1857, there were scores of other people who also responded to the call of rebellion, not necessarily as part of their religious conviction, to throw the British out of India. One such person was Khan Bahadur Khan of Bareilly. He was the scion of the Rohella Sardars who had ruled over the entire region of Rohelkhand for a long time. The last ruler of Rohelkhand was Hafiz Rahmat Khan, the grandfather of Khan Bahadur Khan. Keeping the importance of the Rohella Sardars in mind, Khan Bahadur Khan was made a judicial officer by the British and enjoyed good relations with them. When the rebellion broke out in Rohelkhand, Khan Bahadur Khan was looked upon as the natural choice to lead it and soon he was able to establish his rule over the region with the help of military generals such as Bakht Khan. However, the rebel regime that he established was an all-inclusive one as he assigned prominent positions to Hindus. Shobha Ram was made the Dewan of the regime and there were other prominent Hindus in important positions.[15] The inclusive nature of the regime was so pronounced that it was difficult for the British to break ranks between the Hindus and Muslims of Rohelkhand.[16] With the intention of breaking the unity between the two communities, the colonial government deputed Captain Gawan with Rs. 50,000 to provoke the Hindus of the region against Khan Bahadur Khan, but they declined the offer.[17] As a result, the same amount had to be deposited with the government treasury. In order to keep the base of his regime as broad as possible, Khan Bahadur Khan had secured the support of the *ulemas* and *pandits* alike.[18] It can be surmised that he did not invoke the authority of religion while rebelling against the British and organizing his regime, which was inclusive in every sense of the word. He continued to fight against the British till he was captured along with 257 companions, and they all were hanged from a banyan tree in the compound of the Commissioner of Rohelkhand.[19]

The role played by these three individuals in the Rebellion of 1857 was varied in content and style. Begum Hazrat Mahal and Khan Bahadur Khan played the role of leaders who succeeded in establishing rebellious regimes, while Azizan's role, though equally enthusiastic, was limited in appeal and scope. However, what seems to be common amongst the three is that none of them seemed to have been inspired by the call of *jihad*. Their motto was not to seek a reward in the life hereafter but in the here and now, by driving the British out. They were not ploughing lonely furrows but were keen in taking everybody along with them.

For instance, diverse social groups such as the rajas, jagirdars, peasants, baniyas, dalits, pasis and many others responded to the call of Hazrat Mahal to rebel against the British.[20] It was, thus, a multi-class and multi-religious group's response to the call to overthrow the British.

II

While this was one side of the picture, there was another side to it as well. The other side was represented by the *ulemas*, who tried to articulate the Indians' grievances against the British in religious terms. These *ulemas* have contemptuously been described as *jihadis* by William Dalrymple.[21] It is true that Dalrymple's work essentially focuses on the experience in Delhi and cannot be conflated to other spatial contexts; however, given his approach, it is possible to surmise that he would like others to believe that:

> By and large, however, the people of Delhi, already alarmed by the number of violent, unpaid and hungry *sepoys* gathering within their walls, remained dubious about the pleasure of hosting in addition several thousand fanatical holy warriors. This was specially so, given the *Jihadis*' far from friendly attitude towards Delhi's Hindus—half the city's population—and the importance the Delhi elite placed on not upsetting the delicate equilibrium between Hindus and Muslims in the city.[22]

As regards the role of *jihadis*, he goes on to quote one Sa'id Mubarak Shah that:

> . . . their stated objective was a crusade against the infidels, their real one was plunder. In this manner fully five thousand men from various quarters poured into Delhi as *Ghazees*, the majority armed with *gundasahs* (battle axes) and dressed in blue tunics and green turbans.[23]

Dalrymple leaves no one in doubt that those Muslims who participated in the Rebellion of 1857 were *jihadis*. However, the characteristics of these *jihadis* were that they were 'fanatical holy warriors', had an unfriendly attitude towards the Hindus, behaved more like crusaders against infidels and their only intention was to plunder. It will be interesting to examine these assertions in order to understand and analyse the contribution of Muslims, in particular the *ulemas* in the Rebellion of 1857, whose participation is considered as a *jihad* against the British. It is important to point out the diversity of approaches even among those who took part in the name of Islam. There were some who invoked the authority of Islam with a view to arouse the masses, while others were involved in not only arousing the masses but directly engaging in action on battlefronts.

In this regard, the role of Mufti Sadruddin Azurda is interesting. He had enjoyed proximity with the British for a long time. He was made the *Sadr-i-Amin* of Delhi in 1927 and, by June 1844, was elevated to the status of *Sadarus-Sudoor* of Delhi, drawing a salary of more than Rs. 1,000.[24] Azurda was a man of immense qualities. He was known not only as a serious scholar of Islam, specializing in jurisprudence, *hadith* and exegesis, but also as a poet of *Urdu Rekhta*. Despite the fact that he was serving the British as *Sadarus-Sudoor*, he was against them. He was instrumental in asking Ahmadullah Shah to move to Agra in his campaign against the British and also gave him a letter of introduction, which helped him establish local contacts. It is true that he was not seen on any front in the course of the uprising in Delhi, and yet his sympathies were clearly with the rebels. Munshi Jeevanlal, who was perceived to be an informer of the British, has recorded that on 2 August 1857, when Bahadur Shah Zafar organized a *Darbar-i-Aam*, there many notables present, one of them being Sadruddin Azurda.[25] Apparently, in this gathering, Bahadur Shah Zafar shared some of his poetic reflections, which clearly exhorted everybody, irrespective of their status, to fight against the British till the end. Earlier he had already become a signatory to an important *fatwa* issued against the British, which was widely popularized with the help of Urdu newspapers and individual circulation. After Delhi was recaptured by the British, Sadruddin Azurda, too, was arrested along with others and kept behind bars. Finally, the trial took place; but he was not convicted but released. However, he lost his job as *Sadarus-Sudoor* and his property was confiscated, compelling him to live a life of penury.[26]

Allama Fazli Haq Khairabadi was another of those *ulema*, or religious scholars, who were initially in the service of the British. For instance, despite having been trained in religious studies, he took up a job as head clerk in the office of the Resident of Delhi. Subsequently, he took up employment at Lucknow as *Sadarus-Sudoor* and, later on, became the chief administrator of *Huzoor-i-Tahsil*. However, in due course of time, he quit these jobs and decided to move around as a wandering scholar, enjoying the patronage of different rulers at different points of time. In the course of his travels, he enjoyed the patronage of the Nawab of Jhajhar (Punjab), the Maharaja of Alwar (Rajasthan), the Nawab of Tonk (Rajasthan) and the Nawab of Rampur (Uttar Pradesh).[27] And yet, when the situation became critical, he threw in his lot with those who were rebelling against the British. After the rebellion had broken out, Fazli Haq rushed to Delhi and got in touch with those who were active. He was in regular touch with Bahadur Shah Zafar, who was known to him from before. He actively mobilized the opinion of the *ulema* against the British and finally issued a *fatwa* from the Juma Masjid in Delhi soon after the Friday prayer, which was signed by prominent scholars such as Sadruddin Azurda, Maulvi Abdul Qadir, Qazi Faizullah Dehlavi, Maulana Faiz Ahmad Badauni, Maulvi Wazir Khan Akbarabadi, and Syed Mubarak Shah Rampuri.[28] Even though the *fatwa* came rather late in the day, it had a tremendous effect on the common people, particularly the *sepoys*. By mid-September 1857, the tide was turning against the rebels. The British had mounted a serious challenge and the rebels started conceding ground to them. Finally, by 19 September 1857, Delhi once again fell into the hands of the British. Scores of people were subjected to brutal repression. However, some managed to escape from Delhi. Fazli Haq was one of them. He reached Lucknow and was able to join one Mammo Khan, a close confidant of Begum Hazrat Mahal. He was consulted on important matters. But even at Lucknow the resistance was weakening and the fortunes of rebels were not showing any sign of brightening. In these circumstances, Fazli Haq was captured at Sitapur and finally brought to Lucknow for trial. The charges framed against him were interesting. First, as a part of the rebel governments at Delhi, Awadh and other places, he was responsible for the rebellion and massacre there. Second, he was the chief advisor to the rebel, Sardar Mammo Khan, at

Boondi (Awadh) in May 1858. Third, he conspired in the murder of Abdul Hakim, an employee of the British government in May 1858.[29] Finally, he was convicted and ordered to be deported to Kala Pani (Andaman Islands), where he died in 1861.

Amongst the people who invoked Islam, Maulvi Ahmadullah Shah Faizabadi is a complex but distinct character. His real name was Syed Ahmad Ali Ziauddin Dilawarjung. He was markedly different from the two scholars of Islam discussed above who took part in the Rebellion of 1857. Ahmadullah Shah was cast in the mould of a Sufi, who actively participated on innumerable fronts during the rebellion and was martyred in action. He carried blue blood in his veins, since his ancestry is traced to the Qutub Shahi dynasty of south India. He is said to be the great-grandson of Abul Hasan *Tanashah* who came from Chennapatan.

After travelling through England and other parts of Europe and West Asia, he came in contact with Farman Ilahi of Jaipur and became his disciple. Subsequently, he met Mehrab Shah Qalandar, a Sufi at Gwalior, and developed a close bond with him. It is generally believed that it was Mehrab Shah who inculcated in him the value of *jihad* against the British, which became the mission of his life. Irrespective of the place he visited, he preached *jihad* against them. However, he was not merely confined to preaching. On the advice of Sadruddin Azurda, he settled at Agra for a while, where he used to organize arms training for his disciples near the Agra Fort.[30] Later on, he shifted to Lucknow but, by February 1857, he finally settled in Faizabad. He chose to do so because he hoped to take up the cause of the people of Awadh who were angry at the annexation of their province. He openly preached *jihad* and rebellion to the Muslims and Hindus, respectively, and engaged with the British in a bloody confrontation, which finally resulted in his capture and imprisonment. He was convicted and given a death sentence. However, a rebellion led by Subedar Dileep Singh broke out in Faizabad on 9 June 1857. Dileep Singh successfully freed Ahmadullah Shah from the British jail.[31] Subsequently, Ahmadullah Shah inflicted a crushing defeat on the British at a place called Chinhat, close to Lucknow. In the course of the rebellion, he closely interacted with many rebel leaders such as

Nana Saheb, Azimullah Khan, Bakht Khan, Begum Hazrat Mahal and others. Finally, he was betrayed and killed by one Baldev Singh, brother of the Raja of Pawatin, a small principality in Shahjahanpur. His head was severed and presented to the collector of the district in the hope of a reward, as the British government had put up a reward of Rs. 50,000 for his head. His severed head was hung at the Kotwali for a few days before being buried, although his body was burnt.

In view of the above discussion, some broad conclusions can be drawn. First, in the context of the Rebellion of 1857, the participation of Muslims was not necessarily inspired by Islam as by other historical factors such as exploitation, the cultural arrogance of the British and the fear that, in time to come, they would completely lose out to the British. For these people, the notion of *jihad* was not as important as liberating the country from foreign rule. Second, invoking Islam and the notion of *jihad* in order to liberate the country was not necessarily to earn merits in the life hereafter. Another interesting aspect of the philosophy of *jihad* was that the British, by virtue of being Christians, should have been accepted by the Muslims as *Ahl-i-Kitab (People of the Book)*, but they were invariably described as *kafirs* who must be fought against. The *ulemas* discussed in this paper did not limit the appeal of *jihad* to Muslims alone for they were keen to include everybody, particularly the Hindus. In several cases, Hindus, too, responded to the call of *jihad* in its broader sense. Third, while invoking *jihad*, they did not draw inspiration from any source external to the territorial limits of India as there was hardly any similar resistance to colonial/imperialist domination at this point of time. It has to be noted that European imperialistic penetration had not yet taken place in those countries which were predominantly Muslim. The overall picture that merges in the context of Muslim participation in the Rebellion of 1857, with special reference to those who invoked Islam, is that they were neither inspired by nor drawn to any construction of a pan-Islamic paradigm. On the contrary, the notion of *Ummah*, the community of believers in Islam, was of lesser consideration than that of *Mohibban-i-Watan*, patriots who followed the philosophy of *Hubbul Watani* or love for one's country, which resulted in coalescing communities, particularly the Hindus and Muslims in a united political action.

III

Muslim participation in the anti-colonial struggle in 1857 underwent a transformation towards the end of the nineteenth and beginning of the twentieth century. Their anti-colonial responses were also tinged with growing concern for the declining fate of Turkey, known for being the seat of *Khalifat-ul-Muslimeen.* From this time onwards, pan-Islamism became a factor in galvanizing Muslims against the British, a fact which historians have viewed rather skeptically.[32]

An expression such as pan-Islamism came into currency in the last quarter of the nineteenth century, in European journalistic literature in order to describe unifying tendencies among Muslims on a global scale.[33] This process was accelerated in the wake of the Russo-Turkish war in 1877 in which Turkey was defeated and the Treaty of San Stefano with humiliating conditions was imposed on her. Turkey had to recognize the independence of Romania, Serbia and Montenegro, while ceding certain parts in East Europe to Russia. These developments were hailed by the European press as the liberation of 11 million Christians from Turkish slavery.[34] With this, the growing hegemony of European imperialism was set in motion as the disintegration of the Ottoman Empire had begun. Tunis was captured by France in 1881, Egypt was brought under British control in 1882, Italy invaded Eritrea and, finally, Sudan, too, became a part of the British Empire in 1889.[35] It was around this time that Balkan nationalities were rising against the House of Ottomans and were supported by European powers, particularly Russia, on grounds of religious and ethnic affinities, since a majority of them came from Slavic stock and believed in the Russian Orthodox Church. The growing conflict between Turkey and other European countries, apart from other factors, was also based on religious and ethnic considerations.

These developments caused unease amongst the Muslims and a desire to be united in order to express solidarity with the Sultan of Turkey, who was also perceived as the *khalifa* of the Muslims.[36] A new idea evolved amongst them that Christian Europe was bent upon destroying the last bastion of Muslim power. However, in order to overcome such a predicament, they thought of two ways of reviving the fortune of the Muslims: one was to bring them back to the *Sirat-al-Mustaqeem*, the right path, and the second was to rally around the *khalifa* by accepting him as the central figure of Muslims the world over.[37]

These developments in the Muslim world contained elements of revivalism, which was described as Islamic extremism and lunacy in political as well as journalistic circles in Europe.[38] Such feelings were so strong that even a person like Carlyle suggested that Turkey ought to be thrown out of the Eastern Question immediately and the fate of Bulgaria be decided by the joint leadership of European powers.[39] The underlying motive behind such an articulation was that Islam was against the growing nationalism in the Eastern Europe. While, on the other hand, when an anti-imperialist mobilization had begun rolling in the 1880s in countries such as Egypt and Sudan, it was described as a manifestation of extremism, whereas it was as much an expression of nationalism in these countries.[40] For advocates of European imperialism, the awakening in Muslim societies was projected in an adverse light in two distinct ways: first, it was demonstrated that Islam was against nationalism; second, nationalism in Muslim societies was projected as anti-modern, revivalist and rebellious.[41]

Keeping in view these developments, tension between Muslims and the imperialist West started growing. In order to meet this challenge, ideological preparation was started. It was felt that Islamic culture was in the process of decay which seriously required reforms, and this was not possible without bringing about unity amongst the Muslims in order to confront the West, particularly in the realm of culture.

In this regard, Jamaluddin Afghani emerged as an important ideologue. He was an Islamic scholar, journalist, thinker and reformer of considerable importance. His larger objectives were to remove defeatism and instill a sense of confidence in the hearts and minds of Muslims. He made a strong case for bringing about reforms in Muslim societies, and launching a struggle to free them from colonial and imperialist hegemony. He considered these as inseparable aspect.[42] He emphasized that in order to achieve both, it was important to revitalize Islam, with a worldwide centre of power in the form of the *Khilafat.* Yet Afghani also accepted the realities of particularistic nationalism in view of the anti-colonial struggles which had started emerging in many Muslim countries.[43] It is amply clear that his articulation had elements of contradiction, which, however, was also the case with the whole project of pan-Islamism, an ultimate goal, but the more proximate and vital one being to liberate Muslims from colonial domination.[44] It was in this context that he had argued that Islamic unity was important but more important was national unity in any particular country.[45]

In order to propagate his views, Afghani visited India during 1880-2 and delivered a series of lectures, highlighting the importance of the *Khilafat*. However, while doing so, he also reminded the Muslims of the necessity of fighting against British imperialist domination. In this regard, he forcefully advocated unity between the Hindus and Muslims.[46] He was critical of Sir Syed Ahmad Khan for being friendly with the British and extending support to them. Sir Syed replied to this criticism by arguing that the Sultan of Turkey could not be treated as the *khalifa* of Muslims the world over, particularly by Indian Muslims, because Turkish laws were not applicable to them and they did not enjoy his protection.[47]

The ideological legacies of Jamaluddin Afghani were carried forward by his disciple, Rashid Rida, and, later on, by Sheikh Abduh. In India, it was Maulana Abul Kalam Azad who imbibed the influence of pan-Islamism the most from the writings of Rashid Rida.[48] With the help of *Al-Hilal*, he propagated these ideas in the beginning of the second decade of the twentieth century. Other than Azad, there were many who reflected on similar ideological currents. For instance, Altaf Husain Hali in his famous *Musaddas-i-Hali* had talked about the rise and fall of Islam. Abdul Halim Sharar in his novel *Firdaus-i-Barin* had eloquently presented a picture of revived Islamic values and his characters were presented as following these values with a sense of purpose. Allama Iqbal's poem *Masjid-i-Qartaba* clearly talked about the declining fortunes of the Muslims, which generated a lot of emotion. In one form or the other, intellectuals, writers and thinkers were engaged in addressing this question and the possibilities of reviving the fortunes of Islam.

Other than intellectual responses, there were political responses to the question of pan-Islamism, which were amply manifested through Urdu newspapers, magazines and journals. For instance, when war broke out between Turkey and Greece in 1897, European powers intervened to save Greece from total defeat and placed the island of Crete under international control.[49] Developments related to this war generated a considerable pan-Islamic upsurge among Indian Muslims. In Kanpur, financial contributions were made in support of Turkey, while special prayers were organized in mosques at Agra, Jhansi and other places for her success. The Urdu papers invariably described the Sultan of Turkey as *Khalifat-ul-Muslimeen*. They also criticized Sir Syed for not supporting the cause of pan-Islamism.[50]

The pan-Islamic upsurge slowly started generating anti-British feelings. However, it would not have been able to do so had it not coalesced with other developments which were taking place within the country. The annulment of the partition of Bengal in 1911 was one issue which agitated the minds of the Muslims. It is common knowledge that Bengal was partitioned in 1905 in order to divide the Hindus and Muslims of east and west Bengal; however, it was also seen as an attempt to divide the Hindus on the same line. This was resisted primarily by Hindus but in several places Muslims, too, joined them.[51] Despite this resistance, once the partition was formalized and took place, Muslims were able to benefit as their presence in the bureaucracy and other departments started growing. Thus, the annulment of the partition of Bengal in 1911 was seen as an anti-Muslim act on the part of the British.

Around the same time in July 1912, Italy invaded Tripoli and captured it due to its desperation to join the race of imperialist powers ever since the last quarter of the nineteenth century. This invasion resulted in a war between Turkey and Italy. The palpable feeling among Muslims was that such an invasion would not have been possible without the acquiescence of Britain,[52] and that Russia and France, too, wanted the total disintegration of the Ottoman Empire.[53]

The Ottoman Empire was under threat from different powers in Europe. However, the most serious one arose due to the risings of Balkan nationalities, who wanted to liberate themselves from Turkish control. While these risings had a clear manifestation of nationalism, the elements of religion cannot be denied, for most of these nationalities were followers of the Orthodox Church and enjoyed the support of Russia. Turkey had little option but to defend herself at any cost. These developments in the Balkans had an impact on the Muslims, since they perceived them as an attack by Christian powers on the last surviving Muslim power. They were considerably galvanized and collected huge subscriptions to organize medical aid to Turkey and New York. Finally, they succeeded in sending a medical mission to Constantinople under the leadership of Mukhtar Ahmad Ansari in December 1912.[54] Subsequently, another organization, *Anjuman-i-Khuddam-i-Kaba*, was formed in May 1913 under the leadership of Maulana Abdul Bari Firangi Mahal. The formation of this organization and the medical mission reflected the anxieties of the Muslims of India on the fate of Turkey.

Resentment against the British government was building up in view of other developments too. For instance, in July-August 1913, a portion of a mosque in Kanpur's Machli Bazaar area where Muslims used to perform ablutions was demolished by the government. This incident was widely resented and demonstrated against. However, the government responded in a high-handed manner and fired at the demonstrators, killing many on the spot. This episode generated strong anti-British feelings as several papers described the act of demolition as a part of the anti-Muslim and anti-Islam policies of the British government and appeals were issued against it.[55]

It is important to underline the fact that several developments which were taking place within the country coincided with the issue of pan-Islamism and the fate of Turkey, both of which together produced a lethal combination of anger and resentment, on the one hand, and, on the other, a desire to create a platform which could be used to articulate the Muslim point of view. The All India Muslim League was not considered the right platform to represent the contemporary Muslim point of view because of its demonstrative loyalty to the government. Therefore, in the absence of such a platform, several individuals and papers filled the gap. Maulana Abul Kalam Azad, Maulana Mohammad Ali and Zafar Ali Khan emerged as three prominent figures that made significant use of their journals and papers such as *Al-Hilal* and *Al-Balagh*, *Comrade*, *Hamdard* and *Zamindar* to articulate views on pan-Islamism. In several cases, they used this as an opportunity to launch a scathing criticism of the government. There were other individuals such as Hasrat Mohani, Khaliquzzaman, Shoeb Qureshi and Syed Mahmood who joined this campaign. The academic institutions which came forward in extending support to the cause were Darul Uloom at Deoband, Firangi Mahal and Nadwatul Uloom at Lucknow. However, of all the individuals, Maulana Mohammad Ali and Maulana Abul Kalam Azad emerged as the most articulate voices of this campaign, who, while speaking for pan-Islamism tried to establish its relationship with Indian nationalism.

Maulana Mohammad Ali, after obtaining his higher education from Oxford University, worked for the state of Baroda and Rampur. Thereafter, he joined politics, and became a member of the Muslim League in 1906 but was soon disillusioned by its politics due to its loyalty to the British regime. Later, in 1911, he launched a paper called the *Comrade* which became quite popular. Subsequently, he launched another paper in Urdu called the *Hamdard*. In both, he shared his views on pan-Islamism and tried to instill feelings of patriotism amongst Muslims. He also emphasized Hindu-Muslim unity. After the Balkan wars broke out, Mohammad Ali mobilized not just the Muslim opinion but also financial resources in support of Turkey. While generating political awareness among them, he tried to bridge the gap between the *ulema* and modern, educated Muslims.[56]

Maulana Azad emerged as the most articulate voice who argued the case for Muslim support to Turkey and pan-Islamism. However, it is important to realize that Azad did not begin his political career as a pan-Islamist, as he had joined an underground revolutionary group called Yugantar. Azad had said, 'In those days the revolutionary groups recruited their members exclusively from the Hindu middle class. In fact, all the revolutionary groups were actively anti-Muslim.'[57] Despite these limitations, Azad was able to enter the revolutionary politics of Bengal. During that period, he believed in violence as a means to achieve political goals.[58] This association with underground revolutionary activities amounted to a solitary affair as other Muslims were barely attracted to the philosophy of revolutionary politics. Azad's idea was to take his co-religionists on board and, with this in mind, he decided to launch the *Al-Hilal* in July 1912.

In the *Al-Hilal*, Azad repeatedly wrote that Islam was a force with the help of which the chains of slavery could be broken. He said that under the guidance of Islam, Muslims should launch a *jihad* against the British. He also emphasized Hindu-Muslim unity, without which the struggle against the alien power would remain incomplete. Pan-Islamism was another issue that was discussed. Thus, the *Al-Hilal* emerged as a platform where Maulana Azad struck a relation between pan-Islamism and Indian nationalism. He kept his readers informed about developments regarding the Balkan wars, for he was of the ideological conviction that Muslims must keep their relations with the *khalifa* alive, be friendly with those who were his friends and fight those who were his enemies because, in Islam, friendship and enmity should be maintained for the sake of religion, not personal considerations.[59] Azad gave vent to his resentment against England and other European powers for conspiring against the religious and cultural centre of Muslims in general, and Sunni Muslims, in particular.[60] While highlighting the importance of the *Khilafat*, Azad went on to say that if there was any political centre of the Muslims the world over, it was the *Khilafat*.[61] For a while, it appeared as if Azad was articulating a scheme of supra-national loyalty for the Muslims. This was, however, not true, as he was able to revise his stand when the *Khilafat* movement was underway, a point we shall take up later.

When the First World War broke out, Azad clearly sympathized with Germany, an ally of Turkey. He emphasized that Germans were superior to the British in terms of material resources, as well as discipline and training. His bias in favour of Germany aroused the government's suspicion, who looked upon Azad as a 'dangerous man' and kept 'a close watch on him'. Such a vigil was also initiated because Azad had legally protested against the forfeiture of the security deposits of Mohammad Ali's *Comrade*. Azad's writings in the *Al-Hilal* and his protest against the penalty imposed on the *Comrade* convinced the government that,

> the Editor (Maulana Azad) does his best to make his readers believe in the bad chances of the Allies and in the prospects of German victory. Mohammad Ali in the *Hamdard* is playing the same game. The insidious disloyalty of these people in spite of warning and promises is most discernible. They are unfit to be allowed to publish newspapers, at the present time.[62]

Azad was suspected to be a part of the Turkish and German intrigue not just since the time of the War, but also later when, in the winter of 1911-12, a German emissary moved about in pan-Islamic circles and 'consorted with friends of the editor of the *Al-Hilal*'.[63] Finally, official circles recognized that Abul Kalam Azad, 'the editor of *Al-Hilal*, is a dangerous man, that his private feelings probably lead him to regard Germany as the friend of Turkey and that no chance should be lost in checking his activities.'[64] Consequently, a raid on the *Al-Hilal* was organized on 16 November 1914 and the paper was closed down. After a brief respite, Azad started another paper called the *Al-Balagh* from Calcutta itself. The first issue came out on 12 November 1915 and only lasted till March 1916. Azad had become a thorn in the side of the government and was finally made to leave Calcutta for his continuous exhortation to the people build their self-confidence to resist British rule. Azad was not the only one to have incurred the wrath of the government. There were others, too, such as the Ali Brothers, Maulana Zafar Ali Khan, Hasrat Mohani and Maulana Mahmudul Hasan, all of whom had been treated similarly.

Despite the incarceration of the top advocates of pan-Islamism, the fate of Turkey generated plenty of anxiety in the minds of the Muslims. The government was aware of such feelings and, therefore, made an announcement that the holy places of Islam would not be harmed.[65] However, the defeat of Germany, and

Turkey in particular, ignited strong religious emotion amongst Muslims regarding the fate of Turkey, since it was also the custodian of the holy places of Islam such as Mecca and Medina and was, therefore, the protector of Islam. In order to propagate these ideas, a Khilafat Committee was constituted on 20 March 1919 under the chairmanship of Seth Chotani. The branches of this Committee started mushrooming in different parts of the country and a series of meetings were organized in support of Turkey and the *khalifa*. On 17 October 1919, an all-India 'Khilafat Day' was observed, which was considerably successful. Another 'Khilafat Day' was observed on 20 March 1920, which seriously affected business activities in Bombay. In Sindh, four Muslim magistrates resigned from their job in protest against the government's attitude towards Islam. Punjab, too, was affected by a call for *hartal*. Delhi's Jama Masjid became a major centre of Khilafat-related mobilization. Thus, support for Turkey came from all quarters.[66] However, the Khilafat movement was caught between two diametrically opposite tendencies. From within the Khilafat Committee, one group wanted to keep the movement non-violent and peaceful but another group openly advocated an extremist course. The latter was emerging as more popular with the ordinary masses and enjoyed the support of journalists, *ulema* and others. It was able to spread its influence to wider areas.[67]

The manner in which the Muslims gave vent to their anger and frustration on the question of the *Khilafat* was also gradually affecting other sections of society. Mahatma Gandhi was able to sense it and condemned the terms of peace signed with Turkey. He also said that the only way the wounds of Muslims could be healed was not to cooperate with the government. In a meeting held at Allahabad on 3 June 1920, after a heated debate, it was finally resolved that Indians in general, and Muslims in particular, would not cooperate with the government. It was a victory for the extremist elements within the Khilafat Committee who were supported by Gandhi. It was further resolved that a movement would be launched, whose programme would be divided into four stages; the surrendering of titles, and the boycott of the civil services, police and military. Non-payment of taxes, too, was included in the programme. At this stage, it appeared that Mahatma Gandhi was willing to provide leadership to the proposed movement. Gandhi also attempted to include the Congress leaders. He linked the *Khilafat* issue with the 'Punjab Wrong' and attainment of Swaraj. He explained his present stance as, 'If I kept aloof from the *Khilafat* question, I would consider myself as having lost all my worth. That work is my *dharma par excellence*. It is through the *Khilafat* that I am doing the triple duty of showing what *ahimsa* means, of unity between the Hindus and the Muslims and of coming in contact with one and all.'[68]

Gandhi's stance was not surprising since he had a wide-ranging experience of having worked with Muslims in South Africa and had raised many issues of importance. He had protested seriously when the Ali Brothers were imprisoned.[69] He had enjoyed support from among the Muslims during the Rowlatt Satyagraha. However, this time, he faced a challenge on the question of non-violence as a precondition for launching the movement. Many *Khilafat* leaders protested that non-violence had no sanction within Islam, and it would not be able to control and tame the passion and anger on the *Khilafat* question. However, after an initial protest, it was resolved that it could be accepted as a strategy, as it might help Gandhi to reach out to the other sections of society. Even Gandhi thought on similar lines.[70] He was, however, subjected to severe criticism for espousing a cause, which, in the long run, was likely to pose serious problems, since the issue of the *Khilafat* was essentially a matter of religious emotion for the Muslims. But, for Gandhi, the issue at hand was similar to the one he had espoused in Champaran and Kheda. He was convinced that it would help him in developing an understanding of the masses and in achieving Swaraj.[71] Another objective was to create conditions for the Congress to join the movement, which it finally did with great reluctance.

Despite these efforts to build a large, inclusive framework, bringing various communities together for the cause of India's Independence, historians have remained critical of pan-Islamism and its relationship with Indian nationalism. It is said that in the wake of the Non-Cooperation–Khilafat movement, the objective of Hindu participation was to attain Swaraj, whereas for the Muslims, the objective was not the attainment of Swaraj but Turkey and the *Khilafat*.[72] Other eminent historians do recognize the contributions made by pan-Islamism in generating anti-imperialist sentiments amongst Muslims and yet, the role of pan-Islamism has been viewed as a contributory factor to the growing communalism.[73] Contrary to these perceptions, there were many contemporaries and participants in the movement who were convinced that the issue of Khilafat was a contributory factor to Indian nationalism. In the course of the movement, Maulana Azad had emerged as a major ideologue of pan-Islamism and, for him, it was another way to achieve India's Independence. In one of his speeches, he clearly stated that:

> The first field of action, which was vital for your success, was not something outside India. It was neither Iraq nor Asia Minor nor Smyrna, where blood of Muslims had already been spilt. It was in fact a test of your *Iman* (faith), *Azm* (determination) and *Amal* (action). In place of so many words let me put it in one word, it was a question of your country and its victory and defeat. For the Khilafat movement, India was the field of action for Muslims and other communities living in India. And the world realized that the issue was not confined to any one group as it concerned the whole of India. This was the crux of the issue and thankfully you all have been able to achieve it.[74]

This excerpt makes it adequately clear that for many Muslims, while the issue of Khilafat was important, so was India's Independence. It was perhaps for this reason that they had accepted Gandhi's leadership. Gandhi had asserted that there should be people's participation in the functioning of the government. In case it was not allowed, then they could reject the government, not by force but by popular will.[75] In order to generate this popular will, Gandhi considered it a historic opportunity to launch the Non-Cooperation–Khilafat movement, which would forge Hindu–Muslim unity. He called it Kamadhenu (mythical cow that perennially gave milk). However, the movement was withdrawn as a consequence of the violent Chaura Chauri incident in Gorakhpur district in which twenty constables were burnt alive. Gandhi's Kamadhenu, as a result, started drying up and bitterness in inter-community relations started growing because many Khilafat and other leaders thought it improper on the part of Gandhi to have unilaterally withdrawn the movement.

In the aftermath of the movement, Hindus and Muslims started pulling apart from each other and the bonhomie experienced during the movement was replaced by mutual suspicion, which clouded the political climate. Another development that followed this withdrawal was the feeling that for the mobilization of Muslims, pan-Islamism was almost irrelevant. This was because the new regime in Turkey under Mustafa Kemal Pasha abolished the institution of the Khilafat. Thus, the Muslims in India had very little option but to reconcile to the new situation. The issue of the Khilafat ceased to agitate their minds.

In spite of the fact that pan-Islamism and the Khilafat were no more a force to reckon with, many leaders shifted gear to retain the relevance of Islam. They kept on invoking its authority in mobilizing Muslims to fight for the cause of India's freedom. The 1920s were marred by frequent communal riots and cultural bickering among Hindus and Muslims, which made it difficult to bring about a consensus on many questions that were crucial for advancing the cause of India's Independence. One such issue was the making of a constitution for India in the wake of the formation of an all-white commission known as the Simon Commission in 1927, which was boycotted by a large number of political organizations. A committee was constituted under the chairmanship of Motilal Nehru to draft a constitution. The committee's challenge was to include everybody, which proved rather daunting. Questions were raised about the character of polity: as to whether it should be federal or unitary. Inherent in this question was the security of the Muslims' future. These questions and the attitude of the Hindu Mahasabha of not conceding to recommendations to accommodate Muslim concerns made the Nehru Report largely redundant.

The Muslims were considerably alienated but certainly not from the cause of Independence. Many leaders felt the need for mobilizing Muslims for the cause of Independence, irrespective of the bitter experience in the course of debates on the Nehru Report. New organizations were formed for this purpose and one such body was called the Congress Muslim Party, with its headquarters at Bombay. The larger objectives of this party were to work towards bringing the much-desired Hindu–Muslim unity, helping the Congress to achieve freedom for the country, winning over Muslims to join the Congress, and, finally, carrying out a campaign to propagate the programmes and policies of the Congress.[76] The party had an ambitious job at hand. Their constitution suggested that the Bombay Presidency Congress Muslim Party would be controlling and organizing the divisions or branches in Bombay and its suburbs, Gujarat, Karnataka, Maharashtra, Sind, Ahmedabad, Belgaum, Poona and Hyderabad.[77] The Congress Muslim Party organized several public meetings in different parts of Maharashtra and Gujarat. For instance, one public meeting was organized at Jalgaon, where several leaders spoke on the necessity of Muslims coming forward to take part in the ongoing freedom struggle. Many speakers also invoked the authority of Islam: that it taught the whole world lessons of freedom and that, therefore, the Muslims of India could not afford to stay aloof. They also emphasized Hindu–Muslim unity as vital to India's progress.[78] It was reported that the party had organized another meeting at Dhulia. However, no meeting could take place at Malegaon due to plague. Earlier, while addressing a meeting organized by the Congress Muslim Party at Broach, Maulvi Mohammad Ali, a party leader, argued that 'the Muslims could not claim themselves to be true Muslims so long as India was in bondage'. He added that the fight to free India was not only their national but also their religious duty.[79]

CONCLUSION

In view of the historical experience of the people in India, and Muslims in particular, it is difficult to subscribe to the views of Bernard Lewis that Muslims are keen to draw distinctions between them and others, even in the realm of politics. Historical instances are plenty to show that, while culturally there have been distinctions of all kinds, communities were not lacking in the desire to forge political unity, particularly in the context of the anti-colonial nationalist struggle. Similarly, the essentialist theory of Francis Robinson that separatism is inherent among Muslims, wherever they happen to be in a minority, does not seem to be tenable. Each theoretical formulation needs to be supported by empirical evidence, without which one is likely to reach conclusions that might be contrary to the historical experience of one group or the other.

NOTES

1. Bernard Lewis, *The Political Language of Islam*, Delhi: Oxford University Press, 1988, p. 4.
2. Ibid.
3. Ibid., p. 40.
4. Francis Robinson, *Islam and Muslim History in South Asia*, Delhi: Oxford University Press, 2000.
5. Francis Robinson, 'Islam and Muslim Separatism, A Historical Debate', in Mushirul Hasan, ed., *Communal and Pan-Islamic Trends in Colonial India*, Delhi: Manohar, 1985, p. 356.
6. Shakil Siddiqui, 'Begum Hazrat Mahal', in *Naya Daur*, April-May 2007, p. 61.
7. Ibid. This declaration was issued by Hazrat Mahal on behalf of Birjis Qadar. The translation of this declaration is as follows:
   People belong to God, the country to the King of Delhi but orders are from Brijis Qadar Bahadur. It is declared that God Almighty, who is the Creator of all of us, has kindly restored our reign. Now that the Government is under our control, it is ordered that no one would indulge in loot and acrimony. Violators would be punished by law officers.
8. Ibid., p. 64.
9. Iqbal Husain, ed., *Proclamations of the Rebels of 1857*, Delhi: Indian Council for Historical Research, Draft, 2007, Appendix B, pp. 167-73. The Proclamation stated:
   Victoria, by the grace of God, of the United Kingdom of Great Britain and Ireland and of the colonies and dependencies thereof in Europe, Asia, Africa, America and Australasia, Defender of the faith. Whereas for diverse weighty reasons, we have resolved, by and with the advice and consent of the Lords spiritual and temporal and commons in Parliament assembled, to take upon ourselves the government of the

territories in India heretofore administered in trust for us by the Hon. East India Company. It further said, 'We desire no extension of our present territorial possession and while we will permit no aggression upon our dominions or our rights to be attempted with impunity, we shall sanction no encroachment on those others. We shall respect the rights, dignity and honour of native princes as our own; and we desire that they as well as our subjects, should enjoy that prosperity and that social advancements which can only be secured by internal peace and good government.'

10. Shakil Siddiqui, op. cit., p. 64.
11. Rizwan Qaiser, 'Atharah Sau Santavan ki Bazgasht', in Khurshid Akram, ed., *Aaj Kal*, Delhi: Publications Division, May 2007, p. 12.
12. Ibid.
13. Daya Shankar Surya, 'Pahli Jung-i-Azadi ki Jarri Khatun', in *Naya Daur*, April-May 2007, p. 124.
14. Ibid., p. 125.
15. S.N. Sen, *Eighteen Fifty Seven*, Delhi: Publications Division, 1957, p. 348.
16. Rajat Ray has been cited by Irfan Habib: Khan Bahadur Khan, while moving through Bareilly, carried two banners 'one, the banner of Islam, the green banner and another large banner, the holy *dhvaj*'. For details, see Irfan Habib, *Remembering 1857 in People's Democracy*, 28 January 2007, p. 11.
17. S.N. Sen, op. cit., p. 352.
18. Ibid., p. 349.
19. Pratap Chandar Azad, 'Pahli Jung-i-Azadi ke Mashhoor Rahnuma, Khan Bahdur Khan', in *Naya Daur*, April-May 2007, p. 114.
20. Shakil Siddiqui, op. cit., p. 55.
21. William Dalrymple, *The Last Mughal: The Fall of a Dynasty*, Delhi: Penguin, 2006, p. 440. Dalrymple has used this expression as an omnibus category in order to describe Muslims' participation in the Rebellion of 1857. He does not seem to make a distinction between ordinary Muslims and the *ulema* as a group. His categorization of *sepoys* and *jihadis* is essentially a reflection of the same approach, so much so that even when a Muslim rebel did not necessarily belong to any such religious group, he was still described as a 'civilian *jihadi*'.
22. Ibid., p. 265.
23. Ibid.
24. Yaseen Akhtar Misbahi, *Chand Mumtaz Ulema-i-Inquilab (1857)*, Delhi: Darul Qalam, 2007, pp. 57-8.
25. Ibid., *Roznamcha-i-Jeevanlal*, p. 55.
26. Ibid., p. 59.

27. Ibid., pp. 67-81; Syed Zair Husain Kazmi, 'Azadi ke Matwale Maulana Fazli Haq Khairabadi', in *Naya Daur*, April-May 2007, pp. 94-5.
28. Yaseen Akhtar Misbahi, op. cit., pp. 67-81.
29. Ibid., p. 74.
30. Mumtaz Ahmad Makki, 'Maulvi Ahmadullah Shah (1789-1857)', in *Naya Daur*, April-May 2007, p. 81.
31. Irfan Habib, op. cit., p. 11. Irfan Habib has argued that in 'the *Risala Fathi-i-Islam* (Tract on the Victory of Islam) composed under the supposed aegis of the famous rebel leader and theologian, Ahmadullah Shah, the appeal is repeatedly made to both Hindus and Muslims to fight unitedly to defend their respective faiths against their English oppressors'. Also see Wasim Ahmad Said, 'Mujahid-i-Azam Ahmadullah Shah', in *Naya Daur*, April-May 2007, p. 78.
32. B.R. Nanda, *Gandhi, Pan-Islamism, Imperialism and Indian Nationalism*, Delhi: Oxford University Press, 1989, pp. 372-97. Nanda has argued that Muslim participation in the freedom struggle was possible only due to an emotive issue such as Khilafat, which did not strengthen national unity; instead it generated a sense of exclusivism among the Muslims and, in the long run, the consequences were quite undesirable.
33. Shan Mohammad, *Sir Syed Ahmad Khan: A Political Biography*, Meerut: Minakshi Prakashan, 1969, p. 132.
34. B.R. Nanda, op. cit., p. 10.
35. Ibid.
36. Ibid.
37. Shan Mohammad, op. cit., p. 134.
38. James Piscatori, *Islam in the World of Nation-States*, Cambridge: Cambridge University Press, 1986, pp. 2, 38.
39. Ibid.
40. Ibid.
41. Ibid.
42. Ibid.
43. John L. Esposito, *Islam the Straight Path*, New York: Oxford University Press, 1991, pp. 127-8.
44. Ibid.
45. James Piscatori, op. cit., p. 78.
46. Ian Henderson Douglas, *Abul Kalam Azad: An Intellectual Biography*, Delhi: Oxford University Press, 1988, p. 220. It is surprising that Afghani was highlighting a fact which was already a part of the historical experience of Indians in the context of the Rebellion of 1857, when Hindus and Muslims had joined hands against the British.
47. Shan Mohammad, op. cit., p. 135.
48. Douglas, op. cit., p. 109. *Al-Mannar* was an influential journal started

by Rashid Rida at Cairo in 1897. This journal influenced Azad because of its effort to move away from the influence of the traditional *ulemas* of Al-Azhar in Cairo.

49. B.R. Nanda, op. cit., p. 105.
50. Mushirul Hasan, *Nationalism and Communal Politics in India, 1885-1930*, Delhi: Manohar, 1991, pp. 114-15.
51. Sumit Sarkar, *Swadeshi Movement in Bengal, 1903-1908*, Delhi: People's Publishing House, 1977, p. 79.
52. Mushirul Hasan, 1991, op. cit., p. 45.
53. Ibid.
54. Mushirul Hasan, *A Nationalist Conscience: M.A. Ansari, the Congress and the Raj*, Delhi: Manohar, 1987, p. 45.
55. *Al-Hilal*, vol. 3, no. 7, 13 August 1913. In the editorial commentary, this episode was described as *Karbala-i-Kanpur* with details about the gathering of Muslims to reconstruct the broken portion of the mosque and their being fired upon. It talked about the brutality of the magistrate, Mr. Taylor, and his men who opened fire on unarmed Muslims. In another issue of *Al-Hilal*, vol. 3, no. 8, 20 August 1913, there were many protest letters against the unprovoked firing. In yet another issue of *Al-Hilal*, vol. 3, no. 9, 27 August 1913, the blood-letting at Kanpur was described as a life-regenerating experience, which, by implication, meant organizing resistance to British rule.
56. Aparna Basu, 'Mohammad Ali in Delhi', in Mushirul Hasan, ed., op. cit., 1985, p. 122.
57. Abul Kalam Azad, *India Wins Freedom*, Delhi: Orient Longman, 1988, p. 5.
58. Abdur Razzaq Malihabadi, *Zikre Azad, Maulana Azad ki Rafaqat Mein Anrtees Saal*, Calcutta, 1960, p. 272.
59. *Al-Hilal*, vol. 1, no. 16, November 1912.
60. Maulana Azad, 'Taqreer-i-Ittehad-i-Islami', speech in Calcutta, 27 October 1914, in Malik Ram, ed., *Khutbat-i-Azad*, Delhi: Sahitya Akademy, 1981, pp. 20-5.
61. Ibid.
62. *Home Political A*, no. 178-204, February 1915, p. 4.
63. Ibid., p. 15.
64. Ibid.
65. B.R. Nanda, op. cit., p. 203.
66. Mushirul Hasan, 1991, op. cit., pp. 131-2.
67. Sumit Sarkar, *Modern India*, Delhi: Macmillan, 1983, p. 195.
68. Gandhi, as quoted in Mushirul Hasan, 1991, op. cit., p. 128.
69. Judith Brown, *Gandhi, the Prisoner of Hope*, Delhi: Oxford University Press, 1989, p. 145.
70. Ibid., p. 141.

71. Ibid.
72. B.R. Nanda, op. cit., p. 377.
73. Bipan Chandra, *Communalism in Modern India*, Delhi: Vikas, 1984, p. 233.
74. Maulana Azad, '*Khutba-i-Sadarat Majlis Khilafat*, Agra, 25 August 1921, in Malik Ram, ed., op. cit., p. 44.
75. B.R. Nanda, op. cit., p. 252.
76. *The Bombay Chronicle*, 20 July 1929.
77. Ibid., 29 July 1929.
78. Ibid., 28 September 1929.
79. Ibid., 23 September 1929.

TEN

Christianity and the Mizo Identity

A Review of Sociological and Historical Circumstances

Joy L.K. Pachuau

With over 80 per cent of the population professing to be Christian, Mizoram, today, is one of the few states in India that can claim to be predominantly Christian. This is a very high percentage, especially in comparison with the national average of a little over 2 per cent.[1] Though exact figures are not available, it would probably not be incorrect to say that all 'ethnic' Mizos in Mizoram, at some point in their lives, have professed Christianity as their religion.[2] The non-Christian population within the state, therefore, largely comprises immigrants from neighbouring countries and other states of the Indian Union.

If the numbers that attend church services are any indication, then it can be said that the faith is vibrant and the practice of Christianity has considerable significance in the collective life of the people. 'Sunday schools' (conducted by the church, where Biblical teachings are inculcated at various levels), which admit members from the age of four onwards, are divided into broad age groups. These schools judging from the attendance, are extremely popular. At a Presbyterian church that I visited in the capital city of Aizawl, the attendance in these 'Sunday schools' through August 2004 was over 70 per cent in a church where the membership was almost 3,000.[3] The Sunday school, however, was only one among many services on any given Sunday. There were afternoon and evening services, besides other activities for young people and children that took place between the other 'main' services. This church, as is the custom among Presbyterians in Mizoram, also held at least four meetings during the week with differing objectives and target groups as part of its normal activities, besides 'revival campaigns' that were organized every now and then. Considering the number of meetings that took place, various authors and other observers have commented that the church was not only a place of spiritual renewal but also formed the focal point of socio-cultural interaction. This is even more apparent when Mizos, for various reasons, move out of the state. Mizo welfare associations and Christian fellowships immediately spring up in towns and cities where even a handful of Mizos live. The membership of both is usually identical and it is not uncommon to have the same members as committee members of both associations.[4]

Christianity and its institution, the Church, is, thus, seen by Mizos as drawing them together, uniting them and giving them a sense of cohesion. Despite the rise of several new denominations in recent times and the frictions arising from this, the essential unity that Christianity provides is not lost. The reach of the Church today continues to be greater than ever with the many roles it has assigned for itself in trying to give a comprehensive interpretation of the Bible. For instance, the topics for discussion in the Wednesday evening services of the Presbyterian church of Mizoram in 1993 included themes like materialism and its impact on society, the role of money, the need for diligence in one's work and so on.

Thus, basing itself on the social aspects of Christian teaching, the Church attempts to influence its members in areas that may not appear to be strictly spiritual. The Christian rationale through the institution of the Church is, therefore, pervasive in the explanation of social issues and other problems that are concomitant with modernity. In other words, the Mizos, who once held beliefs associated with traditional societies, have now overwhelmingly come to identify themselves with Christianity such that, to many Mizos, their political identity as 'Mizo' is almost contingent on their being Christian.

Having given a glimpse of the pervasiveness of Christianity among Mizos, this essay essentially looks into the reasons behind this. I believe the issue is also closely related to conversion studies, i.e. the manner in which people around the world have accepted non-indigenous beliefs and adopted it for themselves.

Anthropologists who study religions tend to distinguish between universalizing world religions and community/traditional religions. A characteristic of the former, which sets them apart from the latter according to J. Davis, is that 'the language of divinity is . . . derived . . . from the esoteric discourse of experts organised in many different ways and degrees but confronting similar issues—issues of inclusion and exclusion, of differentiation within the arena created by the organization, of language and texts of the assessment, and control of interior states.'[5] On the other hand, traditional religions show a greater congruity between 'language', the 'practice of the religion', and the 'daily experience of family, political and economic life'. In other words, unlike world religions where the religion itself shows potential for universalizing, the religion of a traditional community is intrinsically one which serves only itself as a political unit, and the language of the religious practice is dependent on the day-to-day practices of the community. Thus, given the differences in the nature of these two kinds of religion, the issue in the context of our area of study is how a practitioner and follower of a traditional religion came to make the shift to a universalizing one. Where is the meeting ground and how does the negotiation take place are some of the questions that need to be asked.

Regarding the contact of traditional religions with world religions, W. James and D. Johnson speak of the need to engage with what they term 'vernacular Christianity', the result of the people's engagement with Christian knowledge and practice at a local level, or the local manifestation of this encounter. This approach, according to them, disengages Christianity from a Western paradigm, which usually includes a comparison with its Western roots and a focus on the dichotomy between the Western and the colonized worlds.[6] They, therefore, seek to focus on the way 'Christianity has been experienced, apprehended in "native" terms' outside of institutions that authorize it, to show that there can be 'subtle variations in the apprehension of truth'.[7] Closely associated with such a concept that seeks to understand local forms of adoption of a world religion is the idea of syncretism, generally regarded as the outcome of the interaction between two forms of belief. Syncretism has sometimes had negative connotations, as it is considered a deviant of what is considered and understood as pure, thereby implying the inauthenticity of what is considered derivative. However, anthropologists do not live under the illusion of the existence of pure cultures and R. Shaw and C. Stewart believe that it is important to direct the enquiry on the process involved in the discourse around syncretism.[8] This includes the entire gamut of agency, power and resistance in the context of which religious interaction takes place. Very often, such studies concentrate on internal structures that facilitate conversion; at the same time, there is a need to look into the role of individuals in syncretic and even 'anti-syncretic' activities. In other words, the study should involve the practical conditions under which syncretism takes place, the human agency that is involved, as well as the politics of the intervention.

Taking such issues into consideration, this paper can perhaps provide answers as to why Christianity has come to be so successful with Mizos, or, in other words, why the faith is such an intrinsic part of Mizo identity. Issues related to this question include the nature and manner in which the Christian message was propagated, and issues related to the conversion experience and links with pre-Christian beliefs. It also encompasses the nature of Christianity that is practised, as well as the colonial context in which the message was proclaimed.

THE ARRIVAL OF MISSIONARIES

The coming of Protestant missionaries to the Lushai Hills followed the arrival of British troops in the north-east in the early nineteenth century. With the expansion of colonial power to India's north-east and, consequently, in accordance with the manner in which the region was made accessible, missionary organizations came to establish themselves here. The Baptists of Serampore under William Carey were the first to send missionaries into the region, more specifically into Assam by 1811. Soon there were other missionary agencies and their zones of work expanded to include the various hills and plains' tribes of the region. For instance, a certain Krishna Chandra Pal from the Serampore Baptist mission visited the Khasis of present-day Meghalaya for the first time in 1813. However, major conversions could take place amongst them only in the second half of the nineteenth century. The first missionaries to go to Nagaland, another state in the north-east, on the other hand, were from the American Baptist Missionary Union and this was as late as 1871.[9]

In the case of the Lushai Hills or Mizoram, soon after military expeditions into the region, a semblance of colonial order and authority were imposed. The Welsh Presbyterian mission (or Calvinistic Methodists) that had already been established in the Khasi-Jaintia Hills sent a missionary, Revd. William Williams, to explore the region in 1891. Due to the political turmoil in the district, he only stayed there for a few weeks. Fresh attempts by another mission followed, but a permanent mission station (Welsh Presbyterian) was established only in 1898. Later, missionaries supported by the Baptist Mission Society of London (1903) joined the Presbyterians and a zone of influence was carved out by mission agencies, amicably following the already existing administrative division. The Baptists set-up their headquarters in the south at Serkawn near Lunglei, while the Presbyterians had their base at Mission Veng (now in Aizawl) in the north. Within the region then demarcated as the Lushai Hills, there was another mission body that worked among the Mara (formerly the Lakher) called the Lakher Pioneer Mission, an independent body, which started work in 1907. The Lakher occupy one of the three autonomous district councils in the state. The Pawi, also known as Lai, are another distinct group that now have an autonomous administration within Mizoram, but their conversion came about as an extension of the work of the Baptist Mission Society that had its headquarters at Serkawn from 1912 onwards.

There were, thus, three main missionary agencies that operated in the state and most of the conversions to Christianity among the people of Mizoram can be attributed to them. Two agencies (Presbyterian and Baptist) worked mainly in regions where the traditional Sailo rulers had held sway (also the major proportion of the state) and used one language, Lushai, that has today come to be known as Mizo. They also generally respected each other's zone of influence and cooperated and consulted with each other in many fields such as creating a script, Bible translation and so on, so that no major differences erupted between the two churches during this period. Consequently, it could also be said that the Christian experience was more or less homogeneous throughout the state. The foreign missionary presence lasted for less than a hundred years, with the last of the missionaries leaving in the 1970s when insurgency overtook the state. Most of my analysis in this essay will be sourced from the letters, reports and articles written by the Presbyterian and Baptist missionaries.

The response to Christianity through the work of these missionaries was overwhelming. In 1901, rough estimates would calculate the percentage of Christians (Presbyterians and Baptists and excluding the Mara Church) at 0.08 per cent of the total population (82,434). By 1911, 3.1 per cent proclaimed themselves to be Christians and this increased to 28 per cent by the next decade. There are no figures available for 1931 but by 1941, 63.26 per cent of the population considered themselves Christian, with a marginal increase to 67.06 per cent by 1951.[10] By the 1960s, it was a well-recognized fact that all those who considered themselves Mizo were Christian, though the state continued to have a substantial non-Mizo non-Christian population.[11]

CHRISTIANITY AND THE POLITICS OF IDENTITY WITHIN THE STATE

I shall now explain the internal dynamics of Mizo identity in relation to Christianity and how this is played out in contemporary politics. Mizo identity, as all ethnic identities, is the product of socio-political agencies and other factors acting in time. In the context of a continual process of incorporating other groups into the Mizo identity, the main criterion today seems to be that of the profession of Christianity. It is almost impossible to find a Mizo who is not a Christian. Even those who are not regular churchgoers or believers are incorporated into a Mizo Christian way of life, as all social practices have Christian overtones.

However, despite the seemingly homogeneous conception of Mizos as one ethnic group, within Mizoram there are four major groups, the Mara, Lai, Chakma and Bru that currently express some form of dissatisfaction with the Mizo identity. The Mara are Christians and from southern Mizoram. While many 'Mizos' would say that the Mara are Mizos, this was not always the case. During my fieldwork, many Maras told me that their being identified as Mizo is a very recent phenomenon and they strongly resisted this identification. There were a few who identified themselves as Mizos but this was more of an exception than the rule. They pointed out that even in the earliest articulation of identity in Mizo writings, the Mara had never been included and that, therefore, there was no reason for them to be included now.

The Lai identity is problematized in various ways. While the Mara are more or less confined to their district (which, in the past, was isolated as it was bounded by a turbulent river, the Koladyne; now there is a major bridge that is a very important link, and this link also has a symbolic significance), the Lai are spread throughout the state. They are known as Pawi outside their district and also as Chins in Burma. Interestingly, those who call themselves Lai do not consider themselves Mizo, while the same people who identify themselves as Pawi are happy to take on the Mizo identity. The reason behind these identifications clearly seems to be the way in which Christianity was organized. The establishment of the Lakher (Mara) Pioneer Mission helped in the crystallization of the Mara identity, whose tools for the maintenance of identity like the preservation of culture, the creation of a script and so on were provided for by the church. On the other hand, the Lai/Pawi conversion was an extension of the work of the Baptist Missionary Society based at Serkawn. Their conversion was also through Mizo converts who extended their language and culture to the Lai/Pawi. In recent times, some Lai in the Lai Autonomous District Council, citing irreconcilable differences with the Baptist Church of Mizoram (BCM), have established a separate Baptist congregation that has come to be known as the Lairam Isua Krista Baptist Kohhran (LIKBK). When I met the leaders of the LIKBK, they were quick to point out that the denomination was not just for Lai people; yet it is through the church that there is an attempt to revive Lai culture. There are attempts to teach the Lai language, which is no longer spoken in Mizoram, in the context of the church. The church, thus, becomes the centre for the preservation and perpetuation of culture as defined and interpreted by the elites.

While locally, the creation of distinct churches becomes a way of expressing identity, the international arena is sought in order to legitimize their claims. Thus, a senior leader of the LIKBK told me that their attempts to gain recognition at Baptist unions both in India and abroad were constantly thwarted by the BCM. On the other hand, the complaint of informants from the BCM was the politicization along ethnic lines of the Christian identity by those from LIKBK. The church, thus, becomes a forum for the contestation of identities and, while incorporation as Mizo, is resisted, it is clear that for those who consider themselves Mizo, the induction of the Mara and Lai is not seen as a problem; sometimes the links with these groups are even considered primordial. On the other hand, there is no problem in deciding who are not Mizos. The faultline, yet again, is religion, and not even recent attempts to broaden the Mizo identity would include Chakmas, who, I was repeatedly told, are more or less recent migrants from Bangladesh, and belong to a different 'stock' altogether. The Chakmas now also have an autonomous district council in Mizoram and are largely Buddhists. Tuikuk/Bru, another group within Mizoram, is also not accepted because of their animist beliefs and conversion to Buddhism.

THE COLONIAL CONTEXT AND ITS IMPLICATIONS

As in many places around the world, the conversion to Christianity occurred in Mizoram in the context of the colonial encounter. This has led to studies concentrating on the nexus between colonialism and missionaries, the implication often being that each contributed substantially to the perpetuation of the other. For instance, John Burton attributes the intransigence of the people and the lack of converts to Christianity in Nilotic Sudan to the disunited front that the church and state showed.[12] Inadvertently, he, thus, emphasizes the contribution that the colonial state could have made to the propagation of the faith.

Jean and John Comaroff, on the other hand, write of more imperceptible ways in which missionaries, by being participants (though often unconsciously) of the modernistic enterprise, were, in fact, aiding the colonizing process.[13] Their main argument is that while the missions (in their case, among the Tswana in South Africa) may not have directly involved themselves in the politics of colonialism, their influence '. . . in such things as aesthetics and religion, built form and bodily presentation, medical knowledge and the mundane habits of everyday life' led to a 'subtle colonization . . . of indigenous modes of perception and practice', which, in turn, contributed to the building of the colonial infrastructure and incorporating them into the capitalist world economy.[14] Thus, whether the nature of the relationship between the church and state is regarded as a surreptitious cooperation, as in the study of the Comaroffs or whether the relationship is seen as more direct, this aspect deserves more attention.

In India, it was the official policy not to aid the propagation of Christianity, yet in the specific case of Lushai Hills, it is clear that the district authorities did not discourage it. There were instances when the missionaries complained that the administrative officer could have been more lenient and sometimes the missionaries directly opposed the colonial authorities. But, more often than not, it was the political administrator's sympathy toward the missionary endeavour that they reported.[15] Colonial officers would also sometimes interfere in religious matters when it was felt that the peace in the district was affected especially in times of revival, when spiritual fervour could cause a commotion leading to problems of law and order.[16] On another occasion, we hear of an administrator facilitating a dialogue between the two mission bodies (Presbyterian and Baptist) to come to a consensus over the translation of biblical concepts.[17]

Conversion in the context of colonialism has also often been attributed to the material benefits that one could acquire as a result of associating with the powerful. These benefits might have taken the form of immediate material needs or the provision of jobs that education and bureaucratization made room for. The evidence for such claims can be seen in the fact that, very often, the powerful in the traditional social structure, especially the chiefs, were usually the last to convert as they believed they had more to lose than gain. Missionaries often noted that the fervour for education amongst Mizos was increased by the realization of the possibility of non-manual work as a result of it. Yet, the extent of Mizo identification with Christianity belies purely utilitarian purposes as the reason for conversion. It can also be argued that the colonial establishment was not really large in Mizoram; the possibilities of government employment were really miniscule so that the lure that modernity posed could not actually have been the main criterion for conversion. Besides, it was found that a large number of the more capable students opted for Christian work (which paid less) rather than posts in the colonial administration.

This, however, is not to deny the impact of colonialism on conversion but merely to say that the influence was indirect. And the nature of this impact is similar to what has been said by Robin Horton in his essay 'On the rationality of conversion'.[18] Horton speaks of a certain inevitability in the adoption of 'world religions', when indigenous groups are brought into contact with a wider, expanding world. He presents the case of Africa, where, according to him, the adoption of Islam or Christianity was the result of a break in the social structure as a result of contact with a wider world. The rationale behind this, for Horton, is that indigenous beliefs present a microcosmic view of the world, which usually cannot hold out against the momentum of an expanding world. The need was, thus, often felt by indigenous groups to adopt a religion that offered the capacity to understand and engage with the changes they were going through. 'World' religions, through their more sophisticated structure and ontology, could, thus, be seen as providing answers to the questions that were posed upon contact with the expanding world.

Similarly, an indirect way in which colonialism aided conversion can perhaps be attributed to the breakdown in traditional structures that followed the introduction of British administration, proving also the efficacy of the latter and all that it was seen to represent. The inefficacy of the power of several chiefs who ruled in the Lushai Hills in the face of superior fire-power was acknowledged everywhere. Despite the fact that the chiefs were allowed to remain in power, their authority had been compromised, with the colonial authorities preventing raids and fixing their territorial boundaries. The arrival of colonial power resulted in the acknowledgement of not only a superior military power but also one that organized the people in relation to the newly-founded authority. With political defeat, the efficacy of their beliefs was easily questioned, considering that one was contingent on the other for the Mizo. It followed that the religion that came along with the new political system was superior to the one that they practised. This comes across clearly in the fact that, for the Mizos, the distinction between the state and the propagators of Christianity was not easily recognizable. Both were identified by the term *sap* (foreigner/white man), though there was a distinction between the *borsap* (or *sap* associated with the government) and *mission sap* (or *sap* associated with the mission); thus, the religion that came with the white man was seen to be an extension of his military superiority, and thereby efficacious. Thus, the adoption of Christianity can be seen to be due to the vacuum created as a result of the break in the traditional powers of authority. It was easy, under such circumstances, for Christianity to take hold.

In addition, we find that most conversions took place in the second and third decades of the twentieth century. The question to ask, in the context of Horton's hypothesis, is whether there could be a link between the recruitment of Mizos as labour corps to work in France during the First World War. The trip, the first for large groups of Mizos to see horizons beyond, had a great impact on them. There were more than 2,000 Mizos in France in 1917 (the population of the Lushai Hills then was 91,204, according to the 1911 census). As a missionary, who was back from furlough after First World War and was with the Mizos in France, noted:

> It is now about two months since I arrived in the country. Although the country itself is much the same, the people have changed. And that not merely in their faces, but their whole outlook on life has altered considerably. I believe that the exodus of 2,000 of them to France and other countries has made a greater impression on the country at large than the presence of 2,000 foreigners in their country for many years.[19]

More and more young people were also going out of the regions, notably to Shillong and Calcutta for higher studies, and reports of them were made through monthly journals that had begun publication as early as in 1902.[20] Thus, with the expansion and broadening of their geographical horizons, there was a likelihood of a weakening of microcosmic boundaries and an 'increased attention to the supreme being'.[21] The gap was filled by the missionaries, who, in many ways, brought the concept of a Supreme Being, already present within the local cosmology, closer to the Mizo reality.

It should, however, be borne in mind that the acceptance of neither colonial rule nor Christianity was as simple as it may appear to be. The colonization of the Lushai Hills was the result of several expeditions between 1843 and 1890, and, thus, occupation was not without armed resistance. The opposition took other forms as well. For instance, native caricatures of the foreigner did the rounds such as *sap â* (crazy foreigner) or *sap vâkvai* (crazy wandering foreigner, in the context of constant tours that were made for purposes of geographical surveys, missionary tours and so on). Opposition to Christianity, usually supported and hosted by chiefs, in the form of *pûma zai* (the singing/songs of *pûma*), was also a cause for great concern to many Christians. Physical harm inflicted on converts at the instigation of a chief, as well as expulsion from villages, was not uncommon and many had to flee to form Christian villages. This was especially common in the early decades of the arrival of the missionaries. The chiefs also often forced Christians to fulfil the obligations that the colonial administration had imposed on the villages such as coolie labour.[22]

SOCIAL STRUCTURE AS AN ARGUMENT FOR IDENTIFICATION WITH CHRISTIANITY

In her work on the Akha highlanders of Burma and Thailand, C.A. Kammerer speaks of the 'indigenous cultural forms and categories' that facilitated conversion to Christianity.[23] From a situation in which Akha conversion (in Burma) was negligible between 1869 and 1909, the number of Akha Christians rose roughly a fifth to a third in approximately 200 villages by the time Kammerer wrote her essay. Missionaries attributed the lack of conversions in the earlier period to the more complex *zahˇ* (glossed as 'religion' by them) that the Akha possessed. However, according to Kammerer, when one understands *zahˇ* as a 'cognitive structure' or a body of knowledge that has 'pragmatic functions' as well as a 'folk model', one can understand why the Akha first responded negatively and then positively to the Christian message. The Akha recognized each ethnic group as having a distinct *zahˇ*. Thus, they believed that their identity was intrinsically associated with their own *zahˇ* and, therefore, could not accept the *zahˇ* of others. The adoption of Christianity became possible in a situation when there was a loosening of this association and, thus, the possibility of associating Christianity with their identity in the same way as the *zahˇ* was associated with their Akha identity. Consequently, Kammerer prefers to call this move 'displacement' rather than conversion. One need not go into the details of her argument but the importance of her work is in highlighting those aspects of social structure that facilitate or prevent conversions. The focus of her work is, therefore, to look at internal religious concepts that promote conversion.[24]

In the case of the Mizos, too, the structural organization and belief patterns in society need to be examined in order to come to an understanding of why conversions occurred in such large numbers. My underlying assumption is that for a society that traditionally acknowledges fluidity in group affiliation and recognizes a set of similar categories in the new form of beliefs, affiliation becomes easier because continuities are recognized. Unlike the Akha, the Mizos were an amalgamation of various tribes. These largely included the Lushai, the Ralte, the Paite and the Pawi. Each tribe had its own *sakhua*. Nowadays *sakhua* is almost always translated as religion but originally it meant a sort of tribe spirit that had to be propitiated through sacrifices. It was said that one did not worship the *sakhua*, rather one made use of it.[25] It was regarded as the one that could cause everything including death, and was said to rule over them.[26] There was a distinct identification of a tribe with a particular *sakhua*, and the more similar the rituals performed by the tribes/clans in propitiating its *sa*, the closer the sense of affinity to that tribe. Given that it was the *sakhua* that gave an individual as well as a tribe an identity, it is not surprising that one could change one's tribe (i.e. one could *sa phun*) by adopting the *sakhua* of the particular tribe that one wanted to be incorporated into. Thus, tribal affiliations and identities were fluid, not watertight.

Two developments were possible as a result of the recognition of this mobility between tribes and the guardian spirit. First, the possibility of the development of a new identity, that of the Mizo (among the various existing tribes, with Lushai predominance), as a result of colonial occupation, was made easier by an indigenous system that recognized the process. Their unification as one single tribe, aided by the colonial process of establishing 'bounded' peace in the region was well-recognized. As a contributor to the monthly *Mizo leh vai*, a government publication, wrote in 1919:

> In days gone by Pawi, Ralte, Paihte, Lusei, *vai* and chiefs and others did not get along; there were wars, and we looked upon each other as enemies. But now, all those who were enemies, or those who were suspicious of each other are now neighbours (or members of the same community/*thenrual*) and no longer behave as enemies. Even those who were enemies now enquire about each other when they meet. This is so valuable.[27]

This process of peace seemed to have simultaneously broadened the Mizo conception of what was their land or territory. As another author mentions,

> henceforth all people, from all places belong to the same territory, we are all siblings (*unau*), we can all support each other now. This being the case, we now have much more freedom than what our ancestors had, people from all lands, villages are all as from one courtyard (*tual khat*). Even those whose heads we used to hunt are now all of one land (*hman a lu an ban khai thin*

te pawh kha tualkhat kan loni vek tawh a). Consequently, we can now live anywhere and we can go anywhere. We no longer say some people belong to somebody else's land and we belong to someone else's, as in the old days [because we all belong to one land]. . . .[28]

Judging from the comments of contemporaries such as the above, it seems that they were aware that colonial intervention did bring about a change in notions of space and territoriality. It was now acceptable to consider those from beyond the confines of one's village as being of one's own and a larger identification may have been sought. This was opposed to the earlier practice of identifying one's self as belonging to a village alone, identified with a certain chief.

Following Kammerer's argument, the adoption of a new religion seems to have been a concomitant part of the process of a new political identity that was developing among the people. To put it differently, the colonial occupation initiated a process of reformulation of an identity in which the adoption of a new religion seemed only natural to the Mizo. This was aided by the fact that the politico-social and religious were not seen as distinct. Therefore, the recognition of changed circumstances facilitated the adoption of something new. *Hmasawn* (or making 'cultural' advancements/moving forward) was valued and Christianity was seen as a way to it. It was noted by one writer in the third decade of the twentieth century that, by then, most people who provided the leadership (whether good or bad) among Mizos were Christians and no longer the chiefs or their elders.[29] Such leadership, according to this writer, was in everyday existence, 'in the way one cut one's hair, the way one dressed, in the manner the youth managed death rituals and other feasts'; all this were now done at the instance of Christians and in the way they thought best.[30] To be sure, this acceptance was, however, not in the nature of a one-way traffic; serious negotiation on the part of Mizos in the practice of Christianity made it much easier for them to identify themselves with the new religion.

Once one recognizes the fact that a changing identity was not in any way new to the traditional Mizo social formation, it is also important to understand that there were, within the indigenous belief system, elements that made the acceptance of Christianity much more plausible. At this point, it may be appropriate to refer to R.G. Lienhardt's (1982) notion of parallax that he believes operated when the Dinka made their transfer to Christianity from their traditional beliefs. While he believes that there are significant categorical similarities between the two modes of faith, what is seen as having clinched the Dinka conversion is the sense in which the same categories were given a fresh meaning in the context of a society that was being opened up to the wider world and becoming more modernized.[31]

Similar to what has been said of the belief system of traditional societies in Africa, and even amongst other tribes in India such as the Nagas, there was a 'two-tiered scheme' with regard to traditional cosmology.[32] Mizo notions of the supernatural were structured around a belief in beings that affected personal fates and destinies, as well as those that affected the general course of nature. Those that affected individual lives (*huai*) were feared and had to be propitiated more than those that were considered distant, both physically and in terms of the roles that they performed. *Huai* inhabited the non-human world in and around the village. They were present in high mountains, springs, trees, precipices, large rocks and so on. Those on land were called by the generic term *ram huai*, while those on water were called *tui huai.* 'Men were always on guard against them. They were easily offended if a man tresspassed on their domain. A man would realize that he had given some offense to some spirit and would need to make formal amends, for they could cause illness and even death.'[33] According to C.L. Hminga, the '*ram huai* was believed to have coveted the properties of men and therefore wanted to take their lives and were thought to have the power of capturing their souls'.[34] Shakespear, an important official and ethnographer in the Lushai Hills (1898-9; 1900-3; 1904-5), says that there were at least fifteen dominant *huai* that were believed to inhabit the land.[35]

While the *huai*, whether those on land or in water, were generally considered malevolent because of the personal harm that they caused, there was also a belief in more benign beings that brought about natural phenomena. There was, thus, a belief in good spirits, as well as in a distant Supreme Deity. Among these, there was *khua nu* or 'mother of *khua*', who was the source of all blessings, *pu vana* or 'grandfather heaven', who caused lightning and thunder, and *vanchung nula* or 'maiden in the heavens above' who caused rain.[36] The one who created the universe was *pathian* but, unlike all the other spiritual and heavenly actors, he was unconcerned about human affairs.[37] *Khua vang*, from amongst the 'heavenly' category was the one concerned with human beings in a direct sort of way. According to Shakespear, 'A Lushai will say "my *khuavang* is bad", if things go wrong with him; he will also tell you that you are his *khuavang* meaning that his fate rests with you.'[38] Thus, the same name was attributed to anyone who was seen as being able to protect one. Judging from the names of these beings, they were physically associated with the skies beyond the immediate surroundings of the Mizo and, thus, their influence was not as direct as those of the *huai*. There was also another ambivalent category, the *lasi*, considered female, residing in precipices and deep jungles, and usually considered as helping hunters in their chase.

The supernatural world was mediated through sacrifices, mainly with domesticated animals and birds, and the priest associated with the sacrifice was either called the *puithiam* or *sadawt*. Shakespear lists eight types of sacrifices depending on the being to which they were dedicated as well as their purpose.[39]

Another area of traditional belief that should be mentioned in order to understand the points at which missionaries intervened was in the entire sphere of the afterlife. When a person died, it was termed *hnuk chat*, *hnuk* being an imaginary cord, while *chat* described the snapping or the breaking of the life-cord.[40] *Thlarau*, derived from *thla* or shadow and *rau*/spirit described the essence of a person, that which travelled when a person died or when his/her life-cord snapped. After death, it was everyone's desire to enter *pial ral* (the land beyond the river *pial*), a veritable land of plenty. But to reach *pial ral*, it was necessary to go through *mithi khua* (settlement of the dead). *Mithi khua*, however, could be reached only if one passed through a lake called the *rih*. Interestingly, this lake corresponded to an actual lake that the Mizos thought they had crossed before arriving at the present location where they were situated. So the land of their origin was also considered a land they went back to once they died. After passing through the lake, the road led to a hill called *hring lang tlang* (hill overlooking the world of the living). From the top of the hill, the travelling spirit looked back and saw the world he had left behind very clearly. But he had to continue his journey, looking back now and then, until he came to a clear mountain stream on which beautiful flowers bloomed. The stream was called *lung loh tui* (heartless pool) and the flowers *hawi lo par* (flower of no return). The spirit plucked the *hawi lo par*, and the desire to go back disappeared. He drank from the *lung loh tui* and all fond memories of his past life would fade away. He could then proceed safely to *mithi khua*. However, Pu Pawla, who was supposed to have been the first man to be born and, thus, the first man to die was believed to have his house at the entrance to the road to *mithi khua*. No one could pass unnoticed, for there was a stone that rocked in front of it every time someone tried to pass. He then came out with a mighty bow in his hand and clay pellets, shooting everyone. Only certain categories of people could pass by him without being shot at: first, those who had earned the coveted *thangchhuah* title, which was obtained either by being successful in the hunting and killing of certain kinds of animals, or by hosting a certain number of feasts; second, those who had died a *hlamzuih* death, i.e. those who had died before they were a year old, and, finally, men who had cohabited with at least three women. Pu Pawla was also said to have always targeted women, since they could not accomplish any of the three criteria, except in the case of *hlamzuih*.[41] This brief description of Mizo beliefs show that there were base categories in the traditional faith similar to Christianity that the missionaries could work on. Thus, for instance, concepts of the afterlife were easily recognizable for the Mizo. *Pial ral* and the *mithi khua* already contained nascent concepts of heaven and hell. According to Revd. Zathanga, the first Christian message he heard was preached by D.E. Jones in 1899, the message that included an exhortation to 'Believe in *Pathian*, Jehovah and worship him, then you don't need to sacrifice to the demons any more. Even when you die you shall go to *pial ral*.'[42]

Pial ral continues to be a poetic form of saying 'heaven' along with *van ram* (literally, 'country in the sky'). It is interesting to note that hell, *hrem hmun*; literally, 'place of punishment' had to be invented. Moreover, one notices that the Mizo creator being was adopted to represent the Christian god, and his distance and relative anonymity were removed by revealing him through the concept of the Christian triune God.

Acceptance of the Christian faith became easier not only because of the recognition of familiar categories but also due to the ability of the missionaries to adapt and make the gospel relevant to them. For instance, J.H. Savidge and F.W. Lorrain (missionaries of the BMS) noted that when Christ was presented as a saviour of sins, the Christian message did not appeal to the people. However, when the emphasis was shifted to Christ as a liberator from the clutches of malevolent spirits, 'as the Vanquisher of the Devil—as the one who had bound the 'strong man' and taken away from him all his armour wherein he trusted . . .', the message struck a chord in the minds of the people.[43]

Furthermore, the missionaries often remarked that the traditional Mizo moral code of *tlawmngaihna* closely approximated to Christian notions of charity, which, in a sense, brought in continuities instead of a disjuncture with the past—the underlying assumption being that people are not always comfortable with change and are more comfortable with the familiar, which makes adoption easier. Thus, identical categories, presented and perhaps experienced as more efficacious, were reasons enough for people to want to convert.

THE PRACTICE OF THE FAITH AND IDENTITY

Identification with Christianity also came about because of the possibility and ease that the Mizos had in engaging with the religion institutionally, as well as in its practice. The missionaries were always careful to take into consideration the opinion of the indigenous and recently-converted lay Christians, who soon came to achieve the status of leaders in the church. Therefore, not only was the concept relevant at work but there was also an early recognition that the faith was theirs, rather than an imposition from outside.

This was aided by the great strides that were made in the fields of literacy and education and the employment of educated people in the propagation of the faith. There were, in any case, never many missionaries. The Mizos, it appears, were extremely receptive to formal education. Mission education was given a great impetus when, in 1904, the Governor of Assam, Sir Bamfield Fuller, visited the Lushai Hills and, impressed by the work of the mission, entrusted all matters of education into its hands. This must have had important consequences since grants were now received from the government by a usually financially-strapped mission for the running of schools which could now be extended to other villages. Students who were trained in these schools became teachers in other villages and, on many occasions, were important messengers of the faith.[44]

Thus, with missionaries fully engaged in the task of education, including Christian education, it was not long before local people took up the leadership of the church. The first ordained minister of the Presbyterian mission was Revd. Chhuahkhama, ordained as early as 1913, while, in the Baptist mission, it was in 1914 that the first minister (Chuautera) was ordained, less than two decades after the missionaries had established themselves. The Welsh missionaries also adopted the system of presbyteries for Mizos, a form of organization that was particular to Presbyterianism, which encouraged lay leadership and involvement. They found that this democratic nature of the presbyteries was particularly suited to the nature of the people, which was essentially egalitarian.[45] For instance, the first presbytery meeting was held in 1910 and there were three elected members from the mission station church besides the missionaries. The secretary of this meeting was a Mizo. Due to the success in giving the leadership of the church to the locals, the Baptist church also moved away from its traditional church organization and established presbyteries.

Such an organization meant that there could be criticism of the mission by the locals. The freedom that was sometimes given made missionaries who were less open to such innovations ask whether this was, indeed, a good thing. For instance, in the 1930s, there was an interesting case where the elders of the church expressed their anger against one particular missionary, Edith Chapman. Opposition took the form of stoning her house and the boarding school she had established, and calling for her expulsion. Personal letters of the missionary speak of the emotional trauma that she had to go through as a result of the insistence of some of the elders that she quit. She, consequently, had to go on leave and her return was agreed upon only after an expressed apology from her to the elders of the church. According to the reports of other missionaries, the local elders were not comfortable that a woman, even though she was *sap*, was appointed the Inspector of Schools (in the absence of a male missionary), wherein she could exercise her authority over them. While the incident can be read in different ways, what is important for our purpose is that the event highlights the recognition by the locals of their place as negotiators and rule-setters within the Christian set-up. They regarded themselves as significant contributors in the articulation of the faith, whether to themselves or to the non-Christians amongst them, so much so that they were negotiating with the *official carriers* of the faith with regard to the manner in which the belief should be practised and, in this particular case, the place of women in the scheme of things.[46]

Besides the ordained ministry, there were several ways in which lay people could contribute to the expansion of the church membership. Lay evangelists who received some theological training did much to propagate the faith and there were many who took up the task. It was said of Khuma, the first convert, that 'there were very few villages in Mizoram that he did not visit in his evangelistic tours. To every person he met on the way he extended an invitation to follow Jesus. In every village he visited, he went from house to house inviting people to believe in the Lord Jesus.'[47] Thus, there were many paid and unpaid, trained and untrained evangelists, itinerant preachers, Bible women and so on who took it upon themselves to proclaim what they believed to be true. Funds for their salaries came from local collections, which could not have been much. A unique fund was created to pay for the Bible women. This came to be called the *buhfai tham* or the 'handful of rice offerings'. Each household would keep aside a handful of rice before a meal was cooked; this was later collected by women volunteers and the proceeds paid to the Bible women.[48] Missionary activity was not only relegated to the Mizos in the Lushai Hills district but, soon enough, the Mizos took upon themselves the task of evangelizing neighbouring tribes. In 1910, three boys were said to have gone to neighbouring Manipur, by 1911, there was a Mizo missionary in Tripura and, by 1913, another in Haflong in Assam.[49] According to these missionaries, there was a compelling need to let others know what they knew and experienced—something that could have risen due to a deep sense of identification and responsibility *vis-à-vis* the faith.

Missionaries also recognized, from the very beginning, the contribution that women could make in the creation of 'Christian homes'. With such goals, a girls' school was initiated in the south Lushai Hills as early as in 1919 and the boarding school that was established provided not only formal education but also helped in formalizing knowledge for daily living.[50] Works in recent times have pointed out the way in which the missionary endeavoured for the creation of a 'Victorian woman'. Habits of everyday living such as notions of cleanliness and hygiene, rearing children, the proper use of money and so on were imparted to girls in the hope that they would make good 'Christian wives'. Edith Chapman, the missionary who was in-charge of girls' education, considered herself a radical in relation to the prevalent discourse that believed that people should be 'brought out' of their existing conditions. Yet she, and others like her who believed in the changes that girls' education provided, considered their work a success. Examples of how some girls took to teaching the Word and how some established schools in their own villages were the success stories that they wrote home.[51] To digress, this idea of education for women was not always appreciated by the local menfolk who were not always receptive to these changes. How could a woman preach when the apostle Paul expressly forbade women to speak in public? Such thinking was the form that resistance to women's education took, as noted by Edith Chapman in the 1930s.[52]

It is generally acknowledged that the provision of formal education, which was initiated through the creation of a script and the establishment of other institutions, such as those to look after health and so on, were all a part of the endeavour to Christianize indigenous groups. This has led many like the Comarroffs to talk of the ways in which the world-view of the people was changed, a process that has come to be referred to as the 'colonization of the mind', the internalization of ideas and ways of living in such a manner that the people accept it as their own. While the intention of such writers is to point to the means by which indigenous peoples were incorporated into the colonial economy and Christian world-view, one perhaps needs to bear in mind that the actors were not always silent spectators to the dialogue; rather they actively engaged with Christianizing agents and contributed to the direction in which change was to take place. For instance, the incorporation of locals into the missionary world meant that the structures through which the missionaries operated had to be made familiar to the natives, such as the adoption of a more sedentary life (as opposed to the earlier migratory lifestyle of the Mizos), as well as a more routinized and predictable lifestyle. One of the ways in which this was done was by the introduction of the Gregorian calendar. The traditional calculation by the Mizos used a calendar that was dependent on the phases of the moon; the solar calendar thus introduced the required creation of the days of the week, and it was a local who was involved in its creation. Sunday was translated as the day of rest, and each day that followed was translated in relation to work against which rest was prescribed on Sunday.[53]

The Comaroff argument also assumes that the missionaries consistently agreed with each other on the cultural implications of their missionizing endeavour. This is seen to be untrue. An example would be the complaints amongst missionaries of the lack of knowledge of anthropology amongst their colleagues. This was usually followed by a deprecation of the aim of making English men and women out of their respective Mizo converts. Moreover, this lack of cohesion can be seen as reflected in the way different generations of converts related to the missionaries' so-called 'civilizing mission'. While some missionaries were keen that they work for the perpetuation of local cultures, a letter written by a local elder speaks of how the focus on this could not be seen as appropriate to Christianity, a response perhaps influenced by some missionaries who held this view.

MIZO RATIONALE FOR CONVERSION

Soon after his arrival in Mizoram in 1921, Enoch Lewis Mendus, in his diary, wrote down a conversation he had with certain Mizos as to the reasons on why they had converted. He writes:

> . . . In examining the grounds of their belief, one of them, a boy from the border of Lushai and belonging to a different tribe, said that the reason for his original belief was that if he obeyed God, God would give him health and satisfy his longings, this he said was an experience shared by the heathen, the reason for his belief at present, he said, was the hope that he would in heaven share the glory of Christ. The second gives as ground of his initial belief the mere fact that as a boy his day school teacher wrote his name down as a Christian; but the ground of his present belief was the knowledge that Christ had redeemed him. The third admitted that his first reason for believing was the fear of Hell, but that his present reason was the love of God as revealed in Christ which he had discovered through the reading of God's word and hearing it preached. Just at that time we met some Lushais coming in single file in the opposite direction. Having discovered that they were Christians I asked one of them the reason for his belief and without the slightest hesitation he gave me this reply: 'Jesus had redeemed us, and so our life's purpose is to please him.'[54]

Mendus seemed to have been pleased by these responses. He was aware that there could have been several circumstances under which the Mizos converted, other than the usual understanding that it was some sort of recognition or belief in what was 'true'. Nevertheless, with teaching, the divide was definitely being closed. It is apparent, thus, that a comprehension of what is 'true' forms an important aspect of the need to convert. However, if one looks carefully into the history of Christianity, 'belief' itself has had different implications. According to Malcolm Ruel, 'belief' is an important concept peculiar to Christianity, not shared (in the way he understands it) by followers either of other world religions or of traditional beliefs.[55] The peculiar historical trajectory in which the concept emerged has meant that there are varied nuances to the way to which Christianity can be adopted. Initially meaning trust (similar to the Hebrew *'mn*) in an all-powerful god, it was followed by belief in an event (the death and resurrection of Christ), which was then followed by the affirmation of a creed, which acted as a form of initiatory declaration as well as a corporately held orthodoxy. In course of time, the semantics of the creed also led the belief in a particular creed to become an inner organizing principle. This understanding is different in contemporary times where, according to Ruel, belief has become totally secularized so that what you believe in no longer becomes important, and the term can, in fact, be replaced by other verbs such as hope, guess and so on.

The recognition of these different categories of belief is helpful in understanding the ways in which Mizos approached the Christian faith or belief system. Mizo belief did involve a level of trust and faith in someone more powerful than the spiritual powers they were accustomed to. In the sermons of the preachers of the early twentieth century that I was able to locate, the focus often is not on what is true or right (*dik*) but rather on what is good (*tha*) and more powerful (*chak*). Missionaries also mention how the Mizos would often say '*A va mak em*', implying something strange, wonderful and incomprehensible. Thus, the 'whiteness' of the missionaries was *mak*, so were their healing powers (medicine), as also their ability to communicate not through speech but through writing; above all, it was the power that Christ was said to have over spirits that was feared, that was considered *mak*. In course of time, 'belief' was not only in manifest power or what was amazing but also in an articulation, in a certain explication that clarified pre-existing beliefs within a Christian cosmology. Thus, as one convert puts it, 'one *had to* believe in Pathian, the One who created heaven and earth; it followed that all other known gods were under him; therefore one had no option, but to believe in him'.

A move from a form of belief that relied on trusting in the power of god and his awesomeness came in times of revivals. While there were several individuals who could give testimony to a personalized understanding of what Christ had done for them, many Mizos would also recognize the turning over to Christianity *en masse* to four major revivals that occurred in 1906, 1913, 1918-19 and 1930. Each of these revivals was said to have had a different emphasis. While, during the first (considered an offshoot of the Welsh revival of 1904-5), there was a general conviction and confession of sin, the second revival focused on Christ's second coming, and the third on his sufferings of the cross. These revivals, thus, helped in the propagation of important tenets of Christianity. Strangely enough, while in the initial phases of missionary activity, it was said that the Mizo could not respond to Christ as the saviour of sins, the 1906 revival had this emphasis. Thus, these revivals are not only seen as leading to numerical growth but were also as periods of spiritual renewal in which the Christian doctrine was further ingrained in the minds of the people. They seemed to have had a deep effect on the people, leading to the strengthening of faith in the believers, while drawing many into the fold.

The revivals were also occasions for innovation and indigenization. After the revival in 1918-19, the traditional Mizo drum came to be used for the first time in church worship. Prior to this, missionaries regarded it as an instrument of pagan feasts that should not be adopted in Christian worship. There were serious discussions on its use but, from this time on, the arguments of the indigenous Christians held sway and it came to be a permanent feature in church worship.

Missionaries did not always welcome the revivals and, at times, it even aroused their suspicion. The fourth revival, for instance, was said to have caused *taksa chetna* or 'involuntary bodily contortions' such occasions were when belief was not in control of the missionaries. As they often came from conservative backgrounds, they worried at its manifestations as well as its theological implications. Gwen Mendus commented:

> But a new and strange element entered into the last revival [1918-1919] . . . and it has taken all sorts of extreme forms, such as 'speaking with tongues' (some say such things as 'one! two! three! right about turn!' knowing no English and thinking they are under the influence of the spirit!), healing, raising the dead even (so they claim!), women giving symbolical birth to Christ, all sorts of weird dancing and bodily contortions in the services,

many of the gestures having some symbolical meaning which they attach to them and so on.[56]

Similarly, E.L. Mendus, in his report on 1938, stated that the revival was the greatest threat that the church had faced and he was even fearful of a split in it. His main reservation was the spiritualization of the Christian faith (which he also recognized as something which should not have been alien to himself as, being a Celt, he was not foreign to mysticism), wherein most people believed that god was speaking to them directly in opposition to the dictates of the church.[57]

FORMS OF OPPOSITION

The narrative in the preceding sections may lead one to think that there was no opposition to the adoption of Christianity. Resistance came from the chiefs, who, if not physically harming the converts, would impose heavy fines on them or even evict them from the village. On the other hand, there were others who felt that they were too old to convert and that the new religion was for the young.[58] It is possible that such people associated the practice of Christianity with education, the meetings in churches and other changes, and they considered themselves too old to start afresh or learn something new. Major opposition to the new faith, however, arose in 1908 in the form of a movement that encompassed the whole country. It was associated with the singing of some couplets, which usually had the refrain *puma* at the end of each line. It was not so much the lyrics of the song, or the meaning of the verse that mattered, for they were more or less frivolous exchanges, but the fact that the singing was accompanied by drinking and dancing in which the entire village would end up in a state of drunken reverie. The disorder and confusion created was anathema to the missionary. A contemporary observer, noting the all-encompassing nature of the *puma* phenomenon, wrote:[59]

> There has never been any composition as popular as the *puma* songs and there will never be any to replace them. It is sung by children, the youth and the old, men and women alike . . . any one who considers her/himself (there is no gender differentiation for the third person in Mizo) a human being in Mizoram sings them!

Big village feasts were held to provide the setting for the singing, which was said to have begun at a place called Ratu in north Mizoram. New couplets were composed as it spread to other villages, making it extremely difficult for Christians to preach. It caught the imagination of the people and many reverted to the old faith. The movement had religious overtones and, true to its opposition to Christianity, its adherents claimed that

> . . . all who acclaimed its advent would be exempted from offering sacrifices to demons, and that the dreaded spirits in future be appeased if such votaries merely offered, when ill, a few hair or feathers instead of the usual sacrifices of animals and birds.[60]

Chiefs, many of whom, in any case, opposed Christianity, made good use of the movement and encouraged it by playing host to the feasting and revelry. Mizos, it was said, had responded greatly to Welsh hymns and, in this light, it is not surprising that the opposition took the form of singing. However, this form of opposition died down by 1912 when a bamboo famine struck the district in 1911 and feasting was no longer possible.[61] It is significant that it was not a concerted action by the missionaries that led to its disappearance but rather an external agency, thus showing that the former were quite powerless in the face of such opposition.

CONCLUSION

This essay began with a brief survey of the ways in which Christianity has come to be an important part of contemporary Mizo identity and society. I have tried to show that the process of conversion and the reasons behind it are notions associated with why the new religion became acceptable. In the case of the Mizos, Christianity did not contradict their traditional concepts, though it did oppose traditional beliefs. Missionary ingenuity in making the gospel relevant and integrating local leadership with the church hierarchy contributed to participation in and identification with the religion. Acceptance of Christianity also coincided with a political reformulation, the formation of the Mizo identity, which, in a sense, necessitated the adoption of a new 'tribe-spirit' or *sakhua*. All this, of course, happened in the context of colonialism and one cannot deny the fact that the seeming order and power that it seemed to represent, including the missionaries who also represented that civilization, were important allurements.

Although the path to conversion was not without impediments, traditional resources (in terms of material or formalized dissent), could not assert themselves and, in the end, Christianity could not be ignored. For the most part, however, people were happy to associate themselves with the new religion. As a chief commented in 1911, he was happy that a lot of progress had been made due to the 'work of the government and God, besides the efforts made by the Sailo rulers and local progressive individuals'. One of the areas of progress, he believed, was the manner in which the Mizos were rallying together around the faith, cognizant of their new identity not only as Mizos but also as Mizo Christians.[62]

NOTES

1. Lalsangkima Pachuau, *Ethnic Identity and Christianity: A Socio-historical and Missiological Study of Christianity in Northeast India with Special Reference to Mizoram*, Frankfurt: P. Lang, 2002, p. 29. The 2001 Census of India does not give figures with regard to religious affiliation. Figures according to the 1991 census are: Hindus 82 per cent; Muslims 12.2 per cent; Christians 2.34 per cent; Sikhs 1.94 per cent; Buddhists 0.76 per cent and Jains 0.46 per cent. This report is not inclusive of the state of Jammu & Kashmir where a census was no conducted.
2. Ibid., p. 78. According to the figures available, the percentage of Christians in the state according to the 1961 general census, was 86.64 per cent; 1971: 86.09 per cent; 1981: 83.71 per cent and 2001: 87 per cent. For details on the 2001 census, see, *Census of India: Data on Religion, 2001 Census*, Mizoram: Director of Census Operations, n.d.
3. The weekly figures were as follows: 29/08/04: 71.31 per cent; 22/08/04: 72.08 per cent; 15/08/04: 73.66 per cent; 8/08/04: 74.47 per cent.
4. I was informed that in Mumbai in 2005, except for the treasurer, the committee membership of the Mumbai Mizo Association and the Bombay Mizo Christian Fellowship was the same. Matters pertaining to both committees were often discussed in the same meeting.
5. J. Davis, ed., *Religious Organization and Religious Experience, ASA Monograph 21*, London: Academic Press, 1982, p. 7.

6. W. James and D. Johnson, eds., *Vernacular Christianity: Essays in the Social Anthropology of Religion*, JASO Occasional Papers, no. 7, Oxford: Anthropological Society of Oxford, 1988.
7. Ibid., pp. 2-3.
8. R. Shaw and C. Stewart, 'Introduction: Problematizing Syncretism', in C. Stewart and R. Shaw, eds., *Syncretism/Anti-Syncretism: The Politics of Religious Synthesis*, London: Routledge, 1994, pp. 1-26.
9. F.S. Downs, *Christianity in Northeast India: Historical Perspectives,* Delhi: ISPCK, 1983.
10. The figures have been calculated by me from data available of the number of Christians in the north and the south and the total population of the district. The 1901 figures of the number of Christians from the south were unavailable, so the 1902 figures were collated instead. Similarly, for the 1951 figure, the total population for that year was taken into consideration, while the number of Christians for the north is taken from the 1950 figures while that of the south is from the 1949 figures. The figures are taken from C.L. Hminga, *The Life and Witnesses of the Church in Mizoram*, Lunglei: Baptist Church of Mizoram, 1987, pp. 347-50. For further details, see, C. Nunthara, *Mizoram: Society and Polity*, Delhi: Indus Publishing, 1996, p. 30.
11. M. Kipgen calculates the percentage of Christians in the district in 1961 as 86.63 per cent. For details, see M. Kipgen, *Christianity and Mizo Culture: The Encounter between Christianity and Zo Culture in Mizoram*, Aizawl: Mizo Theological Conference, 1997, p. 345.
12. J.W. Burton, 'Christians, Colonists and Conversions: A View from Nilotic Sudan', in *The Journal of Modern African Studies*, 23(2), 1985, pp. 349-69.
13. Jean Comaroff and John Comaroff, 'Christianity and Colonialism in South Africa', in *American Ethnologist*, 13(1), 1985, pp. 1-22.
14. Ibid., pp. 1-2.
15. An instance of the opposition to administrative authority was when a missionary took up the cause of the *bawi*, often translated as 'slave'. (A missionary in the early twentieth century commented that it was unfortunate that the word was translated thus it because was opprobrious to British ears.) The working of the system was such that the chief took under his care the poor and orphans; essentially all those who came to him for refuge. They lived in his household and owed him certain dues and obligations unless they could redeem themselves or be redeemed by others. The early missionaries felt it was a good way in which the poor were looked after and felt they were more like retainers than what the term slavery suggested. The administration, for the most part, came to take up this position, as redeeming them would involve too large a sum

and dealing with the poor would cost the administration a fair amount. The cause of the *bawi* was finally taken up by a missionary, Dr. Peter Fraser, who worked for its abolition in the first quarter of the twentieth century with serious opposition from the administration, headed, at that time by Major H.W.G. Cole. For details, see E. Lewis Mendus, *The Diary of a Jungle Missionary*, Liverpool: Foreign Mission Office [n.d.], p. 66; CMA 27291 D.E. Jones File II, *Letter of July 15 1909, D.E. Jones to Mr. Williams*; *2 July 1909, Letter of Savidge and Lorrain to D.E. Jones*, National Library, unpublished, Aberystwyth.

16. For instance, in October 1937, the Superintendent, A.G. McCall, issued a public notice wherein the punishment of a jail term of three years handed out to three people was announced. The three men were sentenced because of their emphasis on 'spiritism' and the resultant disruption of peace and order in the village. According to the order, 'they have made the Christians of one village unable to live their normal lives, and have even troubled several who are not Christians; people dance like monkeys and shake uncontrollably, they say they speak the language of the spirits and they disobey their chiefs and those in authority'. The entire village was also punished in various ways for encouraging the three 'spiritual' leaders. A homily from the Superintendent which followed the notice advised the people to 'stop dancing in the church; you may continue to dance with the drum outside the church, as you once used to do . . . such kind of dancing is good for the body and mind and there is no need for a "spirit" to be present. In the old days the "spirit" was not required [on such occasions], and so even today the "spirit" should not be required. When people play football they do not require a "spirit" and they still play well, similar is the case with dancing. . . . To make the dancing more enjoyable, do sing and compose songs related to cultivation, love, the love of children and animals and do all these with purity and faithfulness. . . . When you do these things you will be closer to happiness. Happiness and peace can be achieved from these things. It is better to pursue peace and satisfaction rather than be under the control of a "spirit"', *Mizo leh Vai*, October 1937. On issues of law and order, see E.L. Mendus, 'The Jungle Diary', in *Glad Tidings*, no. 8, 1939, p. 30.
17. An interesting incident was narrated by Shakespear, of a meeting he convened for the missionaries from the north and south so that they could hold discussions jointly on how they were to translate certain biblical concepts. One of the words in question was 'soul', which the missionaries wanted to translate to a made-up word, namely *Mihring bul* [literally 'shoot/root/origin of man'], the argument being that the soul was the essential part of a man just as the root was of a tree. Not being

able to come to a conclusion, the district superintendent called for some local people to find out what they understood by the term. They came to the conclusion that 'the root is what a tree springs from, so *mihring bul* must mean "father of man"! *Mihring bul* was eventually dropped and instead *thlarau*, from *thla*/shadow and *rau*/spirit was adopted.' *Mss E 361/5*, British Library, unpublished, London.

18. Robin Horton, 'On the Rationality of Conversion', in *Africa: Journal of the International African Institute*, vol. 45, nos. 3 and 4, 1975, pp. 219-35, 373-99.
19. CMA 27292 D.E. Jones File III, National Library, unpublished, Aberystwyth. There were also several articles written by both missionaries and locals about affairs of the world, history, politics and geography in monthly magazines such as *Mizo leh vai.*
20. By 1924, 14 had finished their matriculation at Shillong, in present-day Meghalaya. 1924 was also the year when two Mizos were, for the first time, awarded the B.A. degree.
21. Robin Horton, op. cit., p. 223.
22. CMA HZ1/3/50 E.L. Mendus, National Library, unpublished, Aberystwyth.
23. C.A. Kammerer, 'Customs and Christian Conversion among Akha Highlanders of Burma and Thailand', in *American Ethnologist*, 17(2), 1990, pp. 277-91.
24. Ibid., pp. 277-87.
25. J. Dokhuma, *Hmanlai Mizo Kalphung*, Aizawl: J.D. Press Publication, 1992, p. 24.
26. Dala, 'Sakhua', in *Mizo leh vai*, February 1905.
27. Hrawva, 'Mizoram leh Sawrkar', in *Mizo leh Vai*, June 1919.
28. Makthanga, 'Tui leh ram', in *Mizo leh vai*, January 1926.
29. The word used here was *hruaitu*, which can be translated as a leader, but in this context it meant innovator or trendsetter.
30. Thala, 'Mizo', in *Mizo leh Vai*, December 1938.
31. R.G. Lienhardt, 'The Dinka and Catholicism', in John Davis, ed., *Religious Organization and Religious Experience*, ASA Monograph 21, London: Academic Press, 1982, pp. 81-95.
32. Robin Horton, op. cit., pp. 219-20; R.E. Eaton, 'Conversion to Christianity Among the Nagas, 1876-1971', in *Indian Economic and Social History Review*, 1984, vol. 21, p. 5.
33. J.M. Lloyd, *History of the Church in Mizoram (Harvest in the Hills)*, Aizawl: Synod Publication Board, 1991, p. 9.
34. C.L. Hminga, 'Christianity and the Lushai People: An Investigation of the Problem of Representing Basic Concepts of Christianity in the Language of the Lushai people', M.A. thesis, Manchester University,

1963, p. 35; J. Dokhuma, *Hmanlai Mizo Kalphung*, Aizawl: J.D. Press Publication, 1992, p. 28.

35. J. Shakespear, *The Lushei-Kuki Clans*, Aizawl: Tribal Research Institute, 1988 [1912].
36. Hminga, 1963 op. cit., pp. 29-30; J. Dokhuma, op. cit., p. 28.
37. Shakespear, op. cit., p. 61.
38. Ibid.
39. The categories according to Shakespear include (1) sacrifice to *sakhua* (guardian spirit of the clan/tribe); (2) *khal*: sacrifice to the *huai* supposed to frequent the village and houses; (3) *daibawl*: sacrifice to *huai* that resided in the wild, the jungle, streams, mountains, etc.; (4) sacrifices in times of illness; (5) sacrifices to cure barrenness in women; (6) *nao hri:* this was a once-in-a-lifetime sacrifice; (7) sacrifices connected with hunting and killing; (8) sacrifices connected with the *jhum*/swidden cultivation, Shakespear, op. cit., pp. 69-70.
40. Hminga, 1963, op. cit., p. 66.
41. Ibid., pp. 67-9; Shakespear, op. cit., pp. 62-5.
42. Hminga, 1987, op. cit., p. 62.
43. Ibid., p. 57.
44. The missions for their part can be said to have performed an exemplary task. They set-up primary schools everywhere, using locals as teachers. By 1915, there were 50 Lower Primary Schools, two Upper Primary and one Middle English School in the north, while in the south, there were seven Lower Primary and one Upper Primary and Middle English School. In 1909, six from the north Mission School had passed the Middle English exam. Primary education was, thus, greatly stressed by the missionaries and it is no wonder that Mizoram now has one of the highest literacy rates in the country.
45. CMA 27353 E.L. Mendus, National Library, unpublished, Aberystwyth.
46. BMS IN 65, IN 66, IN 112, Angus Library, unpublished, Regents Park College, Oxford.
47. Rev. Saiaithanga, *Mizo Kohhran Chanchin*, Aizawl: Regional Theological Literature Committee, 1976, p. 50.
48. Ibid., p. 33.
49. S. Nengzakhup, *Amazing Mizo Missions*, Bangalore: SAIACS Press, 2000 [1999], p. 5.
50. BMS IN 113, Angus Library, Unpublished, Regents Park College, Oxford.
51. Ibid., Coming of Age Report of Women's Work in the South Lushai, Hills, 1940.
52. BMS IN 65, *Letter of Edith Chapman to Miss Bowser*, 28.5, Angus Library, unpublished, Regents Park College, Oxford, 1929.

53. Monday was translated as *Thawhtan ni* or 'First day of a (working) week', Tuesday as 'another day of work', Wednesday as the 'middle day of a working week', Thursday as the 'beginning after the middle', Friday as the 'last working/schooling day' and Saturday as the day of preparation (for Sunday).
54. CMA HZ1/3/46 E.L. Mendus, National Library, unpublished, Aberystwyth.
55. Ruel Malcolm, 'Christians as Believers', in J. Davis, ed., *Religious Organization and Religious Experience*, ASA Monograph 21, London: Academic Press, 1982.
56. CMA 27354 E. L. Mendus, National Library, unpublished, Aberystwyth.
57. Mendus, 1939, op. cit., p. 30.
58. Mendus, n.d., op. cit., p. 54.
59. Hrangdawla, 'Puma Zai', in *Chanchin Bu*, April 1911, p. 94.
60. *The Annual Report of BMS on Mizoram, 1901-1938*, Serkawn: Baptist Church of Mizoram, 1993, p. 48.
61. Rev. Saiaithanga, op. cit., p. 24.
62. Lalsailova, 'Mizo Ram Hnam Insuihkhawmna', in *Kristian Tlangau*, Bu No. 1979, 1926, pp. 179-83.

ELEVEN

Religion and Social 'Subversion'

Re-examining Colonial Orissa

Biswamoy Pati

In some of the *garhjats* neighbouring Cuttack a new *dharma* has emerged. Its name is Mahima Dharma. . . . This Dharma does not accept caste and prohibits any form of ritualistic worship and its followers accept only the supreme-being. . . . [1]

[T]he abnormal increase of rent . . . [in Gangpur] . . . engendered intense popular discontent amongst the Christians . . . [who] on account of Christian ideals and influence of missionaries . . . refused to pay bribes and because of this their lands were comparatively highly assessed.[2]

This article focuses on two apparently diverse mass movements of the tribals that interrogated and contested exploitation in colonial Orissa. These were the Mahima movement that developed over the second half of the nineteenth century and attracted large sections of the tribal population, and the Mundas uprising (especially comprising a section of the Mundas who had converted to Christianity) in the princely state of Gangpur in 1938-9.

While analysing the emergence and development of the Mahima movement, I will explore interrelated dimensions of social protest against the hierarchical order of caste. The movement represented an anti-order that sought to delegitimize the rajas and the brahmanas. Its contestory elements invoked *Mahima* and Alekh—which also means unwritten or oral. While inventing 'His' timeless existence that aimed to delegitimize Brahmanical Hinduism, the movement also negotiated the present with an alternative order that included features which were born out of the interactions between pre-colonial dissenting traditions and religious systems and the colonial context. These also drew upon the quotidian existence of the plebeian. Following the devastating famine of 1866, the alternative order of the movement incorporated features that especially stressed upon 'inclusion', thus straining the exclusive and rigid varna hierarchy. As will be discussed, the movement developed certain characteristic problems after the initial phase, the understanding of which make it difficult to accept the romanticized efforts that seek to project it as a 'subaltern revolt' and highlight its so-called attack on the temple of Jagannatha (Puri) in 1881.

The second movement examined in this essay is the Munda (tribal) protest in Gangpur, a princely state of Orissa in 1938-9. Between 1920 and 1934, Orissa had seen two major mass movements, viz., the Non-Cooperation movement and the Civil Disobedience movement. Even though the 'Mahatma' had advocated a policy of 'non-interference' as far as the princely states were concerned and the Congress kept out of these princely states of Orissa, the situation became politically volatile by 1937-8. By this time, some of the princely states saw militant Prajamandal struggles.[3] Although Gangpur did not have a Prajamandal, it was not insulated from the spell of movements in some of the princely states of Orissa. In such a context, one observed the development of a movement among tribal converts to Christianity (Lutherans). This article focuses on the ways in which the tribals incorporated Christianity in order to fight the feudal state and also confront colonialism. The fact that Christianity acquired diverse meanings in the colonial context is not only reflected in the Munda interpretations of Christianity but also in the way the religion was preached and disseminated by certain sections of the church.

This article will attempt to delineate some fascinating aspects of popular imagination and invention. I question and interrogate the elitist pre-occupations of the subaltern historians, especially Ranajit Guha who insists on marginalizing the role of the peasants and tribals on the basis of the rather dubious formulations of 'popular autonomy' and 'territoriality'.[4] As has been argued in this essay, the people associated with the Mahima movement and the 'Christian' Mundas most certainly interacted with the 'world outside'. They borrowed ideas selectively and invented a discourse of equality, even as they fought their immediate oppressors, the princely rulers, as in the case of the Mahima movement, and confronted colonialism, as in the case of the Mundas. This essay also negotiates the issue of colonial modernity that is usually located as a monopoly of the middle classes, especially the urban upper castes or the *bhadraloks*—as is often assumed by some subaltern political scientists and historians.[5] These aspects become crucial not only to come to terms with the limitations of tribal/peasant insurgency, but also to understand and appreciate the various dimensions of protest and dissent in colonial South Asia.

I. THE MAHIMA MOVEMENT

That all religions—the greatest inventions of humankind—seem to have originated in the ancient 'past' is a perception that is a part of a shared 'common sense'. Such a perception is applicable to South Asia as well and can, at most be stretched to the 'medieval past'. In this sense, the colonial period appears to be a frozen site when it comes to the starting point of any religion/religious system. It is here that one needs to see the ideological conditioning of historians that can partly explain why this perception survives. Thus, this perception of the ancient lineage of religious systems can perhaps be traced back to Orientalist writings and the ways in which the Orientalist ideology was subsequently reinforced by both colonialism and Indian nationalism.

Going beyond the religious frame, one needs to perhaps probe the 'making' of this plebeian movement and the diversities it negotiated in a colonial setting.[6] In addition, my effort would be to weave in dimensions of social history ranging from the world of the pre-colonial to the fall-out of the process of colonization in the region. While probing the specificities of the movement, I situate it within the general framework of the survival strategies of the poor. The essay will also further examine why the Mahima movement could not impact the society in a way so as to alter it, in spite of its alternative perceptions and visions that contained dreams and ideas based on egalitarianism and equality, contesting the established order.

The Mahima movement was rather broadbased if one takes into account the geographical area that it influenced. We can include here the diverse regions that together constituted colonial Orissa, including the coastal tract and the western 'interior'. One of the methodological problems related to studying this movement is the set of paradigms that scholars have almost unquestioningly accepted while studying it. A major component of these analyses involves associating various aspects of the movement in some way or the other with religion, especially in relation to the Jagannatha cult and Puri.[7] In fact, both Jagannatha and Puri assumed a different form in colonial Orissa, and what is often overlooked is that a host of players contributed to 'make' it this way. Significantly, they ranged from the colonialist and his feudal allies (associated with the process of Orissa's colonization) and missionaries to the upper caste, urban and coastal-centric Oriya middle-class discourse and those associated with the pilgrim traffic to transform the Jagannatha cult in its colonial context. In fact, the cult of Jagannatha gained unprecedented importance with Puri's colonization.[8] However, most scholars working on the Mahima movement do not take these features into account. This leads them to locate Jagannatha as 'Orissa's deity' and, in the process, they Hinduize the region and its identity. Needless to say, such a method—which makes a historic block out of Jagannatha and Puri—fetters the possibilities of studying something like the Mahima movement.

Talking in particular about the pre-colonial period, especially the early medieval in Orissa, historians highlight the dynamics of the feudalization of this region. According to them, the manifestations of this process included, at one end, the emergence of intermediaries and superior landlords and, at the other, the reduction of peasants and artisans to the position of semi-serfs. As suggested, the caste system developed late in Orissa and when it did (approximately around the tenth-eleventh century AD), certain specificities and differences in comparison with the Indo-

Gangetic plain model marked it. This was primarily because of the preponderant tribal population and the geographical variations in the region (viz., the coastal tract and the hilly/forested interior). As a result, land grants to brahmanas and the extension of agriculture, especially in the forest areas, led to the conversion of most of the tribes into shudras, which converged with the process of their subsequent peasantization. Alongside this, tribal chiefs were absorbed as kshatriyas into the varna system. This implied the absence of any rigid polarization. The classic fourfold varna system continued to remain largely notional, as in practice, the two-tier structure of the brahmana and shudra with the numerous intermediary occupational castes constituted the functional reality. Consequently, one witnesses the evolution of these two strata as clearly identifiable varnas. The vaishyas were not really visible in society, though men of material substance appropriated this status for themselves. The epigraphical references to the vaishyas show that they became important only occasionally in times of trade. Similarly, the kshatriyas never had local roots and were created in this period of state formation in early medieval Orissa. In the process of transition from a clan to caste society that influenced state formation, there were shifts in the identity of adivasi chieftains, who started claiming for themselves the status of kshatriyas. The rise of the kshatriyas/karanas was a feature associated with the emergence of feudalism. As delineated, the varna system was a major legitimizing force in the process of state formation.[9]

The process of consolidation of the caste system continued and, in fact, the varna order was considerably reinforced with Orissa's colonization. Orissa was colonized during 1803-4 and this was followed by large-scale colonial interventions that specifically focused on land settlements.[10] A major aspect of the land settlements involved incorporating pre-existing propertied classes and social hierarchies associated with caste into the freshly imposed colonial administration, thus reinforcing them. Without going into details, it needs to be articulated that this drive stabilized revenue incomes and created a set of dependable political allies.[11] In fact, the stabilization of the process of surplus generation in colonial

Orissa was, to a large extent, dependent on the Hinduization of the region. One should also add here that this process was intimately associated with land settlements that had the distinct imprints of and were founded on the pillars of property, caste and inequality. Besides, these were accompanied by terror strikes and large-scale displacements of tribes in the hills of Orissa, which saw their subsequent conversion into Brahmanical Hinduism.[12]

The *Naanka Durbikhya* or the Famine of 1866 was a major milestone in the history of colonial Orissa. On the basis of official reports, it wiped out approximately one-third to one-fourth of the population of the coastal tracts of Cuttack, Puri and Balasore. Unfortunately, there is no available estimate about the manner in which the famine affected the western interior, especially the princely states. It led to serious dislocations and the rigid crystallization of caste norms. We also witness the emergence of new castes, like the *chatara khia*. It comprised excommunicated people who had accepted food from the relief centres opened by the colonial establishment.[13]

The intellectual inspiration of the Mahima movement was provided by several pre-colonial movements of dissent and protest that were primarily concentrated around the coastal tract. These elements of protests can be traced back to Sarala Dasa, who lived in the second half of the fifteenth century. He was a shudra peasant cultivator who wrote the *Mahabharata* in spoken Oriya. This shift from the formal Sanskrit language to the spoken one—which had a local flavour and contained additions by the poet—simultaneously unleashed a distinct rebellious tradition of protest and dissent. Thus, such a shift implied challenging the brahmanas who monopolized Sanskrit (*debabhasa*—the language of the gods) and making it accessible to the common people. This was further highlighted by Dasa's ideas on inequality, women and the tribal folk, and his effort to turn the epic (viz., the *Mahabharata*) 'upside down' by making it inclusive.[14]

Sarala Dasa was followed by the *panchasakhas*—'five friends'—who became famous in the first quarter of the sixteenth century. These were Shudramunis Balarama Dasa, Jagannatha Dasa, Achyutananda Dasa, Jasabanta Dasa and Ananta Dasa.

Interestingly, it appears that all of them were not shudras but the power of the movement swept them to sympathize and identify themselves with the poor and downtrodden.[15] It needs to be emphasized that all the Shudramunis—as they were called—are from Puri and Cuttack—a factor that by and large is not taken seriously by historians working on medieval Orissa. The association of Shudramunis primarily with Puri and Cuttack implied that their ideology remained confined largely to the coastal tracts, even though we are told that they travelled to different places. This also implied vital limitations insofar as the ideological fallout of their movement was concerned. The rebellious tradition associated with the Shudramunis advocated a crusade against the system that hierachically arranged society on the basis of birth and gave importance to idolatry and rituals, and emphasized the need for mediators between humans and God. As a counterpoint to all these elements of social and religious beliefs, the Shudramunis stressed upon both monotheism and bhakti.[16] Buddhism, Islam, and Vaishnavism also influenced the world-views of this pre-colonial movement of social protest.[17]

While discussing the intellectual background of the Mahima movement, it is vital to examine its association with colonial modernity. Historians and political scientists normally assume that colonial modernity was an exclusive domain monopolized by the middle classes.[18] Here, they generally focus on the urban, upper castes—more specifically the *bhadraloks*. Nevertheless, colonial modernity was rather nuanced and complex, and co-existed with colonization and the terrible blows dealt by it.[19] In fact, from the point of view of the Mahima movement, it assumed serious significance. One needs to understand here the way in which colonial modernity impacted the poor and led them to invent survival strategies in a context that threatened to decimate them. This can be illustrated especially by focusing on the ways in which Christianity and missionary activities introduced a discourse of 'equality' and humanism in colonial Orissa.

With reference to the Mahima movement, what usually goes unnoticed in a historical analysis is the effort made by it to draw upon pre-colonial rebellious and dissenting traditions and synthesize it with new features that came in with colonialism and the development of colonial modernity. In fact, the Mahima movement, through such a synthesis, marked an attempt to invent a discourse of equality and humanism in order to build a rebellion of the poor tribals and outcastes through an interrogation of their exploitation, inequalities and sufferings. The magnitude of the movement was widely felt in the region. Unlike pre-colonial movements of social protest, the impact generated by it was felt both in the coastal tract as well as the western 'interior'. The latter aspect assumes significance since the footprints of regional diversities clearly marked the movement.

With reference to the western tract, comprising twenty-six princely states, it is worth mentioning that many of the durbars did try to reach out to the world of the adivasis by incorporating some of their practices and rituals. This was perhaps a response to the fallout of the crisis posed by the famine and involved a strategy to draw in the large adivasi population affected by it.[20] Thus, one needs to locate the efforts of some of the princely states like Sonepur, Rairakhol, Dhenkanal, Athgarh, Sukinda and Keonjhar to associate themselves with the movement from this angle. At the same time, the movement also faced some opposition. For instance, attacks launched on the caste system by it supporters (with the intention of 'destroying it') made the Madhupur zamindar declare the movement 'anti-Hindu' and take steps to expel some of rebels who had entered the estate.[21] The movement seems to have been attracted the attention of the urban world of colonial Orissa from as early as 1867. Reports of the movement having involved as many as 20,000 to 30,000 followers shocked the urban elite.[22]

Although it is not really possible to look for the accurate chronology of the birth of the movement, one can see its beginnings with Mukunda Dasa, who seems to have been a Vaishnava and had spent some years in Puri. Between 1840 and 1850, he established himself in the Kapila hills of the princely state of Dhenkanal. He seemed to have possessed 'magical healing powers'. Moving around from place to place—almost like a missionary—Mukunda popularized the movement and hence, came to be known as Mahima Gosain. Mukunda Dasa's transformation into Mahima

Gosain was accompanied by his deification before his death in 1876. He was buried at Joranda—in line with what can be seen as the standard tribal practice.[23]

The Mahima movement had fascinating features that explain its diversities. A very vital component included its emphasis upon the creator of the universe who was *Alekha* (which literally means unwritten) or *Mahima* (viz., glorious). These two features delineated certain characteristics of the movement's rather complex cosmology. *Alekha* or *Mahima* was the 'Supreme Being', who was 'timeless', 'formless', 'omnipresent' and 'omniscient'. The movement stressed upon monotheism and clearly rejected caste and idol worship, as well as the rituals associated with Brahmanical Hinduism. It also stressed upon bhakti or devotion, and denied the need for any intermediary between the 'Supreme Being' and an individual in the form of the brahmanas or the priestly section. The primary targets were the kings and brahmanas. The criticism against these two groups co-existed harmoniously with upper castes like the brahmanas and karanas, along with the hadis (outcastes), joining the movement.[24] Going by a report of the *tahsildar* of Angul, the movement aided the colonial administration when it came to negotiating with the panas, who were regarded as 'hard core criminals'. In fact, we are told that the *tahsildar* initiated them into 'Alekhaism', after which they gave up their 'criminal' past.[25] A lot of importance seems to have been attached to common feasting. The movement advocated a rather simplified logic of marriage, with the bride garlanding the bridegroom and the gathering of relatives/friends calling out loudly to 'Alekh' to bless them.[26]

What needs to be emphasized is the importance attached to the oral—not the textual or the scriptural—that transcended the logic of time and space. And, if seen along with the importance attached to some of the attributes of the 'Supreme Being'—especially the 'timeless' and 'formless' component—one can see this as a strategy aimed at de-legitimizing Brahmanical Hinduism. The emphasis upon monotheism, bhakti, and the obliteration of any intermediaries between 'Him' and the human beings also formed a part of this agenda. One can also see how these features incorporated certain diversities that have already been discussed. Nevertheless, the tribal affinities and linkages need emphasis as they usually remain unnoticed in scholarly enterprises that attempt to Hinduize pre-colonial as well as colonial movements of dissent and protest.[27]

The person who popularized the movement after this was Bhima Bhoi. Bhima was a blind *kandha* (adivasi), who was most probably from the princely state of Sonepur. He seems to have been exposed to the movement in 1862, after which he accepted its doctrines and became associated with it and its propagation. His association with it reflects its diversities that shocked the upper caste, especially as he is reported to have had about four or five women consorts and two children.[28] Of course, it is clear that the movement attracted a large following of women.

Bhima is reported to have had 'magical healing powers' and was associated with the composition of a host of fascinating *bolis* or songs that delineated compassion and humanism. Many of these songs also projected apocalyptic notions about *kaliyuga*—the moral and social decay and the ensuing crisis. These were attributed to the falling values of the brahmanas and kings.[29] Bhima's basic postulates marked a crusade against the varna system with the aim of de-legitimizing it. After all, this was the only way of getting some space for the poor tribals and shudras. The logic of the system of *nirbeda* that was supposed to be the hallmark of the movement represented a virtual antithesis of Brahmanical hegemony that was based upon the Vedas. Bhima's effort at integration on the basis of numbers is significant. He articulates: 'All the devotees of Alekha are One. . . . Fifty-six crores of lives go in one.'[30] This stress on numbers assumes significance especially as this period coincided with the census operations that had started in Orissa by 1869. Besides, the interaction with bourgeois-humanism and Christianity is visible in a *boli* where he articulates:

> Boundless is the anguish and misery of the living,
> Who can see and tolerate it
> Let my soul be condemned to Hell,
> But let the Universe be redeemed.[31]

Interestingly, post-modern twenty-first century scholarship, given its class predilections and admiration of caste, cannot accept this blind tribal as an intellectual. In fact, we are categorically told that Bhima Bhoi 'was *not* an intellectual'.[32]

Everyday Life and the Movement

One needs to mention here that it is impossible to be precise about the time-wise location of anything associated with the Mahima movement. Many of the issues that will be subsequently delineated here could well be aspects that were drawn into the movement at a much later stage, when it had become institutionalized. For example, most probably at the initial stages, the movement did not have the three categories of followers that we hear of—viz., *kumbhipatias*, *kamapatias* (*sannyasis*) and *grihasthas* (householders). Besides, features like regional variations need to be borne in mind while negotiating this dimension. This is significant because of the prominent following of tribals and shudras outside the coastal tract of Cuttack, Puri and Balasore.

Nevertheless, some aspects can perhaps be traced to the origin of the movement. One of the aspects worth mentioning was the importance attached to the deletion of memory related to one's past. Thus, the newly initiated were expected to forget their 'past'. Some scholars see this as an effort to set-up a rival order to the Jagannatha cult.[33] I would argue that this was a strategy aimed at transcending the varna order that had been subjected to extreme dislocation in the context of the famine. Consequently, the dislocation of the order created the basis of a new beginning independent of one's birth and social status—these two features being crucial in determining one's social position, according to the logic of the varna system.

Another significant feature was the intrinsic connection between the movement and the everyday life of the people who joined it. The idea of eating before sunrise and sunset was probably tuned to the daily work routine of the plebeian. It is worth mentioning that this appears to have had some association with the 'clock time' of the agrarian world of colonial capitalism, with which the peasants and agricultural labourers were linked. Surprisingly, scholars working on this area have failed to see the broader linkages and associations of the movement with certain practices. For example, the daily practise of prostrating to Alekha seven times in the morning and five times in the evening if seen along with the daily eating routine probably suggests some influence of and interactions with Islam.[34] Interestingly, the movement does not prohibit any food except the flesh of domestic animals. Even the Mahima *sannyasis* are allowed to eat dried fish and other wild animals that form a typical plebeian diet in Orissa. Although efforts are made to locate meat-eating as a feature that developed at a later phase, it is most likely that, given its social base, this was a regular part of the diet of the followers of the movement.[35] Further, with regard to the spread of the movement and the establishment of the monastic order, one observes imprints of Christian missionaries and their activities in colonial Orissa. Here, we can also cite the missionary zeal with which the movement was propagated and spread. It included a network of *tungis* (outposts) and also incorporated the logic of 'sin' and 'confession', with the *sannyasis* confessing to the chief patriarch.

The movement was rigid as far as *sannyasis* were concerned. It drew upon the concept of renunciation which they were expected to abide by and, hence, were celibates. Besides, they were not supposed to have any fixed place of residence or possess any property.[36] Perhaps the movement got codified with the setting-up of the monastic establishment at Joranda that institutionalized it. This institutionalization inaugurated a new chapter in the life of the movement. The Oriya upper caste order and the colonial establishment took keen interest in knowing about a movement that had threatened to turn the world upside down. Besides, some durbars, like the Dhenkanal durbar, attempted to establish links with it. This also heralded the process of Hinduizing and Oriyaizing the movement that had actually started as a movement of the adivasis and shudras. In such a context, the efforts at textualization which can be traced to the 1930s reinforced the process of Hinduization and Oriyaization. This climaxed with the high priest of this movement—Biswanath Baba—scripting his work.

Without going into any sort of textual study or analysis, some typical features of this drive need to be highlighted. This would enable us to grasp some features associated with what was undoubtedly one of the most powerful movements that challenged Brahmanical Hinduism in colonial Orissa. Biswanath Baba, we are told, got associated with Mahima when he was 21 years old. This also needs to be located simultaneously as an effort to give a 'modern' façade to what was left of the movement. It is this 'modern-ness' that co-exists and illustrates its negotiations with Brahmanical Hinduism.[37] On the whole, textualization creates three epochs of the Mahima movement. These are associated with Mahima Swami who died in 1875 and was buried at Joranda in Dhenkanal (a major centre of the movement); Bhima Bhoi, who died in 1895 and was buried at Khaliapali, Sonepur (a major centre of the movement); and Biswanath Baba. One of the efforts to textualize it was to focus on its creator, Mahima Swami, the 'Supreme Being' who, we are told, also created the 'trinity' of Brahma, Vishnu and Maheshwara. Needless to say, it indicated an effort to show the origins of Brahmanical Hinduism as rooted in the Mahima.

We are not told anything about Mahima Swami's life story and 'He' fits into the 'timeless'/'formless' genre. This enabled 'Him' to transcend both Brahmanical Hinduism in terms of its origins and the varna system. The texts inform us that the Swami moved around from place to place (Himalayas, etc.) and entered Utkal in 1826. The initial references are from his presence in Puri, his debates with the brahmanas in the temple of Jagannatha and of them finally accepting him. For twelve years, according to the textual sources (from 1826 onwards), he lived on water (*jalahari*) and for the next twelve, he ate fruits (*phalahari*). After leaving Puri, he roamed around Dhauligiri, Khandagiri and Udayagiri. It needs to be noted here that these places are important Buddhist and Jaina sites. From these places, the Swami went to the Kapilas hill in the princely state of Dhenkanal (in 1838) and finally sat in meditation. The chronology, in terms of the Swami's entry into Utkal, is quite clear. This assumes significance if one keeps in mind the 'formless' and 'timeless' one's presence in this worldly form as a 'messiah'.

In the course of his meditation, the Swami established contacts with a Sabara (tribal)—Sadananda, who provided 'Him' with fruits and roots. Incidentally, Sadananda seems to be a rather Hinduized name. What is striking is that 'Lord' Jagannatha became the first disciple of the Swami. In fact, we are told that the 'Lord' left the temple at Puri to serve him and spread his message. This reflected an attempt to prove the superiority of the new order that was propounded by the Swami.[38] As is obvious, one witnesses an attempt to both incorporate and de-legitimize the Jagannatha cult. This account also highlights a connection with the chief of Dhenkanal, hence indicating an effort to gain legitimacy, patronage and respect.

Thus, the Mahima needs to be located as a powerful movement that challenged the kings and the brahmanas. Its opposition to both were premised on the exploitative order that both perpetuated. Most scholars working on the movement tend to Hinduize it. An effort is also made to compare it with the Arya Samaj and the Brahmo Samaj in colonial Punjab and Bengal, respectively.[39] We should perhaps wait for more research to be done before making any such comparisons. However, one basic difference that is evident was the predominant involvement of the tribal folk in this movement and the contextual setting that had distinct specificities.

Interestingly, Ishita Banerjee-Dube, while referring to the so-called attack on the Jagannatha temple in 1881, concludes that the movement was directed against Jagannatha. What we are expected to believe is that twelve men and three women, who were unarmed sympathizers of the movement, attempted this 'subaltern' revolt by entering the temple at Puri.[40] Their aim was to take the three idols of Jagannatha, Balabhadra and Subhadra out of the temple and burn them. Besides the obvious fact that such a position echoes the colonial and upper caste fears of the time (reflected in the Oriya newspapers), it also presupposes that poor people are naïve since fifteen of them went unarmed to accomplish this 'task'. Besides attempting to legitimize her position on the basis of the 'members of subaltern studies', Banerjee-Dube invokes and quotes D.W. Sabean selectively, blanking out what is articulated just before the tract she chooses to quote. Here, as Sabean puts it:

> What appears as direct testimony in a judicial text may well be a paragraph redaction of something that took quite a long time to say. In addition, evidence about what peasants thought or how they acted is largely anecdotal in character and subject to distortion that story telling brings to a situation. . . . [T]wo problems . . . the entanglement of peasant views in sources deriving from various levels of authority and the nature of the evidence as anecdote—present issues of great importance to the student of popular culture.[41]

Even more significantly, she fails to comprehend the magnitude of upper caste prejudices and how they impacted both colonial jurisprudence and the way of collecting testimonies from prisoners in colonial (or even contemporary) India, or the possibilities of communication problems. She seems to assume that Orissa was populated by everyone who spoke (and hence could understand) one version of Oriya—a point that is difficult to sustain even in the twenty-first century.

Interactions with Brahmanical Hinduism, especially after the movement got institutionalized and began to draw upon the support of princes, seems to have affected revolutionary zeal.[42] One can its highlight features like the 'otherizing' of the washerfolk (*dhobis*) and barbers (*bhandaris*) within the movement to prove this point.[43] If seen along with its ambiguity *vis-à-vis* colonialism, one can easily grasp how these together contributed significantly towards compromising its contestatory potentialities.

II. THE MUNDA REBELLION

The Munda rebellion developed in the princely state of Gangpur in 1938. Orissa had by this time seen two mass movements in the form of the Non-Cooperation and Civil Disobedience movements. Moreover, although the Gandhian policy of 'non-interference' in princely states had been the declared policy of the Congress, a spell of major mass movements in some of the princely states over the 1937-8 had altered the situation considerably.[44] Gangpur had remained comparatively isolated from the Prajamandal (State Peoples' movement) and the state did not have one. Nevertheless, as will be seen, the fallout of the movements in other princely states impacted the people of Gangpur as well.

Those who rebelled against the Gangpur durbar were the Mundas, who had been converted to Christianity around the 1880s.[45] Although largely a less-researched area, it needs to be emphasized that, unlike what is normally projected, the association between Christianity and the tribals is rather complex and nuanced. For example, in a colonial context that bred uncertainties and insecurities, the Oraons explained their attraction to Christianity by pointing out that it protected them from witches and ghosts, who were powerless against this system.[46] Moreover, like the converts to Hinduism who participated in Hindu as well as tribal festivals, tribal converts to Christianity observed certain customs and beliefs that were antithetical to its basic tenets. They participated in tribal festivals and, when asked about their identity, very often mentioned their tribe, overlooking the Christian connection.[47]

In the case of Gangpur, the Munda rising of 1938-9 was precipitated by the sudden increase in the rate of rent (between 100 and 150 per cent after the 1910 settlement) by the durbar. In the absence of a Prajamandal, Christianity became a source of strength for the Mundas, in the sense that it united them in their fight against their oppressors. There was a campaign for a no-rent movement around January-February 1939, which was led by Nathaniel Munda.[48] The Regent Rani announced some meagre concessions (which were not satisfactory), perhaps to prevent any untoward events as in the case of the other princely states.[49]

Most probably as 'good Christians' who had partly accepted the hegemony of the colonial administrative system, the Mundas submitted a petition to the Rani, the *diwan* and the *tahsildar* at a meeting on 2 February 1939. This was attended by about 5,000 people from nearly thirty villages. Besides desiring that the rent structure should remain at the 1910 level, this petition articulated the anti-feudal sentiments that had been generated through contacts with anti-imperialist and anti-feudal movements in other princely states in the province of Orissa, the Orissa States Enquiry Committee (which had toured the states to gather information about the conditions of the people) and Christianity (especially the activities of the 'native' preachers). Thus, the petition also included the abolition of *bethi* (forced labour), customary levies, restriction on land transfers and the use of forests and forest products, the right to use roads, irrigation and employment facilities, and the freedom to buy and sell (since this was the only state which levied an income tax).[50]

Since the durbar did not respond to this petition, the tribals appealed to the Viceroy—the 'good Christian'—which failed to produce any result.[51] It was only after these developments that a no-rent movement was launched in the state. Out of a population of 60,000 Mundas, 17,000 were Lutherans and the rest were Roman Catholics. What needs to be emphasized is that only the Lutheran Mundas rebelled. It is quite possible that they were translating into action the plebeian version of Christianity that was preached by their 'native' preachers. The preaching of the native missionaries appears to have matched the Munda perceptions and, thus, had relevance for them. This was significant as the Lutheran mission was initially indifferent to the Munda sentiments and demands.

In contrast, the Roman Catholic Church of Gangpur considered the hike in rent to be reasonable. In fact, it felt that this would be 'beneficial' for the people in the long run as it would force the cultivators to work their lands better. The hold of the church over its following seems to have been quite strong, since the latter seems to have accepted the position of the Catholic establishment. The no-rent movement was launched by the end of March 1939.[52] Nearly 5,000 Lutheran Mundas refused to pay the second *kist* to the durbar. The rest of the Lutherans and the Catholic Mundas continued to petition against the settlement. As the no-rent movement gathered momentum, there was a shift in the position of the Lutheran establishment—from indifference to anxiety. However, its 'holy' intervention proved to be ineffective. Its following seems to have been influenced by two Munda pleaders of Ranchi and 'native' preachers. This reflects the complexities of rural and urban linkages, as well as the popular interpretations of Christianity, both at the level of the 'native' preachers and the Munda followers.[53]

In its anxiety, the durbar approached the Lutheran Church Council (Ranchi) to send a deputation to Gangpur to impress upon the rebellious Mundas that the path of the durbar was correct. The deputation reached Gangpur around the beginning of April 1939 but failed to achieve the desired results. The secretary of the church, in fact, advised the *diwan* that only strong action would make the Mundas 'see reason'.[54] In fact, Reverend Schultz, the head of the Lutheran Mission at Gangpur, informed the durbar that the German government would recall the German members of the Lutheran Mission to Germany in September 'on the plea that they can no longer afford the present subsidy'.[55]

The durbar, the colonial administration and the church establishment viewed the situation seriously.[56] On 25 April 1939, about ninety troops and sixty state policemen led by the Assistant Political Agent went over to village Sikmo, a mile and a half away from the village of the 'rebellious' Mundas. The state police were ordered to advance and arrest Nirmal Munda for assaulting a *chaukidar*. On the arrival of the police, the Mundas collected and refused to surrender Nirmal.[57]

At this point, the Assistant Political Agent addressed the gathering of about eight people who were asked to keep away their *lathis*, bows and arrows and proceed to a nearby *maidan* for a meeting to discuss their grievances. The Mundas agreed to this proposal and reached the *maidan*. Here they were surrounded by the military and policemen and were asked to surrender Nirmal. The tribals refused to be cowed down and threats of firing did not deter them. One man exposed his chest saying, 'Let us see how you will shoot us'. At this point, a gunshot was heard and one of the villagers hit the Assistant Political Agent with a stick. After this, a firing was ordered which left thirty-two dead and nineteen injured.[58] The leaders were arrested. Subsequently, the movement was shattered in the context of its relative isolation from other movements in the states and the Province, the atmosphere of repression (especially from about September 1939) and the retreat of the Congress.[59]

The Munda rebellion reflects the changing nature of Christianity, its association with a struggle against oppression and its role as an instrument of solidarity. The way in which Christianity, which was a product of the West, became a rallying point to fight both internal and external exploitation suggests an obvious transformation or even a possible inversion of its fundamentals. After all, in the state of Gangpur, a social historian would expect it to have been an instrument of legitimization of both colonialism and the structure of internal exploitation. That the Mundas sought to set things right in this world through Christianity is both representative of the changing nature of Christianity in a colonial context, as well as the dynamism of popular militancy.

CONCLUSION

The two movements that we have discussed reflect the inventive power of the common people. When it comes to the Mahima movement, it hardly needs any reiteration that it had a predominantly tribal and shudra social base, and that it affected different parts of Orissa. Interestingly, the former aspect has led some present-day scholars to even look down upon it.[60] In such a context, what needs to be appreciated is the way in which a plebeian order invented a movement, drawing upon a host of diversities in colonial Orissa. As can be seen, these included the medieval outcaste protest tradition, Islam, Christianity and aspects of Brahmanical Hinduism. These became the basis of a struggle against their oppressors. Dreams of equality, absent in the real world, were incorporated to fight the 'sinful' order of exploitation epitomized by the kings and brahmanas.

Nevertheless, the failure of the Mahima movement was perhaps conditioned by the swiftness with which the durbars both incorporated and patronized it. This enabled them to re-establish themselves *vis-à-vis* their tribal/outcaste population that had been swayed by the movement in order to legitimize their rule. The movement also hierarchized low castes as it developed and got institutionalized. Here, one can cite the examples of *dhobis* (washerfolk) and barbers who were 'otherized', the movement thus betraying distinct footprints of the Brahmanical order. Thus, even though it had started by declaring a war on brahmanas and the varna system, after a point, it seems to have been affected by the shadow of Brahmanical Hinduism. Interestingly, any reference to the so-called 'raid' on the Jagannatha temple at Puri embarrasses its followers today, who define it as a '*succha* (true) Hindu *dharma*', and who articulate apocalyptic notions about what would happen if women devotees came into the *tungis*. Perhaps this illustrates how Brahmanical Hinduism has integrated and hierarchized the cult, and erased its interrogative and elements. One also observes an ambiguity *vis-à-vis* colonialism. In the specific context that this article focused on, this feature severely limited its interrogative and contestatory potentialities. Regarding the Munda rebellion, one witnesses the changing nature of Christianity in a princely state in colonial Orissa. This was due to its association with a struggle against oppression, as well as its role as an instrument of solidarity. This in fact shows the dynamism and inventive power of popular militancy.

NOTES

* I would like thank the South Asia Institute, Heidelberg, and R.P. Bahuguna for sharing his fascinating ideas and research related to the Sant movement that swept medieval north India. I am grateful to the University Grants Commission for a research award that has helped me work on this project.

1. *Utkala Dipika*, 1 June 1867. The translation is mine.
2. H.K. Mahtab, B.R. Mehta and L.M. Patnaik, *Report of the Enquiry Committee: Orissa States*, Cuttack: Orissa Mission Press, 1939.
3. The Prajamandal movement was affiliated to the All India State People's movement. It took up the cause of people in the princely states.
4. These are the hallmarks of an unsustainable method; for details, see Ranajit Guha, *Elementary Aspects of Peasant Insurgency in Colonial India*, Delhi: Oxford University Press, 1983.
5. See, for example, Partha Chatterjee, 'A Religion of Urban Domesticity: Sri Ramkrishna and the Calcutta Middle Class', in Partha Chatterjee and Gyanendra Pandey, eds., *Subaltern Studies VII: Writings on South Asian History and Society*, Delhi: Oxford University Press, 1992,

pp. 40-68; Gyan Prakash, *Another Reason: Science and the Imagination of Modern India*, Princeton: Princeton University Press, 1999.

6. I would leave it to other scholars to resolve if the Mahima movement was a cult or a sect. The only point that needs to be mentioned here is that the pseudo-Hindu, fascist thinking locates Hinduism as a religion and everything else as a sect. One should add that western Orissa was touched by the Satanamipanth (viz., Sambalpur) and forms of tribal protest like the rebellion of Birsa Munda, which did invoke the world of 'religion', 'magic' and a host of other complexities.
7. See for details, A. Eschmann, 'Mahima Dharma: An Autochthonous Hindu Reform Movement', in A. Eschmann, Hermann Kulke and G.C. Tripathi, eds., *The Cult of Jagannatha and the Regional Tradition of Orissa*, Delhi: Manohar, 1978, pp. 375-410; Ishita Banerjee-Dube, 'Taming Traditions: Legalities and Histories in Twentieth-Century Orissa', in Gautam Bhadra, Gyan Prakash and Susie Tharu, eds., *Subaltern Studies X: Writings on South Asian History and Society*, Delhi: Oxford University Press, 1999, pp. 98-125; Ishita Banerjee-Dube and J. Beltz, eds., *Popular Religion and Ascetic Practices: New Studies on Mahima Dharma*, Delhi: Manohar, 2008. See especially the general tone of the introduction, pp. 13-29.
8. For details, see especially Hermann Kulke, 'Juggernaut under British Supremacy and the Resurgence of the Khurda Rajas as Rajas of Puri', in A. Eschmann et al., eds., 1978, op. cit., pp. 345-58. Also see, Biswamoy Pati, '"Ordering Disorder" in a Holy City: Colonial Health Interventions in Puri During the Nineteenth Century', in Biswamoy Pati and M. Harrison, eds., *Health Medicine and Empire: Perspectives on Colonial India*, Delhi: Orient Longman, 2001, pp. 270-98.
9. Bhairabi Prasad Sahu, 'Orissan Society: Past and Present Manifestations', paper presented at the Training for Development of Scholarship Society, Pune, 1987; and 'The Brahminical Model Viewed as an Instrument of Socio-Cultural Change: An Autopsy', in the *Proceedings of the Indian History Congress*, 1985, Delhi: Indian History Congress, 1986, pp.180-92. Swati Datta, *Migrant Brahmanas in Northern India: Their Settlement and General Impact c.* AD *475-1030*, Delhi: Motilal Banarsidass, 1989 does refer to the phenomenon of land grants to brahmanas. It is emphasized here that they also emerged from within the stratified adivasi society. Hermann Kulke, 'Kshatriyaisation and Social Change: A Study in Orissa Setting', in S.D. Pillai, ed., *Aspects of Change in India: Studies in Honour of Prof. G.S. Ghurye,* Bombay: Popular Prakashan, 1976, pp. 398-411 focuses on the issue of Kshatriyaization in the context of medieval Orissa and extends its relevance up to the seventeenth-eighteenth century AD. He emphasizes this as a more relevant way of analysis than Brahmanization and the functional reality. Surajit Sinha,

'State Formation and the Rajput Myth in Central India', in Hermann Kulke, *The State in India, 1000-1700*, Delhi: Oxford University Press, 1995, pp. 304-42 feels that the diffusion of the Rajput model of the state and indigenous developmental processes could gain ground only among those tribal groups that had attained the technological level of settled agriculture. Thus, as he puts it, we do not find shifting cultivating groups like the Juangs or the Hill Bhuiyas of Orissa developing a kingship supported mainly by their primitive techniques of cultivation. However, he makes it clear that it was not essential for the use of the plough to determine the rise of kingship. Sumit Guha, *Environment and Ethnicity in India, 1200-1991*, Cambridge: Cambridge University Press, 1999, pp. 110-16 also refers to certain aspects of 'Rajputization' affecting some of the adivasi communities. Interestingly, H. Beverley, *Report on the Census of Bengal (1872)*, Calcutta: Bengal Secretariat Press, 1872, p. 193, mentions the absence of a 'pure' kshatriya caste in Orissa and refers to the *khandaits* (swordsmen) who formed the erstwhile militia and who took their caste from their profession, which corresponds to the military class in the fourfold division of northern India.

10. The grant of the Diwani (1764) had initiated this process of colonization, with the Company under Clive getting the right to collect revenue from Orissa—along with Bengal and Bihar—from Shah Alam, the Mughal emperor.
11. For details related to Orissa's colonization, agrarian interventions and allied changes, see Sanjib Rout, 'Rural Stratification in Coastal Orissa, 1866-1900', in *Social Science Probings*, 3: 1, 1986, pp. 136-50; Pradipta Chaudhury, 'Peasants and British Rule in Orissa', *Social Scientist*, 19: 7, 1991, pp. 28-56; Biswamoy Pati, *Resisting Domination: Peasants, Tribals and the National Movement in Orissa,1920-50*, Delhi: Manohar, 1993, Ch. 1, pp. 1-60; Shakti Prasad Padhi, *Land Relations and Agrarian Development in India: A Comparative Historical Study of Regional Variations*, Thiruvananthapuram: Centre for Development Studies, 1999, especially for the variations between the coastal and the western tract.
12. For details, Biswamoy Pati, *Identity, Hegemony, Resistance: Towards a Social History of Conversions in Orissa, 1800-2000*, Delhi: Three Essays, 2003.
13. For details related to the 1866 famine, see Gorachand Patnaik, *The Famine and Some Aspects of the British Economic Policy in Orissa, 1866-1905*, Cuttack: Vidyapuri, 1980. For the way it impacted society, see Bidyut Mohanty, 'Orissa Famine of 1866: Demographic and Economic Consequences', *Economic and Political Weekly*, 28: 1-2, 1993, pp. 55-66, and 'Migration, Famines and Sex Ratio in Orissa Division

between 1881 and 1921', *Indian Economic Social History Review*, 29, 1992, pp. 507-28.

14. For details, see B.K. Mallik, *Paradigms of Dissent and Protest: Social Movements in Eastern India*, Delhi: Manohar, 2004, especially chapter 2, 'The Dissenter Within: Sarala Dasa and his Oriya Mahabharata', pp. 69-109.
15. Ibid., pp. 110-50. Sarala Dasa was a shudra by birth. Interestingly, Balarama Dasa's family's caste origins is a matter of debate, viz., bauri or brahmana. Jagannatha Dasa was a brahmana who was initiated into Vaishnavism by Shudramuni Balarama Dasa, whose lineage is again debated, viz., brahmana or bauri. Achyutananda Dasa did not have a shudra origin, though he identified himself as one. Ananta Dasa had a karana lineage and Jasobanta Dasa had a shudra lineage. One can perhaps interpret the 'dual identity' of some Shudramunis as associated with the logic of incorporation associated with Brahmanical Hinduism. Although this is an area that needs to be researched, the *panchasakhas* seem to have been far more radical than Sarala Dasa.
16. For details, see ibid.
17. It is indeed amusing to see scholars almost wishing away the possibilities of any interaction between Brahmanical Hinduism and Islam, especially Islam influencing the former. A classic example would be Sheldon Pollock, 'Ramayana and Political Imagination in India', in D.N. Lorenzen, *Religious Movements in South Asia 600-1800*, Delhi: Oxford University Press, 2006, pp. 153-208, who argues that unlike the earlier phase that witnessed assimilation, the fallout in the case of Islamized invaders of the eleventh and twelfth centuries witnessed attempts to codify what he identifies as a 'Hindu way of life'. The Bhakti, or the Sant movement, with its stress on monotheism, can be cited here to contradict this position. See, for example, Irfan Habib, 'Medieval Popular Monotheism and its Humanism: The Historical Setting', *Social Scientist*, 21: 3-4, 1993, pp. 77-88; and also his 'Kabir: The Historical Setting', in Irfan Habib, ed., *Religion in Indian History*, Delhi: Tulika, 2007, pp. 133-57. Besides, an effort to compartmentalize interactional possibilities and syncretism is methodologically unsustainable. See, for example, Axel Michaels, *Der Hinduisms: Geschichte and Gegenwart*, Munich: Beck, 1998. According to him, the fifth and sixth periods of Hinduism, viz., 1100-1850 and post-1850, respectively, was characterized by syncretism (viz., Islamic/Hindu and then Christian/Hindu), cited in H.W. Wessler, 'Idolatry, Syncretism, and Anti-syncretism in Hindu Reform Movements of the Nineteenth Century', in G. Beckerlegge, ed., *Colonialism, Modernity and Religious Identity*, Delhi: Oxford University Press, 2008, p. 76. Besides being a

classic example of looking at history and society 'from above', such a formulation rules out the possibilities for interactions and syncretism between Brahmanical Hinduism, Islam and Christianity, which, as will be seen, is visible in the case of the Mahima movement in the context of the post-1850s, which falls under Michaels' so-called 'sixth period' of Hinduism.

18. The focus is normally on elite discourses that narrow the boundaries and complexities of colonial modernity.
19. We have already discussed the process of Orissa's colonization. It implied obliterating large sections of the tribal population through terror strikes in the hills, undermining their identity through the process of their conversion and a sharpening of caste/class, which was reinforced by the 1866 famine.
20. One can cite here the example of the Keonjhar durbar that created a virtual cult out of an adivasi method of curing leprosy in the latter half of the nineteenth century; for details, Biswamoy Pati and C.P. Nanda, 'The Leprosy Patient and Society: Colonial Orissa, 1870s-1940s', in Biswamoy Pati and M. Harrison, eds., *The Social History of Health and Medicine in Colonial India*, London: Routledge, 2009, pp. 113-28.
21. Joranda in Dhenkanal emerged as a major *gadi*, viz., centre—of the Mahima movement; *Utkala Dipika*, 6 September 1873, specifically mentions the princely states of Dhenkanal, Sukinda and Keonjhar where about 400 to 500 people were associated with this 'community'; The *Utkala Putra*, 3 September 1873, refer to the presence of the supporters of the movement in Athgarh.
22. This is visible from a news item in *Utkala Dipika*, 1 June 1867, which mentioned 'the propagation of a new religion in some of the princely states adjoining Cuttack' (translation mine), and that it had as many as 20 to 30 *sahasra* (thousand) followers. After this, a letter to the editor of *Utkala Dipika* on 20 August 1871, expressed the fears and insecurities associated with the rapid development of this religious system, and prayed that the government took appropriate steps to abolish it or else the people of Orissa would abandon their *gehastha dharma*. The *Utkala Dipika* (26 August 1871) mentioned the reaction of the Commissioner who took steps to see that the administration was vigilant about these people.
23. For details, *Proceedings of the Asiatic Society of Bengal*, January 1882; M. Laeequddin (Census Officer, Mayurbhanj State), *Census of Mayurbhanj State (1931), Vol. I, Report*, Calcutta: Calendonian Printing Company, 1937, pp. 120-1.
24. *Utkala Dipika*, 6 September 1873; the report is from Jajpur.

25. *Utkala Dipika*, 19 November 1881. The effort to incorporate panas seems to have been part of a major drive of the colonial establishment in Angul. Thus, R. Clarke refers to a plan to start a Pana settlement at Angul, and giving them 'good' lands and loans, which would be written off. For details, see R. Clarke, 'Panas of Orissa', in M. Kennedy, *The Criminal Classes in India*, Delhi: Mittal, 1985 (1907) rpt., Appendix, pp. 324-9.
26. For details, *Proceedings of the Asiatic Society*, January 1882; Laeeq-uddin, *Census of Mayurbhanj State (1931)*, pp. 120-1.
27. For a critique of this trend related to the medieval *sants*, see R.P. Bahuguna, 'Modern Labels on Medieval Sants: The Sant Movement and Limits of Hindu Identity', in *Social Science Probings*, December 2005, pp. 31-59. This attempt to Hinduize the Mahima movement is a major problem of most scholarly studies on it that we have already cited. For instance, for details on this issue, see A. Eschmann, in A. Eschmann et al., eds., 1978, op. cit., pp. 375-410; Ishita Banerjee-Dube, in Gautam Bhadra et al., eds., 1999, op. cit., pp. 98-125; Ishita Banerjee-Dube and J. Beltz, eds., 2008, op. cit .
28. A set of counter-myths seem to have emerged to counter this image and, in fact, J. Beltz and K. Mishra provide fascinating details related to this dimension. See J. Beltz and K. Mishra, 'Ascetic, Layman or Rebellious Guru?: Bhima Bhoi and his Female Consorts', in Ishita Banerjee-Dube and J. Beltz, eds., 2008, op. cit., pp. 132-57.
29. We get initial references to *bolis* from the *Proceedings of the Asiatic Society*, January 1882. Nevertheless, one needs to be cautious about locating them as a source. This is especially so because the ones that are available today are in Oriya, and the possibility of additions or deletions, while scripting what was essentially an oral tradition would, most likely have taken place. The process of codifying them began in the 1930s.
30. Bhima Bhoi, '*Stutichintamani*', 163-4, in Siddhartha Das, tr., *Mahima Dharma: A Cultural Dissent*, Cuttack: Arya Prakashan, 1997, p. 68.
31. Sitakanta Mahapatra, *Bhima Bhoi: Makers of Indian Literature*, New Delhi: Sahitya Akademi, 1983, p. 31. I have slightly modified it.
32. J. Beltz and K. Mishra, 'Ascetic, Layman or Rebellious Guru?', in Ishita Banerjee-Dube and J. Beltz, eds., op. cit., 2008, p. 151 (emphasis added).
33. See for example, Siddhartha Das, *Mahima Dharma: A Cultural Dissent,* Cuttack: Arya Prakashan, 1997, pp. 33-4.
34. It is amazing that most scholars working on Orissa wish away any possibility of interactions between Brahmanical Hinduism and Islam. They seem to be particularly amnesic about Salabega—a household

name in many parts of coastal Orissa—who, we are told, lived in the first half of the seventeenth century and was a 'great devotee' of Jagannatha.

35. Priyadarsi Kar, *Against the Tyranny of Society: Reflections on a Protest Movement*, Delhi: Academic Excellence, 2006, p. 40. In fact, Kar himself sees meat-eating as a phenomenon that developed at a later stage, forgetting that, for the poor, vegetarianism is a rather expensive option.
36. Interview with Biswanath Baba, Cuttack, October 1989. Along with stressing the importance of these rules, he responded apocalyptically and told me that there would be *pralaya* (deluge) when I asked him what would happen if women entered the *tungis*.
37. Biswanath Baba, *Satya Mahima Dharmara Itihasa* (Oriya: 'The True History of the Mahima Dharma'), (no publication details), pp. 1-11; rpt. (Cuttack: Mahima Dharma Alochana Samiti, 1975). The following part is based on this text.
38. This particular point is cited in *The Collected Works of Bhima Bhoi*, Cuttack: Dharma Grantha Store, 1990, p. 37, translated and cited in Siddhartha Das, tr., 1997, op. cit., pp. 43-8.
39. J. Beltz and Mishra, in Ishita Banerjee-Dube and J. Beltz, eds., op. cit., 2008, p. 152.
40. Ishita Banerjee-Dube, in Gautam Bhadra et al., 1999, pp. 98-125. The upper caste order was severely threatened through this and, besides failing to comprehend what had happened, concluded that these 'semi-naked', 'barbarous', people had rushed into the temple to take out and burn the idols of the three deities (Jagannatha, Balabhadra and Subhadra). Interestingly, in the ensuing clash between them and the 'protectors' of Jagannatha, one of the men, Dasaram (who was about thirty-five years old), died. As explained in the post-mortem report, this was not because he was badly beaten as he had marks on his body but as he had fallen down after a heavy meal. For details, 'Old Correspondence Regarding Juggernath Temple at Pooree, Part VI (1880-1884)', Orissa State Archives; *Utkala Dipika*, 12 March 1881, and 26 March 1881. This so-called 'attack' on the Jagannatha temple is also upheld as 'historically . . . correct by Bhagirathi Nepak. See Bhagirathi Nepak, *Bhima Bhoi: The Adivasi Poet Philosopher*, Bhubaneswar: Publication Committee, 1987, p. 66.
41. David Warren Sabean, *Power in the Blood: Popular Culture and Village Discourse in Early Modern Germany*, Cambridge: Cambridge University Press, 1984, p. 2.
42. Fanindam Deo also refers to this feature. Fanindam Deo, 'Institutionalization of *Mahima Samaja*', in Ishita Banerjee-Dube and J. Beltz, eds., op. cit., 2008, pp. 173-88.

43. This relates to the non-acceptance of food from *dhobis* (washerfolk) and *bhandaris* (barbers); it seems to be based on the logic that *dhobis* washed clothes of 'sinful people' while *bhandaris* shaved the 'sinners'. This is not really an exceptional case and there are other examples of conflicts between the Hinduized adivasis and outcastes in Orissa. Thus, the *kandhas* (adivasis) in Phulbani clashed with the panas (outcastes) in 1994, denying them entry into a Hindu (Shiva) temple. For details, see Biswamoy Pati, 2003, op. cit., p. 28.
44. For details related to the exploitative system in the princely states of Orissa, see H.K. Mahtab et al., 1939, pp. 144-8. For this and the Prajamandal Movement, see Biswamoy Pati, 1993, op. cit., Ch. 3, 'Of Movements, Compromises and Retreats, Orissa, 1936-39', pp. 85-142; and 'Interrogating Stereotypes: Exploring the Princely States in Colonial Orissa', *South Asia Research*, 28: 1, 2005, pp. 165-82.
45. Home Political Fortnightly Report, National Archives, Delhi (hereafter HP), 18/3/1939; *National Front*, 18 June 1939.
46. E.T. Dalton, *Descriptive Ethnology of Bengal*, Calcutta: Government Press, 1872, p. 247.
47. N. Senapati and N.K. Sahu, eds., *Orissa District Gazetteers: Koraput*, Cuttack: Orissa Government Press, 1966, pp. 121-2.
48. HP, 18/2/1939; 18/3/1939.
49. *National Front*, 18 June 1939.
50. H.K. Mahtab et al., 1939, pp. 146-8; *Orissa States News Bulletin*, 27 April 1939, in the All India State People's Conference, file no. 127, Nehru Memorial Museum & Library, Delhi (NMML).
51. All India Congress Committee (AICC), file no. G12/1937-39, NMML; *National Front*, 18 June 1939.
52. HP, 18/3/1939.
53. HP, 18/3/1939. In fact, it was suspected that initially Reverend Schultz (the head of the Lutheran council of Gangpur) 'may possibly have encouraged his community in their resistance'.
54. *National Front*, 18 June 1939.
55. HP, 18/6/1939.
56. This was in the aftermath of the murder of Bazellgate, the Political Agent of Orissa (at Ranpur on 5 February 1939). For details, see Biswamoy Pati, 1993, op. cit., pp. 124-6.
57. *National Front*, 18 June 1939.
58. HP, 18/2/1939; 18/3/1939; AICC Private Papers G12/1937-39, NMML; *National Front*, 18 June 1939.
59. For details, Biswamoy Pati, 1993, op. cit., Ch. 3, pp. 85-141.
60. As J. Beltz and K. Mishra boldly assert: 'One of the major differences between Mahima Dharma and the other reform movements is its *non-intellectual basis*'. See J. Beltz and K. Mishra in Ishita Banerjee-Dube

and J. Beltz, eds., 2008, op. cit., p. 152 (emphasis added). In fact, this position harmonizes perfectly with the ideas of colonial officials and the upper caste tradition in colonial Orissa (which was shocked by the movement), as well as the elitist notions of some of the subalterns—cited at the outset—who seem to locate thinking and 'colonial modernity', respectively, as exclusive preserves of the urban-centric, upper caste/class population.

TWELVE

Religious Rhetoric, Mercantile Strategies and a Community in Revolt

A Study on the Conflicts between the St. Thomas Christians and the Portuguese *Padroado*

Pius Malekandathil

The type of religious rhetoric used in any belief system is conditioned considerably by the socio-economic and political milieu with which the drafters of the rhetoric normally wish to enter into a dialogue. Some of the religious idioms and languages used by the Portuguese were fabricated within the frames of their larger mercantile interests and were often used for creating an atmosphere that would, in turn, help them to expand their political and commercial frontiers. One of the most striking examples of how languages of religion charged with new meanings and logic were used for establishing the hegemony of external powers over resourceful indigenous groups is seen in Portuguese engagements for about a century and a half to bring the spice-producing St. Thomas Christians of Kerala under the Portuguese *Padroado* through repeated accusations on them of heresy and dogmatic perversions.[1]

A chain of accusations of 'Nestorian heresy' was levelled against the spice-producing indigenous Christians of Kerala.[2] Their age-old customs and practices as well as rituals were labelled as 'heretical' by the Portuguese, a rhetoric which was intensively used by the latter for erasing the culture, ritual practices and traditions prevalent among indigenous Christians in order to facilitate the transplantation of European culture, rites and practices instead.

The entire exercise of 'Europeanization' was meant for realizing the standardization and homogenization needed for mercantile penetration, whereby the spice-producing St. Thomas Christians would be permanently made subservient to the interests of the Portuguese trading community. Though there was an apparent and evident commonality amongst them because of their adherence to one and the same belief system (Christianity), the St. Thomas Christians of Kerala resisted and vehemently defied the Portuguese attempts of Lusitanization and Europeanization for more than 150 years, making the core areas of conflict and resistance often move from diverse religious platforms to the domain of economics. As a part of the struggle of resistance, the spice-producing Christians blocked the flow of pepper and other spices from inland production centres to the Portuguese factories on the Kerala coast and diverted them instead to the ports of Coromandel through several Ghat-routes. However, the final phase of this conflict was their open revolt against the Portuguese in 1653. This long history of resistance by the indigenous Christians against the Portuguese also unravels the saga of the struggles waged for having multiple voices and pluralism within the same belief system. This paper focuses on the nuanced and continuous struggles of resistance that the indigenous Christians of Kerala waged against the Portuguese, mainly for the purpose of preserving their own ways of practising religion, and for fighting against the forceful Lusitanization and cultural domination thrust upon them as a part of the Portuguese strategy for their mercantile penetration.

THE ST. THOMAS CHRISTIAN COMMUNITY

The St. Thomas Christians trace back their origins to the apostolic work of St. Thomas.[3] They formed the most important spice-producing-cum-trading community in central Kerala, to which they were geographically confined for the entire medieval period.[4] This community was spiritually catered to, initially, by the Archbishop of Rew Ardashir from the Fars region of Iran and later, by the Patriarch of Seleucia-Ctesiphon and Mossul. Consequently, their trading activities were linked principally with the ports of the Persian Gulf region.[5] Pahlavi-inscribed granite crosses dating back to the sixth century AD that have been obtained from their principal settlements of Kottayam, Alengad, Kadamattom, Kothanalloor and Muttuchira, besides the one obtained from Mylapore, attest to the age-old linkage that these Christians maintained with the church of Rew Ardashir, where the ecclesiastical language was Pahlavi till the eighth century.[6] The subsequent dispersal of Christians to other places like Quilon and Mylapore was later referred to in the accounts of Marco Polo.[7] Similar details of migration can also be found in the accounts of John of Monte Corvino, Friar Jordanus and John Marignoli.[8]

The increasing involvement of Christians in the overseas trade is indicated by the Tharisappally copper plate (AD 849) of Quilon, granted by Ayyanadikal Thiruvadikal, a feudatory of the Cera ruler, Sthanu Ravi Varma.[9] The copper plate speaks of the various economic privileges and concessions conferred upon the church of Tharisa of Quilon. This church was set up by Mar Sapor and Mar Prodh, who, as migrant traders from Persia, seem to have linked the trade of Kerala with the vast commercial networks already spread all over the Indian Ocean with the help of former Sassanid merchants of Persia.[10] The Thazhekkadu inscription (AD 1024), which refers to the Christian traders of Chathan Vadukan and Iravi Chathan, also members of the Manigramam merchant guild, is suggestive of their involvement in inland exchange centres.[11] However, the travellers of the fourteenth century like John Marignoli,[12] and the Portuguese documents of the sixteenth and seventeenth centuries, referred to them as *Cristãos de São Tome* (Christians of St. Thomas).[13] They also referred to them as owners of pepper plantations in central Kerala.[14]

However, the increasing participation of this community in trading activities enabled them to occupy the vacuum created by the absence of vaiśyas in Kerala, socially making them evolve almost as a caste group with a great amount of ethnic exclusiveness.[15] In this social process, they imbibed a lot of elements from the neighbouring cultural space and developed the practice of untouchability, wearing of the sacred thread and *kudumi* (tuft-with a cross), observance of birth-related pollution, as well as *pula* (perception of the family as being under pollution, after the death of a member), *pulakuli* (the feast usually held on the tenth day after a funeral) and *sraddham* (feast held one year after the funeral, when the souls were believed to come back).[16] Those Christians claiming a brāhmaṇa origin also used to wear the Brahmanical sacred thread (*punūl*), a custom later quoted by Robert de Nobili for justifying his own wearing of the sacred thread as a part of his acculturation in Madurai.[17] This Christian community used to follow the East Syrian liturgy, which had originally taken shape in Seleucia-Ctesiphon. The ritual content of this liturgy was widely different from the Latin liturgy introduced in India by the Portuguese in the sixteenth century.[18] Till the Portuguese intervention, the churches of these indigenous Christians were all built on temple models, the only distinguishing sign being the huge granite cross erected in front of them.[19] All these varieties of customs, rituals and practices, together with their theological and spiritual notions that were developed among these Christians over centuries, were collectively called *Thomayude Margam* or the Law of Thomas.[20]

The principal settlements of the St. Thomas Christians were Kaduthuruthy, Alengad, Parur, Kottayam, Diamper, Angamali, Kayamkulam, Cranganore, Quilon, Changanacherry, Palai, Kuravilangadu and so on.[21] Giovanni Empoli, who came to Quilon in 1503, estimates that there were more than 3,000 St. Thomas Christians in Quilon alone, and who were called *Nazareni*.[22] The same was the number of Christians (that is, 3,000) in Quilon, according to the estimate given by the German artillerist who accompanied Vasco da Gama in 1502/3.[23] However, it is Tome Pires, the author of *Suma Oriental* (1512-15), who gives the demographic strength of this community for the first time for the entire region of Kerala. According to his estimates, the population of these Christians varied between 60,000 and 75,000.[24] In 1564 and in 1568, the number of St. Thomas Christians was estimated to be about 1,00,000.[25]

The bishops coming from West Asia became the spiritual heads of the church, while the actual head of the community was *jathikkukarthaviyan* or Archdeacon.[26] Thus, the Archdeacon wielded a great amount of power because of being the administrative head and the key decision-taking figure of this Christian community that was engaged in trade, agriculture and military activities.[27] The priests and the members of the community owed their loyalty principally to him rather than to the foreign bishop from Babylon, who was often unfamiliar with the local language and customs. The native rulers of Kerala never wanted to antagonize the Archdeacon, fearing the alienation of this resourceful Christian community.[28] However, the Archdeacon's decisions were conditioned mostly by the pulse and views of the representative bodies of the community, including *palli yogams*, whose membership then was restricted only to the aristocratic families and landed gentry. Any matter that was vetoed by the *yogam* had little scope of being implemented at any level of church activities. However, this arrangement infused into the church administrative system, elements of democratic practice, making decisions emerge from the grass-root levels. The local church as a body enjoyed the prerogative to judge certain key matters, including the admission of people to the priesthood, issues related to excommunication and so on. Thus, the Archdeacon emerged as the key figure in the general administrative system of the St. Thomas Christians and the *yogams* became powerful mechanisms at all levels of decision-making.[29] This was more so due to the relative uncertainty of the availability of bishops from West Asia at different time periods for catering to the spiritual needs of the Christians. Besides, these bishops' stay in Kerala was temporary and they had little knowledge of the language of the land. Since the feudal European notion of episcopacy as a benefice for a noble obtained from the ruler was absent in Kerala, temporality was detached from the episcopal post, which, according to oriental tradition, was meant to be exclusively spiritual. Thus, the type of church administration that evolved amongst this community was different and distinct.

FROM ECONOMIC COLLABORATORS TO 'HERETICS'

The Portuguese, on their arrival in Kerala, found the St. Thomas Christian community, which was actively engaged in spice-production and trading activities, as potential partners for realizing their mercantile designs, particularly against the backdrop of the commonality of their religion. St. Thomas Christian traders like Taraka Thoma (Traqe Thoma) and Mathias were the initial suppliers of spices to the Portuguese factory at Cochin.[30] The Lusitanians also sought the help of their bishop, Mar Jacob Abuna, to persuade the community members to sell spices only to the Portuguese at Cochin.[31] However, a rupture in the relationship between the St. Thomas Christians and the Portuguese began to appear by the middle of the second decade of the sixteenth century, especially when Padre Alvaro Penteado, a Portuguese priest, started accusing the former of Nestorian heresy in 1517 because of the indigenous customs, practices and rites that they maintained.[32] With the outbreak of the Protestant Reformation in Germany in 1517, these accusations of heresy were viewed in Portugal with great seriousness and caution.[33]

Despite the commonality of religion, there eventually emerged a feeling that the spice-producing St. Thomas Christians and the trading group of the Portuguese were not actually brothers in the 'same faith' because of the differences in their customs and practices. It was a time when such cultural differences were looked upon with suspicion and homogeneity was considered the best way to ensure orthodoxy. Things became further complicated as different patterns of customs, traditions and ritual practices prevalent among the Indian Christians became stumbling blocks against the Portuguese attempts to realize their mercantile integration and penetration.[34] In the meantime, the Lusitanians also realized that the centuries-old ecclesiastical and commercial linkages, which the St. Thomas Christians had been maintaining with the Persian Gulf regions, had facilitated the unhindered flow of spices from the hinterland of central Kerala to the ports of the Safavids and Ottomans in the Persian Gulf, undermining the very Portuguese claims of monopoly and their subsequent trading interests.[35] This made the Portuguese authorities resort to wider, long-term strategies and policies that would de-link the connections of the spice-producing St. Thomas Christians with the ecclesiastical and commercial centres of the Persian Gulf region. The local customs and the East Syrian ritual traditions that the indigenous Christians observed amongst themselves provided, for the Lusitanians, an opportunity to interfere in their affairs under the pretext of correcting 'the errors of faith'. Consequently, the Portuguese authorities launched several attempts, including frequent accusations of 'Nestorian heresy', on the St. Thomas Christians to reshape and re-formulate the cultural and liturgical expressions of this community in a way that would erase the differences and divisive elements between them and would, therefore, keep the customs, ritual traditions and cultural practices of the latter similar to those of the Lusitanians.

It was Padre Alvares Penteado who first accused the St. Thomas Christians of 'Nestorian heresy' in his letter written to the king of Portugal in 1517. While working among them for a short while, he found that their customs and practices were strange and entirely different from those of the Portuguese. He thought that these differences must have occurred because of the influence of Nestorian heresy.[36] Eventually, repeated allegations of 'Nestorian heresy' were levelled against them and the rhetoric of 'orthodoxy' was resorted to by different segments of the Lusitanians. This provided the Portuguese an opportunity of getting justification, legitimacy and sanction for their continued interference in the affairs of the indigenous Christians and for silencing the voices of their resistance.[37] In public displays and public sacramental demonstrations, only the Portuguese ways of administering baptism and other sacraments were projected as correct rituals, and the practice among indigenous Christians was depicted as lacking in basic ritual components.[38] The Bishop of the indigenous Christians, Mar Jacob Abuna, was even pressurized to follow Latin practices and customs. By the 1520s, he eventually took a pro-Lusitanian and Latin policy against the background of increasing Turkish threats on Mossul, the seat of the Chaldean patriarch.[39] However, Mar Denha, the second bishop, then working in the inland part of central Kerala fearing attacks from the Portuguese, resisted and opposed their moves to introduce Latin and Lusitanian practices. In this resistance, he was supported by a large number of spice-producing Christians in the interior parts of upland Kerala where the Portuguese had no hold. Till about the mid-1530s, Mar Denha was the rallying point for the anti-Portuguese struggles of the St. Thomas Christians, fighting for the preservation of their age-old traditions and practices.[40]

In fact, the Portuguese wanted the St. Thomas Christians to submit to the patronage of the king of Portugal through the *Padroado* system. This system would compel the indigenous Christian community to be weaned away from its ecclesiastical and commercial linkage with West Asia. Finally, this would also convert them into pliable agents for the Portuguese penetration into inland production centres.[41] The Portuguese patronage system took shape from a series of Papal Bulls and Briefs beginning with the Bull *Inter Caetera* of Pope Calixtus II (1456) and culminating in the Bull *Praecelsae devotionis* (1514), whereby the king of Portugal was given spiritual patronage over newly-discovered and conquered territories. By these Bulls, the Popes transferred the responsibility of evangelization in newly-discovered territories to the Portuguese crown, as a result of which the king of Portugal got the right to select and present his own men as bishops and superiors to monastic institutions.[42] Though *Padroado* did function greatly as an ecclesiastical arrangement for evangelization, it was often used for the extension of the 'glory of Portugal' over and above the 'glory of God'. Through the *Padroado* right, both the temporal and spiritual powers were combined in the crown of Portugal. Under this arrangement, religious activities were not restricted to the spiritual realm alone but were extended to the farthest possible temporal realms. The temporal activities were not confined to the secular realm alone but were stretched to farthest possible of religious spheres to empower the national monarch of Portugal.[43] Thus, for all practical purposes, *Padroado*, which was set up for conducting evangelization work and serving God better, became a pliable tool in the hands of the Portuguese for implementing their mercantilist designs and for carrying out the expansion of Portuguese power and influence in areas, where in the normal course of action, the power of weapons would not succeed.[44] It is against this larger context that one should look at the rhetoric of the *Padroado* authorities regarding the 'dogmatic perversions' of the St. Thomas Christians, whose practices and traditions they tried to replace by Portuguese ones. The entire purpose behind this was to realize the homogenization and standardization needed for the purpose of converting the spice-producing indigenous Christians into a religious appendage of the *Padroado*, as well as an economic appendage of the Lusitanian commercial system.[45]

DEPORTATION OF BISHOPS, FORMATION OF SUICIDE SQUADS AND THE SYNOD OF DIAMPER

From the mid-1550s onwards, the Portuguese resorted to the strategy of deporting the East Syrian bishops coming to Kerala from West Asia. The primary purpose was to reduce the linkage of the St. Thomas Christians with the ecclesiastical and economic centres of West Asia, and ensure their speedy integration with the *Padroado* system. In 1555, a new bishop, Mar Joseph, came from West Asia to Kerala to take over the charge of the community. He was sent by Patriarch Mar Simon Sulaqa of Seleucia, who was reunited with the Catholic Church in 1552. The Portuguese, who did not want West Asian bishops to work in India, accused him of Nestorian heresy and tried to arrest him.[46] The St. Thomas Christians, who were agitated over this development, formed a suicide squad (*chaverpada*) of 2,000 soldiers to protect their bishop and to resist Portuguese attempts to arrest and deport him to farther places.[47] However, the suicide squad could not prevent the bishop from being arrested and he was finally deported to Lisbon, where he managed to convince the crown and church authorities of his innocence and orthodoxy in faith. However, the moment he reached India, he was once again captured, accused of heresy and sent first to Goa, then to Lisbon and finally to Rome. In Rome, he was set free by the church authorities because of his piety and learning but he died in 1569.[48] The Portuguese found that their penetration into the spice-producing areas of central Kerala would remain impossible as long as West Asian bishops were allowed to exercise spiritual jurisdiction over the St. Thomas Christians. Consequently, they made efforts to prevent the entry of bishops from the Chaldean church into Kerala, for which directives were given to major ports on the west coast of India. The ultimate purpose of this attempt was to break the bond existing among this Christian community with the Persian Gulf regions.[49]

In 1568, a new bishop, Mar Abraham, came to India from West Asia. He had received valid episcopal consecration from the Patriarch of Venice, and had with him letters of the Pope and the Patriarch addressed to the authorities of Portuguese India, besides recommendation letters of the superiors-general of the Franciscans, Dominicans and Jesuits. In spite of all these documentary proofs and certificates, he was detained at Goa under the charges of heresy and impersonation, and was accused of not having authorization from the Portuguese king, Sebastian, to come to India.[50] However, on the night of Maundy Thursday, he managed to escape from the place of detention at Goa and secretly made his way to Kerala. There, he joined hands with the members of the Indian Christians and vehemently resisted interventions made by the Lusitanians, both in their culture and liturgical practices.[51] When he was later invited to attend the second Provincial Council of Goa (1575), he refused to go, raising doubts about his safety. However, he attended the third Provincial Council of Goa (1585) on the assurance of his safety by the Pope.[52] In the Council, Mar Abraham refused to accept the decrees, saying that he had to consult the Archdeacon and important Christian leaders before doing so. However, the Portuguese intimidated and threatened him and finally extracted a promise from him, that the council decisions would be implemented among the St. Thomas Christians.

After coming back to Kerala, he did not collaborate with the efforts of Fr. Francis Roz to correct the Syriac books.[53] This was an exercise which was carried out to make the St. Thomas Christians of Kerala conform to the Latin rituals. Further, Mar Abraham refused to ordain the pro-Latin students of Vaipincotta Jesuit Seminary who he feared, in the long run, would be made use of as tools to sever the ties of Malabar with the West Asian Church traditions.[54] Allegations of heretical practices were increasingly attributed to him. In 1595, Pope Clement VIII ordered an inquiry into the life and orthodoxy of Mar Abraham.

This was followed by another brief of the same Pope addressed to Archbishop Dom Alexis Menezes of Goa to appoint a Vicar Apostolic for Angamali after the death of Mar Abraham.[55] Thus, finally, as a result of frequent accusations of heresy against the Chaldean bishops working among the St. Thomas Christians, the Portuguese managed to make the West Asian bishops unacceptable before the Pope and to project the bishops of *Padroado* as the only alternative possible at this stage.[56]

The death of Mar Abraham in 1597 finally gave the Portuguese the opportunity they were long looking for. In the absence of any other bishop from West Asia, the Portuguese *Padroado* authorities immediately took up the governance of the indigenous Christians. They launched an agenda for the erasure of the Oriental rites and practices of the indigenous St. Thomas Christians, and the introduction of Latin liturgical rites and Lusitanian practices instead. The entire exercise was legitimized by the controversial Synod of Diamper held in 1599 under the leadership of Dom Alexis de Menezes, the Archbishop of Goa.[57] The Archbishop knew very well that the change of customs and ritual practices of the St. Thomas Christians through the platform of the Synod of Diamper would not be an easy task, as the majority of this community resented change. Hence, he allowed only his people to take part in the Synod and differences of opinion were not entertained in its discussions. Out of the 153 priests who took part as delegates, more than hundred were his men, ordained by him within a period of two-three months for this purpose alone, without even a proper training.[58] The dissenting clergy of the community was not given a chance to defend their age-old traditions in the Synod, as they were kept outside the proceedings.

Bishop Roz S.J., who was a close associate of Dom Alexis de Menezes in the conduct of the Synod and who was made the first Latin bishop for the St. Thomas community in 1599, later confessed that some of the decrees of the Synod of Diamper were added by the Archbishop himself after its conclusion.[59] John Campori, another Jesuit, also says that Dom Alexis de Menezes himself had added certain things to the actual document which were never discussed in the Synod.[60] This shows that at least in the case of certain crucial matters, things were presented in one way in the Synod, probably to get the approval of the delegates, and later recorded differently to suit their designs.[61] However, through the instrumentality of the Synod of Diamper, every cultural element comprising the diverse social customs and ritual traditions of the St. Thomas Christians that appeared to be non-European and not conforming to Portuguese practice was changed, The vast range of powers and authority enjoyed by the Archdeacon was cut down and he was reduced to the status of an ordinary priest. The patriarch of Babylon and the bishops sent by him to India were condemned in the Synod as heretics perpetuating Nestorian heresy on Indian soil. The most significant part of this development was that the Synod used 'Nestorian heresy' as a convincing rhetoric device to also suppress the ecclesiastical linkages of Indian Christians with the Chaldean church of West Asia. It legitimized Portuguese attempts to keep the spice-producing Christians under the *Padroado* system in a way that would ensure the integration and cohesion required for the mercantilist ventures of the Lusitanians.[62]

HEIGHTENED TENSIONS AND ECONOMIC FORMATS OF COLLECTIVE RESISTANCE

The convocation of the Synod of Diamper in 1599 and the cultural grafting done by it among the spice-producing Christians did not silence the voice of resistance; instead it only intensified the conflicts, making the indigenous Christians look for various channels for ventilating their anger. The St. Thomas Christians who formed the principal pepper producers and traders in the hinterland of central Kerala, besides being a fighting force, also used to get support and protection from the rulers of Thodupuzha, Vadakkenkur, Thekkenkur, Alengadu, Parur, Porca and Cochin in their resistance against the Portuguese.[63] This was mainly because the strength of these rulers of central Kerala depended upon the wealth coming from Christian agriculturists and traders. This made many of them argue vehemently in favour of their Christian subjects to the Portuguese Archbishop, Dom Alexis Menezes. They also tried to dissuade the Archbishop from imposing Portuguese customs and Latin ritual traditions among indigenous Christians against their wish. These discussions often invited the wrath of the Portuguese.[64] The political support from local rulers emboldened the St. Thomas Christians and the entire spice-growing hinterland of central Kerala appeared to be a highly tense zone, with many of them carrying swords, lances and guns wherever they went, including the churches that they used to visit for worship.[65] *Jornada* repeatedly refers to the frequent attempts of indigenous Christians to kill the Archbishop, Dom Alexis de Menezes, whom they considered the most important person keen on imposing Latin ritual traditions and Lusitanian social customs on them by erasing their indigenous practices and traditions.[66] In the midst of heightened tensions and conflicts, there were instances of attacks on Latin priests. For example, the St. Thomas Christians of Angamali attempted to kill a Latin priest who had gone there.[67] At Kaduthruthy, some of the St. Thomas Christians even kept two cobras near the sleeping cell of two Latin priests visiting the place, so that the snakes might kill them.[68] These were some of the visible forms by which they channellized their resentment and anger in different parts of central Kerala against the cultural colonialism to which they were being subjugated.

Though the weight of cultural colonialism was felt greatly among the spice-producing St. Thomas Christians, many others, including the Nairs and Muslims, sympathized with them and took active part in these struggles in different parts of central Kerala. Thus, we find a group of Nairs going with guns in two vessels all the way to Kulasekharamangalam for the purpose of killing the Archbishop, Dom Alexis de Menezes. Even though they were not successful in their attempt, they clearly spoke out, before their escape, that they had tried to kill the Latin Archbishop to free the indigenous Christians from the Latin enslavement that he had imposed on them.[69]

It is quite interesting to note here that the Ravuthar Muslims of Kanjirappally, who were chiefly engaged in the Ghat-route trade between Kanjirappally and Madurai and the Tamil ports, also turned against the Portuguese in the midst of these struggles, for reasons linked with developments in the spice-hinterland.

While visiting the inland parts of central Kerala, the Archbishop, Alexis de Menezes, realized that a large volume of pepper was flowing from various production centres through the Kumily pass to Madurai and to the Coromandel ports. Hence, he ordered the construction of a fortress equipped with artillery at Periate (Vandiperiyar), which was the most important junction for the Ghat-route trade, commencing from the spice hinterland of central Kerala and terminating in the Coromandel ports. However, the Portuguese attempts at the construction of the fortress to thwart the flow of spices to Tamil ports were initiated under the guise of erecting a church at Vandiperiyar. The Ravuthar Muslims of Kanjirappally, who were involved in the process of purchasing pepper from the St. Thomas Christians of the region and sending it to Madurai and the Coromandel ports through this Ghat-route, made a hue and cry about the new construction and requested the king of Thekkenkur to destroy this fort-structure of the Portuguese.[70] Though the Portuguese did not complete the project, the clamour that the Muslims of Kanjirappally had made merged into the voices of resistance that were heard in the habitats of the spice-producing Christians. In fact, among the Ghat-route traders, especially those from the Ravuthar Muslim community and the spice-producers belonging to the St. Thomas Christian community, there was a great amount of economic collaboration and cooperation, particularly in places like Kanjirappally, Erattupetta and Thodupuzha. It was from these inland markets that the St. Thomas Christians used to send a large volume of pepper to the Coromandel ports of Mylapore, Nagapattinam, Pulicat and Masulipattanam. In this process of commodity movement between Kerala and Tamil Nadu, the Ravuthar Muslim traders played a vital role as the principal carriers of cargo up to Madurai. From Madurai, the cargo was taken through a variety of routes to the Coromandel ports by Tamil traders.[71]

With the intensification of conflicts between the St. Thomas Christians and the Portuguese, the flow of pepper from predominantly Christian spice-producing centres to Tamil ports increased unprecedentedly. From the Kanjirappally market alone, about 3,220,000 kg (9,000 *bhars*) of pepper were taken through the

Ghat-route to the Coromandel ports, while from Erattupetta 1,66,830 kg (1,000 *bhars*) of pepper moved to the Tamil country through the Ghat-routes. About 5,00,490 kg (3,000 *bhars*) were taken from Erumely to the Coromandel ports via the Ghat. From Thodupuzha, about 8,34,150 kg (5,000 *bhars*) of pepper were taken to inland parts of the subcontinent for domestic consumption and for overseas trade from the Coromandel ports. From Koratty, about 5,00,490 kg (3,000 *bhars*) of pepper and another 5,00,490 kg (3,000 *bhars*) from Palghat were diverted to the routes terminating in the Coromandel ports.[72]

With the translation of anger and resistance into an economic realm, the supply of pepper in Cochin for the Portuguese trade with Europe also dwindled significantly. The Portuguese authorities in Lisbon had also taken note of the damages caused to their European trade following the estrangement of the St. Thomas Christians, who had resorted to the diversion of cargo to the Coromandel ports with the help of Muslim traders. As early as January 1601, the crown sent two letters to Aires de Saldanha, the Viceroy, asking him to specially favour the St. Thomas Christians and to win over their goodwill.[73] Between 1603 and 1605, the pepper supply to the Portuguese factory in Cochin became scanty. In 1602, only 7598 quintals of pepper were transhipped from Cochin to Portugal.[74] Between 1606 and 1609 (both years inclusive), no ship departed from Cochin to Lisbon, as the Portuguese got very little pepper during this period. Whatever they collected during these years was only 4170 quintals, which they only sent to Portugal in 1610.[75] Against this background of the estrangement of the pepper-producing St. Thomas Christians and the dwindling spice-trade, Portuguese vessels also stopped visiting Cochin from 1611 onwards.[76] Consequently, the Portuguese *casado* traders, who found little commercial opportunities in Cochin, started migrating from the city in large numbers to Mylapore, Nagapattinam and Pulicat, where the pepper trade that was diverted from central Kerala finally took place through the Ghat-routes.[77] By 1615/16, almost two-thirds of the population of Cochin moved out of the city and proceeded to the eastern coast of India for taking part in this redirected trade.[78] Thus, a project that was initially carried out with the help of cultural devices for the purpose of keeping the spice-producers within the trajectories of mercantile integration bounced back, affecting the core of the economic activities of the Portuguese.

In fact, the process of collective resistance involving the participation of different segments of Kerala society at varying degrees and levels, particularly between 1599 and 1615, had begun to shake the foundations of the Portuguese commercial edifice. The multiple voices of protest and resistance from a large multitude of social groups and classes seemed so overwhelming that the Portuguese found themselves incapable of containing them. The collective resistance caused large damages to the Portuguese commerce and economy. Both the St. Thomas Christians and the Ravuthar Muslims had developed a social rapport for the purpose of materializing the project of pepper-diversion, which they had developed as an economic device for ventilating their anger towards and resistance to the Portuguese.

OPEN REVOLT OF 1653 AND THE FINAL BREAKING AWAY

Tensions brewed amongst the spice-producing Christians over the ritual changes and cultural modifications that were thrust upon them through the Synod of Diamper and subsequent ecclesiastical exercises. These tensions escalated, eventually got intensified and finally burst out into an open revolt in 1653. The immediate cause for the open revolt against the Portuguese was a series of events that were linked to the expectations of the members of the St. Thomas Christian community about the arrival of a bishop from West Asia. These expectations rose especially with the antagonistic and hostile policies of the various Jesuit bishops appointed for the community.[79] The St. Thomas Christians collectively resented the administration of Bishop Francis Garcia, whose policies and stubbornness alienated a major segment of indigenous Christians. They earnestly believed that a bishop belonging to the East Syrian liturgical tradition from West Asia would come to their land one day to cater to their spiritual needs, as well as to help them restore their old practices and customs, and throw away the yoke of spiritual subjugation thrust upon them by the Portuguese.[80]

As early as 1652, stories about the arrival of a West Asian bishop by the name of Ahatullah spread among the Nazarani settlements of Kerala through seminarians who had gone to Mylapore for a pilgrimage.[81] On hearing this, a large crowd of St. Thomas Christians flocked together at Cochin to receive him. Seeing the size of the crowd and keeping in mind the fomenting of tensions in Cochin, the Portuguese did not allow Ahatullah to land there and forced him go further towards Goa. As there was no sign of the West Asian bishop, the St. Thomas Christians who had gathered at the port-site to receive him became highly excited and agitated. To worsen the situation, a rumour spread that the Portuguese had already drowned the bishop in the deep sea. This disturbed the members of the community.[82] Angry and disappointed, they first went to the Portuguese city of Cochin and stormed and battered the gates.[83] Nothing could contain their emotional outburst which they ventilated while running amok, thus disturbing the law and order conditions in the region between Cochin and Mattancherry. Finally, they gathered round a granite cross planted in Mattancherry and took an oath that they would no longer remain under the *Sampalur pathiris*, or the Portuguese priests belonging to the Jesuit Order.[84] This oath taken in 1653 is generally referred to as the 'Oath of Coonan Cross'. Since all could not touch the granite cross, the agitated mob tied ropes onto it and took the oath while holding these. Interestingly, instead of resorting to weapons to ventilate their anger and frustration, the indigenous Christians rallied around the cross as their final alternative and took their oath by it. This was important as the cross, with which Jesus is said to have liberated the world from evil forces, has been considered by the Christian world as a tool for fighting against evil forces, oppression and hegemony. Similarly, the collective oath by the cross was a powerful device amongst Christian circles, with which the utterly helpless and frustrated segment of society fought the last round of battles against the forces of oppression.[85] The usage of the religious symbol of the cross by the St. Thomas Christians as a mechanism to ventilate their feelings of anger, frustration, and helplessness was significant in the entire process of conflict between the spice-producing Christians and the trading Portuguese Christians, who often used to hide their politico-commercial agenda behind well-articulated religious rhetoric. After a long war of words and symbolisms, the community started developing divisive tendencies from within. This became more obvious in the days following the Coonan Cross Oath and the developments subsequent to it. A major chunk of the St. Thomas Christians broke away from the Portuguese *Padroado* administration and Catholicism. The breakaway group known as *Puthunkur* eventually embraced the West Syrian ecclesiastical and liturgical traditions. These traditions were later instrumental in the introduction of the Jacobite faith amongst them. Those who were supportive of the Portuguese *Padroado* system and continued to adhere to Catholicism came to be known as *Pazhayakur*.[86]

Meanwhile, the Portuguese made serious attempts to contain the split and end the schism by capturing the Archdeacon and his leading men, including Ittithommen *kathanar*, who was responsible for preparing a fake letter from the Pope and for spearheading the division. However, they escaped the Portuguese trap under the guise of Nair soldiers.[87] By moving away from the areas controlled by the Portuguese, the leaders of the *Puthenkur* faction managed to enlist the support of the leading Christian spice-producers of central Kerala. Their main purpose was to mobilize the grassroots to revolt. Except for a small minority that continued to adhere to the Portuguese, the majority of the St. Thomas Christians were eventually made to become anti-Portuguese and non-Catholic.[88] In the course of time, separate administrative arrangements evolved among the *Puthenkur* and *Pazhayakur.* The doctrinal and theological differences between the two only emerged later. From 1748 onwards, these differences became evident, especially with the increasing transplantation of West Syrian ecclesiastical traditions amongst the breakaway group.[89] It is pertinent to note here that it was the ambitious design of the Portuguese mercantile state to control the spice producing Christians to their advantage that brought in splits and divisions in the indigenous Christian community. The scars still remain among them even after the passage of 350 years.

What is significant in the entire development was that both the parties resorted to religious rhetoric, and ritual symbols and platforms for ventilating their ideology. The Portuguese made use of religious rhetoric for legitimizing and realizing their mercantile designs. Allegations of heresy and the rhetoric of orthodoxy were repeatedly harped upon for facilitating the process of Lusitanization among the spice-producing indigenous St. Thomas Christians, and for ensuring standardization and homogenization among them in a way that would facilitate the Portuguese penetration of the spice-production centres. The response of the St. Thomas Christians to these Portuguese attempts was manifold. Initially, it was a simple withdrawal from the overarching power entity and a move to the interior areas located outside Portuguese control. Later, when their bishop was arrested on charges of heresy, their resistance took the form of quasi-military obstructions and resistance. Eventually, when decisions were taken in the religious Synod of Diamper to effect changes in the socio-cultural life of the entire community in a manner that suited Portuguese mercantile designs, the spice-producers reacted *en masse*, translating their resistance into the economic domain by not supplying cargo for the Portuguese trade and diverting it to Tamil ports instead. However, the culmination of tensions was the open revolt where the St. Thomas Christians also started using religious symbols like the cross as a justifiable device to legitimize their collective resistance, and also as a validating instrument for their struggles of liberation from the religious and cultural domination of the Portuguese. In the clash of interests and the fight against hegemonic motives, religious symbols and rhetoric were given usages and meanings other than spiritual ones, enabling them to evolve as tools of assertion.

NOTES

1. *Padroado Real* was a unique experiment in the Catholic church, which developed as an institutional arrangement for evangelical activities in the newly-discovered territories of the Portuguese in Asia, Africa and Brazil. The Portuguese *Padroado Real* (patronage system) took the shape out of

a series of Papal Bulls and Briefs beginning with the Bull *Romanus Pontifex* of 1455 and the *Inter Caetera* of Pope Calixtus II (1456), culminating in the Bull *Praecelsae devotionis* (1514). For details on the *Padroado* System, see Josef Wicki, 'The Portuguese Padroado in India in the Sixteenth Century and Francis Xavier', in E.R. Hambye and H.C. Perumalil, eds., *Christianity in India*, Alleppey: Prakasham Publications, 1972, p. 49; C.R. Boxer, *The Portuguese Sea-borne Empire, 1415-1825*, London: Hutchinson, 1969, p. 228; Ino Godinho, *The Padroado of Portugal in the Orient (1454-1860*), Bombay, 1924, pp. 1-3. According to this system, the king of Portugal was given the right to rule over spiritual matters in the newly-discovered territories as patron of the missions, and to set-up dioceses, religious institutions as well as houses in such territories, where they also held the right of presenting prelates and office holders to vacant seats, religious houses and other ecclesiastical institutions. Virtually, the patronage rights made the Portuguese crown a sole power that could send missionaries to Asia, Africa and Brazil, where the temporal and spiritual domains were made to merge together. This further strengthened the power of the crown. C.R. Boxer, *The Portuguese Sea-borne Empire*, London: Hutchinson, 1975, pp. 129 and 228-9; Pius Malekandathil, 'Cross, Sword and Conflicts: A Study on the Political Meanings of the Conflicts between Padroado Real and Propaganda Fide in India (1623-1800)', paper presented in the National seminar on The Dynamics of Religious Pluralism: Conflicts, Assimilation and Innovation in Pre-modern India, organized by Jawaharlal Nehru Institute of Advanced Study and Centre for Historical Studies, Jawaharlal Nehru University, 18-19 February 2009, pp. 1-3.

2. Nestorian heresy includes the teachings of Nestorius who was a patriarch of Constantinople, and the famous Antiochene theologians like Theodore of Mopseustia and Diodorus. According to them, Jesus Christ had two natures (divine and human) and hence, he had two persons. Further, they believed that Mary was the mother of Jesus, the human person, and not of the divine person. Consequently, they held the view that the reference to her as the 'mother of God' is wrong. Their teachings were condemned by the Catholic church as heretical views in the Council of Ephesus held in AD 431. In fact, the origin of this heresy is traceable to the clashes between the theological schools of Alexandria and Antioch on certain phrases and usages to explain the relation between the humanity and divinity of Jesus Christ. For details, see Arthur Vööbus, *History of the School of Nisibis*, CSCO, vol. 266, Louvain, 1965; Assemani, *Bibliotheca Orentalis*, III, Parts 1 and 2, Rome, 1728; Fendt, *Die Christologie des Nestorius*, Münich,

1910. From Edessa and Nisibis, their teachings eventually spread to the Seleucia and Ctesiphon regions, from where bishops used to come to India to cater to the spiritual needs of the St. Thomas Christians. Against this background of Seleucian connections, the indigenous practices and ritual traditions of the St. Thomas Christians were suspected by the Portuguese to be of Nestorian origin.

3. For details on the origin of Indian Christians, see Mathias Mundadan, *Sixteenth Century Traditions of St. Thomas Christians*, Bangalore: Dharmaram College, 1970, pp. 38-67; Joseph C. Panjikaran, 'Christianity in Malabar with Special Reference to the St. Thomas Christians of the Syro-Malabar Rite', in *Orientalia*, vol. VI, 1926, pp. 103-5; Jonas Thaliath, *The Synod of Diamper*, Rome, 1958; Fr. Bernard, *The History of the St. Thomas Christians*, Pala, 1916; Placid J. Podippara, *The Thomas Christians*, Bombay, 1970.
4. St. Thomas Christians were described as the major cultivators of pepper in central Kerala, See Henri Yule, ed., *Cathay and the Way Thither*, vol. III, Delhi/Liechtenstein: Asian Educational Services, 1967, pp. 216-18 and 248-57. See also ANTT, *Cartas dos Vice-Reis da India*, doc. 95. See also E.R. Hambye, 'Medieval Christianity in India: The Eastern Church', in E.R. Hambye and H.C. Perumalil, ed., *Christianity in India*, Alleppey: Prakasham Publications, 1972, p. 34; Samuel Matteer, *The Land of Charity: A Descriptive Account of Travancore and its People*, Delhi: Asian Educational Services, 1991, pp. 237-8.
5. Pius Malekandathil, 'The Sassanids and the Maritime Trade of India during the Early Medieval Period', in the *Proceedings of the Indian History Congress*, 63rd Session, Amritsar, 2002, Kolkata, 2003, pp. 157-66.
6. Gerd Gropp, 'Christian Maritime Trade of Sassanian Age in the Persian Gulf', in *Archaeologia*, 6, 1997, pp. 85-6; E. Schau, 'Vom Christentum in der Persis', in *Sitzungsberichte Preußischen Akademie der Wissenschaften*, Berlin, 1916, pp. 958-80; Richard N. Frye, 'Bahrain under the Sassanians', in Daniel Potts, ed., *Dilmun: New Studies in the Archaeology and Early History of Bahrain*, Berlin, 1983, p. 169.
7. Henry Yule and Henry Cordier, eds., *The Book of Ser Marco Polo*, vol. II, Delhi: Asian Educational Services, 1998, pp. 375-6.
8. Henry Yule and Henry Cordier, eds., *Cathay and the Way Thither*, vol. III, Delhi: Asian Educational Services, 1998, pp. 63ff.
9. For details on the content of the copper plate, see T.A. Gopinatha Rao, *Travancore Archaeological Series*, vol. II, Madras, 1916, pp. 66-75.
10. Pius Malekandathil, 2002, op. cit., pp. 160-5. The various privileges included a gift of four Ezhava families, four Vellala families, one

thachan and one Vannan (*mannan*) family to the Church of Tharisa. Further, the privileges also included the right of the Church to collect taxes like *thalakkanam*, *enikkanam* (professional taxes from toddy tappers and tree-climbers), *manai meypan kollum ira* (housing tax), *chantan mattu meni ponnu* (tax for using the title *chantan* [channan or Shanar] to show his high social status), *polipponnum* (tax given on special occasions), *iravuchorum* (*balikaram* or tax collected to feed the brahmanas, refugees and destitutes), and *Kudanazhiyum*, collection of a *nazhi* [a type of liquid-measurement] of toddy as tax from each pot tapped). Moreover, the church-men might collect eight *kasu* from each cart that used to take merchandise by land into the market of Kollam (*vayinam*) and four *kasu* from each boat that was used to carry cargo to the port (*vediyilum*). T.A. Gopinatha Rao, 1916, op. cit., pp. 63-71.

11. A. Sreedhara Menon, *Kerala Charitram*, Kottayam: National Book Stall, 1973, p. 135. The grant made to these two Christian merchants was recorded in the form of a *vattezhuthu* inscription on a granite slab, 74 inches by 51 inches, lying at the foot of the open-air cross in front of the Catholic Church at Thazhekkadu near Irinjalakuda.
12. Henri Yule, ed., 1967, op. cit., pp. 216-18 and 248-57. The active involvement of St. Thomas Christians in spice-production was testified by Bishop John Marignoli, who visited Malabar on his way back from Cambulac (Peking in China) and referred to the Christians of Quilon as 'rich people' and as 'owners of pepper plantations'.
13. See Antonio Gouvea, *Jornada do Arcebispo*, Coimbra, 1604; Biblioteca Nacional de Lisboa (BNL), *Reservados*, Cod. 464, 'Vida do Illustrissimo Dom Francisco Garcia Arcebispo de Cranganore por Francisco Teixeira', 1659, Fols. 8-70; João Paulo Oliveira e Costa, 'Os Portugueses e a Cristandade Siro-Malabar (1498-1530)', in *Studia*, 52, Lisboa, 1994.
14. In Portuguese documents, the St. Thomas Christians were described as the major cultivators of pepper in central Kerala. For example, see ANTT, *Cartas dos Vice-Reis da India*, doc. 95; Antonio da Silva Rego, ed., *Documentação para a Historia das Missões*, vol. II, Lisboa: Agencia Giraldas Colonias, 1948, pp. 175-6. See also E.R. Hambye, 'Medieval Christianity in India: The Eastern Church', in E.R. Hambye and H.C. Perumalil, eds., 1972, op. cit., p. 34; Samuel Matteer, *The Land of Charity: A Descriptive Account of Travancore and its People*, Delhi: Asian Educational Services, 1991, pp. 237-8.
15. Antonio de Gouvea, *Jornada do Arcebispo*, Coimbra, 1606 tr. and ed. Pius Malekandathil under the title *Jornada of Dom Alexis de Menezes: A Portuguese Account of the Sixteenth Century Malabar*, Kochi: LRC Publications, 2003 (hereafter as Antonio de Gouvea, *Joranada*), p. 258; Pius Malekandathil, 'Christians and the Cultural Shaping of India in

the First Millennium AD', in *Journal of St. Thomas Christians*, vol. 17, no. 1, January-March 2006, p. 11.

16. Antonio de Gouvea, *Jornada*, pp. 258, 251, 257; Leslie Brown, *The Indian Christians of St. Thomas*, Cambridge: Cambridge University Press, 1982, pp. 205-6.
17. Leslie Brown, 1982, op. cit., p. 177; Ines G. Zupanov, *Disputed Mission*, Delhi: Oxford University Press, 2001, pp. 58 and 93-8; D. Ferroli, *The Jesuits in Malabar*, vol. I, Bangalore, 1939, pp. 300-60.
18. Eugene Tisserant, *Eastern Christianity in India*, tr. E.R. Hambye, Calcutta: Newman Press, 1957; Placid Podipara, *The Thomas Christians*, Bombay, 1970.
19. Antonio de Gouvea, *Jornada*, p. 244.
20. Antonio de Gouvea, *Jornada of Dom Alexis de Menezes*, pp. 57, 124, 212-14.
21. For details on the Christian concentration in the sixteenth and seventeenth centuries, see Biblioteca Nacional de Lisboa (BNL), *Reservados*, Cod. 464, 'Vida do Illustrissimo Dom Francisco Garcia Arcebispo de Cranganore por Francisco Teixeira', 1659, fols. 8-10; Antonio Gouvea, *Jornada do Arcebispo*, Coimbra, 1606.
22. Giovanni di Empoli, 'Viaggio fatto nell'India per Gionni da Empoli fattore su la nave del serenissimo re di Portugallo per conto de marchioni di Lisbona', in G.B. Ramusio, ed., *Delle Navigationi et Viaggi nel qual si contiente la descrittione dell'Africa, et del Paese del Prete Joanni, con varii Viaggi, dal Mar Rosso a Calicut, et in fin all'isole Molucche, dove nascono le Spetieri, et la Navigatione attorno il Mondo*, Venice, 1550, fol. 57; Pius Malekandathil, 'The Portuguese and the St. Thomas Christians: '1500-1570', in K.S. Mathew, Teotonio R. de Souza and Pius Malekandathil, eds., *The Portuguese and the Socio-Cultural Changes in India, 1500-1800*, Lisboa: Fundação Oriente, 2001, p. 128.
23. See the report of the German artillerists given in Gernot Giertz, *Vasco da Gama, die Entdeckung des Seewegs nach Indien: ein Augenzeugenbericht 1497-1499*, Tübingen, 1980, p. 188. For the detailed report of the same, see, Horst G.W. Nüsser, *Frühe Deutsche Entdecker: Asien in Berichten unbekannter deutscher Augenzeugen (1502-6)*, München, 1980, pp. 126-40.
24. Tome Pires, *A Suma Oriental de Tome Pires e o Livro de Francisco Rodrigues*, Armando Cortesão, ed., Coimbra, 1978, p. 180. In this connection, recent research works of Portuguese scholars like João Teles e Cunha, João Paulo Oliveira e Costa and Luis Filipe F.R. Thomaz deserve special mention because of the objective, painstaking research undertaken by them. See João Teles e Cunha 'De Diamper a Mattancherry: Caminhos e Encruzilhadas da Igreja Malabar e Catolica

na India: Os Primeiros Tempos (1599-1624)', in *Anais de Historia de Alem-Mar*, vol. V, 2004, pp. 283-368; João Paulo Oliveira e Costa, 'Os Portugueses e a Cristandade Siro-Malabar (1498-1530), in *Studia*, 52, Lisboa, 1994; Luis Filipe F.R. Thomaz, 'Were Saint Thomas Christians Looked upon as Heretics?', in K.S. Mathew et al., eds., 2001, pp. 27-92.

25. Josef Wicki, ed., *Documenta Indica*, vol. VI, Roma, 1948, p. 180; vol. VII, p. 475. However, in 1607, Fernão Guerreiro estimates the number to be 80,000. See Fernão Guerreiro, *Relação Annual*, vol. II, p. 338; João Teles e Cunha, 2004, op. cit., p. 289.
26. Jacob Kollaparambil, *The Archdeacon of All India*, Rome: Lateran University, 1972.
27. Antonio de Gouvea, *Jornada*, pp. 116-17.
28. Ibid., pp. 162; 164-5; 176; 190; 200-4; 220-1.
29. Ibid., pp. 42-54; see also Jacob Kollaparambil, 1972, op. cit.
30. Raymundo Antonio Bulhão Pato, ed., *Cartas de Affonso de Albuquerque seguidas de documentos que as elucidam*, tom. II, Lisboa, 1884, p. 268; tom. III, pp. 30; 258-9; tom. VI, pp. 114; 398-9.
31. Antonio da Silva Rego, ed., *Documentação para a Historia das Missões do Padroado Portugues do Oriente*, vol. II, Lisboa, 1991, p. 175.
32. For details see João Paulo e Costa, 'Os Portugueses e a cristandade siro-malabar (1498-1530)', in *Studia*, no. 52, Lisboa, 1994, pp. 145-67. For details on the debate on whether the St. Thomas Christians were Nestorians, see Luis Filipe F.R. Thomaz, 'Were Saint Thomas Christians looked upon as Heretics', in K.S. Mathew et al., eds., 2001, pp. 27-91.
33. The news of the Protestant Reformation in Germany reached Cochin by 1521, where there were some sympathizers of Martin Luther. For details, see the letter of Jorge Pock sent to Michael Behaim from Cochin on 1 January 1522 in Ghillany, *Geschichte des Seefahrers Ritter Martin Behaim, Urkunde XXXIV*, Nürnberg, 1853, p. 121; Pius Malekandathil, *The Germans, the Portuguese and India*, Münster: LIT Verlag, 1999, p. 65.
34. For details, see Antonio de Gouvea, *Jornada*, pp. XX-LXXI.
35. Pius Malekandathil, *Portuguese Cochin and the Maritime Trade of India, 1500-1663* (A volume in the South Asian Study Series of Heidelberg University, Germany), Delhi: Manohar, 2001.
36. For details on the accusations levelled by Alvaro Penteado, see Antonio da Silva Rego, ed., 1948, op. cit., vol. III, pp. 543-53; João Paulo e Costa, 1994, op. cit., pp. 145-67.
37. In 1522, Padre Alvares Penteado came back from Portugal with a mission to Europeanize and Latinize indigenous Christians. See Antonio da Silva Rego, ed., 1948, op. cit., vol. II, pp. 357-61.

38. Ibid., pp. 358ff.
39. Teotonio R de Souza, 'The Indian Christians of St. Thomas and the Portuguese Padroado: A Rape Only After a Century-long Dating (1498-1599)'. A paper presented in the International Seminar on Christians and Spices, Freising, University of Munich, 14-17 January 1997, p. 2, no. 3; Pius Malekandathil, in K.S. Mathews et al., 2001, op. cit., pp. 133-5.
40. Ibid., pp. 135-7: George Schurhammer, *The Malabar Church and Rome during the Early Portuguese Period and Before*, Trichinopoly, 1934, pp. 17-19.
41. Antonio de Gouvea, *Jornada*, pp. XLVIII-XLIX.
42. Thomas Pallippurathukkunnel, *A Double Regime in the Malabar Church*, Alwaye, 1982, pp. 3-4. See also Isabel dos Guimaraes Sa, 'Ecclesiastical Structures and Religious Action', in Francisco Bethencourt and Diogo Ramada Curto, eds., *Portuguese Oceanic Expansion, 1400-1800*, Cambridge: Cambridge University Press, 2007, pp. 255-80; João Paulo e Costa, 'The Padroado and the Catholic Mission in Asia during the 17th Century', in Ernst van Veen and Leonard Blusse, eds., *Rivalry and Conflict: European Traders and Asian Trading Networks in the 16th and 17th Centuries*, Leiden: CNWS Publications, 2005, pp. 71-88.
43. Antonio de Gouvea, *Jornada*, pp. LIV-LV.
44. The defects in the functioning of the *Padroado* system later made Pope Gregory XIV set up *Propaganda Fide* in 1622. He entrusted a major portion of Asia to the ecclesiastical administrative arrangement of *Propaganda*. However, in 1838, *Padroado* was suppressed by the Pope despite severe opposition from the Portuguese crown, and the strained relationship between Rome and Portugal continued up to 1886. For more details, see Dominic, 'The Latin Missions under the Jurisdiction of Propaganda (1637-1838)', in H.C. Perumalil and E.R. Hambye, 1972, op. cit., pp. 102-3.
45. Pius Malekandathil, in K.S. Mathews et al., eds., 2001, pp. 123-30; Mathias Mundadan, *St. Thomas Christians, 1498-1552*, Bangalore: Church History Association of India, 1967, pp. 76-120.
46. Josef Wicki, *Missionskirche im Orient*, 1976, p. 204; Josef Wicki, *Documenta Indica*, vol. III, Roma: Monumenta Historica Societatis Iesu, 1948, pp. 800-1; 754. Joseph Thekkedath, *History of Christianity in India*, vol. II, Bangalore: Church History Association of India, 1988, p. 48.
47. Josef Wicki, *Documenta Indica*, vol. III, p. 801.
48. Giuseppe Beltrami, *La Chiesa Caldea nel Secolo dell'Unione, Orientalia Christiana*, vol. 29, Rome, 1933, pp. 89-93.
49. Antonio de Gouvea, *Jornada*, pp. XLVI-LXIV.

50. Josef Wicki, *Documenta Indica*, vol. XI, Rome, 1950, pp. 62; 65. Mar Abraham was in Malabar for some time during Mar Joseph's time. He went to Venice to get valid Episcopal consecration so that he might not be ousted by the Portuguese on charges of heresy.
51. Antonio da Silva Rego, ed., *Documentação para a Historia das Missões*, vol. XII, Lisboa, pp. 321-2; 411-12; Joseph Thekkedath, 1988, op. cit., pp. 53-5; Cyriac Thevarmannil, 'Mar Abraham, the Archbishop of St. Thomas Christians in Malabar, 1506-1597', Ph.D. thesis submitted to the Gregorian University, Rome, 1965, pp. 162-4; Giuseppe Beltrami, 1933, op. cit., pp. 115-16.
52. In fact, the king of Cochin came forward to defend Mar Abraham by sending a letter to the Pope, saying that the prelate did not attend the council because of the fear of Portuguese persecution and ill-treatment. In 1578, Pope Gregory XIII asked Mar Abraham to attend the next councils assuring him of safety, to which effect the Pope had also written to the Portuguese bishops of India and the king of Portugal. Antonio da Silva Rego, ed., *Documentação para a Historia das Missões*, vol. XII, pp. 321-2; 411-12.
53. Joseph Thekkedath, 1988, op. cit., pp. 53-5.
54. Cyriac Thevarmannil, 1965, op. cit., pp. 162-4.
55. Giuseppe Beltrami, 1933, op. cit., pp. 115-16.
56. With the frequent allegations of heretical practices against Mar Abraham, Pope Clement VIII ordered an inquiry into the life and teachings of the bishop in 1595. Mar Abraham eventually died in 1597. See Giuseppe Beltrami, 1933, pp. 115-16.
57. Jonas Thaliath, *The Synod of Diamper*, Rome, 1958.
58. Ibid., p. 24.
59. *Archivum Romanum Societatis Iesu*, Goa-Mal, XV, fols. 155-6 (Letter of Bishop Roz S.J. dated 20-11-1603 addressed to Claudius Aquaviva, the Jesuit General in Rome), fols.176-8; Jonas Thaliath, 1958, op. cit., pp. 139-42.
60. *Archivum Romanum Societatis Iesu*, Goa-Mal, XV, fols. 182-3 (Letter of John Campori dated 1-1-1604 addressed to John Alvarez, the Portuguese Assistant to the Jesuit General in Rome).
61. Antonio de Gouvea, *Jornada*, p. LXX.
62. Ibid., pp. XXVI-LXIV
63. Antonio de Gouvea, *Jornada*, pp. 116-17; 176; 179; 177-8; 426-8; 229; 128ff; 231-4; 341-58; 148-51 and 200-4.
64. Ibid., pp. 120-92; 293-449.
65. Antonio de Gouvea, *Jornada of Dom Alexis de Menezes*, pp. 129-30.
66. Ibid., p. 134.
67. Ibid., p. 57.

68. Ibid.
69. Ibid., pp. 166-8.
70. Antonio de Gouvea, *Jornada do Arcebispo*, Coimbra, 1606, pp. 208-9. The Ravuthar Muslims of Kanjirappally, an interior marketplace of central Kerala, trace back their origin to Moosavannan Ravuthar, Kulasekhara Khan and Mollamiya Labha who came to Kanjirappally from Madurai in AD 1373. From there, these Ravuthar Muslims eventually spread to Erumely, Erattupetta and Thodupuzha. For details, see Jacob Aerthail, *Kanjirappally Noottandukaliloode*, 1985, pp. 88-97. Even now they use certain Tamil words in their daily Malayalam conversations.
71. Pius Malekandathil, 'The Portuguese and the Ghat-Route Trade: 1500-1663', in *Pondicherry University Journal of Social Sciences and Humanities*, vol. I, nos. 1 & 2, Pondicherry, 2000, pp. 137-48.
72. The report of Francisco da Costa, 'Relatorio sobre o Trato da Pimenta', in Antonio da Silva Rego, *Documentação Ultramarina Portuguesa*, vol. III, Lisboa, 1972, p. 315.
73. HAG, *Livro das Monções*, no. 7 (1601-3), royal letter sent to Viceroy Aires de Saldanha dated 2 January 1601, fols. 21-4; another letter dated 22 January 1601, fols. 27-30.
74. Niels Steensgaard, *Carracks, Caravan and Companies: The Structural Crisis in the European-Asian Trade in the Early Seventeenth Century*, Kopenhaven, 1973, p. 166.
75. AHU, *Caixas da India*, Caixa 1, doc. 101, dated 25 February 1611.
76. Pius Malekandathil, 2001, op. cit., p. 254.
77. AHU, *Caixas India*, Caixa 2, doc. 107. The letter of the city council of Cochin sent to Philip II (Philip III of Spain) giving an account of the economic condition of Cochin dated 21-12-1613; Pius Malekandathil 2000, op. cit., pp. 145-6.
78. AHU, *Caixas da India*, Caixa 2, doc. 107; AHU, *Caixas da India*, Caixa 3, doc. 29, dated 25-1-1615; AHU, *Caixas da India*, Caixa 3, doc. 31, dated 25-1-1615. The Viceroy, D. Jeronimo de Azevedo, in his letter addressed to the Portuguese crown, refers to the reduction of the population of Cochin to one-third following these developments. HAG, *Livro das Monções*, no. 12 (1613-17), fols. 254-80, dated March 1617.
79. Since the time of Bishop Roz (1599-1624), Jesuits were appointed as spiritual heads of the St. Thomas Christian community. Stephen Britto, another Jesuit, was made a bishop in 1624 and on his death in 1641, Francis Garcia was appointed. He died in 1659. See Joseph Thekkedath, 1988, op. cit., pp. 75-99.
80. Joseph Thekkedath, *The Troubled Days of Francis Garcia S.J., Arch-*

bishop of Cranganore (1641-59), Rome: Universita Gregoriana, 1972, pp. 40-52; 73-82.

81. Ibid., pp. 51-2; 73-82.
82. Ibid., pp. 52-62.
83. AHU, *Caixas da India*, Caixa 22, doc. 23, dated 4 March 1653, Caixa 23, doc. 20, dated 5 February 1655.
84. There are differences of opinion among scholars about the nature of the oath. Some hold the view that the rebels pledged not to remain under the Pope. Others say that they did not rebel against him. What they did was refuse to subjugate themselves to the Jesuit ecclesiastical authorities and priests, who were then known as *Sampalur pathiris*, a term that denoted priests from the Jesuit college of São Paulo of Goa. The probability lies with the second view, as the breakaway group did not change the Catholic teachings at least till 1748, when it was necessitated by the demands of the West Syrian bishops.
85. There were more or less similar cases of Christians using churches and crosses as a mechanism to resist and oppose the arbitrary decisions of rulers and the oppression of the Portuguese authorities in Cochin. When the Portuguese officials raised the customs duty levied on the private traders of Cochin in 1583, about 15,000 Christians (10,000 local Christians and 5,000 Portuguese), some of them carrying crosses, marched into the church of St. John, clamouring for the reduction of customs duty. For details, see Diogo do Couto, *Asia dos feitos que os Portuguezes fizeram na Conquista e Descobrimento das Terras e Mares do Oriente*, part I, liv. IV, Decada XIII, Lisboa, 1973, pp. 472-80.
86. For details, see Jacob Kollaparambil, *The St. Thomas Christians' Revolution in 1653*, Kottayam, 1981; Jacob Kollaparambil, 1972, op. cit.; Joseph Thekkedath, 1972, op. cit.
87. Joseph Thekkedath, 1972, op. cit., pp. 152-9; Joseph Thekkedath, 1988, op. cit., pp. 99-100.
88. Many of these breakaway Christians were later brought back to Catholicism with the appointment of an indigenous bishop, Mar Alexander Parambil, from the community of St. Thomas Christians. Through his efforts many *Puthenkur* parishes were made to become Catholic. See Joseph Thekkedath, 1988, pp. 100-9.
89. West Syrian bishops used to intervene decisively in the affairs of the *Puthenkur* Christians from 1748 onwards when Mar Ivanios launched attempts to change their liturgy and theology. Konat MSS No. 34, J.P.M. van der Ploeg, *The Syriac Manuscripts of St. Thomas Christians*, Bangalore, 1983, pp. 255-64. He also burned crucifixes and images of saints used in the churches (evidently used by both the Jacobites and

Catholics) as a part of the attempts to introduce West Syrian theology. Paulinus Bartholomeo, *India Orientalis Christiana*, Rome, 1796, p. 86. Later, in 1751, a team of West Syrian prelates led by Mar Baselius Sakrallah came to Kerala. They organized and made systematic moves to introduce Jacobite ideology and West Syrian ritual practices among the *Puthenkur* faction on an extensive scale. See also M. Kurian Thomas, *Niranam Grandhavari*, Kottayam, 2000, pp. 85-100.

THIRTEEN

Sufis and Communal Harmony

A Case Study of Indian Sufis

S.M. Azizuddin Husain

A dictionary of Islam defines *Sufiyah* as a man of the people who professes the mystic principles of *Tasawwuf*. Such men in popular parlance were known as the Sufis. The origin of the word Sufi can be traced to various roots, for example, to the Arabic *Suf* which means wool. This was on account of the woollen dress worn by the Eastern ascetics. The word Sufi is also derived from the Arabic *Safu*, meaning purity, with reference to the effort to attain metaphysical purity. According to the *Ghiyaas-ul-lughaat*, it is derived from the *Sufah*, the name of a tribe of Arabs who in the time of ignorance separated themselves from the world and engaged themselves exclusively in the service of the Makkah Temple.[1]

It would not have been very easy to engraft mysticism over Quranic lessons. However, it is generally admitted by the Sufis that one of the great founders of their system, was the son-in-law of the Prophet and the fourth Caliph, Ali-ibn-Abu-Talib. All the Sufi *silsilahs* with the exception of the Naqshbandiyya, start with Ali because he never discriminated between the Arabs and non-Arabs and behaved impartially towards them. He was also very sympathetic towards the downtrodden in society and lived an exemplary, simple life. It was for this reason that Ali became the point of attraction for the Sufis who traced their source of inspiration to him. Ali shifted the capital of the Islamic state from the Arab-dominated town of Madina to Kufa. Kufa was a military cantonment and also the most planned urban centre, and was, thus, the confluence of people belonging to different religious and social groups. More than 50 per cent of the population was of non-Arab origin and were mostly slaves or liberated slaves. Most Sufis accept that their religious system had always existed in the world, even prior to the rise of Islam. Indeed, mysticism as a way of religious emotionalism and simple spirituality can be traced to other religions as well like the bhakti stream of Hinduism, or in the writings of the philosophers of Greece such as Plato.[2]

The rise of Sufism in Arabia was prompted by its own socio-cultural context. However, amongst the reasons of political hue, one issue was that Islam believed in democracy and the democratic functioning of the state, which continued up to Ali, the fourth Caliph. But in AD 661, Muawiyah converted the Caliphate into *mulukiyat* (absolute monarchy). After the assassination of Ali, Muawiyah laid the foundation of Umayyad rule. Yazid, the son and successor of Muawiyah, openly violated the tenets of Islam. In AD 681, Imam Husain protested against this and he, along with his family members and companions, was killed. In 682, Madina and Mecca were attacked and plundered, and the result was the rape and massacre of innocent people.[3] Abdullah bin Zubair was executed.[4] Kufa and Basra were the main targets of barbarism and tyranny since AD 661. It is likely that the Sufi movement originated in these very towns as a fallout of the challenging political and socio-cultural circumstances.

It is obvious that diverse inter and intra-religious systems have their own powerful mechanisms for confirming to a particular belief. Often, the confirmation comes from the past experiences of the community or communities in question. In such cases, the present starts manipulating the past. This could happen through a systematic way of selection, reduction or enhancement of evidence and facts. There might be an overplay or underplay of incidents that may be useful in justifying a current demand or situation. The development of consciousness and identity are complex issues, and their evolution cannot be studied in a simplistic manner. Exactly why and how religious philosophers feel and think in a certain way at a certain point in time may remain unclear, but what sometimes is comparatively clear and probably more important is the positive impact of their thought process. The cognitive science of religion is a new approach to the scientific study of religion. Cognitive science is the set of disciplines that investigate the mind-brain process involved in human thought and behaviour. Scholars in the cognitive science of religion explain features of religious thought and behaviour that recur across cultures and eras in terms of mental processes involved in their production and transmission. Religion, along with other forms of culture like music, art and literature, is understood by cognitive scientists as a natural by-product of the way our mind-brain functions. Cognitive scientists of religion are primarily interested in explaining religion, which they distinguish from theology. Religion for them is a set of actual religious concepts that people have in their heads and the behaviour they perform. Theology is the set of creeds that the clergy instruct people to believe in. Islamic Sufism is an interesting mix of this 'religion' and 'theology'. The early Sufis of Arabia were probably designing, consciously or unconsciously, an emotional revolt against the exploitation of religious systems for perpetuating imperialism, separatism and corruption. Their mission was to establish peace and harmony in the society. Sufi scholars like Shaikh Ali Hajweri (b. AD 1072), the author of *Kashful Mahjub*, Shaikh Muhiuddin Ibn-i-Arabi (b. AD 1248), the author of *Futuhat-i-Makkiya* and *Fususul Hikam*, Shaikh Shahabuddin Suhrawardi (b. AD 1234) and Maulana Jalaluddin Rumi (b. AD 1273) created a treasure of philosophy of religious emotionalism. The Sufis divided the universe into their *vilayats* (spiritual territories) and India was one of these. They played a significant and positive role in Indian society.

The famous doctrine of Mohiuddin Ibn-i-Arabi's *Wahdatul Wujud* (Unity of Being) was a revolutionary doctrine as far as harmony between the followers of different religions was concerned. This doctrine implied that the entire mankind is one and reflects the glory of god. It meant that the essential being is one and we all are its manifestations. When put to practical and emotional use, the doctrine of *Wahdatul Wujud* inculcates a sense of unity amongst all human beings. It also induces respect for nature and other objects in the universe, as everything in the universe is a reflection of divine glory. Ibn-i-Arabi's verses have always fascinated students of his thought:

> Within my heart, all forms may find a place, the cloister of the monk, the idol's frame, a pasture of gazelles, the Sacred Home of God, to which all Muslims turn face: The Table of the Jewish Law, the world of God revealed unto His Prophet true. Love is the faith I hold, and wheresoever His camels turn, the one true faith is there.

Thus, the doctrine of *Wahdatul Wujud* was instrumental in promoting communal harmony by eliminating all formal differences of faiths. This attitude was of great importance in the context of the Indian subcontinent because of the heterogeneous religious milieu of the place.

Shaikh Ahmed Sirhindi refuted the doctrine of *Wahdatul Wujud* and propounded the doctrine of *Wahdatush Shuhud* (Unity of Witnessing) instead. What was implied was that though we witness such unity, it does not exist. Existence does not emanate from God since he is distant and transcendent. However, it was the all-embracing and all-inclusive *Wahdatul Wujud* which was the accepted popular notion in India. *Wahdatush Shuhud* could never compete successfully with it. Although Shah Waliullah tried to work out a synthesis of the two divergent philosophies, it did not find many takers and remained confined to a small section of scholars. Akbar's policy of *Sulh-i-kul* (Peace with all) was also based on *Wahdatul Wujud.* So was Abul Fazl and Faizi's religious outlook. This implies that the popularity of this notion had cut across class structures, and commoners as well as the most brilliant scholars of the age were influenced by it.

Maulana Jalaluddin Rumi sums up the substance of the story in his own characteristic way. According to him, 'The religion of love is apart from all religions. The lovers of God have no religion but God alone.' Hafiz Shirazi echoes it in his own superb way when he says: 'The good of this world and that can be summed up in a few words: that is kindness towards friends and hospitality towards enemies.' The noted Persian and Urdu poet, Mirza Ghalib (b.1797), highlighting the doctrine of unity of being and one creed, says: 'to renounce all formalities (of faith) the (different) communities, when obliterated, became ingredients of (my) faith'.

Mir Anis (1805-74), a famous *marsiya* poet, sums up the essence of *Wahdatul Wujud* in his *rubai*. Shii *mujtahids* of Lucknow who were *usulis* asked Mir Anis to give an explanation of his religion because Maulana Dildar Ali (b. 1752), a Shii *alim*, had declared the Sufis as *kafirs* in his work *Shihab-i-Saqib* as they believed in *Wahdatul Wujud*. Mir Anis was also the descendent of a famous Sufi saint, Saiyid Muhammed Gaisu Daraz of the Deccan. This is why Anis says:

Har rang main jalwa hai teri qudrat ka
Jis phool ko sunghta hou bu teri hai

Each colour bears the splendour of your Essence. Whichever flower I smell, the fragrance is yours.

So the Sufis never hesitated to assimilate spiritual insights from other faiths. Their ideas were more akin to those in the Quranic verse which emphasized that 'for everyone there is direction to which one turns, so view with each other in good deeds'.

Once Shaikh Nizamuddin Aulia went for a morning walk to Ghiyaspura, along the banks of the river Yamuna. There he saw some Hindu women worshipping the rising sun. On seeing these women in the act of worship, he told his poet disciple, Amir Khusrau, that 'for every people there is religion and direction to which they turn to pray'. These words were a literal translation of the Quranic verse quoted above and deeply reflected Auliya's approach towards other religions. Auliya used to recite this verse often.

Another idea that had an impact on the Sufis was taken from the Quranic verse: 'He who is not my friend—May God be his friend! And he who bears ill-will against me, may his joys increase. He, who puts thorns in my way on account of enmity, may every flower that blossoms in the garden of his life, be without thorns.'

Sufis adopted an attitude of sympathy and understanding towards all creeds. They said that, 'O you, who sneer at the idolatry of the Hindu, learn also from him how worship is done.' Sufis believed in universal brotherhood and never made any individual distinction between the people of different creeds, races, communities and sects. The concept of god, people and the existence of the universe is very clear and lucid in the Koran. This enlightened and influenced the Sufis and they put it to use through preaching and practice. As Jami explains: 'Jami, you have become the slave of love, so you just forbade pride in genealogy because in the path of love, you are the son of such and such is meaningless.'

The fundamentals of Sufi ideology rested on the relationship of love that exists between god and man. They helped in developing a more humanitarian approach in religious life with a stress on service to mankind and a belief that the love of God was not possible without love for mankind. The Sufis, unlike the *ulemas*, did not keep themselves aloof from the Indian masses. They knew Arabic and Persian but they adopted the local idiom, and preached the message of love and universal brotherhood in the local languages. They also adopted local customs and traditions and, thus, drew the Indian masses towards Islam. Thus, they played a greater role in spreading the universal values of Islam than the doctrinaire *ulemas*. As Ibn Hujveri rightly commented: 'You will not find God in the books on jurisprudence; see the mirror of your heart, because no book is better than this.'

Islam, as practised by the Sufis, was somehow more influential than the Islam of the ambitious Turkish conquerors. The Sufis believed in equality and fraternity of mankind. They abjured narrowness of the mind and opposed communal, sectarian and caste barriers, which caused conflict and destroyed social harmony. The outstanding Sufis who played a revolutionary role in the social, cultural and religious life of India were Khwaja Moinuddin Chishti of Rajasthan, Shaikh Fariduddin Ganj-i-Shakar of Punjab, Shaikh Bahaduddin Zakariya of Punjab, Shaikh Nizamuddin Aulia of Delhi, Mir Saiyid Ali Hamedani of Kashmir, Saiyid Muhammed Gaisu Daraz of Deccan, Shaikh Latif, Shaikh Jalal Thanesri and others. These Sufis had divided the whole of north India and some parts of the south up to the Deccan into their *vilayats*. They worked in Kashmir, Sindh, Punjab, Bihar, Bengal, Gujarat, Maharashtra, Awadh and the Deccan. On the basis of their unparalleled moral standards and sweet spiritual voice, they propagated Islam in India and opened a new epoch in Islamic history for a better understanding of other religions and cultures. Human values and good interreligious relations were stressed upon.

Shaikh Fariduddin Ganj-i-Shakar established his *khanqah* at Ajodhan, a town in Punjab. He was the first Indian Sufi who had cordial relations with Hindu thinkers. He wrote excellent poetry in Arabic, Persian, Punjabi and the local Hindavi dialect. His *shlokas* and *shabads* have been incorporated into the *Guru Granth Sahib* by the fifth *guru*, Arjun Singh. Baba Farid adopted Punjabi and, in turn, the Sikhs adopted Persian. Baba Farid's poetry was a means of creating a congenial moral atmosphere in Punjab. His *shlokas* and *shabads* won the hearts of the Punjabi people. His Punjabi and Hindavi poetry became immortal and, even today, his verses are sung in Punjab.

Amir Khusrau (1253-1325), born of an Indian mother and Turkish father, personified the diffusion of these two cultures, imbibing the best of both. Extremely proud of being an Indian and intensely devoted to Hindavi, he occupies a prominent position as one of the spiritual benefactors of mankind on the basis of his love towards the common people of India. Khusrau endeavoured to transform the common speech of the people into a literary language, 'Hindavi', which he regarded as not being second to either Arabic or Persian. Khusrau also brought about a synthesis of Indian and Iranian music.

In the socio-religious life of the Deccan, Burhanuddin Gharib, Saiyid Zainuddin Daood, Shaikh Ainuddin Bijapuri, Saiyid Muhammed Gaisu Daraz and Shaikh Sirajuddin Junaidi played a significant role. One of the most celebrated figures in the early history of Sufism in the Deccan was Saiyid Muhammed Gaisu Daraz, who played a conspicuous role there. Hindus frequently visited him and stayed in his *khanqah* without any inhibition.[5] He also read Sanskrit books to know about the mythologies of the Hindus.[6] Saiyid Muhammed Gaisu Daraz's father, Saiyid Yusuf, composed the *Manan Suhagan Nama* in Dakkani. Gaisu Daraz also wrote the *Mairajul Ashiqin* in Dakkani, which is a symbol of composite culture and social integration. The liberal attitude of the Sufis created a harmonious atmosphere, and their *khanqahs* became the centres of cultural synthesis and communal harmony. That is why a new language known as Dakkani originated in the *khanqahs* of the Sufis of the Deccan.

Shaikh Muhammed Baba of Shirgonda of the Ahmednagar district gave his message in Marathi. With Marathi, the Sufis established a dialogue with and within the entire Marathi-knowing community of Maharashtra. Shivaji's grandfather, Maluji's wife was barren and he went to a Sufi, Shah Sharif, and sought his blessings for having children. Subsequently, two sons were born to her whom he named after the Sufi as Shahji and Shivaji.[7] The nineteenth-century reformer, M.G. Ranade, is of the opinion that some Mohammedan *fakirs* have been ranked with Hindu saints in general veneration, and there are some saints who are venerated by both communities alike. These features of tolerance and moderation have been developed in the course of centuries and they constitute some of the most stable elements in the national character.[8]

Sufism had a deep impact on Sindhi life and literature. The humanist outlook and harmonious approach, especially through the liberal poetry of the Sufi poets like Qazi Qadan, Abdul Karim, Shah Inayat, Shah Latif, Sarmast, Sami, Bedil, Bekas, Dalpat and others from the middle of the sixteenth to the nineteenth century, reflects the impact. All these poets had condemned communal hatred and religious bigotry, and preached communal harmony and social integration. Shah Latif (1690-1750) and Sachal (1739-1829) were influential and are household names for both Sindhi Muslims and Hindus till today. Sachal was a multilingual poet of Sindhi, Persian and Urdu, and used Persian prosody along with indigenous forms. He boldly spoke in favour of a classless and peaceful society, which would form a base for communal harmony. He warned the people against rising British power as well. He had said: 'Hindus and Muslims unite in bond of love. Before it is too late and the Sun sets in the west.' And indeed, Sachal's fears proved true because we did suffer many losses due to the 'policy of divide and rule', which the British administrators followed in the Indian subcontinent.

Several Sufis authored epic romances. Through the *Padmavat*, Jaysi tried to open the eyes of all those who advocated separation between followers of different religions. He said that the *viyog* of Ratna Sen for Padmavati was the same as that of Alauddin for her. The text evokes emotions and feelings for different characters, irrespective of their caste, colour or religion. Jaysi asserts that all humans emote in the same way. Basic human responses to situations do not have much to do with formal religion. During the course of humanitarian interaction, bonds of religion, caste, sect and nationality break down automatically, and there emerges a perfect being whose heart is tender, liberal, permissive and powerful. Jaysi wrote thousands of verses in Avadhi but in the Persian script. His description of events appear to be close to the cultural and social reality, as they were narrated without any modifications. Jaysi followed the tradition of Khusrau's *masnavis* in the *Chandayan.* Similarly, Shaikh Qutban of Jaunpur wrote the *Mrigawati* (1503), an epic of love and romance. Qutban utilized Hindu mythology, astrology and many religious symbols to weave a wonderful tale which culminated in preaching oneness and the unity of god.

In retrospect, we can see that as the basic ideas and attitudes of Sufism were translated from Arabic to Persian, they were expressed in Hindavi, Rajasthani, Punjabi, Marathi, Sindhi and Dakkani. The Sufis promoted communal harmony with their devoted activities, and attracted the casteridden and oppressed lower sections to their organizational fold. Titus rightly said that, 'It was through Sufism that Islam really found a point of contact with Hinduism and an effective entrance to the Hindu heart.'[9] R.K. Megh holds the opinion that, 'We can thus conclude that whenever there is a crisis of cultural identity, or the romantic spirit is resurrected, the Sufi heritage would speak with a thousand tongues to us all.'[10]

We see that following the death of Muhammed Ghori, the Ghorid empire broke up. His favourite slave, Yalduz, succeeded him at Ghazni, while another slave, Qubecha, seized control of

Multan and Uchh. Another of his slaves, Qutubuddin Aibak, became the Sultan of Delhi in 1206 and India was divided. But the dream of united India was seen by a Sufi, Shaikh Bahauddin Zakaria of the Suhrawardi order. After the death of Aibak, Iltutmish became the Sultan of Delhi in 1210. Shaikh Bahauddin Zakaria had his *khanqah* in Multan and invited Iltutmish to attack Multan. Iltutmish followed the direction given by the Sufi and Qubecha was defeated. The whole of Punjab came under the direct rule of Delhi.[11] So we see that the Sufis played an important role in uniting India and Punjab during the thirteenth century, whereas Indian scholars educated at Cambridge, Oxford and other Indian universities agreed to the partition of Punjab, Bengal as well as India, which resulted in bloodbaths and communal hatred.

Some of the poets joined the romantic group of liberals who composed works on love and beauty. All of them believed that love could not be realized without beauty and that one must sacrifice oneself in the fire of love. Yet they were clearly against lust. They transformed their *Ishq-i-Majaz* into *Ishq-i-Haqi* and elevated the woman of pleasure and dance into a spiritual symbol. Amongst such prominent romantic rebels of the eighteenth and nineteenth century were Bodha (eighteenth century), Thakur (eighteenth century) and Ghananand (nineteenth century). Almost all of them were under the deep influence of the Sufis. *Ishq Nama* by Bodha and *Ishq Lata* by Ghananand are glowing examples. It appears that Sufi influence had become a strong archetype in our cultural pattern. The *Rubaiyat-i-Umar Khaiyam* is popularly tinted with Sufi thought and it has been variously translated by Hindi poets of different schools and periods. Bhagwati Charan Verma and Jaya Shankar Prasad have intimately drawn from Sufi idioms.

The Sufis refrained from hollow argumentation and lived a life of poverty, piety, trust, patience, resignation and love. They practised and preached these values and thereby created a peaceful and progressive society. The Sufis were never sectarian because they never identified with any particular sect. All the Sufi poets condemned communal hatred and religious bigotry, and preached communal harmony and social integration. They stood for cultural co-existence and this Sufi idea became the norm of mutual community relations during the medieval period in India. This is the great legacy which Sufis left for succeeding generations in India. Respect for cultural diversity is perhaps their greatest contribution to Indian civilization.

Today, when we are facing a great challenge from communal and divisive forces bent upon promoting conflict in the name of creed, sect and caste, it is necessary to revive the spirit of the Sufi and bhakti saints. Real spiritualists can play a vital role in the spiritual evolution of a pluralistic society which will promote peace, harmony and humanitarianism. We need them again.

NOTES

1. Thomas Patrick Hughes, *Dictionary of Islam*, Delhi: Rupa, 1993, pp. 608-9.
2. Ibid.
3. Jurji Zaydan, *History of Islamic Civilization*: *Umayyads and Abbasids*, Pt. 4, D.S. Margoliouth, tr., 1987, Delhi: Kitab Bhavan, p. 139; *Tarikh-i-Ibn Khalladun*, 2 vols., Beirut: Dar Ibn Hazm, 2003, pp. 139-40.
4. Ibid., vol. II, pp. 184-94.
5. Syed Shah Khusro Husaini, *Sayyid Muhammed al-Husayni Gaisu Daraz*, Delhi: Idarah-i-Adabiyat-i-Delhi, 1985, p. 7.
6. M. Sulaiman Siddiqi, 'Origin and Development of Chishti Order in the Deccan', in *Islamic Culture*, vol. I, L1, no. 3, July 1977, p. 218.
7. P.V. Ranade, *Binocular Glossary of Vedanta and Tasawwuf of Shaikh Muhammed*, Bombay: Natraj Books, 1973, p. 74.
8. B. Nemade, *Tukaram*, Bombay: Popular Prakashan, 1980, p. 8.
9. Murray T. Titus, *Islam in India and Pakistan*: *A Religious History of Islam in India and Pakistan*, Delhi: Munshiram Manoharlal, 1959, p. 36.
10. R.K. Megh, *The Influence of Sufism in the Growth of Hindi Poetry*, p. 208.
11. M.M. Khizr, *Sufism and Social Integration*, a publication of SAARC literary wing, New Delhi, p. 119; P.D. Jassal, *The Life and Message of Guru Ravidas*, Delhi: National Book Shop, 1999, p. 169.

Contributors

S.M. AZIZUDDIN teaches at the Department of History and Culture at Jamia Millia Islamia, New Delhi. He is currently the Dean of the Faculty of Humanities and Languages, Jamia Millia Islamia. S.M. Azizuddin's research interests include religion and religious ideas in Islam, art and architecture in pre-colonial India, the history of social medicine, and the study of archives. He has authored seven books, which include *Kalimat-i-Taiyabat Idara-i-Adabiyat-i-Delhi* (1982); *Structure of Politics under Aurangzeb* (2002) and *1857 Revisited* (2007).

RAMESHWAR PRASAD BAHUGUNA teaches at the Department of History and Culture at Jamia Millia Islamia, New Delhi. His research interests include the history of the sant movement and the religion of marginalized sections in pre-colonial South Asia.

UMA CHAKRAVARTI taught history at Miranda House College, University of Delhi. Her areas of interest are gender, caste and the study of Buddhism with a focus on early India. Uma Chakravarti is also a well-known social activist. Her publications include *Everyday Lives and Everyday Histories: Beyond the Kings and Brahmanas of Ancient India* (2006), *Delhi Riots: Three Days in the Life of a Nation* (co-ed. Nandita Haksar, 1996), *The Social Dimensions of Early Buddhism* (1987), *Rewriting History: The Life and Times of Pandita Ramabai* (2000), *From Myths to Markets: Essays on Gender* (co-ed. Sudesh Vaid, 1999) and *Gendering Caste: Through a Feminist Lens* (2003).

RANJEETA DUTTA teaches at the Department of History and Culture, Jamia Millia Islamia, New Delhi. Her research interests are religion and religious identities in pre-colonial India with special emphasis on the peninsular region. Currently she is a Fellow at the Indian Institute of Advanced Study, Shimla.

N.R. FAROOQI teaches in the Department of Medieval and Modern History at the University of Allahabad and is currently the Dean of the Faculty of Arts there. He was a Junior Fulbright Fellow at the University of Wisconsin-Madison from 1978-9, Fellow at the American Institute of Indian Studies, Chicago, USA, from 1981-2, Senior Leverhume Fellow at the Oxford Centre for Islamic Studies, Oxford University, from 1994-5 and Fulbright Visiting Specialist at the University of Pennsylvania, Pittsburgh, in 2004. His publications include *Mughal Ottoman Relations: A Study of Political and Diplomatic Relations Between Mughal India and the Ottoman Empire 1556-1748* (1989), and *Medieval India: Essays on Sufism, Diplomacy and History* (2006).

R. MAHALAKSHMI teaches at the Centre for Historical Studies, Jawaharlal Nehru University, New Delhi and specializes in the history of Peninsular India. Her doctoral dissertation was on 'The Making of the Goddess Korravai-Durga in the Tamil Religious Traditions, *c.* AD 600-1300. Her forthcoming publications are 'From Independent Deity to Divine Consort: The Goddess in the Tamil Saiva Tradition', and 'The Book of Lakshmi' She is currently researching on aspects of early Sri Lankan history.

PIUS MALEKANDATHIL teaches at the Centre for Historical Studies, Jawaharlal Nehru University, New Delhi and specializes in maritime history in pre-colonial South Asia with a focus on the Indian Ocean and trading societies. He has been a recipient of several fellowships, including the Instituto Camões Fellowship, Lisboa (1992-3), Comissão Nacional para as Comemorações dos Descobrimentos Portugueses, Lisboa (1993-6) for doctoral research and the DAAD Fellowship (1996-8) for postdoctoral research at the South Asian Institute, Heidelberg University. He has published numerous papers and monographs. Some of his publications include *The Germans, the Portuguese and India:*

(1999); *Portuguese Cochin and the Maritime Trade of India, 1500-1663 (A Volume in the South Asian Study Series of Heidelberg University, Germany)* (2001); *Maritime India: Trade, Religion and Polity* (2010).

FARHAT NASREEN teaches at the Department of History and Culture, Jamia Millia Islamia, New Delhi. Her research interests are gender and religion, and her doctoral dissertation was on understanding Vaishnavism in the pre-colonial Braj region. Currently she is working on the representation of women in Islam. She has published a book *Kashful Baghaavat Gorakhpur* which is based on an eyewitness account of the Revolt of 1857.

JOY L.K. PACHUAU teaches at the Centre for Historical Studies, Jawaharlal Nehru University, New Delhi. Her research interests include the role of religion, the formation of regional identities and issues related to the conversion to Christianity. She has worked on these areas in the context of coastal India in the sixteenth and seventeenth centuries, as well as north-east India in the nineteenth and twentieth centuries.

BISWAMOY PATI teaches at the Department of History, University of Delhi. His research interests are various aspects of social history with emphasis on colonial and post-colonial South Asia. His latest publications include an edited book, *The 1857 Rebellion: Debates in Indian History and Society* (2007) and a co-edited book *The Social History of Health and Medicine in Colonial India* (2009). He has also edited *The Great Rebellion of 1857 in India: Exploring Transgressions, Contests and Diversities* (2010).

RIZWAN QAISER teaches at the Department of History and Culture, Jamia Millia Islamia, New Delhi. He has published a book *Resisting Colonialism and Communal Politics: Maulana Azad and the Making of Indian Nation* (2011). In this work he has discussed the ideology and politics of Maulana Azad, and his attempts to create an ideological framework to enable communities to coalesce into the nation.

AMIYA SEN teaches at the Department of History and Culture, Jamia Millia Islamia, New Delhi. He has been an Agatha Harrison Fellow to the University of Oxford, and Visiting Fellow to the Indian Institute of Advanced Study, Shimla, and the Nehru Memorial Museum & Library, New Delhi. During 2007-8, he was Tagore Professor at Visva Bharati, Santiniketan. Amiya Sen's research interests are focused on the intellectual and cultural history of modern India. He has authored six books and three more are to be published soon. Some of his publications include *Social and Religious Reform: The Hindus of British India* (ed. 2005), *The Indispensable Vivekananda: An Anthology of Our Times* (2006), *Bankimchandra Chattopadhyaya: An Intellectual Biography* (2008).

HEERAMAN TIWARI teaches at the Centre for Historical Studies, Jawaharlal Nehru University, New Delhi. He was educated at Lucknow, Delhi and Oxford, and specializes in Sanskrit language, literature and philosophy. He has edited with Jonardon Ganeri, *The Character of Logic in India* by B.K. Matilal (1999) and revised and edited B.K. Matilal's *Logical and Ethical Issues* (1982). He is preparing for publication a volume titled 'From Word to the World: A Study of Classical Indian Philosophy of Meaning'.